Revolutionary Patriots

of

Caroline County

Maryland

1775-1783

Henry C. Peden, Jr.

HERITAGE BOOKS
2012

HERITAGE BOOKS
AN IMPRINT OF HERITAGE BOOKS, INC.

Books, CDs, and more—Worldwide

For our listing of thousands of titles see our website at
www.HeritageBooks.com

Published 2012 by
HERITAGE BOOKS, INC.
Publishing Division
100 Railroad Ave. #104
Westminster, Maryland 21157

Copyright © 1998 Henry C. Peden, Jr.

All rights reserved. No part of this book may be reproduced or transmitted in any form or by any means, electronic or mechanical, including photocopying, recording or by any information storage and retrieval system without written permission from the author, except for the inclusion of brief quotations in a review.

International Standard Book Numbers
Paperbound: 978-1-58549-479-8
Clothbound: 978-0-7884-9340-9

INTRODUCTION

This book has been compiled for the purpose of serving as a research tool for locating the men and women of Caroline County, Maryland who served in the military, rendered material aid to the army or navy, took the Oath of Allegiance and Fidelity, served in an office or on a committee at the town, county or state level, or in some fashion contributed and supported the fight for freedom by the American colonies from the rule of Great Britain during the Revolutionary War, 1775-1783.

It is hoped that this book, which is the thirteenth in a series on Revolutionary War patriots and soldiers in Maryland, will encourage and enable interested persons to become members of such patriotic organizations as The Sons of the American Revolution, The Daughters of the American Revolution, The Sons of the Revolution, and The Society of the Cincinnati.

Information for this book has been gleaned from many primary and secondary sources, which makes this book far more than just a listing of names and ranks. Many of the approximately 2,500 persons named herein have genealogical data included with their respective entries, such as places of residence and dates of birth, death, and marriage, names of wives, husbands, children and other relatives, plus descriptions, occupations, and other information gleaned from church registers, military lists, pension files, tax lists, probate accounts, equity cases, and marriage records.

Each entry in this book has been documented and a key to that documentation has been implemented within the text to enable the reader to review the cited source. A letter followed by a number is the code used for a source and the page within that source. For example, [Ref: D-555] would indicate that the information can be found on page 555 of Reference D, which is *Archives of Maryland, Volume 18*. The coded sources cited herein are as follows:

A = *Archives of Maryland, Volume XI*. "Journal of the Maryland Conventions, July 26 - August 14, 1775, and Journal and Correspondence of the Maryland Council of Safety, August 29, 1775 - July 6, 1776" (Baltimore: Maryland Historical Society, 1892)

B = *Archives of Maryland, Volume XII*. "Journal and Correspondence of the Maryland Council of Safety, July 7, 1776 - December 31, 1776" (Baltimore: Maryland Historical Society, 1893)

C = *Archives of Maryland, Volume XVI*. "Journal and Correspondence of the Council of Safety, January 1, 1777 - March 20, 1777" and "Journal and Correspondence of the State Council, March 20, 1777 - March 28, 1778" (Baltimore: Maryland Historical Society, 1897)

D = *Archives of Maryland, Volume XVIII*. "Muster Rolls and Other Records of Service of Maryland Troops in the American Revolution, 1775-1783" (Baltimore: Maryland Historical Society, 1900)

E = *Archives of Maryland, Volume XXI*. "Journal and Correspondence of the Council of Maryland, April 1, 1778 - October 26, 1779" (Baltimore: Maryland Historical Society, 1901)

F = *Archives of Maryland, Volume XLIII*. "Journal and Correspondence of the State Council of Maryland, 1779-1780" (Baltimore: Maryland Historical Society, 1924)

G = *Archives of Maryland, Volume XLV*. "Journal and Correspondence of the State Council of Maryland, 1780-1781" (Baltimore: Maryland Historical Society, 1927)

H = *Archives of Maryland, Volume XLVII*. "Journal and Correspondence of the State Council of Maryland, 1781" (Baltimore: Maryland Historical Society, 1930)

I = *Archives of Maryland, Volume XLVIII*. "Journal and Correspondence of the State Council of Maryland, 1781-1784" (Baltimore: Maryland Historical Society, 1931)

J = *Revolutionary War Military Collection, Manuscript MS.1814, Box 4* (Baltimore: Maryland Historical Society, Manuscript Division)

K = Wright, F. Edward. *Maryland Eastern Shore Vital Records, 1751-1775* (Westminster, Maryland: Family Line Publications, 1984)

L = Miller, Richard B. "Some Little Known Data Regarding Maryland Signers of the Oath of Fidelity," *Maryland Genealogical Society Bulletin*, Volume 27, No. 1, pp. 101-124 (Winter, 1986)

M = Clements, S. Eugene and Wright, F. Edward. *The Maryland Militia in the Revolutionary War* (Westminster, Maryland: Family Line Publications, 1987)

N = *Caroline County Court Minutes, 1777-1781* (Original Records at the Maryland State Archives, Accession No. MdHR10066)

O = *Calendar of Maryland State Papers, The Red Books, No. 4, Part 1* (Annapolis: The Hall of Records Commission, 1950)

P = Papenfuse, Edward C., et al. *An Inventory of Maryland State Papers, Volume I*, "The Era of the American Revolution, 1775-1789" (Annapolis: The Hall of Records Commission, 1977)

Q = *Maryland Genealogical Society Bulletin* (as cited)

R = Papenfuse, Edward C., et al. *A Biographical Dictionary of the Maryland Legislature, 1635-1789* (Baltimore: The Johns Hopkins University Press, 1979), 2 volumes

S = *Sketches of Maryland Eastern Shoremen*: Genealogical Extracts from *Portrait and Biographical Record of the Eastern Shore of Maryland* (Westminster, Maryland: Family Line Publications, 1988)

T = Harper, Irma. *Heirs and Legatees of Caroline County* (Westminster, Maryland: Family Line Publications, 1989)

U = *Maryland Historical Magazine* (as cited)

V = *Accounts Received by Giles Hicks 3rd, Commissary, 1782* (Original records at the Maryland State Archives, Accession No. MdHR6636-42-7/9)

W = White, Virgil D. *Genealogical Abstracts of Revolutionary War Pension Files* (Waynesboro, Tennessee: The National Historical Publishing Company, 1990), 4 volumes

X = Cranor, Henry Downes. *Marriage Licenses of Caroline County, Maryland, 1774-1815* (Baltimore: Genealogical Publishing Company, Inc., 1975; originally published in Philadelphia in 1904)

Y = *DAR Patriot Index, Centennial Edition* (Washington, D. C.: Daughters of the American Revolution, 1990), 3 volumes

Z = *Caroline County Court Minutes, 1775-1776* (Original records at the Maryland State Archives, Accession No. MdHR10064)

It must be noted that it is not possible to know who all of the patriots were who served in or from Caroline County during the entire Revolutionary War period. This is especially true for those who joined the Maryland Line and served in the Continental Army. Due to the constant reorganization of the Maryland troops during the war, it is not easily determinable which soldier served from which county. It appears, however, that most men from Caroline County served in the 5th Maryland Continental Line. Also, since Caroline County was created out of Dorchester County and Queen Anne's County in 1773, one should also consult my books entitled *Revolutionary Patriots of Dorchester County, Maryland, 1775-1783*, and *Revolutionary Patriots of Kent and Queen Anne's Counties, Maryland, 1775-1783*, which are available from Family Line Publications in Westminster, Maryland.

Finally, as may be the case in works such as this, it is possible that some patriots and soldiers may have been omitted inadvertently; thus, additional research will be necessary before drawing conclusions. Therefore, one should check the *Archives of Maryland,* especially Volume 18, for perhaps even more names of soldiers who served from Caroline County in the Maryland Line during the Revolutionary War era, 1775 to 1783.

Henry C. Peden, Jr.
Bel Air, Maryland
July 11, 1998

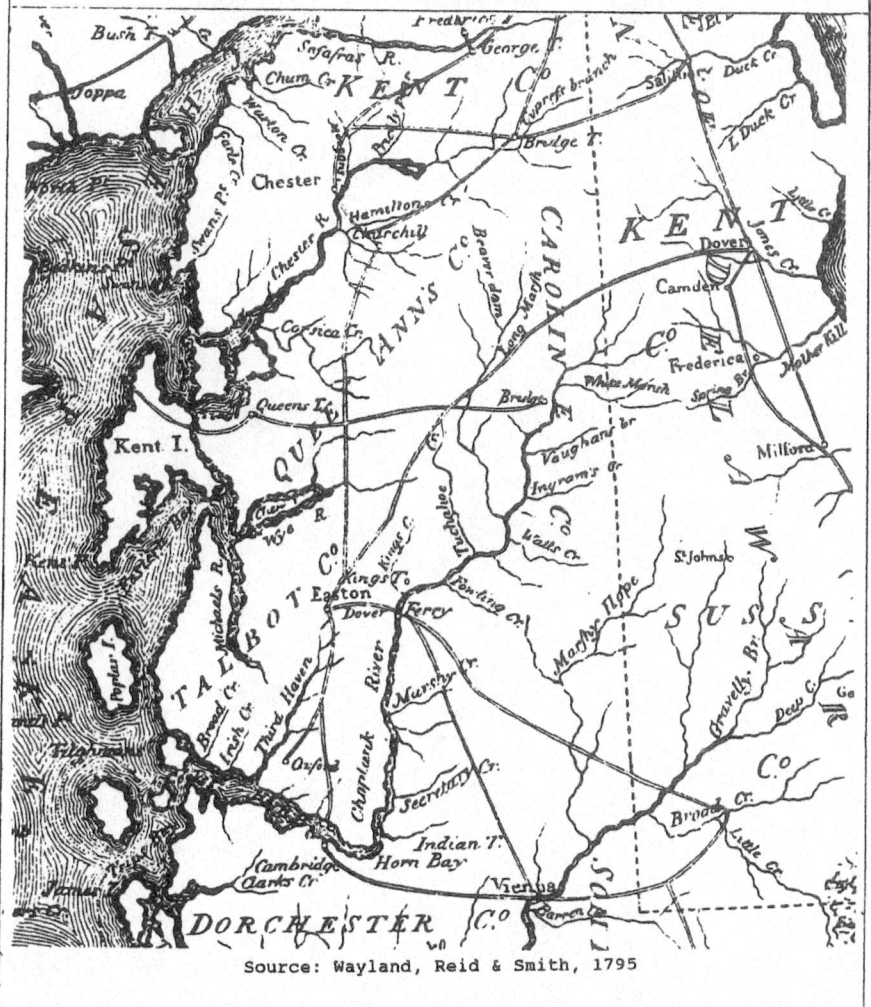

CAROLINE COUNTY, MARYLAND AND ENVIRONS, 1795

Source: Wayland, Reid & Smith, 1795

REVOLUTIONARY PATRIOTS OF CAROLINE COUNTY, MARYLAND, 1775-1783

--?--, Ann. See "John Dillen," q.v.
--?--, Elizabeth. See "James Kirkman," q.v.
--?--, Elizabeth. See "George Kirkman," q.v.
--?--, Elizabeth. See "William Molleston," q.v.
--?--, Elizabeth. See "Alexander Waddell," q.v.
--?--, Esther. See "Asa Banning," q.v.
--?--, Esther. See "Jeremiah Colston," q.v.
--?--, Frances. See "William Coursey," q.v.
--?--, Hebijah. See "Hephzebah Guild," q.v.
--?--, Lydia. See "Robert Dwigans," q.v.
--?--, Mary. See "William Dulaney," q.v.
--?--, Mary. See "James Edgell," q.v.
--?--, Mary. See "William Lister," q.v.
--?--, Mary. See "Samuel Martindale," q.v.
--?--, Mary. See "William Whitely," q.v.
--?--, Rachel. See "Benjamin Chance," q.v.
--?--, Rachel. See "Rachel Meeds," q.v.
--?--, Rebecca. See "Benjamin Edgell," q.v.
--?--, Sabina. See "Asa Banning," q.v.
--?--, Sarah. See "Thomas Dukes," q.v.
--?--, Sarah. See "Valentine Green," q.v.
--?--, Sarah. See "Daniel Higgnutt," q.v.
--?--, Sarah. See "William Keene," q.v.
--?--, Sarah. See "Richard Mason," q.v.
--?--, Sarah. See "Hugh McBryde," q.v.
--?--, Tamson. See "Robert Hardcastle," q.v.
ABBITT, Thomas. Private, Militia, Capt. Thomas Hughlett's Company, 28th Battalion, by August 13, 1777 [Ref: M-152].
ABLE, John. Private, Militia, Capt. John Fauntleroy's Company, 28th Battalion, by August 13, 1777 [Ref: M-154].
ADAMS, Boaz. Private, Militia, Capt. Shadrack Liden's Company, 14th Battalion, by August 13, 1777 [Ref: M-155].
ADAMS, Ann. See "William Adams," q.v.
ADAMS, Chaney. See "William Adams," q.v.
ADAMS, Charles. See "Thomas Hughlett," q.v.
ADAMS, Elizabeth. See "William Adams," q.v.
ADAMS, John. See "William Adams," q.v.
ADAMS, Levin. See "William Adams," q.v.
ADAMS, Mary. See "Thomas Hughlett," q.v.

ADAMS, Nathan. See "William Adams," q.v.

ADAMS, Peter. Attended the Maryland Convention in 1775. Captain, 6th Company, 1st Maryland Line, commissioned January 3, 1776. Captain, General Smallwood's Maryland Regiment, 1776. Major, 7th Maryland Line, 1777. Lieutenant Colonel, 1777. Lieutenant Colonel-Commandant, 1st Maryland Line, 1779; transferred to 3rd Maryland Line, 1781. He served until 1783, in spite of the fact that Gen. William Smallwood had written to Gov. Thomas Sim Lee in 1781 complaining that Col. Adams was "commonly activated by avarice and invincible obstinancy" and that he refused to obey orders. Peter died testate by September 5, 1785, and his brother William Adams was his executor and sole legatee [Ref: D-13, R-98, R-99, O-4, O-71, A-4]. See "William Adams," q.v.

ADAMS, Ralph. Private, Militia, Capt. Vincent Price's Company, 28th Battalion, by August 13, 1777 [Ref: M-151]. Subscribed to the Oath of Allegiance and Fidelity before the Hon. Henry Downes, Jr. on March 2, 1778 [Ref: J-1814].

ADAMS, Sarah. See "William Adams," q.v.

ADAMS, William. Officer, Maryland Line, who lived in Caroline County, never married, and died circa 1789. "John Adams and brother William Adams filed for land [bounty land warrant #373-200] of Capt. Nathan Adams, deceased, of Delaware Line, also Peter Adams and Lt. William Adams, both of Maryland Line. John and William were sons of Nathan Adams and were the only heirs, the said William Adams died leaving a widow Chaney and children: Elizabeth, Ann, Sarah, and Levin Adams. The widow married second William Clarke and lived at Dover, Delaware. Both brothers John and William Adams were doctors. Nathan, Peter and William were brothers. Nathan was killed in battle of White Plains, Peter died about 1788, and William died about 1789. Peter and William Adams never married according to Abner Dill on February 18, 1808, and William Adams, son of Nathan and nephew of Capt. William Adams, married Chaney, a daughter of Abner Dill." [Ref: W-17]. See "Peter Adams," q.v.

ADCOCK, Agga. See "William Holland," q.v.

ADCOCK, Lovy. See "William Holland," q.v.

ADCOCK, Niminah. See "William Holland," q.v.

ADCOCK, Tiry. See "William Holland," q.v.

ADCOCK, William. See "William Holland," q.v.

AITKEN, William. Private, 6th Company, Capt. Peter Adams, 1st Maryland Line, enlisted May 7, 1776 [Ref: D-15].

ALCOCK, Samuel. Private, Militia, 14th Battalion, Capt. Joseph Richardson's Company, by August 13, 1777 [Ref: M-154].

ALCOCK (ALLCOCK), William. Private, Maryland Troops, enrolled by Lieut. Thomas Wynn Loockerman in Caroline County in July, 1776 [Ref: D-69].

ALEXANDER, Robert. Private, Militia, Capt. William Haslett's Company, 28th Battalion, by August 13, 1777 [Ref: M-152]. Subscribed to the Oath of Allegiance and Fidelity before the Hon. Benson Stainton on February 6, 1778 [Ref: J-1814].

ALFORD, Aaron. Private, Militia, Capt. John Mitchell's Company, 14th Battalion, by August 13, 1777 [Ref: M-154].

ALFORD, Ann. See "John Ireland," q.v.

ALFORD, Eleanor. See "Robert Thomas," q.v.

ALFORD, Elizabeth. See "Daniel Valliant," q.v.

ALFORD, Henrietta. See "Risdon Bozman," q.v.

ALFORD, John. See "Mathias Alford," q.v.

ALFORD, Lilly. See "Mathias Alford," q.v.

ALFORD, Maccabeus (1733 - after 1786). Subscribed to the Oath of Allegiance and Fidelity before the Hon. Peter Richardson on February 28, 1778 [Ref: J-1814]. Private, Militia, 14th Battalion, Capt. Joseph Richardson's Company, by August 13, 1777 [Ref: M-154, which listed the name as "Maccobins(?) Alford"]. Aged 53 in a 1786 deposition [Ref: T-12]. "MacCabee Alford" married Rachel Bozman by license dated August 3, 1774 [Ref: X-3].

ALFORD, Mathias (1756 - after 1823). Private, Militia, 14th Battalion, Capt. Joseph Richardson's Company, by August 13, 1777 [Ref: M-154, which spelled his name "Mathyas"]. John Alford, aged 34, died on December 13, 1823, "son of Mathias and Lilly Alford [and] worthy to remark they had been married 40 years, have had 7 children and this is the first death that has occurred in the family, father is now 66 and the mother 63 years of age." [Ref: *Easton Gazette*, December 20, 1823].

ALFORD, Moses. Private, Militia, 14th Battalion, Capt. Joseph Richardson's Company, by August 13, 1777 [Ref: M-154].

ALFORD, Sarah. See "Richard Cooper" and "William Ryon," q.v.

ALL, Elizabeth. See "John Wootters," q.v.

ALLEN, Nathan. See "John Thomas," q.v.

ANDERSON, Ann. See "John Stevens," q.v.

ANDERSON, Elizabeth. See "John Dawson," q.v.

ANDERSON, Isaac. Private, Militia, 14th Battalion, Capt. Richard Andrew's Company, by August 13, 1777 [Ref: M-156]. Rendered patriotic service by providing wheat for the use of the military in August, 1782, as verified by Giles Hicks 3rd, Commissary for Caroline County [Ref: V-6636].

ANDERSON, James. Private, Militia, Capt. Joseph Douglass' Company, 14th Battalion, by August 13, 1777 [Ref: M-156]. James Anderson married Celia Harris by license dated January 4, 1792 [Ref: X-23].

ANDERSON, Michael. Private, Militia, Capt. Shadrack Liden's Company, 14th Battalion, by August 13, 1777 [Ref: M-155].

ANDERSON, Thomas. See "John Dawson," q.v.

ANDERSON, William. Private, Militia, Capt. Shadrack Liden's Company, 14th Battalion, by August 13, 1777 [Ref: M-155].

ANDREW, Amos, of Choptank Hundred. Subscribed to the Oath of Allegiance and Fidelity (made his "X" mark) before the Hon. Benson Stainton on February 2, 1778 [Ref: J-1814].

ANDREW, Ann. See "Thomas Turner," q.v.

ANDREW, Beauchamp or Beatchum or Beachum (1752 - after 1798). Private, Militia, Capt. Nehemiah Andrew's Company, 14th Battalion, by August 13, 1777 [Ref: M-155]. Second Lieutenant, Militia, Capt. Andrew's Company, 14th Battalion, December 17, 1781 [Ref: M-48, I-27]. Aged 46 in a 1798 deposition [Ref: T-18].

ANDREW, Bromwell. Private, Militia, 14th Battalion, Capt. Joseph Richardson's Company, by August 13, 1777 [Ref: M-154]. Ensign, Militia, Capt. Alexander Waddle's Company, 14th Battalion, December 17, 1781 [Ref: M-48, I-27].

ANDREW, Curtis (Curtice). Private, Militia, Capt. Shadrack Liden's Company, 14th Battalion, by August 13, 1777 [Ref: M-155]. Rendered patriotic service by providing wheat for the use of the military in August, 1782, as verified by Giles Hicks 3rd, Commissary for Caroline County [Ref: V-6636].

ANDREW, George. Private, Militia, 14th Battalion, Capt. Richard Andrew's Company, by August 13, 1777 [Ref: M-156]. Rendered patriotic service by providing wheat for the use of the military in August, 1782, as verified by Giles Hicks 3rd, Commissary for Caroline County [Ref: V-6636]. Subscribed to the Oath of Allegiance and Fidelity before the Hon. Nathaniel Potter on March 2, 1778 [Ref: J-1814].

ANDREW, Isaac (1741 - after 1798). Rendered patriotic service by providing wheat for the use of the military in May, 1782, as verified by Giles Hicks 3rd, Commissary for Caroline County [Ref: V-6636]. Isaac Andrew, son of John, was aged 57 in a 1798 deposition [Ref: T-20].

ANDREW, James (1754 - after 1798). Captain, Militia, 14th Battalion, December 17, 1781 [Ref: M-48, I-27]. Aged 44 in a 1798 deposition [Ref: T-19].

ANDREW, Jeremiah. Private, Militia, Capt. Nehemiah Andrew's Company, 14th Battalion, by August 13, 1777 [Ref: M-155]. Ensign, Militia, Capt. James Andrew's Company, 14th Battalion, December 17, 1781, [Ref: M-48, I-27]. Rendered patriotic service by providing wheat for the use of the military in June, 1782, as verified by Giles Hicks 3rd, Commissary for Caroline County [Ref: V-6636]. Subscribed to the Oath of Allegiance and Fidelity before the Hon. Charles Dickinson on March 1, 1778 [Ref: J-1418].

ANDREW, John. Rendered patriotic service by providing wheat for the use of the military in August, 1782, as verified by Giles Hicks 3rd, Commissary for Caroline County [Ref: V-6636]. See "John Andrews," q.v.

ANDREW, John Sr. Rendered patriotic service by providing wheat for the use of the military in May, 1782, as verified by Giles Hicks 3rd, Commissary for Caroline County [Ref: V-6636].

ANDREW, Luke. Private, Militia, Capt. Shadrack Liden's Company, 14th Battalion, by August 13, 1777 [Ref: M-155]. Rendered patriotic service by providing wheat for the use of the military in August, 1782, as verified by Giles Hicks 3rd, Commissary for Caroline County [Ref: V-6636]. Luke Andrew married Mary Rowins by license dated September 1, 1778, and Luke Andrew married Rhody Blades by license dated January 14, 1790 [Ref: X-9].

ANDREW, Mark. Rendered patriotic service by providing wheat for the use of the military in August, 1782, as verified by Giles Hicks 3rd, Commissary for Caroline County [Ref: V-6636]. "Mark Andrews" married Ann Manning by license dated June 7, 1779 [Ref: X-10].

ANDREW, Nehemiah (1729 - after 1782). Captain, Militia, 14th Battalion, by August 13, 1777 [Ref: M-155]. Captain, Militia, 14th Battalion, April 9, 1778, and resigned June 12, 1781 [Ref: M-48, E-23]. Subscribed to the Oath of Allegiance and Fidelity before the Hon. Nathaniel Potter on March 2, 1778 [Ref: J-1814]. Age 53 in a 1782 deposition [Ref: T-4].

ANDREW, Nehemiah Jr. (1756 -   ). Private, Militia, Capt. Nehemiah Andrew's Company, 14th Battalion, by August 13, 1777 [Ref: M-155]. Age 42 in a 1798 deposition [Ref: T-19]. Nehemiah Andrew married Anna Davis by license dated November 23, 1791 [Ref: X-23, which listed the name without the "Jr."].

ANDREW, Richard. Captain, Militia, 14th Battalion, 1776- 1777 [Ref: M-156, B-449, C-65]. This notice appeared in the *Republican Star* newspaper on April 14, 1812: "Richard Andrew, aged 89 years, now living at the Walnut Trees. Caroline County, can probably boast of what few men can equal in the following posterity: 11 children, 110 grandchildren, 84 great-grandchildren; some of his children having sometime since removed to the westward, addition no doubt might be made to the above." One "Richard Andrews" was a captain in the militia, 14th Battalion, on May 14, 1776, and reportedly deceased by June 12, 1781 [Ref: M-48, A-11, I-28]. One "Richard Andrew" married Mary Hill by license dated April 3, 1788 [Ref: X-18]. There appears to have been more then one man with this name, so additional research will be necessary before drawing conclusions.

ANDREW, Samuel. Second Lieutenant, Militia, Capt. Richard Andrew's Company, 14th Battalion, May 14, 1776 to at least August 13, 1777 [Ref: M-48, A-424, M-156]. Subscribed to the Oath of Allegiance and Fidelity before the Hon. Nathaniel Potter on March 2, 1778 [Ref: J-1814].

ANDREW, Sarah. See "Jesse Grayless," q.v.

ANDREW, William (1742 - after 1797). Private, Militia, Capt. Shadrack Liden's Company, 14th Battalion, by August 13, 1777 [Ref: M-155]. Rendered patriotic service by providing wheat for the use of the military in August, 1782, as verified by Giles Hicks 3rd, Commissary for Caroline County [Ref: V-6636]. Aged 55 in a 1797 deposition [Ref: T-19]. One William Andrew married Rachel Prouce or Pronce by license dated June 29, 1782, and a William Andrew married Margaret Beauchamp by license dated December 10, 1790 [Ref: X-14, X-21].

ANDREW, William. Private, Militia, 14th Battalion, Capt. Richard Andrew's Company, by August 13, 1777 [Ref: M-156]. See the other "William Andrew," q.v.

ANDREWS, Amos. Private, Militia, Capt. Thomas Hughlett's Company, 28th Battalion, by August 13, 1777 [Ref: M-152].

ANDREWS, Eleanora. See "Nathan Manship," q.v.

ANDREWS, John (Reverend). Served on the Committee of Observation for Caroline County in June, 1776 [Ref: A-481].
ANDREWS, Mark. See "Mark Andrew," q.v.
ANDREWS, William. Private, Militia, Capt. Joseph Douglass' Company, 14th Battalion, by August 13, 1777 [Ref: M-156].
ANTHONY, Ann. See "Nicholas Bright," q.v.
ANTHONY, Elonor. See "John Smith," q.v.
ANTHONY, Morgan. Private, Militia, Capt. Vincent Price's Company, 28th Battalion, by August 13, 1777 [Ref: M-151].
ANTHONY, Nathan. Private, Militia, Capt. Vincent Price's Company, 28th Battalion, by August 13, 1777 [Ref: M-151]. Rendered patriotic service by providing wheat for the use of the military in September, 1782, as verified by Giles Hicks 3rd, Commissary for Caroline County [Ref: V-6636].
ARSMWITH, McCalvey. Private, Militia, Capt. Andrew Fountain's Company, 14th Battalion, by August 13, 1777 [Ref: M-157].
ASKIN, Solomon. On November 5, 1779, the Treasurer of Maryland's Western Shore was directed to "pay to Henry Downes four pounds, nine shillings and two pence for the use of Solomon Askin per account passed by the Deputy Auditor." [Ref: F-9].
AUSTIN, Henry. Private, Militia, 14th Battalion, Capt. Joseph Richardson's Company, by August 13, 1777 [Ref: M-154].
AUSTON, William. Private, Militia, Capt. William Chipley's Company, 28th Battalion, by August 13, 1777 [Ref: M-153].
BAGGS, --?--. See "Richard Mason," q.v.
BAGGS, Abram. See "James Roe," q.v.
BAGGS, Elizabeth. See "James Roe" and "Thomas Hardcastle," q.v.
BAGGS, Esther. See "Henry Mason," q.v.
BAGGS, Henry. See "James Roe," q.v.
BAGGS, Isaac. Private, Militia, Capt. John Fauntleroy's Company, 28th Battalion, by August 13, 1777 [Ref: M-153]. Ensign, Capt. William Haslett's Company, 1777 [Ref: J-1814]. Subscribed to the Oath of Allegiance and Fidelity in 1780 [Ref: L-104]. Isaac Baggs married Elizabeth Cook by license dated January 31, 1786 [Ref: X-17].
BAGGS, James. Private, Militia, Capt. Samuel Jackson's Company, 28th Battalion, by August 13, 1777 [Ref: M-153]. Second Lieutenant, Militia, Capt. Jackson's Company, 28th Battalion, April 9, 1778 [Ref: M-49, E-21]. Subscribed to the Oath of Allegiance and Fidelity before the Hon. Richard Mason on March 2, 1778 [Ref: J-1814]. James Boggs [Baggs?] married Ann Mason by license dated December 4, 1778, and James Baggs married Nancy Mason by license dated October 15, 1779 [Ref: X-9].
BAGGS, John. Subscribed to the Oath of Allegiance and Fidelity before the Hon. Richard Mason on March 2, 1778 [Ref: J-1814]. See "Thomas Baggs," q.v.
BAGGS, Mary. See "Thomas Roe," q.v.

BAGGS, Nancy. See "William Mason," q.v.

BAGGS, Pebbles. Rendered patriotic service by providing wheat for the use of the military in August, 1782, as verified by Giles Hicks 3rd, Commissary for Caroline County [Ref: V-6636].

BAGGS, Thomas (1709 - after 1790). Subscribed to the Oath of Allegiance and Fidelity in 1780 [Ref: L-104]. Aged 73 in a 1782 deposition and aged 81 in a 1790 deposition, noting that he was the son of John Baggs [Ref: T-10, T-14]. See "Richard Mason," q.v.

BAGGS, Thomas (c1740 - before November 12, 1793). On January 14, 1779, he filed a certificate in Caroline County Court that he had subscribed to the Oath of Allegiance and Fidelity before the Hon. Richard Mason [Ref: N-85, Y-114].

BAKER, Benjamin. See "John Voss Baker," q.v.

BAKER, Esther. See "John Voss Baker," q.v.

BAKER, Henry. Private, Militia, Capt. William Hopper's Company, 28th Battalion, by August 13, 1777 [Ref: M-151].

BAKER, James. Private, Militia, Capt. William Hopper's Company, 28th Battalion, by August 13, 1777 [Ref: M-151].

BAKER, John. Subscribed to the Oath of Allegiance and Fidelity before the Hon. Henry Downes, Jr. on March 2, 1778 [Ref: J-1814]. Rendered patriotic service by providing wheat for the use of the military in September, 1782, as verified by Giles Hicks III, Commissary for Caroline County [Ref: P-552]. John Baker married Sarah Broadaway by license dated November 18, 1779 [Ref: X-11]. See "John Voss Baker," q.v.

BAKER, John Voss. Private, Militia, 14th Battalion, Capt. Joseph Richardson's Company, by August 13, 1777 [Ref: M-154]. In an 1802 land commission record it stated that John Voss Baker died on April 15, 1790, seized of tracts called "Hobb's Folly," "Clay Swamp" and "Addition to Clay Swamp," and leaving heirs as follows: John Baker (of age), Thomas Baker (of age), Esther Baker (minor), Benjamin Baker (minor), and Ann Chance, wife of Elijah Chance [Ref: T-22].

BAKER, Thomas. See "John Voss Baker," q.v.

BALEY, Nathan. Rendered patriotic service by providing wheat for the use of the military in August, 1782, as verified by Giles Hicks 3rd, Commissary for Caroline County [Ref: V-6636].

BALL, Elizabeth. See "Robert Waddle (Waddell)," q.v.

BALL, Levin. Subscribed to the Oath of Allegiance and Fidelity before the Hon. Henry Downes, Jr. on March 2, 1778 [Ref: J-1814].

BALL, Samuel, of Talbot County. "Marriner, belonging to Capt. Thomas Noel's sloop now lying at his wharf," subscribed to the Oath of Allegiance and Fidelity before the Hon. Peter Richardson on March 1, 1778 [Ref: J-1814]. Samuel Ball married Lydia Kerap by license dated June 5, 1783 in Caroline County [Ref: X-15].

BANCKES, Deborah. See "William Banckes," q.v.

BANCKES, William, of Queen Anne's County. On December 10, 1779, he filed a certificate in Caroline County Court that he had subscribed to the Oath of Allegiance and Fidelity [Ref: N-67]. William Banckes and Deborah Hawkins were married on January 14, 1744. William Banckes, son of William and Deborah Banckes, was born August 24, 1754 in Queen Anne's County (now Caroline County) as recorded in the register of St. John's P. E. Church [Ref: K-25, K-26].

BANKS, James. Private, Militia, Capt. John Fauntleroy's Company, 28th Battalion, by August 13, 1777 [Ref: M-154]. Rendered patriotic service by providing wheat for the use of the military in August, 1782, as verified by Giles Hicks 3rd, Commissary for Caroline County [Ref: V-6636].

BANNING, Ann. See "William Banning, Jr.," q.v.

BANNING, Anthony. Private, Militia, Capt. John Mitchell's Company, 14th Battalion, by August 13, 1777 [Ref: M-154].

BANNING, Asa (c1742-1818). Private, Militia, Capt. William Hopper's Company, 28th Battalion, by August 13, 1777 [Ref: M-151]. Ensign, Militia, Capt. Allenby Jump's Company, July 24, 1780 [Ref: M-50, F-230, G-28]. Subscribed to the Oath of Allegiance and Fidelity before the Hon. Matthew Driver on February 1, 1778 [Ref: J-1814]. Rendered patriotic service by providing wheat for the use of the military in August, 1782, as verified by Giles Hicks 3rd, Commissary for Caroline County [Ref: V-6636]. Asa Banning married first to Sabina --?--, second to Esther --?--, and died in 1818 in Virginia [Ref: Y-144].

BANNING, Elizabeth. See "Joseph Stack," q.v.

BANNING, Esther. See "Asa Banning," q.v.

BANNING, Henry. Private, Militia, Capt. John Mitchell's Company, 14th Battalion, by August 13, 1777 [Ref: M-154].

BANNING, Sabina. See "Asa Banning," q.v.

BANNING, Sarah. See "Richard Smith," q.v.

BANNING, Thomas. Private, Militia, 14th Battalion, Capt. Richard Andrew's Company, by August 13, 1777 [Ref: M-156].

BANNING, William. Private, Militia, Capt. John Mitchell's Company, 14th Battalion, by August 13, 1777 [Ref: M-154].

BANNING, William. Private, Militia, Capt. Vincent Price's Company, 28th Battalion, by August 13, 1777 [Ref: M-151].

BANNING, William. Subscribed to the Oath of Allegiance and Fidelity (made his "W" mark) before the Hon. Henry Downes, Jr. on March 2, 1778 [Ref: J-1814]. One William Banning married Rebecca Cheez by license dated June 21, 1774 [Ref: X-3].

BANNING, William Jr. Subscribed to the Oath of Allegiance and Fidelity before the Hon. Henry Downes, Jr. on March 2, 1778 [Ref: J-1814]. William Banning, son of William and Ann Banning, was born March 17, 1750 in Queen Anne's County (now Caroline County) as recorded in the register of St. John's P. E. Church [Ref: K-25, which spelled the name "Baning"].

BARCROSS, William. Private (recruit), Maryland Troops, enrolled in Caroline

County by William Whiteley, County Lieutenant, on August 14, 1781 to serve in the Maryland Line until December 10, 1781 [Ref: D-385].

BARKLEY, James. Private, 6th Company, Capt. Peter Adams, 1st Maryland Line, enlisted May 7, 1776 [Ref: D-14].

BARNETT, Sarah. See "Thomas Goldsborough," q.v.

BARNICASSLE, Fradrick. Private, Maryland Troops, enrolled by Lieut. Levin Handy in Caroline County and passed by Col. William Hopewell on August 4, 1776 [Ref: D-69].

BARNS, James. Private, Militia, Capt. William Chipley's Company, 28th Battalion, by August 13, 1777 [Ref: M-153].

BARNS, Thomas. Private, Militia, Capt. John Mitchell's Company, 14th Battalion, by August 13, 1777 [Ref: M-154].

BARROW, James. Private, 5th Maryland Line, enlisted June 16, 1778 and reported missing on August 16, 1780 at the Battle of Camden in South Carolina [Ref: D-186].

BARROW, Thomas. Private, Militia, Capt. Vincent Price's Company, 28th Battalion, by August 13, 1777 [Ref: M-151].

BARTLETT, Daniel. Rendered patriotic service by providing wheat for the use of the military in August, 1782, as verified by Giles Hicks 3rd, Commissary for Caroline County [Ref: V-6636].

BARTLETT, James. Private, Militia, Capt. Thomas Hughlett's Company, 28th Battalion, by August 13, 1777 [Ref: M-153]. Rendered patriotic service by providing wheat for the use of the military in August, 1782, as verified by Giles Hicks 3rd, Commissary for Caroline County [Ref: V-6636].

BARTON, Andrew. See "William Kelly," q.v.

BARTON, James. Private, Militia, 14th Battalion, Capt. Richard Andrew's Company, by August 13, 1777 [Ref: M-156]. Rendered patriotic service by providing wheat for the use of the military in August, 1782, as verified by Giles Hicks 3rd, Commissary for Caroline County [Ref: V-6636].

BARWICK, Ann. See "James Barwick," q.v.

BARWICK, Edward. Private, Militia, Capt. William Hopper's Company, 28th Battalion, by August 13, 1777 [Ref: M-151]. Rendered patriotic service by providing wheat for the use of the military in August, 1782, as verified by Giles Hicks 3rd, Commissary for Caroline County [Ref: V-6636]. See "James Barwick," q.v.

BARWICK, James (post?). Private, Militia, Capt. John Stafford's Company, 14th Battalion, by August 13, 1777 [Ref: M-156].

BARWICK, James. Private, Militia, Capt. Andrew Fountain's Company, 14th Battalion, by August 13, 1777 [Ref: M-157].

BARWICK, James. Private, Militia, Capt. William Hopper's Company, 28th Battalion, by August 13, 1777 [Ref: M-151].

BARWICK, James. Rendered patriotic service by providing wheat for the use of the military in July, 1782, as verified by Giles Hicks III, Commissary for

Caroline County [Ref: P-527]. "James Barwick, son of Edward" was aged 56 in a 1791 deposition. In an 1806 land commission record it stated that James Barwick had died (date not given) seized of tracts called "Jump's Choice," "Fisher's Plains," and "Roe's Fancy," and leaving heirs as follows: Edward Barwick, James Barwick, John Barwick, Letitia Barwick, Rebecca Barwick (minor), Joshua Barwick (minor), Ann Barwick (minor), and Mary Thawley (wife of John Thawley). [Ref: T-15, T-23]. Since there was more then one man named James Barwick, additional research will be necessary before drawing conclusions. One James Barwick married Cordelia Hynson by license dated February 25, 1778 [Ref: X-8].

BARWICK, John. Private, Militia, Capt. William Hopper's Company, 28th Battalion, by August 13, 1777 [Ref: M-151]. "John Barrwick" married Rachel Webber by license dated May 31, 1779 [Ref: X-10]. See "James Barwick," q.v.

BARWICK, Joshua. Private, Militia, Capt. Andrew Fountain's Company, 14th Battalion, by August 13, 1777 [Ref: M-157]. See "James Barwick," q.v.

BARWICK, Letitia. See "James Barwick," q.v.

BARWICK, Margaret. Rendered patriotic service by providing wheat for the use of the military in August, 1782, as verified by Giles Hicks 3rd, Commissary for Caroline County [Ref: V-6636].

BARWICK, Rebecca. See "James Barwick," q.v.

BARWICK, Sidney. See "Nehemiah Draper," q.v.

BATCHELOR, Nathan. Private (draft), Maryland Troops, furnished in Caroline County by William Whiteley, County Lieutenant, on April 16, 1781, and on August 14, 1781 reported "run" although he had enrolled to serve in the Maryland Line until December 10, 1781 [Ref: D-368, D-385].

BATCHELOR, Rhody. See "Henry Willis," q.v.

BATCHELOR, William. Private, Militia, Capt. John Fauntleroy's Company, 28th Battalion, by August 13, 1777 [Ref: M-153]. William Batchelor married Margaret McCan by license dated December 12, 1774 [Ref: X-5].

BATES, Marlene Strawser. See "John Cooper," q.v.

BAUGHSTICK, Nathan. Private, Militia, Capt. Samuel Jackson's Company, 28th Battalion, by August 13, 1777 [Ref: M-153].

BAXTER, John. Private (recruit), Maryland Troops, enrolled in Caroline County by William Whiteley, County Lieutenant, on August 14, 1781 to serve in the Maryland Line until December 10, 1781 [Ref: D-385].

BAXTER, Thomas. Private (recruit), Maryland Troops, enrolled in Caroline County by William Whiteley, County Lieutenant, on August 14, 1781 to serve in the Maryland Line until December 10, 1781 [Ref: D-385]. Thomas Baxter married Mary Hughes by license dated February 2, 1790 [Ref: X-20].

BAYLEY, Margaret. See "Robert Orrell," q.v.

BAYNARD, Daniel. On December 27, 1776 he joined a company of men in Caroline County who marched to Talbot County to obtain a supply of salt [Ref: B-564, B-565, which spelled the name "Bayner"]. Private, Militia, Capt. Vincent

Price's Company, 28th Battalion, by August 13, 1777 [Ref: M-151]. Subscribed to the Oath of Allegiance and Fidelity before the Hon. Richard Mason on March 2, 1778 [Ref: J-1814].

BAYNARD, Eliza. See "John Allen Sangston," q.v.

BAYNARD, Elizabeth. See "Thomas Baynard," q.v.

BAYNARD, Henry. See "John Allen Sangston," q.v.

BAYNARD, John. Private, Militia, Capt. William Haslett's Company, 28th Battalion, by August 13, 1777 [Ref: M-152]. See "Thomas Baynard," q.v.

BAYNARD, John Pratt. See "Matthew Driver," q.v.

BAYNARD, Levin. Private, Militia, Capt. William Haslett's Company, 28th Battalion, by August 13, 1777 [Ref: M-152]. Rendered patriotic service by providing wheat for the use of the military in August, 1782, as verified by Giles Hicks 3rd, Commissary for Caroline County [Ref: V-6636].

BAYNARD, Lydia. See "Thomas Baynard," q.v.

BAYNARD, Margaret. See "Henry Downes" and "Thomas Baynard," q.v.

BAYNARD, Martha. See "Thomas Baynard," q.v.

BAYNARD, Mary. See "Thomas Hardcastle" and "John Allen Sangston," q.v.

BAYNARD, Rebecca. See "John Allen Sangston," q.v.

BAYNARD, Sarah. See "Thomas Hardcastle," q.v.

BAYNARD, Thomas. Rendered patriotic service by providing wheat for the use of the military in August, 1782, as verified by Giles Hicks 3rd, Commissary for Caroline County [Ref: V-6636]. "Thomas Baynard, Jr." married Rebekah Sangston by license dated August 30, 1784, and "Thomas Baynard" married Elizabeth Slaughter by license dated July 28, 1789 [Ref: X-16, X-20]. There was also a Thomas Baynard, son of John Baynard, who married Hannah Clarke on January 19, 1747 at St. John's P. E. Church in Queen Anne's County (now Caroline County) and had three daughters: Elizabeth (born November 14, 1748), Lydia (born May 10, 1750), and Margaret (born May 7, 1752). [Ref: K-25]. One Thomas Baynard died on May 27, 1752 [Ref: K-27]. Additional research will be necessary before drawing conclusions. See "Philemon Downes" and "John Allen Sangston," q.v.

BAYNARD, William. Private, Militia, Capt. William Haslett's Company, 28th Battalion, by August 13, 1777 [Ref: M-152].

BEACH, Jeremiah. Rendered patriotic service by providing wheat for the use of the military in August, 1782, as verified by Giles Hicks 3rd, Commissary for Caroline County [Ref: V-6636].

BEADLEY, Nelly. See "Thomas Harvey," q.v.

BEAUCHAMP (BEACHAMP), Ann. Rendered patriotic service by providing wheat for the use of the military in August, 1782, as verified by Giles Hicks 3rd, Commissary for Caroline County [Ref: V-6636].

BEAUCHAMP (BEACHAMP), John. Private, Militia, Capt. Shadrack Liden's Company, 14th Battalion, by August 13, 1777 [Ref: M-155]. Rendered patriotic service by providing wheat for the use of the military in June, 1782, as verified

by Giles Hicks 3rd, Commissary for Caroline County [Ref: V-6636].
BEAUCHAMP, Margaret. See "William Andrew," q.v.
BECK, Aquilla (Aquila). Private, Militia, Capt. William Chipley's Company, 28th Battalion, by August 13, 1777 [Ref: M-153]. Rendered patriotic service by providing wheat for the use of the military in August, 1782, as verified by Giles Hicks 3rd, Commissary for Caroline County [Ref: V-6636].
BECK, Edward. Private, Militia, Capt. William Chipley's Company, 28th Battalion, by August 13, 1777 [Ref: M-153].
BECK, Lenry(?). Private, Militia, Capt. William Chipley's Company, 28th Battalion, by August 13, 1777 [Ref: M-153].
BELL, Ann. See "William Bell" and "Robert Bell," q.v.
BELL, Cyrus. See "John Dawson," q.v.
BELL, Daniel. See "William Bell," q.v.
BELL, Diana. See "Ezekiel Dean," q.v.
BELL, Elenor. See "James Fountain," q.v.
BELL, Fanny. See "Thomas Lecompte," q.v.
BELL, George (1737 - after 1782). Subscribed to the Oath of Allegiance and Fidelity before the Hon. Nathaniel Potter on March 2, 1778 [Ref: J-1814]. Aged 45 in a 1782 deposition [Ref: T-5].
BELL, Henry. See "William Bell," q.v.
BELL, James. Private, 6th Company, Capt. Peter Adams, 1st Maryland Line, enlisted January 30, 1776 [Ref: D-14]. Private, Militia, Capt. Vincent Price's Company, 28th Battalion, by August 13, 1777 [Ref: M-151]. James Bell married Margaret Willoughby by license dated July 12, 1779 [Ref: X-10].
BELL, Joseph. See "Thomas Lecompte," q.v.
BELL, Lydia. See "Benjamin Whitby," q.v.
BELL, Margaret. See "William Bell," q.v.
BELL, Mary. See "William Bell," q.v.
BELL, Nancy. See "William Bell," q.v.
BELL, Rebecca. See "Matthew Chilton," q.v.
BELL, Robert (1759 -   ). Private, Militia, Capt. William Hopper's Company, 28th Battalion, by August 13, 1777 [Ref: M-151]. Robert Bell married Mary Fountain by license dated April 9, 1782 [Ref: X-14]. Robert Bell, son of William and Ann Bell, was born June 3, 1759 [Ref: K-25]. See "William Bell," q.v.
BELL, Sarah. See "John Dawson," q.v.
BELL, Thomas. See "William Bell," q.v.
BELL, William (1736-1815). Served on the Committee of Observation for Caroline County on August 2, 1775 [Ref: A-48]. Rendered patriotic service by providing wheat for the use of the military in August, 1782, as verified by Giles Hicks 3rd, Commissary for Caroline County [Ref: V-6636, which listed the name as "Sr."]. Aged 52 in a 1788 deposition [Ref: T-12]. William Bell married Ann Hardcastle on April 14, 1755. Daniel Bell (born March 6, 1763) and Ann Bell (born December 25, 1766) were children of William and Ann Bell. Thomas Bell (born

November 18, 1768) and Margaret Bell (born September 5, 1770) were children of William and Margaret Bell [Ref: K-26, K-27]. In an 1819 land commission record it stated that one William Bell had died in 1815 and owned tracts called "Mill Security," "Plowyard," "Fountain's Addition to White's Beginning," "Piney Neck Regulated," "Exchange," "Lyconium," "Lecompte's Lot," "Cape Ann," "Hallock's Cow Pasture," "Sand Hill," "Byrn's Bower" and "Parrott's Lookout," and left the following heirs: Daniel Bell, Jr., Nancy Bell, Mary Bell (who married Levin Smith), William Bell (minor), Margaret Bell (minor), Robert Bell (minor), and Henry Bell (minor). [Ref: T-32]. One William Bell was a private in the militia, Capt. William Hopper's Company, 28th Battalion, by August 13, 1777 [Ref: M-151]. Additional research will be necessary before drawing conclusions. See "Robert Bell" and "William Bell, Jr.," q.v.

BELL, William Jr. (1757 -   ). Private, Militia, Capt. William Hopper's Company, 28th Battalion, by August 13, 1777 [Ref: M-151]. William Bell, Jr. married Margaret Talbott by license dated October 10, 1783 [Ref: X-15]. William Bell, son of William and Ann Bell, was born July 17, 1757 [Ref: K-25].

BELLWOOD, Henry. Private, Militia, Capt. Vincent Price's Company, 28th Battalion, by August 13, 1777 [Ref: M-151].

BENDING (BENDEN), Thomas. Private, Militia, Capt. William Haslett's Company, 28th Battalion, by August 13, 1777 [Ref: M-152]. Rendered patriotic service by providing wheat for the use of the military in August, 1782, as verified by Giles Hicks 3rd, Commissary for Caroline County [Ref: V-6636].

BENNEY, William. Private, Militia, Capt. John Fauntleroy's Company, 28th Battalion, by August 13, 1777 [Ref: M-154].

BENSTON, John. Private, Maryland Troops, enrolled by Lieut. Levin Handy in Caroline County and passed by Col. William Hopewell on August 4, 1776 [Ref: D-69].

BEWLEY, Joseph. See "Edward Turner," q.v.

BILLETOR (BILLETER, BILLERTOR), James (c1740 - after 1798). Private, Militia, 14th Battalion, Capt. Joseph Richardson's Company, by August 13, 1777 [Ref: M-154]. Subscribed to the Oath of Allegiance and Fidelity (made his "X" mark) before the Hon. Peter Richardson on February 26, 1778 [Ref: J-1814]. Joseph Billeter was aged 57 or 58 in a 1798 deposition [Ref: T-20].

BILLETOR (BILLITOR), Joseph. Private, Militia, 14th Battalion, Capt. Joseph Richardson's Company, by August 13, 1777 [Ref: M-154].

BILLETOR (BILLITOR), Zebdiah. Private, Maryland Troops, enlisted by Capt. Joseph Richardson in Caroline County and passed by Col. William Richardson on August 31, 1776 [Ref: D-69]. "Zebdiah Billeter" married Anna Seward, lived in Maryland, and died after November 21, 1813 in North Carolina [Ref: Y-253].

BISHOP, Mary Ann. Rendered patriotic service by providing wheat for the use of the military in August, 1782, as verified by Giles Hicks 3rd, Commissary for Caroline County [Ref: V-6636].

BISHOP, Robert. Private, Militia, Capt. John Stafford's Company, 14th Battalion,

by August 13, 1777 [Ref: M-156].
BISHOP, William. Private, Militia, Capt. John Stafford's Company, 14th Battalion, by August 13, 1777 [Ref: M-156].
BLACK, James. Private, Militia, Capt. John Fauntleroy's Company, 28th Battalion, by August 13, 1777 [Ref: M-154]. James Black, Jr. married Tacy Oldfield by license dated February 9, 1780 [Ref: X-11].
BLADES, Anderton. Private, Militia, Capt. Shadrack Liden's Company, 14th Battalion, by August 13, 1777 [Ref: M-155]. "Omderton Blades" married Sarah Bowdle by license dated March 8, 1780 [Ref: X-11].
BLADES, Arnold (1754 -   ). Private, Militia, Capt. William Haslett's Company, 28th Battalion, by August 13, 1777 [Ref: M-152, which spelled the name "Arnill Blades"]. Aged 28 in a 1782 deposition [Ref: T-11].
BLADES, George. Private, Militia, 14th Battalion, Capt. Joseph Richardson's Company, by August 13, 1777 [Ref: M-154].
BLADES, Hannah. See "Samuel Southerly," q.v.
BLADES, James. Rendered patriotic service by providing wheat for the use of the military in August, 1782, as verified by Giles Hicks 3rd, Commissary for Caroline County [Ref: V-6636]. James Blades married Sidney Jordan by license dated September 1, 1778 [Ref: X-9].
BLADES, John. Private (draft), Maryland Troops, enrolled in Caroline County by William Whiteley, County Lieutenant, on August 14, 1781 (although reported sick at the time) to serve in the Maryland Line until December 10, 1781 [Ref: D-385]. John Blades married Lucretia Turner by license dated May 30, 1785 [Ref: X-16].
BLADES, Joseph. Private, Militia, Capt. Nehemiah Andrew's Company, 14th Battalion, by August 13, 1777 [Ref: M-155].
BLADES, Levin (1755 -   ). Private, Militia, 14th Battalion, Capt. Joseph Richardson's Company, by August 13, 1777 [Ref: M-154]. Aged 31 in a 1786 deposition [Ref: T-12]. Levin Blades married Betsey Newman by license recorded January 28, 1775 [Ref: X-5].
BLADES, Rhody. See "Luke Andrew," q.v.
BLADES, Sarah. See "Henry Turner," q.v.
BLADES, Thomas (1753 -   ). Private, Militia, 14th Battalion, Capt. Joseph Richardson's Company, by August 13, 1777 [Ref: M-154]. Aged 33 in a 1786 deposition [Ref: T-12]. Thomas Blades married Keziah Cromean (Cremeen) by license dated January 24, 1784 [Ref: X-15].
BLADES, Tilghman. Private, Militia, Capt. Andrew Fountain's Company, 14th Battalion, by August 13, 1777 [Ref: M-157]. Tilghman Blades married Ann Lawfull by license dated September 7, 1779 [Ref: X-10].
BLADES, Tilley. See "James Dillen (Dilling)," q.v.
BLAIR, Charles. See "John Stevens," q.v.
BLAND, Ann. See "Charles Manship, Jr.," q.v.
BLAND, Joseph. Private, Militia, Capt. Andrew Fountain's Company, 14th

Battalion, by August 13, 1777 [Ref: M-157].

BLAND, Joseph (1718 - after 1798). Rendered patriotic service by providing wheat for the use of the military in August, 1782, as verified by Giles Hicks 3rd, Commissary for Caroline County [Ref: V-6636]. Aged 80 in a 1798 deposition [Ref: T-19].

BLAND, Sarah. See "Aaron Manship" and "Charles Manship, Jr.," q.v.

BLAND, Tamsey. See "James Towers," q.v.

BLOOD, Robert. Private (recruit), Maryland Troops, enrolled in Caroline County by William Whiteley, County Lieutenant, on August 14, 1781 to serve in the Maryland Line for 3 years [Ref: D-385].

BLUNT, Benjamin. First Lieutenant, Militia, Bridgetown Volunteers, January 3, 1776 [Ref: M-50].

BLUNT, Benjamin. Private, Militia, Capt. William Haslett's Company, 28th Battalion, by August 13, 1777 [Ref: M-152].

BLUNT, Benjamin. Rendered patriotic service by providing wheat for the use of the military in August, 1782, as verified by Giles Hicks 3rd, Commissary for Caroline County [Ref: V-6636].

BLUNT, Levi. See "Richard Fisher," q.v.

BLUNT, Lydia. See "Richard Fisher," q.v.

BOGGS, James. See "James Baggs," q.v.

BOOKER, Samuel. Private, Militia, Capt. John Fauntleroy's Company, 28th Battalion, by August 13, 1777 [Ref: M-154].

BOON, Ann. See "Isaac Boon," q.v.

BOON (BOONE), Foster. Private, Militia, Capt. William Chipley's Company, 28th Battalion, by August 13, 1777 [Ref: M-153]. Rendered patriotic service by providing wheat for the use of the military in August, 1782, as verified by Giles Hicks 3rd, Commissary for Caroline County [Ref: V-6636].

BOON (BOONE), Isaac. Private, Militia, Capt. Thomas Hughlett's Company, 28th Battalion, by August 13, 1777 [Ref: M-152]. Rendered patriotic service by providing wheat for the use of the military in August, 1782, as verified by Giles Hicks 3rd, Commissary for Caroline County [Ref: V-6636]. Isaac Boon married Ann Boon by license dated August 7, 1792 [Ref: X-24]. See "James Boon" and "William Boon, Jr.," q.v.

BOON (BOONE), Jacob. Private, Militia, Capt. Thomas Hughlett's Company, 28th Battalion, by August 13, 1777 [Ref: M-152]. Jacob Boon married Catharine Whitby by license dated July 26, 1788 [Ref: X-19].

BOON (BOONE), James. Ensign, Militia, Capt. William Chipley's Company, 28th Battalion, by August 13, 1777 [Ref: M-153].

BOON (BOONE), James. Private, Militia, Capt. Thomas Hughlett's Company, 28th Battalion, by August 13, 1777 [Ref: M-152].

BOON (BOONE), James. Private, Militia, Capt. Thomas Hughlett's Company, 28th Battalion, by August 13, 1777 [Ref: M-153].

BOON (BOONE), James. Private, Militia, Capt. Thomas Hughlett's Company, 28th

Battalion, by August 13, 1777 [Ref: M-153].

BOON (BOONE), James. Ensign, Militia, Capt. Hughlett's Company, 28th Battalion, April 9, 1778 [Ref: M-50, E-23]. Rendered patriotic service by providing wheat for the use of the military in August, 1782, as verified by Giles Hicks 3rd, Commissary for Caroline County [Ref: V-6636]. "James Boon, Sr., son of Isaac" was aged 44 in a 1790 deposition [Ref: T-9]. One James Boon married Mary Toolson by license recorded October 30, 1775, and a James Boon married Sarah Boon by license dated November 13, 1792 [Ref: X-6]. Since there was more then one man named James Boon, additional research will be necessary before drawing conclusions.

BOON (BOONE), John. Private, Militia, Capt. Thomas Hughlett's Company, 28th Battalion, by August 13, 1777 [Ref: M-152]. Private, 5th Maryland Line, enlisted June 8, 1778 [Ref: D-185]. Rendered patriotic service by providing wheat for the use of the military in August, 1782, as verified by Giles Hicks 3rd, Commissary for Caroline County [Ref: V-6636].

BOON (BOONE), Joseph. Private, Militia, Capt. William Chipley's Company, 28th Battalion, by August 13, 1777 [Ref: M-153]. On December 10, 1779, he filed a certificate in Caroline County Court that he had subscribed to the Oath of Allegiance and Fidelity before the Hon. Samuel Ridgeway in Queen Anne's County [Ref: N-67]. Rendered patriotic service by providing wheat for the use of the military in August, 1782, as verified by Giles Hicks 3rd, Commissary for Caroline County [Ref: V-6636]. Joseph Boone married Rebekah Cox by license dated January 26, 1778 [Ref: X-8].

BOON (BOONE), Letaetia. Rendered patriotic service by providing wheat for the use of the military in August, 1782, as verified by Giles Hicks 3rd, Commissary for Caroline County [Ref: V-6636]. See "Andrew Jump," q.v.

BOON (BOONE), Mary. See "John Deroachbrune" and "Moses Boon," q.v.

BOON (BOONE), Moses (1742 -   ). Private, Militia, Capt. Thomas Hughlett's Company, 28th Battalion, by August 13, 1777 [Ref: M-152]. Rendered patriotic service by providing wheat for the use of the military in August, 1782, as verified by Giles Hicks 3rd, Commissary for Caroline County [Ref: V-6636]. Moses Boon, son of Isaac, was aged 42 in a 1784 deposition [Ref: T-9]. Rebecah Boon, daughter of Moses and Mary Boon, was born July 29, 1766 in Queen Anne's County (now Caroline County) as recorded in the register of St. John's P. E. Church [Ref: K-25].

BOON (BOONE), Perry. Private, Militia, Capt. William Chipley's Company, 28th Battalion, by August 13, 1777 [Ref: M-153].

BOON (BOONE), Prudence. See "Ezekiel Hunter, Jr.," q.v.

BOON (BOONE), Rebecca. See "Peter Chance" and "Moses Boon," q.v.

BOON (BOONE), Sarah. See "James Boon," q.v.

BOON (BOONE), Susanna. See "Henry Covington," q.v.

BOON (BOONE), Thomas. Rendered patriotic service by providing wheat for the use of the military in August, 1782, as verified by Giles Hicks 3rd, Commissary for Caroline County [Ref: V-6636].

BOON (BOONE), William (Joiner). Rendered patriotic service by providing wheat for the use of the military in August, 1782, as verified by Giles Hicks 3rd, Commissary for Caroline County [Ref: V-6636]. William Boon, Sr. was aged 51 in a 1784 deposition [Ref: T-9].

BOON (BOONE), William Jr. (1737 - after 1786). Private, Militia, Capt. Thomas Hughlett's Company, 28th Battalion, by August 13, 1777 [Ref: M-152]. William Boon, Jr., son of Isaac, was aged 48 in a 1784 deposition and aged 49 in a 1786 deposition [Ref: T-10].

BOON (BOONE), Willson. Private, Militia, Capt. Thomas Hughlett's Company, 28th Battalion, by August 13, 1777 [Ref: M-152].

BOOTMAN, Joseph. Private, 6th Company, Capt. Peter Adams, 1st Maryland Line, enlisted January 30, 1776 [Ref: D-14].

BOSTICK, James. Private, Militia, Capt. William Haslett's Company, 28th Battalion, by August 13, 1777 [Ref: M-152].

BOSTICK, Nathan. See "Nathan Baughstick," q.v.

BOSTICK, Thomas. Private, Militia, Capt. William Haslett's Company, 28th Battalion, by August 13, 1777 [Ref: M-152].

BOWDLE, Henry. Private, Militia, Capt. John Mitchell's Company, 14th Battalion, by August 13, 1777 [Ref: M-154]. Ensign, Militia, Capt. Mitchell's Company, August 14, 1779 [Ref: M-51, E-493]. Subscribed to the Oath of Allegiance and Fidelity before the Hon. Peter Richardson on February 28, 1778 [Ref: J-1814].

BOWDLE, Mary. See "James Sisk," q.v.

BOWDLE, Sarah. See "Anderton Blades," q.v.

BOZMAN, --?--. See "Charles Daffin," q.v.

BOZMAN, Rachel. See "Maccabeus Alford," q.v.

BOZMAN, Risdon. Private, Militia, 14th Battalion, Capt. Joseph Richardson's Company, by August 13, 1777 [Ref: M-154]. Rizdon Bozman married Henrietta Alford by license dated December 20, 1780 [Ref: X-13]. See "Charles Daffin," q.v.

BRADLEY, Jonah. Private, Militia, Capt. William Haslett's Company, 28th Battalion, by August 13, 1777 [Ref: M-152].

BRADLEY, Nathaniel. Private, Militia, Capt. William Chipley's Company, 28th Battalion, by August 13, 1777 [Ref: M-153].

BRADLEY, Sarah. See "John Culbreth," q.v.

BRADLEY, Thomas. Rendered patriotic service by providing wheat for the use of the military in August, 1782, as verified by Giles Hicks 3rd, Commissary for Caroline County [Ref: V-6636].

BRADLEY, Thompson. Private, Militia, Capt. William Chipley's Company, 28th Battalion, by August 13, 1777 [Ref: M-153].

BRANNOCK, Sarah. See "Cornelius Johnson," q.v.

BRANTON, Jacob. Private (substitute), Maryland Troops, furnished in Caroline County by William Whiteley, County Lieutenant, on April 16, 1781 [Ref: D-

368].

BREEDING, John. Private, Militia, Capt. John Stafford's Company, 14th Battalion, by August 13, 1777 [Ref: M-156].

BRICE, Benedict. Employed to haul corn for the State of Maryland, as certified by Richard Keene, Commissary for Caroline County, on June 1, 1780 [Ref: P-293].

BRICE, Mary. See "James Cohee," q.v.

BRIGHT, Ebenezer. Private, Militia, Capt. Vincent Price's Company, 28th Battalion, by August 13, 1777 [Ref: M-151].

BRIGHT, George. Private, Militia, Capt. Andrew Fountain's Company, 14th Battalion, by August 13, 1777 [Ref: M-157]. George Bright married Rachel Chapman by license dated August 10, 1778 [Ref: X-9].

BRIGHT, James. Private, 5th Maryland Line, enlisted June 14, 1777 and discharged by Col. Forrest on May 14, 1780 [Ref: D-184].

BRIGHT, Jonas. Private, Militia, Capt. Andrew Fountain's Company, 14th Battalion, by August 13, 1777 [Ref: M-157]. Rendered patriotic service by providing wheat for the use of the military in August, 1782, as verified by Giles Hicks 3rd, Commissary for Caroline County [Ref: V-6636, which listed the name as "Jones Brite"].

BRIGHT, Nicholas. Private, Militia, Capt. Andrew Fountain's Company, 14th Battalion, by August 13, 1777 [Ref: M-157]. Nicholas Bright married Ann Anthony by license dated February 20, 1780 [Ref: X-11].

BRILEY, Benjamin. Subscribed to the Oath of Allegiance and Fidelity before the Hon. Richard Mason on March 2, 1778 [Ref: J-1814].

BRILEY, William. Subscribed to the Oath of Allegiance and Fidelity before the Hon. Richard Mason on March 2, 1778 [Ref: J-1814]. Rendered patriotic service by providing wheat for the use of the military in August, 1782, as verified by Giles Hicks 3rd, Commissary for Caroline County [Ref: V-6636].

BRITE, Jones. See "Jonas Bright," q.v.

BROADAWAY, Sarah. See "John Baker," q.v.

BROADWAY, Ann. See "Richard Cooper" and "Nehemiah Cooper," q.v.

BRODY (BROADEY), William. Private, Militia, Capt. Samuel Jackson's Company, 28th Battalion, by August 13, 1777 [Ref: M-153]. Subscribed to the Oath of Allegiance and Fidelity before the Hon. Richard Mason on March 2, 1778 [Ref: J-1814].

BRODY (BROADY), James. Rendered patriotic service by providing wheat for the use of the military in August, 1782, as verified by Giles Hicks 3rd, Commissary for Caroline County [Ref: V-6636]. Subscribed to the Oath of Allegiance and Fidelity before the Hon. Richard Mason on March 2, 1778 [Ref: J-1814].

BROOKS, Benjamin. Private, Militia, Capt. John Mitchell's Company, 14th Battalion, by August 13, 1777 [Ref: M-154].

BROOKS, Dennis. Private, Militia, Capt. John Mitchell's Company, 14th Battalion, by August 13, 1777 [Ref: M-154].

BROOME, Ann. See "Matthew Driver," q.v.

BROOME, James. See "Matthew Driver," q.v.
BROUGHTEN, Isaac. Private, Maryland Troops, enrolled by Lieut. Levin Handy in Caroline County and passed by Col. William Hopewell on August 4, 1776 [Ref: D-69].
BROWN, Jessee. Private, Militia, Capt. Joseph Douglass' Company, 14th Battalion, by August 13, 1777 [Ref: M-156].
BROWN, John. Private (draft), Maryland Troops, enrolled in Caroline County by William Whiteley, County Lieutenant, on August 14, 1781 to serve in the Maryland Line until December 10, 1781 [Ref: D-385]. One John Brown married Fanney Coursey by license dated November 13, 1789 [Ref: X-20].
BROWN, John. Private, Militia, Capt. Henry Downes' Company, 28th Battalion, by August 13, 1777 [Ref: M-152].
BROWN, John. Private, Militia, Capt. Samuel Jackson's Company, 28th Battalion, by August 13, 1777 [Ref: M-153].
BROWN, Levi. Private, Militia, Capt. Joseph Douglass' Company, 14th Battalion, by August 13, 1777 [Ref: M-156]. Rendered patriotic service by providing wheat for the use of the military in June, 1782, as verified by Giles Hicks 3rd, Commissary for Caroline County [Ref: V-6636].
BROWN, William. Private, Maryland Troops, enlisted by Capt. Joseph Richardson in Caroline County and passed by Col. William Richardson on August 31, 1776 [Ref: D-69]. Private, Militia, Capt. Thomas Hughlett's Company, 28th Battalion, by August 13, 1777 [Ref: M-152]. "William Brown, of Choptank Hundred" subscribed to the Oath of Allegiance and Fidelity before the Hon. Benson Stainton on February 2, 1778 [Ref: J-1814].
BROWNING, Richard. Private (draft), Maryland Troops, enrolled in Caroline County by William Whiteley, County Lieutenant, on August 14, 1781 to serve in the Maryland Line until December 10, 1781 [Ref: D-385]. Richard Browning married Rebekah Camp by license dated May 12, 1778 [Ref: X-8].
BRUFF, Rachel. See "Foster Goldsborough," q.v.
BRYAN, John. Private, 6th Company, Capt. Peter Adams, 1st Maryland Line, enlisted February 15, 1776 [Ref: D-14]. Private, Militia, Capt. William Chipley's Company, 28th Battalion, by August 13, 1777 [Ref: M-153, which spelled the name "Bryann"].
BRYLEY, Samuel. Private, Militia, Capt. William Chipley's Company, 28th Battalion, by August 13, 1777 [Ref: M-153].
BRYLEY, William. Private, Militia, Capt. John Fauntleroy's Company, 28th Battalion, by August 13, 1777 [Ref: M-154].
BUCKINHAM, Isaac. Private, Militia, Capt. Thomas Hughlett's Company, 28th Battalion, by August 13, 1777 [Ref: M-153].
BULEY, William. Private, Militia, Capt. William Chipley's Company, 28th Battalion, by August 13, 1777 [Ref: M-153].
BULLOCK, John. Private, Militia, Capt. Shadrack Liden's Company, 14th Battalion, by August 13, 1777 [Ref: M-155].

BURK, Edward. Private, Militia, Capt. Henry Downes' Company, 28th Battalion, by August 13, 1777 [Ref: M-152]. Subscribed to the Oath of Allegiance and Fidelity before the Hon. Henry Downes, Jr. on March 2, 1778 [Ref: J-1814]. Rendered patriotic service by providing wheat for the use of the military in August, 1782, as verified by Giles Hicks 3rd, Commissary for Caroline County [Ref: V-6636].

BURK, Thomas. Ensign, Militia, Capt. Henry Downes' Company, 28th Battalion, by August 13, 1777 [Ref: M-152]. Captain, Militia, April 9, 1778 [Ref: M-51. E-23]. Rendered patriotic service by providing wheat for the use of the military in August, 1782, as verified by Giles Hicks 3rd, Commissary for Caroline County [Ref: V-6636]. Thomas Burk married Elizabeth Turner by license dated January 3, 1781 [Ref: X-13].

BURN, Carbry. Private, 6th Company, Capt. Peter Adams, 1st Maryland Line, enlisted January 23, 1776 [Ref: D-14].

BURT, Henry. Rendered patriotic service by providing wheat for the use of the military in August, 1782, as verified by Giles Hicks 3rd, Commissary for Caroline County [Ref: V-6636].

BURT, James. Private, Militia, Capt. Samuel Jackson's Company, 28th Battalion, by August 13, 1777 [Ref: M-153].

BURT, William. Private, Militia, Capt. Samuel Jackson's Company, 28th Battalion, by August 13, 1777 [Ref: M-153]. Rendered patriotic service by providing wheat for the use of the military in August, 1782, as verified by Giles Hicks 3rd, Commissary for Caroline County [Ref: V-6636].

BURTICE, James. Private, Militia, Capt. William Hopper's Company, 28th Battalion, by August 13, 1777 [Ref: M-151].

BURTON, William (1734 - after 1799). Private, Militia, Capt. Vincent Price's Company, 28th Battalion, by August 13, 1777 [Ref: M-151]. Aged 65 in a 1799 deposition [Ref: T-21].

BUSH, John. On December 27, 1776 he joined a company of men in Caroline County who marched to Talbot County to obtain a supply of salt [Ref: B-564, B-565]. Private, Militia, Capt. Henry Downes' Company, 28th Battalion, by August 13, 1777 [Ref: M-152]. One John Bush married Rachell Curtis on November 3, 1756 [Ref: K-26].

BUSH, Penelope. See "Richard Collison," q.v.

BUSICK, Caleb. Private, Militia, Capt. Nehemiah Andrew's Company, 14th Battalion, by August 13, 1777 [Ref: M-155].

BUSICK, Keziah. See "Nicholas Stubbs," q.v.

CAHALL, Elizabeth. See "William Cahall," q.v.

CAHALL, John. Private, Militia, Capt. Andrew Fountain's Company, 14th Battalion, by August 13, 1777 [Ref: M-157]. See "William Cahall," q.v.

CAHALL, Mary. See "William Cahall," q.v.

CAHALL, Noah. See "William Cahall," q.v.

CAHALL, Solomon. See "William Cahall," q.v.

CAHALL, William (c1750-1812). Private, Militia, Capt. Andrew Fountain's Company, 14th Battalion, by August 13, 1777 [Ref: M-157]. In an 1815 land commission record it stated that William Cahall had died in 1812 seized of a tract called "Maiden's Forrest" and leaving heirs as follows: John Cahall (eldest son, of age), Esther Cahall (of age), Winnafred Cahall (minor), Solomon Cahall (minor), Noah Cahall (minor), Elizabeth Cahall (minor), and Mary Cahall (minor). [Ref: T-30].
CAHALL, Winnafred. See "William Cahall," q.v.
CAIN, Manasseh. Subscribed to the Oath of Allegiance and Fidelity before the Hon. Henry Downes, Jr. on March 2, 1778 [Ref: J-1814].
CALDECORD, Edward, of Choptank Hundred. Subscribed to the Oath of Allegiance and Fidelity before the Hon. Benson Stainton on February 2, 1778 [Ref: J-1814].
CALDWELL, Ann. See "Thomas Hughlett," q.v.
CALDWELL, James. See "Thomas Roe," q.v.
CALDWELL, Mary. See "Thomas Roe," q.v.
CALDWELL, Timothy. See "Thomas Hughlett," q.v.
CALLAHAN, Cornelius. Private, 5th Maryland Line, enlisted June 10, 1778 and reportedly "deserted" on June 30, 1779 [Ref: D-193].
CALLAHAN (CALAHAN), Dennis. Private, Militia, Capt. Henry Downes' Company, 28th Battalion, by August 13, 1777 [Ref: M-152]. Private, 5th Maryland Line, enlisted June 6, 1778 and discharged March 19, 1779 [Ref: D-193].
CALLISON, Richard. See "Richard Collison," q.v.
CALSTON, Lydia. See "Thomas Leverton," q.v.
CAMP, Rebekah. See "Richard Browning," q.v.
CAMPBELL, Elizabeth. See "Benson Stainton," q.v.
CAMPBELL, John. See "Benson Stainton," q.v.
CAMPBELL, Margaret. See "Benson Stainton," q.v.
CAMPER, William. Private, Militia, Capt. Joseph Douglass' Company, 14th Battalion, by August 13, 1777 [Ref: M-156].
CANNON, James. Private, Militia, Capt. William Chipley's Company, 28th Battalion, by August 13, 1777 [Ref: M-153].
CANNON, Sarah. See "Solomon Jump," q.v.
CANNON, Solomon. Private, Militia, Capt. William Chipley's Company, 28th Battalion, by August 13, 1777 [Ref: M-153].
CANNON, Thomas. Private, 5th Maryland Line, enlisted August 28, 1777 [Ref: D-191].
CANNON, William. Private, Militia, Capt. William Chipley's Company, 28th Battalion, by August 13, 1777 [Ref: M-153]. Rendered patriotic service by providing wheat for the use of the military in August, 1782, as verified by Giles Hicks 3rd, Commissary for Caroline County [Ref: V-6636]. William Cannon married Henrietta Wheatley by license dated November 19, 1784 [Ref: X-16].

CAPEROON, Rebecca. See "Thomas Roe," q.v.

CAPEROON, William. See "Thomas Roe," q.v.

CAREY, Francis. Private, Militia, 14th Battalion, Capt. Richard Andrew's Company, by August 13, 1777 [Ref: M-156].

CAREY, Hannah. Rendered patriotic service by providing wheat for the use of the military in August, 1782, as verified by Giles Hicks 3rd, Commissary for Caroline County [Ref: V-6636].

CAREY, William. Private, Militia, Capt. Andrew Fountain's Company, 14th Battalion, by August 13, 1777 [Ref: M-157]. Second Lieutenant, Militia, Capt. Rich's Company, April 9, 1778 [Ref: E-23 (which spelled the name "Cary"), M-60]. Subscribed to the Oath of Allegiance and Fidelity before the Hon. Matthew Driver on February 1, 1778 [Ref: J-1814].

CAREY, William Jr. Subscribed to the Oath of Allegiance and Fidelity before the Hon. Matthew Driver on February 1, 1778 [Ref: J-1814].

CARLILE, Samuel. Private, Militia, Capt. John Stafford's Company, 14th Battalion, by August 13, 1777 [Ref: M-156].

CARMICHAEL, James. Private, 6th Company, Capt. Peter Adams, 1st Maryland Line, enlisted February 24, 1776 [Ref: D-15].

CARNEY, Alice. See "Thomas Carney," q.v.

CARNEY, George. Private (recruit), Maryland Troops, enrolled in Caroline County by William Whiteley, County Lieutenant, on August 14, 1781 to serve in the Maryland Line for 3 years [Ref: D-385].

CARNEY, Grace. See "Thomas Carney," q.v.

CARNEY, Rebecca. See "Thomas Carney," q.v.

CARNEY, Thomas (c1759-1828). Private, Maryland Line, who applied for pension (S35203) in Caroline County on February 24, 1819, aged about 60. In 1822 he had a wife Grace (aged 57 or 58) and daughters Alice (aged 17 to 18) and Rebecca (aged about 14). Thomas appeared on the pension rolls under the Act of March 18, 1818, and was placed on rolls on March 5, 1819. His pension commenced May 7, 1819, at $96 per year, was suspended under the Act of May 1, 1820, and then restored to the rolls commencing March 9, 1823. He died on June 30, 1828 [Ref: *Maryland Pension Rolls, 1835 Report*, page 33, reprinted in 1968 by the Genealogical Publishing Company, Inc.]

CARPENTER, William. See "William Douglass," q.v.

CARRINGTON, Thomas. Rendered patriotic service by providing wheat for the use of the military in August, 1782, as verified by Giles Hicks 3rd, Commissary for Caroline County [Ref: V-6636].

CARROLL, Anne. See "Richard Kennard," q.v.

CARTER, Edward. Ensign, Militia, Capt. Thomas Knotts' Company, 28th Battalion, December 17, 1781 [Ref: M-60, I-27]. "Edward Carter, Jr., of Choptank Hundred" subscribed to the Oath of Allegiance and Fidelity before the Hon. Benson Stainton on February 7, 1778 [Ref: J-1814]. Rendered patriotic service by providing wheat for the use of the military in August, 1782, as verified by Giles Hicks 3rd, Commissary for Caroline County [Ref: V-6636]. Edward Carter married Mary Webb by license dated February 7, 1782 [Ref: X-14].

CARTER, Edward Sr. Rendered patriotic service by providing wheat for the use of the military in August, 1782, as verified by Giles Hicks 3rd, Commissary for Caroline County [Ref: V-6636]. "Edward Carter, of Choptank Hundred" subscribed to the Oath of Allegiance and Fidelity before the Hon. Benson Stainton on January 23, 1778 [Ref: J-1814].

CARTER, Eliza. See "Hezekiah Coxell," q.v.

CARTER, John (1735 -   ). Subscribed to the Oath of Allegiance and Fidelity before the Hon. Charles Dickinson on March 1, 1778 [Ref: J-1418]. Aged 51 in a 1786 deposition [Ref: T-11]. See the other "John Carter," q.v.

CARTER, John. Private, Maryland Troops, enrolled by Lieut. Thomas Wynn Loockerman in Caroline County in July, 1776 [Ref: D-69]. Private, Militia, Capt. John Mitchell's Company, 14th Battalion, by August 13, 1777 [Ref: M-154]. John Carter married Lydia Hubbert by license dated August 6, 1779, and John Carter, Jr. married Lavinia Rumbley by license dated December 18, 1792 [Ref: X-10, X-24].

CARTER, Mary. See "John Stant," q.v.

CARTER, Sarah. See "Richard Mitchell," q.v.

CARTER, Sidney. See "Benjamin Jump," q.v.

CARTER, Solomon. Rendered patriotic service by providing wheat for the use of the military in August, 1782, as verified by Giles Hicks 3rd, Commissary for Caroline County [Ref: V-6636]. Solomon Carter married Rhoda Webster by license dated October 28, 1780 [Ref: X-12].

CARTWRIGHT, William. Private, Militia, 14th Battalion, Capt. Joseph Richardson's Company, by August 13, 1777 [Ref: M-154].

CASSON, David. Private, Militia, Capt. William Haslett's Company, 28th Battalion, by August 13, 1777 [Ref: M-152].

CASSON, Esther. See "Matthew Driver," q.v.

CASSON, Ferdinando. Private, Militia, Capt. William Haslett's Company, 28th Battalion, by August 13, 1777 [Ref: M-152]. See "Matthew Driver," q.v.

CASSON, Henry (1709 - after 1782). Appointed a Judge of Elections for Caroline County at the Maryland Convention on November 8, 1776 [Ref: O-55]. Subscribed to the Oath of Allegiance and Fidelity before the Hon. Matthew Driver on February 30 [sic], 1778 [Ref: J-1814]. Aged 73 in a 1782 deposition [Ref: T-6]. See "Matthew Driver," q.v.

CASSON, Henry Jr. First Lieutenant, Militia, Capt. William Hopper's Company, 28th Battalion, by August 13, 1777 [Ref: M-151, J-1814, and M-60, which latter source listed a Henry Casson, Jr. with the rank of captain on January 5, 1776]. One Henry Casson married Polly Nabb by license dated February 12, 1791 [Ref: X-22].

CASSON, James. Second Lieutenant, Militia, Capt. Thomas Casson's Company, 28th Battalion, April 9, 1778 [Ref: M-60, E-23]. First Lieutenant, Militia, Capt.

Allenby Jump's Company, July 24, 1780 [Ref: M-60, F-230, G-28]. Subscribed to the Oath of Allegiance and Fidelity before the Hon. Henry Downes, Jr. on March 2, 1778 [Ref: J-1814].

CASSON, John. Lieutenant in Capt. William Brown's Maryland Artillery, 1780-1781 [Ref: G-287]. See "Matthew Driver," q.v.

CASSON, Margaret. See "Matthew Driver," q.v.

CASSON, Mary. See "Daniel Skinner," q.v.

CASSON, Myers. See "Matthew Driver," q.v.

CASSON, Philip. Ensign, Maryland Troops, 1776; resigned, exact date not given in the record [Ref: D-68]. Appointed as the "Commissary of Purchases" on December 23, 1780 and "Purchaser of Cloathing" for Caroline County on June 5, 1781 by the Council of Maryland, and was subsequently referred to as "Philip Casson, Esquire, Commissary of Caroline County." On August 1, 1781 he was also Procurer of Horses for the Light Horse Troops in Caroline County; a number of horses he "took into possession from non-jurors." [Ref: G-254, G-462, G-593, G-610, G-200 (which misspelled the name as "Carson"), H-305, H-384, I-35].

CASSON, Robert. See "Matthew Driver," q.v.

CASSON, Thomas. Captain, Militia, 28th Battalion, April 9, 1778, and succeeded on July 24, 1780 and December 17, 1781, both dates were given in different sources [Ref: M-60, E-23, F-230, G-28, I-27]. See the other "Thomas Casson," q.v.

CASSON, Thomas. Private, Militia, Capt. William Hopper's Company, 28th Battalion, by August 13, 1777 [Ref: M-151]. Subscribed to the Oath of Allegiance and Fidelity before the Hon. Henry Downes, Jr. on March 2, 1778 [Ref: J-1814]. One Thomas Casson married Martha Baynard by license dated November 18, 1778 [Ref: X-9]. There was also a Thomas Casson who was a first lieutenant in the 5th Battalion of Militia in Queen Anne's County on June 7, 1781 [Ref: G-465]. Also see the other "Thomas Casson," q.v. Additional research may be necessary before drawing conclusions.

CAULK, Benjamin. Private, Maryland Troops, enlisted by Capt. Joseph Richardson in Caroline County and passed by Col. William Richardson on August 31, 1776 [Ref: D-69]. Private, Militia, 14th Battalion, Capt. Joseph Richardson's Company, by August 13, 1777 [Ref: M-154].

CAULK, Frances. Rendered patriotic service by providing wheat for the use of the military in August, 1782, as verified by Giles Hicks 3rd, Commissary for Caroline County [Ref: V-6636].

CAULK, Francis. Rendered patriotic service by providing wheat for the use of the military in May, 1782, as verified by Giles Hicks 3rd, Commissary for Caroline County [Ref: V-6636].

CAULK, John. Private, Militia, Capt. Nehemiah Andrew's Company, 14th Battalion, by August 13, 1777 [Ref: M-155].

CAULK, Lawrence. Rendered patriotic service by providing wheat for the use of the military in August, 1782, as verified by Giles Hicks III, Commissary for

Caroline County [Ref: P-539].

CAULK, Levin. Private, Militia, Capt. John Stafford's Company, 14th Battalion, by August 13, 1777 [Ref: M-156]. Rendered patriotic service by providing wheat for the use of the military in August, 1782, as verified by Giles Hicks 3rd, Commissary for Caroline County [Ref: V-6636].

CAULK, Mary. See "Matthew Paulson," q.v.

CAULK, Peter. Private, Militia, Capt. John Mitchell's Company, 14th Battalion, by August 13, 1777 [Ref: M-154].

CAULK, Sarah. See "John Jones," q.v.

CAUSEY, Ann. See "Beacham Causey," q.v.

CAUSEY (CAWSEY), Beacham or Beachamp (1740-1802). Private, Militia, 14th Battalion, Capt. Richard Andrew's Company, by August 13, 1777 [Ref: M-156]. Rendered patriotic service by providing wheat for the use of the military in August, 1782, as verified by Giles Hicks 3rd, Commissary for Caroline County [Ref: V-6636]. Aged 45 in a 1785 deposition [Ref: T-9]. In an 1817 land commission record it stated that Beacham Causey had died in 1802, leaving a widow "who has since died" and the following children: Eliza or Elizabeth Dawson (wife of Asa Dawson), Robert Causey (who died leaving a daughter Eliza, wife of Samuel Long of Talbot County, and is about age 19), Curtis Causey, Eleanor Reed (wife of Andrew Reed of Talbot County), Beachamp Causey, Nancy Jester (widow of William Jester), and Ann Causey [Ref: T-31, which spelled the name "Betchim Causay"].

CAUSEY, Curtis. See "Beacham Causey," q.v.

CAUSEY, Ezekiel (1759-c1821). Born in Maryland, married Elizabeth Clary, and served in the Revolutionary War in Georgia, where he died before 1821 [Ref: Y-519].

CAUSEY (CAWSEY), Frederick. Ensign, Militia, 14th Battalion, Capt. Richard Andrew's Company, by August 13, 1777 [Ref: M-156]. Rendered patriotic service by providing wheat for the use of the military in August, 1782, as verified by Giles Hicks 3rd, Commissary for Caroline County [Ref: V-6636].

CAUSEY (CAWSEY), Hubbert. Private, Militia, 14th Battalion, Capt. Richard Andrew's Company, by August 13, 1777 [Ref: M-156].

CAUSEY (CAWSEY), Isaac. Private, Militia, 14th Battalion, Capt. Richard Andrew's Company, by August 13, 1777 [Ref: M-156].

CAUSEY (CAWSEY), Isaac. Rendered patriotic service by providing wheat for the use of the military in August, 1782, as verified by Giles Hicks 3rd, Commissary for Caroline County [Ref: V-6636].

CAUSEY (CAWSEY), Nehemiah. Private, Militia, Capt. John Stafford's Company, 14th Battalion, by August 13, 1777 [Ref: M-156].

CAUSEY, Robert. See "Beacham Causey," q.v.

CAUSEY (CAWSEY), Solomon (1735 -   ). First Lieutenant, Militia, Capt. John Stafford's Company, 14th Battalion, by August 13, 1777 [Ref: M-156]. Rendered patriotic service by providing wheat for the use of the military in August, 1782, as verified by Giles Hicks 3rd, Commissary for Caroline County [Ref: V-6636]. Aged 40 in a 1775 deposition and aged 49 in a 1784 deposition [Ref: T-1, T-7].

CAUSEY (CAWSEY), Thomas. Private, Militia, Capt. John Stafford's Company, 14th Battalion, by August 13, 1777 [Ref: M-156]. Rendered patriotic service by providing wheat for the use of the military in August, 1782, as verified by Giles Hicks 3rd, Commissary for Caroline County [Ref: V-6636].

CAUSEY (CAWSEY), William (1744-c1828). Private, Militia, 14th Battalion, Capt. Richard Andrew's Company, by August 13, 1777 [Ref: M-156]. Ensign, Militia, Capt. Andrews' Company, 14th Battalion, August 14, 1779 [Ref: M-60, E-493]. Born in June, 1744 in Ireland, married second to Susannah Jackson (first wife unknown), and died before July 21, 1828 in Mississippi [Ref: Y-519].

CAUSEY (CAWSEY), Zebulon (Zebelon). Private, Militia, Capt. John Stafford's Company, 14th Battalion, by August 13, 1777 [Ref: M-156]. Rendered patriotic service by providing wheat for the use of the military in August, 1782, as verified by Giles Hicks 3rd, Commissary for Caroline County [Ref: V-6636].

CHAFFINCH, James. Second Lieutenant, Militia, Capt. Andrew Fountain's Company, 14th Battalion, by August 13, 1777 and April 9, 1778; resigned some time in 1779, exact date not given in the record [Ref: M-61, M-156, E-23]. Subscribed to the Oath of Allegiance and Fidelity before the Hon. Nathaniel Potter on March 2, 1778 [Ref: J-1814].

CHAFFINCH, Sarah. See "John Morgan," q.v.

CHALMERS, Margaret. See "Giles Hicks," q.v.

CHANCE, Absalom (1742 -   ). Private, Militia, Capt. Thomas Hughlett's Company, 28th Battalion, by August 13, 1777 [Ref: M-153]. Rendered patriotic service by providing wheat for the use of the military in August, 1782, as verified by Giles Hicks 3rd, Commissary for Caroline County [Ref: V-6636]. Aged 42 in a 1784 deposition [Ref: T-9].

CHANCE, Ann. See "John Voss Baker," q.v.

CHANCE, Batchelor. Private, Militia, Capt. Thomas Hughlett's Company, 28th Battalion, by August 13, 1777 [Ref: M-152]. Batchelor Chance, Jr. married Nancy Dunning by license dated June 20, 1781 [Ref: X-13]. He may have been the son of or related to "Bachelor Chance, Quaker" who was aged 61 in a 1782 deposition [Ref: T-11].

CHANCE, Benjamin (c1753-c1816). Born in Maryland, married Rachel --?--, rendered patriotic service during the Revolutionary War in North Carolina, and died after November 29, 1816 [Ref: Y-531].

CHANCE, Elijah. See "John Voss Baker," q.v.

CHANCE, Levi. Private, Militia, Capt. William Haslett's Company, 28th Battalion, by August 13, 1777 [Ref: M-152]. "Levy Chance" was a private (draft), Maryland Troops, enrolled in Caroline County by William Whiteley, County Lieutenant, on August 14, 1781 (although reported "run" at the time) to serve in the Maryland Line until December 10, 1781 [Ref: D-385]. See "Thomas Roe," q.v.

CHANCE, Peter. Private, Militia, Capt. William Chipley's Company, 28th Battalion, by August 13, 1777 [Ref: M-153]. Peter Chance married Rebecca Boone by license dated February 23, 1785 [Ref: X-16].

CHANCE, Rachel. See "Benjamin Chance," q.v.

CHANCE, Rich. Private, Militia, Capt. Thomas Hughlett's Company, 28th Battalion, by August 13, 1777 [Ref: M-152].

CHANCE, Richard. Private, Militia, Capt. John Stafford's Company, 14th Battalion, by August 13, 1777 [Ref: M-156]. Private (draft), Maryland Troops, furnished in Caroline County by William Whiteley, County Lieutenant, on April 16, 1781 [Ref: D-368].

CHANCE, Sarah. See "Thomas Roe," q.v.

CHANCE, Stephen (c1760-c1820). Born in Maryland, married Lillie Hood, served as a musician and private in the Revolutionary War in North Carolina, and died after 1820 in Georgia [Ref: Y-531].

CHANCE, Thomas. Private, Militia, Capt. William Haslett's Company, 28th Battalion, by August 13, 1777 [Ref: M-152]. Rendered patriotic service by providing wheat for the use of the military in August, 1782, as verified by Giles Hicks 3rd, Commissary for Caroline County [Ref: V-6636]. Thomas Chance married Mary Richardson and Thomas Chance married Rebecca Price, both by licenses dated June 15, 1779 [Ref: X-10]. Additional research will be necessary before drawing conclusions.

CHANCE, Tilghman. Private, Militia, Capt. Thomas Hughlett's Company, 28th Battalion, by August 13, 1777 [Ref: M-153].

CHANCE, Vinson (1758-c1824). Born on March 17, 1758 in Maryland, married Sarah Taylor, served as a drummer in the Revolutionary War in North Carolina, and died after November 25, 1824 in Louisiana [Ref: Y-531].

CHAPLAIN, James. See "John Harvey," q.v.

CHAPMAN, Rachel. See "George Bright," q.v.

CHEESLY, John. On December 27, 1776 he joined a company of men in Caroline County who marched to Talbot County to obtain a supply of salt [Ref: B-564, B-565]. Private, Militia, Capt. Henry Downes' Company, 28th Battalion, by August 13, 1777 [Ref: M-152, which listed the name as "John Chestell?"].

CHEEZ, Rebecca. See "William Banning," q.v.

CHEEZUM (CHEZUM), John. Ensign, Militia, Capt. John Mitchell's Company, 14th Battalion, by August 13, 1777 and April 9, 1778 [Ref: E-23 (which listed the name as "John Chizmn"), M-62 (which reported "Jno. Chiezum" as deceased, but gave no date of death), M-154].

CHEEZUM (CHEZUM), Samuel. Private, Militia, Capt. John Mitchell's Company, 14th Battalion, by August 13, 1777 [Ref: M-154].

CHEEZUM (CHEZUM), William. Private, Militia, Capt. John Mitchell's Company, 14th Battalion, by August 13, 1777 [Ref: M-154].

CHESTELL, John. See "John Cheesly," q.v.

CHILCUTT, John. Private, Militia, Capt. John Stafford's Company, 14th Battalion, by August 13, 1777 [Ref: M-156]. "John Chelcott" married Eliza Hill by license recorded October 30, 1775 [Ref: X-6].

CHILCUTT, Joshua. Private, Militia, Capt. William Chipley's Company, 28th Battalion, by August 13, 1777 [Ref: M-153].

CHILCUTT, Thomas. Private, Militia, Capt. John Mitchell's Company, 14th Battalion, by August 13, 1777 [Ref: M-155]. Rendered patriotic service by providing wheat for the use of the military in August, 1782, as verified by Giles Hicks 3rd, Commissary for Caroline County [Ref: V-6636, which spelled the name "Chilcut"].

CHILTON, Able (Abel). Private, Militia, Capt. William Hopper's Company, 28th Battalion, by August 13, 1777 [Ref: M-151]. Abel Chilton married Mary Swann by license dated October 17, 1780 [Ref: X-12].

CHILTON, Anthony. Private, Militia, Capt. Thomas Hughlett's Company, 28th Battalion, by August 13, 1777 [Ref: M-153].

CHILTON, John. Private, Militia, Capt. Thomas Hughlett's Company, 28th Battalion, by August 13, 1777 [Ref: M-153].

CHILTON, Matthew. Private, Militia, Capt. William Chipley's Company, 28th Battalion, by August 13, 1777 [Ref: M-153]. Matthew Chilton married Hannah Wootters by license dated October 19, 1784 [Ref: X-16]. There was also a Matthew Chilton, Jr. who married Rebecca Bell on May 9, 1751 [Ref: K-26]. See "William Chilton," q.v.

CHILTON, Rebecca. See "William Chilton," q.v.

CHILTON, William (1752 -   ). Private, Militia, Capt. Thomas Hughlett's Company, 28th Battalion, by August 13, 1777 [Ref: M-153]. William Chilton, son of Matthew and Rebecca Chilton, was born January 8, 1752 [Ref: K-25].

CHILTON, William. Rendered patriotic service by providing wheat for the use of the military in August, 1782, as verified by Giles Hicks 3rd, Commissary for Caroline County [Ref: V-6636]. William Chilton married Rebecca Talbot by license dated September 14, 1774 [Ref: X-4].

CHIPLEY, James. Private, Militia, Capt. John Mitchell's Company, 14th Battalion, by August 13, 1777 [Ref: M-154].

CHIPLEY, John. Second Lieutenant, Militia, Capt. John Mitchell's Company, 14th Battalion, December 17, 1781 [Ref: M-62, I-27]. Subscribed to the Oath of Allegiance and Fidelity before the Hon. Charles Dickinson on March 1, 1778 [Ref: J-1418].

CHIPLEY, William. Served on the Committee of Observation for Caroline County on August 2, 1775 [Ref: A-48]. Ensign, promoted to Second Lieutenant, Militia, Capt. Thomas Hughlett's Company, 28th Battalion, June 19, 1777; Captain, by August 13, 1777 until June 21, 1781, when reported as "moved from the county." [Ref: M-62, M-153, C-294, E-493, J-1814]. Subscribed to the Oath of Allegiance and Fidelity before the Hon. Richard Mason on March 2, 1778 [Ref: J-1814]. See "William Shiply," q.v.

CHIPPY, Joshua. Second Lieutenant, Militia, Capt. Hughlett's Company, 28th

(8th?) Battalion, April 18, 1780; First Lieutenant, Militia, Capt. Robert Hardcastle's Company, December 17, 1781 [Ref: M-62, F-144, I-27]. Subscribed to the Oath of Allegiance and Fidelity before the Hon. Thomas Hardcastle on February 20, 1778 [Ref: J-1814].

CLARK, Anne. See "Joshua Clark," q.v.

CLARK, Caleb (1746 -   ). Private, Militia, 14th Battalion, Capt. Joseph Richardson's Company, by August 13, 1777 [Ref: M-154]. Aged 40 in a 1786 deposition [Ref: T-12].

CLARK, Celia. See "John Cohee," q.v.

CLARK, Chaney. See "William Adams," q.v.

CLARK, Edward. See "Joshua Clark," q.v.

CLARK, Elijah. Private, Maryland Troops, enrolled by Lieut. Thomas Wynn Loockerman in Caroline County in July, 1776 [Ref: D-69]. Private, Militia, 14th Battalion, Capt. Joseph Richardson's Company, by August 13, 1777 [Ref: M-154]. Ensign, Militia, Capt. Thomas Loockerman's Company, April 9, 1778; Second Lieutenant, Militia, Capt. Vincent Price's Company, July 24, 1780; First Lieutenant, Militia, Capt. Alexander Waddle's Company, December 17, 1781 [Ref: M-62, E-23, F-230, G-27, I-27]. "Eliza Clark" married Elizabeth Robinson by license dated March 9, 1785 [Ref: X-16].

CLARK, Elizabeth. See "Joshua Clark" and "Jacob Loockerman" and "Isaac Baggs," q.v.

CLARK, Jane. See "Henry James," q.v.

CLARK, John. Private, 6th Company, Capt. Peter Adams, 1st Maryland Line, enlisted January 22, 1776 [Ref: D-14]. John Clark married Martha Lyden by license dated January 14, 1784 [Ref: X-15].

CLARK (CLARKE), Joshua. First Lieutenant, Militia, Capt. Vincent Price's Company, 28th Battalion, 1777, but "resigned from his bad state of health." [Ref: J-1814]. Subscribed to the Oath of Allegiance and Fidelity before the Hon. Henry Downes, Jr. on March 2, 1778 [Ref: J-1814]. A son of Joshua Clarke who died by 1741, Joshua married by 1764 to Anne Oldham and their children were Joshua, Edward Oldham, Philip, Ann, Elizabeth, Mary, and Margaret. Joshua represented Caroline County at the Maryland Conventions in 1775 and 1776. He served as a Justice in Queen Anne's County from 1768 to 1773 and a Justice in Caroline County from 1774 to 1777. He also served on the Committee of Observation in Queen Anne's County in 1774, Justice of the Orphans' Court of Caroline County in 1777, and Justice of the Peace in 1778. Joshua Clarke died by February, 1781 in Caroline County [Ref: R-223, R-224, R-70, R-71, R-72, E-249, O-1, O-4, O-28, A-4, Z-2, Z-26].

CLARK, Margaret. See "John Freeman" and "Joshua Clark," q.v.

CLARK, Mary. See "Joshua Clark," q.v.

CLARK, Philip. See "Joshua Clark," q.v.

CLARK, Richard (1743 -   ). Private, Militia, 14th Battalion, Capt. Joseph Richardson's Company, by August 13, 1777 [Ref: M-154]. Subscribed to the

Oath of Allegiance and Fidelity (made his "|" mark) before the Hon. Peter Richardson on February 28, 1778 [Ref: J-1814]. Aged 43 in a 1786 deposition [Ref: T-12].

CLARK, Solomon. On October 18, 1780, he filed a certificate in Caroline County Court that he had subscribed to the Oath of Allegiance and Fidelity [Ref: N-90]. "Solomon Clarke" married Sarah Swift by license dated August 14, 1793 [Ref: X-25].

CLARK, William. Private, Maryland Troops, enrolled by Lieut. Thomas Wynn Loockerman in Caroline County in July, 1776 [Ref: D-69].

CLARK, William. Private, 6th Company, Capt. Peter Adams, 1st Maryland Line, enlisted May 7, 1776 [Ref: D-15].

CLARKE, Elizabeth. See "James Hardcastle," q.v.

CLARKE, Hannah. See "Thomas Baynard," q.v.

CLARKE, Joshua. See "Joshua Clark," q.v.

CLARKE, William. See "William Adams," q.v.

CLARKSON, Thomas. Private, Militia, Capt. Joseph Douglass' Company, 14th Battalion, by August 13, 1777 [Ref: M-156]. Private (draft), Maryland Troops, enrolled in Caroline County by William Whiteley, County Lieutenant, on August 14, 1781 (although reported "run" at the time) to serve in the Maryland Line until December 10, 1781 [Ref: D-385].

CLARY, Elizabeth. See "Ezekiel Causey," q.v.

CLARY, John. Sergeant, 5th Maryland Line, enlisted on December 4, 1776 and was either discharged on April 10, 1777 or deceased on July 20, 1777 [Ref: D-191].

CLEMENTS (CLEMMONS, CLEMENT), Abner (1755 -   ). Private, Militia, Capt. Vincent Price's Company, 28th Battalion, by August 13, 1777 [Ref: M-151]. On May 26, 1780, he filed a certificate in Caroline County Court that he had subscribed to the Oath of Allegiance and Fidelity before the Hon. Richard Mason [Ref: N-78]. Abner Clements, son of John and Jane Clements, was born November 27, 1755 [Ref: K-25]. "Abner Clemmons" married Margaret Morgan by license dated September 22, 1780, and "Abner Clements" married Lydia Stewart by license dated January 27, 1785 [Ref: X-12, X-16].

CLEMENTS (CLEMONS), James. Subscribed to the Oath of Allegiance and Fidelity before the Hon. Richard Mason on March 2, 1778 [Ref: J-1814].

CLEMENTS, Jane. See "Abner Clements," q.v.

CLEMENTS, Joel. See "James Roe," q.v.

CLEMENTS (CLEMMONS), John (1751 - after 1832). Private, Militia, Capt. Samuel Jackson's Company, 28th Battalion, by August 13, 1777 [Ref: M-153]. Applied for pension (S8215) in Richmond County, North Carolina on July 18, 1832, stating he was born in Queen Anne's County, Maryland on December 12, 1751 and lived in Caroline County at the time of his enlistment in the Maryland troops; also served in the North Carolina Line during the war [Ref: W-673]. "John Clemments" married Rebekah Rogers in Caroline County by license dated

April 14, 1779 [Ref: X-10]. See "Abner Clements," q.v.
CLEMENTS, Margaret. See "James Roe," q.v.
CLEMENTS (CLEMENT), Richard. Subscribed to the Oath of Allegiance and Fidelity (made his "R" mark) before the Hon. Richard Mason on March 2, 1778 [Ref: J-1814].
CLEMENTS, Unicey. See "William Satterfield," q.v.
CLIFT, Abroll(?). Private, Militia, Capt. Henry Downes' Company, 28th Battalion, by August 13, 1777 [Ref: M-152].
CLIFT, Crisenberry. Private, 6th Company, Capt. Peter Adams, 1st Maryland Line, enlisted May 15, 1776 [Ref: D-15].
CLIFT, Henry. Private, 6th Company, Capt. Peter Adams, 1st Maryland Line, enlisted February 6, 1776 [Ref: D-14]. Private, Militia, Capt. Vincent Price's Company, 28th Battalion, by August 13, 1777 [Ref: M-151]. Henry Clift married Elizabeth Cronnoon [Cromean?] by license dated November 2, 1778 [Ref: X-9].
CLIFT, Joseph. Private, Militia, 14th Battalion, Capt. Joseph Richardson's Company, by August 13, 1777 [Ref: M-154]. Subscribed to the Oath of Allegiance and Fidelity before the Hon. Peter Richardson on February 23, 1778 [Ref: J-1814].
CLIFT, Mark. Private, Militia, Capt. John Mitchell's Company, 14th Battalion, by August 13, 1777 [Ref: M-154].
CLIFT, Sarah. See "John Morgan," q.v.
CLOUGH, Elizabeth. See "Jeremiah Monticue," q.v.
CLOVE, John. Private, Militia, Capt. Thomas Hughlett's Company, 28th Battalion, by August 13, 1777 [Ref: M-153]. Rendered patriotic service by providing wheat for the use of the military in August, 1782, as verified by Giles Hicks 3rd, Commissary for Caroline County [Ref: V-6636].
CLOVE, Nathan. Private, Militia, Capt. John Fauntleroy's Company, 28th Battalion, by August 13, 1777 [Ref: M-154].
CLYMER, James. Private, Militia, Capt. Vincent Price's Company, 28th Battalion, by August 13, 1777 [Ref: M-151]. "James Climer" subscribed to the Oath of Allegiance and Fidelity (made his "J" mark) before the Hon. Henry Downes, Jr. on March 2, 1778 [Ref: J-1814].
CLYMER, John. Private, Militia, Capt. Nehemiah Andrew's Company, 14th Battalion, by August 13, 1777 [Ref: M-155].
CLYMOR, Francis. Private, Militia, Capt. Henry Downes' Company, 28th Battalion, by August 13, 1777 [Ref: M-152].
COGHILL, James. Private, Militia, Capt. William Chipley's Company, 28th Battalion, by August 13, 1777 [Ref: M-153].
COGHILL, Solomon. Private, Militia, Capt. William Chipley's Company, 28th Battalion, by August 13, 1777 [Ref: M-153].
COHEE, Amos. Private, Militia, 14th Battalion, Capt. Joseph Richardson's Company, by August 13, 1777 [Ref: M-154].
COHEE, James (1746 - after 1798). Private, Militia, Capt. John Mitchell's

Company, 14th Battalion, by August 13, 1777 [Ref: M-154]. "James Cohee, of Dorchester County" was aged 52 in a 1798 deposition taken in Caroline County [Ref: T-19]. A James Cohee married Mary Brice by license dated August 28, 1787 [Ref: X-18].

COHEE, John. Private, Maryland Troops, enrolled by Lieut. Thomas Wynn Loockerman in Caroline County in July, 1776 [Ref: D-69]. Private, Militia, 14th Battalion, Capt. Joseph Richardson's Company, by August 13, 1777 [Ref: M-154]. John Cohee married Celia Clark by license dated November 18, 1777 [Ref: X-7].

COLEMAN, John. Private, Militia, 14th Battalion, Capt. Joseph Richardson's Company, by August 13, 1777 [Ref: M-154]. Subscribed to the Oath of Allegiance and Fidelity before the Hon. Charles Dickinson on March 1, 1778 [Ref: J-1418]. Gave a deposition on January 20, 1777 (age not given) before the Committee of Observation, and signed with his "X" mark [Ref: C-66].

COLLINS, Abraham or Abram (1743 - after 1809). Private, Militia, 14th Battalion, Capt. Richard Andrew's Company, by August 13, 1777 [Ref: M-156]. Rendered patriotic service by providing wheat for the use of the military in August, 1782, as verified by Giles Hicks 3rd, Commissary for Caroline County [Ref: V-6636]. "Abraham Collins, Sr." was aged 66 in an 1809 deposition [Ref: T-26].

COLLINS, Emory (Emmory). Private, Militia, Capt. John Mitchell's Company, 14th Battalion, by August 13, 1777 [Ref: M-154]. Seaman, enlisted June 2, 1782 to serve on the barge "Fearnaught" under Capt. Edward Spedden, and was paid £3 bounty for enlisting; physical description given as 5' 6" tall with a dark complexion [Ref: D-612].

COLLINS, Isaac. Private, Militia, 14th Battalion, Capt. Richard Andrew's Company, by August 13, 1777 [Ref: M-156].

COLLINS, James. Seaman, enlisted June 11, 1782 to serve on the barge "Fearnaught" under Capt. Edward Spedden, and was paid £3 bounty for enlisting; physical description given as 6' 1" tall with a fair complexion [Ref: D-612]. A "James Cohlins" married Sarah Perry by license dated May 15, 1786 [Ref: X-17].

COLLISON, Peter. Private, Militia, Capt. Shadrack Liden's Company, 14th Battalion, by August 13, 1777 [Ref: M-155]. Rendered patriotic service by providing wheat for the use of the military in August, 1782, as verified by Giles Hicks 3rd, Commissary for Caroline County [Ref: V-6636]. Peter Collison married Sarah Johnson by license dated January 5, 1790 [Ref: X-20].

COLLISON, Richard (1739 -   ). Second Lieutenant, Militia, Capt. John Mitchell's Company, 14th Battalion, by August 13, 1777 and commissioned again on April 9, 1778; First Lieutenant, August 14, 1779 [Ref: M-154, E-493, E-23, M-51, which latter two sources spelled the name "Callison"]. Aged 48 in a 1787 deposition [Ref: T-14]. Richard Collison married Penelope Bush by license dated November 13, 1787 [Ref: X-18].

COLLISON, William. Private, Militia, Capt. Shadrack Liden's Company, 14th Battalion, by August 13, 1777 [Ref: M-155]. Rendered patriotic service by providing wheat for the use of the military in August, 1782, as verified by Giles Hicks 3rd, Commissary for Caroline County [Ref: V-6636].

COLSCOTT, John Jr. Private, Militia, Capt. Henry Downes' Company, 28th Battalion, by August 13, 1777 [Ref: M-152].

COLSCOTT, William. Private, Militia, Capt. Henry Downes' Company, 28th Battalion, by August 13, 1777 [Ref: M-152]. Rendered patriotic service by providing wheat for the use of the military in August, 1782, as verified by Giles Hicks 3rd, Commissary for Caroline County [Ref: V-6636]. "William Colescott" married Mary Wheatley by license recorded August 9, 1775 [Ref: X-5].

COLSTON, Anne. See "Thomas Hardcastle" and "William Keene," q.v.

COLSTON, Elizabeth. See "Jeremiah Colston" and "Thomas Cooper, Jr.," q.v.

COLSTON, Esther. See "Jeremiah Colston," q.v.

COLSTON, Jeremiah (1725 - after 1780). Served on the Committee of Observation for Caroline County in June, 1776 [Ref: A-481]. Attended the Maryland Convention on July 3, 1776 for the "express purpose of forming a new government." [Ref: O-35]. On December 27, 1776 he joined a company of men in Caroline County who marched to Talbot County to obtain a supply of salt [Ref: B-564, B-565]. On May 26, 1780, he filed a certificate in Caroline County Court that he had subscribed to the Oath of Allegiance and Fidelity before the Hon. Richard Mason [Ref: N-78]. Rendered patriotic service by providing wheat for the use of the military in September, 1782, as verified by Giles Hicks 3rd, Commissary for Caroline County [Ref: V-6636]. Aged 57 in a 1782 deposition [Ref: T-4]. Jeremiah Colston married Esther --?-- and had at least two daughters: Elizabeth (born May 27, 1755) and Mary (born October 9, 1757). [Ref: K-25].

COLSTON (CALSTON), Lydia. See "Thomas Leverton," q.v.

COLSTON, Mary. See "Jeremiah Colston" and "Giles Hicks, Jr.," q.v.

COLTRON, Henry. Private, Militia, Capt. Vincent Price's Company, 28th Battalion, by August 13, 1777 [Ref: M-151].

COLWELL, David. Private, Militia, Capt. William Hopper's Company, 28th Battalion, by August 13, 1777 [Ref: M-151].

COLWELL, Edward. Private, Militia, Capt. William Hopper's Company, 28th Battalion, by August 13, 1777 [Ref: M-151].

COMERFORD, Thomas. Private, Maryland Troops, enlisted by Capt. Joseph Richardson in Caroline County and passed by Col. William Richardson on August 31, 1776 [Ref: D-69].

CONNAWAY, Samuel. Rendered patriotic service by providing wheat for the use of the military in August, 1782, as verified by Giles Hicks 3rd, Commissary for Caroline County [Ref: V-6636].

CONNELLY, Celia. See "John Willoughby," q.v.

CONNELLY, Eli. See "Levin Johnson," q.v.

CONNELLY, Jesse. See "Henry Willis," q.v.

CONNELLY, Owen. See "Owen Connerly," q.v.

CONNELLY (CONNERLY), Roger. Private (draft), Maryland Troops, furnished in Caroline County by William Whiteley, County Lieutenant, on April 16, 1781 [Ref: D-368]. Private (draft), Maryland Troops, enrolled in Caroline County by William Whiteley, County Lieutenant, on August 14, 1781 to serve in the Maryland Line until December 10, 1781 [Ref: D-385]. Honorably discharged from the service on December 5, 1781 [Ref: I-10, which spelled the name "Connerly"].

CONNER, Daniel. Private (draft), Maryland Troops, enrolled in Caroline County by William Whiteley, County Lieutenant, on August 14, 1781 to serve in the Maryland Line until December 10, 1781 [Ref: D-385]. Honorably discharged from the service on December 5, 1781 [Ref: I-10].

CONNER, Hughett. Private, Maryland Troops, enlisted by Capt. Joseph Richardson in Caroline County and passed by Col. William Richardson on August 31, 1776 [Ref: D-69].

CONNER, James. Private, Militia, Capt. Samuel Jackson's Company, 28th Battalion, by August 13, 1777 [Ref: M-153].

CONNER, Rachel. See "John Cooper, Jr.," q.v.

CONNER, Thomas (1732 - after 1782). Private, Militia, Capt. John Mitchell's Company, 14th Battalion, by August 13, 1777 [Ref: M-154]. Aged 50 in a 1782 deposition [Ref: T-4].

CONNERLY, Allin or Allen (1738 - after 1785). Private, Militia, Capt. Nehemiah Andrew's Company, 14th Battalion, by August 13, 1777 [Ref: M-155]. Aged 47 in a 1785 deposition [Ref: T-12].

CONNERLY, Ann. See "Henry Willis," q.v.

CONNERLY (CONNELLY), Owen. "Owen Connerly" was a private in the militia, 14th Battalion, Capt. Joseph Richardson's Company, by August 13, 1777 [Ref: M-154]. "Owen Connelly" married Elizabeth Layton by license dated August 25, 1788 [Ref: X-19].

CONNERLY, Reubin. Private, Militia, Capt. Shadrack Liden's Company, 14th Battalion, by August 13, 1777 [Ref: M-155]. Reuben Connerly married Rebekah Pritchett by license dated October 13, 1778 [Ref: X-9].

CONNERLY, Roger. See "Roger Connelly," q.v.

CONNOWAY, Benjamin. Rendered patriotic service by providing wheat for the use of the military in August, 1782, as verified by Giles Hicks 3rd, Commissary for Caroline County [Ref: V-6636].

COOCK, William. Private, Militia, Capt. William Haslett's Company, 28th Battalion, by August 13, 1777 [Ref: M-152]

COOK, Risdon. Private, Militia, Capt. William Haslett's Company, 28th Battalion, by August 13, 1777 [Ref: M-152].

COOK, Thomas. Private, Militia, Capt. William Haslett's Company, 28th Battalion, by August 13, 1777 [Ref: M-152].

COOK, William. Private, Militia, Capt. John Mitchell's Company, 14th Battalion, by August 13, 1777 [Ref: M-154].

COOK, William. Private, Militia, Capt. William Haslett's Company, 28th Battalion,

by August 13, 1777 [Ref: M-152].
COOK, William. Private, Maryland Troops, enlisted by Capt. Joseph Richardson in Caroline County and passed by Col. William Richardson on August 31, 1776 [Ref: D-69].
COOPER, Aaron. On December 27, 1776 he joined a company of men in Caroline County who marched to Talbot County to obtain a supply of salt [Ref: B-564, B-565]. Private, Militia, Capt. Vincent Price's Company, 28th Battalion, by August 13, 1777 [Ref: M-151].
COOPER, Abram. Private, Militia, Capt. William Haslett's Company, 28th Battalion, by August 13, 1777 [Ref: M-152].
COOPER, Ann. See "Nathan Downes" and "Nehemiah Cooper" and "Abner Roe," q.v.
COOPER, Catharine. See "Vinson Penkend," q.v.
COOPER, Cloudsberry (1752 -   ). Private, Militia, Capt. Vincent Price's Company, 28th Battalion, by August 13, 1777 [Ref: M-151]. Aged 47 in a 1799 deposition [Ref: T-20].
COOPER, Ezekiel. See "Richard Cooper," q.v.
COOPER, Ignatius. See "Richard Cooper," q.v.
COOPER, James. Constable, 1775 [Ref: Z-2].
COOPER, John. Private, Militia, Capt. Andrew Fountain's Company, 14th Battalion, by August 13, 1777 [Ref: M-157].
COOPER, John. Private, Militia, Capt. Henry Downes' Company, 28th Battalion, by August 13, 1777 [Ref: M-152].
COOPER, John. Private, Militia, Capt. Vincent Price's Company, 28th Battalion, by August 13, 1777 [Ref: M-151].
COOPER, John. On May 26, 1780, he filed a certificate in Caroline County Court that he had subscribed to the Oath of Allegiance and Fidelity before the Hon. Richard Mason [Ref: N-78]. Rendered patriotic service by providing wheat for the use of the military in August, 1782, as verified by Giles Hicks 3rd, Commissary for Caroline County [Ref: V-6636]. One John Cooper married Eliza Lucas by license dated April 27, 1774, and a John Cooper married Sarah Cooper by license dated July 14, 1787 [Ref: X-3, X-18]. One John Cooper was aged 27 in a 1775 deposition [Ref: T-1]. Since there was more then one man named John Cooper, additional research will be necessary before drawing conclusions. One should refer to an excellent family genealogy article entitled "Descendants of John Cooper of Tuckahoe Neck," by Marlene Strawser Bates [Ref: Q-32:2 (Spring, 1991), pp. 137-151]. See "James Curtis," q.v.
COOPER, John Jr. Private, Militia, Capt. Vincent Price's Company, 28th Battalion, by August 13, 1777 [Ref: M-151]. John Cooper, Jr. married Rachel Conner by license dated June 22, 1781 [Ref: X-14].
COOPER, Mark. Private, Militia, Capt. William Haslett's Company, 28th Battalion, by August 13, 1777 [Ref: M-152]. "Mark G. Cooper" rendered patriotic service by providing wheat for the use of the military in August, 1782, as verified by

Giles Hicks 3rd, Commissary for Caroline County [Ref: V-6636].

COOPER, Mary. See "Thomas Meeds," q.v.

COOPER, Nehemiah (1760-1789). Private, Militia, Capt. Henry Downes' Company, 28th Battalion, by August 13, 1777 [Ref: M-152]. Nehemiah Cooper, son of Richard Cooper and Ann Broadway, was born September 14, 1760 and married Elizabeth Morgan by license dated December 13, 1780. Their two children were Thomas Morgan Cooper (1787-1848) and Ann (Nancy) Cooper. Nehemiah died November 22, 1789 and Elizabeth died November 24, 1789, just two days later [Ref: X-13, Q-32:2 (Spring, 1991), p. 140].

COOPER, Owen (Owin). Private, Militia, Capt. Andrew Fountain's Company, 14th Battalion, by August 13, 1777 [Ref: M-157]. Rendered patriotic service by providing wheat for the use of the military in August, 1782, as verified by Giles Hicks 3rd, Commissary for Caroline County [Ref: V-6636].

COOPER, Rebecca. See "James Curtis" and "John Cooper," q.v.

COOPER, Rhody. See "Thomas Smith," q.v.

COOPER, Richard. On October 10, 1780, "Richard Cooper and other non-jurors filed a certificate of their having furnished a horse for the use of the State." However, his name alone was listed in the Caroline County Court record [Ref: N-86]. Richard Cooper, son of Richard Cooper and Ann Broadway, was born September 10, 1755. He married first to Sarah Alford or Allford by license dated January 21, 1782, and second to Clarissa Taylor (who died in Dover, Delaware in 1841). Richard's children were Ezekiel Cooper, Sarah Cooper, Richard Jenifer Cooper, Ignatius F. Cooper, and William Hughlett Cooper [Ref: X-14, Q-32:2 (Spring, 1991), pp. 140-143]. See "Nehemiah Cooper" and "Henry Ward," q.v.

COOPER, Sally. See "George Wilson," q.v.

COOPER, Sarah. See "James Wilson" and "Richard Cooper," q.v.

COOPER, Stephen. Private, Militia, Capt. Andrew Fountain's Company, 14th Battalion, by August 13, 1777 [Ref: M-157]. Stephen Cooper married Priscilla Scott by license dated April 19, 1786 [Ref: X-17].

COOPER, Thomas. Private, 6th Company, Capt. Peter Adams, 1st Maryland Line, enlisted February 6, 1776 [Ref: D-14]. On December 27, 1776 he joined a company of men in Caroline County who marched to Talbot County to obtain a supply of salt [Ref: B-564, B-565]. On May 26, 1778, he filed a certificate in Caroline County Court that he had subscribed to the Oath of Allegiance and Fidelity before the Hon. Richard Mason [Ref: N-78]. Thomas Cooper married Elizabeth Whirritt by license dated January 3, 1792 [Ref: X-23]. See "Nehemiah Cooper," q.v.

COOPER, Thomas Jr. Private, Militia, Capt. Henry Downes' Company, 28th Battalion, by August 13, 1777 [Ref: M-152]. Subscribed to the Oath of Allegiance and Fidelity before the Hon. Henry Downes, Jr. on March 2, 1778 [Ref: J-1814]. Thomas Cooper, Jr. married Elizabeth Colston by license dated May 15, 1781 [Ref: X-13].

COOPER, William. Private, Maryland Troops, enrolled by Lieut. Thomas Wynn

Loockerman in Caroline County in July, 1776 [Ref: D-69]. See "Richard Cooper," q.v.

CORKRIN, James. Private, Militia, Capt. John Mitchell's Company, 14th Battalion, by August 13, 1777 [Ref: M-154].

CORNISH, Charles. Private (recruit), Maryland Troops, enrolled in Caroline County by William Whiteley, County Lieutenant, on August 14, 1781 to serve in the Maryland Line until December 10, 1781 [Ref: D-385].

CORRIE, William. See "John Stevens," q.v.

COSILL, Ezekiel. Private, Militia, Capt. William Hopper's Company, 28th Battalion, by August 13, 1777 [Ref: M-151].

COSTEN, Polly. See "John Hardcastle" and "Thomas Hardcastle," q.v.

COTTERAL, William. Private, Militia, Capt. Nehemiah Andrew's Company, 14th Battalion, by August 13, 1777 [Ref: M-155].

COU(?), Thomas. Private, Militia, Capt. William Haslett's Company, 28th Battalion, by August 13, 1777 [Ref: M-152].

COUNTESS, Peter. Private, Militia, Capt. William Chipley's Company, 28th Battalion, by August 13, 1777 [Ref: M-153].

COUNTISS, James. Private, Militia, Capt. Samuel Jackson's Company, 28th Battalion, by August 13, 1777 [Ref: M-153].

COUPES, John, of Choptank Hundred. Subscribed to the Oath of Allegiance and Fidelity (made his mark that resembled an "I" with a line draw horizontally through the center) before the Hon. Benson Stainton on February 2, 1778 [Ref: J-1814]. See "John Kopes," q.v.

COURSEY, Fanney. See "John Brown," q.v.

COURSEY, Frances. See "William Coursey," q.v.

COURSEY, Hampton. Private, 2nd Maryland Line, recruited in April, 1780 [Ref: F-132].

COURSEY, Mary. See "William Coursey," q.v.

COURSEY, Thomas. See "William Coursey," q.v.

COURSEY, William. Captain, Militia, 14th Battalion, December 17, 1781 [Ref: M-65, I-27]. William Coursey, Jr. married Mary Thomas by license dated December 30, 1783 [Ref: X-15]. William Coursey, son of William and Frances, was born August 17, 1759 [Ref: K-25, which spelled the name "Corsey"]. Since there was more then one William Coursey, additional research will be necessary before drawing conclusions.

COURSEY, William. First Lieutenant, Militia, Capt. Thomas Knotts' Company, 28th Battalion, December 17, 1781 [Ref: M-65, I-27].

COURSEY, William. Rendered patriotic service by providing wheat for the use of the military in August, 1782, as verified by Giles Hicks 3rd, Commissary for Caroline County [Ref: V-6636]. One William Coursey was aged 52 in an 1812 deposition [Ref: T-27]. One William Coursey (Corsey) married Frances --?-- and had these children: William (born August 17, 1759), Frances (born December 12, 1761), Mary (born April 1, 1764), and Thomas (born August 10, 1766). [Ref: K-

25]. See the other "William Coursey," q.v.

COVENTON, Thomas. Rendered patriotic service by providing wheat for the use of the military in August, 1782, as verified by Giles Hicks 3rd, Commissary for Caroline County [Ref: V-6636].

COVEY, Francis. Rendered patriotic service by providing wheat for the use of the military in August, 1782, as verified by Giles Hicks 3rd, Commissary for Caroline County [Ref: V-6636].

COVEY, John. Private, Militia, Capt. Nehemiah Andrew's Company, 14th Battalion, by August 13, 1777 [Ref: M-155].

COVEY, William. Private, Militia, Capt. Nehemiah Andrew's Company, 14th Battalion, by August 13, 1777 [Ref: M-155].

COVINGTON, Henry. Private, 6th Company, Capt. Peter Adams, 1st Maryland Line, enlisted January 22, 1776 [Ref: D-14]. Private, 5th Maryland Line, enlisted December 10, 1776, promoted to corporal on July 1, 1779, and discharged on January 12, 1780 [Ref: D-192]. Henry Covington married Susanna Boone by license dated May 8, 1787 [Ref: X-18].

COVINGTON, Sarah. See "James Culbreth," q.v.

COVINGTON, Thomas. Private, Militia, 14th Battalion, Capt. Richard Andrew's Company, by August 13, 1777 [Ref: M-156].

COX, Ann. See "William Hopper," q.v.

COX, Anthony. Private, Militia, Capt. William Chipley's Company, 28th Battalion, by August 13, 1777 [Ref: M-153]. He may have been the son of Anthony Cox who was aged 64 in a 1782 deposition [Ref: T-11].

COX, Daniel. See "William Hopper," q.v.

COX, Rebekah. See "Joseph Boon," q.v.

COX, Thomas. Private, Militia, Capt. William Haslett's Company, 28th Battalion, by August 13, 1777 [Ref: M-152].

COX, Thomas Stradley. Private, Militia, Capt. Andrew Fountain's Company, 14th Battalion, by August 13, 1777 [Ref: M-157].

COXELL, Hezekiah. Subscribed to the Oath of Allegiance and Fidelity before the Hon. Henry Downes, Jr. on March 2, 1778 [Ref: J-1814]. "Hezekiah Coxill" married Eliza Carter by license dated October 31, 1774 [Ref: X-4].

COXELL, Thomas, of Choptank Hundred. Subscribed to the Oath of Allegiance and Fidelity before the Hon. Benson Stainton on February 2, 1778 [Ref: J-1814].

CRAFTON, Joseph. Private, Militia, Capt. John Fauntleroy's Company, 28th Battalion, by August 13, 1777 [Ref: M-154]. Rendered patriotic service by providing wheat for the use of the military in August, 1782, as verified by Giles Hicks 3rd, Commissary for Caroline County [Ref: V-6636].

CRAIG, James. Private, 6th Company, Capt. Peter Adams, 1st Maryland Line, enlisted February 22, 1776 [Ref: D-14].

CRAIG, John. See "Hugh McBryde," q.v.

CRANMER, Rhody. See "Joshua Hobbs," q.v.

CRANOR (CRAYNOR), Aaron. Private, Militia, Capt. Shadrack Liden's

Company, 14th Battalion, by August 13, 1777 [Ref: M-155].
CRAYNOR, Elizabeth. See "Solomon Wilson," q.v.
CRANOR (CREYNOR), Charles and Dorcas. See "Joshua Cranor," q.v.
CRANOR (CRAYNOR), Emanuel. Private, Militia, Capt. Henry Downes' Company, 28th Battalion, by August 13, 1777 [Ref: M-152]. "Emanuel Crayner" married Susannah Wadman by license dated November 28, 1791 [Ref: X-23].
CRANOR (CRAYNOR), John. Private, Militia, Capt. Shadrack Liden's Company, 14th Battalion, by August 13, 1777 [Ref: M-155].
CRANOR (CRANER, CREYNOR), Joshua (1757 -   ). Rendered patriotic service by providing wheat for the use of the military in August, 1782, as verified by Giles Hicks 3rd, Commissary for Caroline County [Ref: V-6636]. Joshua Creynor, son of Charles and Dorcas Creynor, was born May 16, 1757 [Ref: K-25].
CREMEEN, John, and others. See "John Cromean," q.v.
CROCK, George. Rendered patriotic service by providing his wagon and team for the use of the State of Maryland, as certified by Richard Keene, Commissary for Caroline County, on June 22, 1780 [Ref: P-297].
CROMEAN (CREMEEN), Curtice. Private, Militia, Capt. Nehemiah Andrew's Company, 14th Battalion, by August 13, 1777 [Ref: M-155].
CROMEAN (CREMEEN), Elijah. Private, Militia, Capt. Shadrack Liden's Company, 14th Battalion, by August 13, 1777 [Ref: M-155].
CROMEAN (CRONNOON), Elizabeth. See "Henry Clift," q.v.
CROMEAN (CREMEEN), Jacob. Private, Militia, Capt. Nehemiah Andrew's Company, 14th Battalion, by August 13, 1777 [Ref: M-155].
CROMEAN (CREMEEN), John. Private, Militia, 14th Battalion, Capt. Joseph Richardson's Company, by August 13, 1777 [Ref: M-154].
CROMEAN (CREMEEN), John. Private, Militia, Capt. Shadrack Liden's Company, 14th Battalion, by August 13, 1777 [Ref: M-155].
CROMEAN (CREMEAN), John (Taylor). Rendered patriotic service by providing wheat for the use of the military in August, 1782, as verified by Giles Hicks 3rd, Commissary for Caroline County [Ref: V-6636]. One John Cromean was aged 39 in a 1786 deposition [Ref: T-12].
CROMEAN (CREMEEN), Justina. See "James Morgan," q.v.
CROMEAN (CREMEEN), Keziah. See "Thomas Blades," q.v.
CROMEAN (CREMEEN), Salathiel. Private, Militia, Capt. Nehemiah Andrew's Company, 14th Battalion, by August 13, 1777 [Ref: M-155].
CROMPTON (CRUMPTON), John. Private, Militia, Capt. John Mitchell's Company, 14th Battalion, by August 13, 1777 [Ref: M-154].
CROMPTON, Thomas. Private (recruit), Maryland Troops, enrolled in Caroline County by William Whiteley, County Lieutenant, on August 14, 1781 to serve in the Maryland Line for 3 years [Ref: D-385].
CRONNOON, Elizabeth. See "Henry Clift," q.v.
CRUNAN, Rebecca. See "William Walker," q.v.

CULBRETH, Ann. See "John Hardcastle," q.v.

CULBRETH, James. Private, Militia, Capt. Samuel Jackson's Company, 28th Battalion, by August 13, 1777 [Ref: M-153]. Subscribed to the Oath of Allegiance and Fidelity (made his large "+" mark) before the Hon. Richard Mason on March 2, 1778 [Ref: J-1814]. James Culbreth married Sarah Covington by license dated October 2, 1781 [Ref: X-14].

CULBRETH, John. Private, Militia, Capt. Samuel Jackson's Company, 28th Battalion, by August 13, 1777 [Ref: M-153]. John Culbreth married Sarah Bradley by license dated August 17, 1774 [Ref: X-4].

CULBRETH, Jonathan. Subscribed to the Oath of Allegiance and Fidelity before the Hon. Richard Mason on March 2, 1778 [Ref: J-1814].

CULBRETH, Thomas. See "John Hardcastle," q.v.

CURRY, Henry. Private, Militia, Capt. William Chipley's Company, 28th Battalion, by August 13, 1777 [Ref: M-153].

CURRY, John. Private, Militia, Capt. John Stafford's Company, 14th Battalion, by August 13, 1777 [Ref: M-156].

CURRY, William. Private, Militia, Capt. William Chipley's Company, 28th Battalion, by August 13, 1777 [Ref: M-153].

CURTICE, Thomas. Private, Militia, Capt. Henry Downes' Company, 28th Battalion, by August 13, 1777 [Ref: M-152].

CURTIS, James (1747 -   ). Subscribed to the Oath of Allegiance and Fidelity before the Hon. Henry Downes, Jr. on March 2, 1778 [Ref: J-1814]. Aged 36 in a 1783 deposition which stated he was the son-in-law of John Cooper and wife Rebeccah, aged 70 [Ref: T-5].

CURTIS, Rachell. See "John Bush," q.v.

DABSON, Edward. Subscribed to the Oath of Allegiance and Fidelity (made his "L" mark) before the Hon. Richard Mason on March 2, 1778 [Ref: J-1814]. See "Edward Dobson," q.v.

DAFFIN, Charles. Son of George Daffin of St. Mary's County, Charles married in 1775 to Mabel Sherwood, daughter of Philip Sherwood and widow of --?-- Ridgway and Risdon Bozman (died 1774). Their children were Capt. Thomas B. Daffin, Joseph G. Daffin, Charles Daffin, and Susannah Wilson. His stepchildren were William Ridgway and Sarah Ridgway. Charles represented Caroline County in the Lower House of the Maryland General Assembly from 1779 to 1780, served as Court Justice from 1779 to at least 1785, Justice of the Peace from 1778 to at least 1784, and Justice of the Orphans' Court from 1781 to at least 1785. He was a Coronet, Light Horse Troops, Capt. Henry Dickinson's Company, on June 12, 1781. Charles died intestate in Caroline County in November, 1794, and his brother Joseph Daffin died testate in Dorchester County in June, 1796 [Ref: R-247, R-248, R-82, R-87, M-157, F-20, G-475, I-45, I-341, I-371, I-503]. "Charles Doffin married --?-- Bozman" by license recorded January 28, 1775 [Ref: X-5].

DAFFIN, Joseph. See "Charles Daffin," q.v.

DAFFIN, Rebecca. See "Henry Dickinson," q.v.

DAFFIN, Thomas. See "Charles Daffin," q.v.

DARDEN, Mary. See "Richard Loockerman," q.v.

DARNELL, James. Private (recruit), Maryland Troops, enrolled in Caroline County by William Whiteley, County Lieutenant, on August 14, 1781 to serve in the Maryland Line until December 10, 1781 [Ref: D-385].

DAVIS, Anna. See "Nehemiah Andrew," q.v.

DAVIS, Aquilla. Private, Militia, Capt. Joseph Douglass' Company, 14th Battalion, by August 13, 1777 [Ref: M-156].

DAVIS, Baptist (Baptiz). Private, Militia, Capt. Joseph Douglass' Company, 14th Battalion, by August 13, 1777 [Ref: M-156]. Baptist Davis married Ann Genn by license dated November 17, 1783 [Ref: X-15].

DAVIS, David. Private, Militia, Capt. Thomas Hughlett's Company, 28th Battalion, by August 13, 1777 [Ref: M-152]. Subscribed to the Oath of Allegiance and Fidelity before the Hon. Thomas Hardcastle on January 29, 1778 [Ref: J-1814].

DAVIS, John. Private, Militia, Capt. Samuel Jackson's Company, 28th Battalion, by August 13, 1777 [Ref: M-153].

DAVIS, Mary. See "John Ryall," q.v.

DAVIS, Phillimon. Private, Militia, Capt. John Fauntleroy's Company, 28th Battalion, by August 13, 1777 [Ref: M-154].

DAVIS, Samuel. Private, Militia, Capt. Joseph Douglass' Company, 14th Battalion, by August 13, 1777 [Ref: M-156].

DAVIS, Solomon. Private, Militia, Capt. John Fauntleroy's Company, 28th Battalion, by August 13, 1777 [Ref: M-154].

DAWSON, Asa. See "Beacham Causey," q.v.

DAWSON, Asbury. See "John Dawson," q.v.

DAWSON, Edward. See "John Dawson," q.v.

DAWSON, Elijah. Private, Militia, 14th Battalion, Capt. Richard Andrew's Company, by August 13, 1777 [Ref: M-156].

DAWSON, Elizabeth. See "Beacham Causey," q.v.

DAWSON, Enoch. See "John Dawson," q.v.

DAWSON, George. Private (draft), Maryland Troops, enrolled in Caroline County by William Whiteley, County Lieutenant, on by August 13, 1781 to serve in the Maryland Line until December 10, 1781. The Council was informed that "if you are in want of officers for the drafts, there is a young man amongst them by the name of George Dawson, if you think him capable, should be glad you would give him an Ensign's commission." [Ref: D-384, D-385]. See "John Dawson," q.v.

DAWSON, John. Ensign, Militia, Capt. Joseph Douglass' Company, 14th Battalion, May 14, 1776 and by August 13, 1777. Second Lieutenant, Militia, Capt. Hugh McBride's Company, April 9, 1778 [Ref: M-68, M-156, A-424, E-23]. In an 1819 land commission record John Dawson was noted as having died testate in April or May, 1798 and devised tracts called "Black Level Enlarged" and "Addition to Rawleight" to his son John Dawson "and other lands to other persons." His widow Sarah "since deceased, leaving four sons and two daughters" as follows: (1) George Dawson, who died intestate before his brother John Dawson, leaving Enoch Dawson, William Dawson, Medford Dawson, Sarah Dawson (minor), Mary Dawson (minor), and Asbury Dawson (minor); (2) Noah Dawson, who died before his brother John Dawson, leaving Ritta Graham (wife of John Graham), Elizabeth Anderson (wife of Thomas Anderson), Edward Dawson, Mary Dawson, Richard Dawson (minor), Zaccheus Dawson (minor), John Jefferson Dawson (minor), and Sarah Dawson (minor, who has since died); (3) Sovren (Severn?) Dawson; (4) John Dawson, who died intestate, without heirs; (5) Mary Derickson, wife of James Derickson; and, (6) Sarah Bell, wife of Cyrus Bell [Ref: T-32]. Since there was more then one man named John Dawson, additional research will be necessary before drawing conclusions. It must be noted that a chancery court case involving members of this Dawson family appeared in the *Republican Star* newspaper on April 6, 1819 and should be consulted for further information. See "Nicholas Stubbs," q.v.

DAWSON, John. Private, Light Horse Troops, Capt. Henry Dickinson's Company, June 12, 1781 [Ref: M-157].

DAWSON, John. Private, Militia, Capt. Shadrack Liden's Company, 14th Battalion, by August 13, 1777 [Ref: M-155].

DAWSON, John. Private, Militia, Capt. Henry Downes' Company, 28th Battalion, by August 13, 1777 [Ref: M-152].

DAWSON, John, of John. See "Nicholas Stubbs," q.v.

DAWSON, John, of Richard. Subscribed to the Oath of Allegiance and Fidelity before the Hon. Nathaniel Potter on March 2, 1778 [Ref: J-1814].

DAWSON, Jonas. Private, Militia, Capt. Shadrack Liden's Company, 14th Battalion, by August 13, 1777 [Ref: M-152]. Rendered patriotic service by providing wheat for the use of the military in August, 1782, as verified by Giles Hicks 3rd, Commissary for Caroline County [Ref: V-6636].

DAWSON, Manus (Manas). Private, Militia, 14th Battalion, Capt. Joseph Richardson's Company, by August 13, 1777 [Ref: M-154]. Subscribed to the Oath of Allegiance and Fidelity before the Hon. Charles Dickinson on March 1, 1778 [Ref: J-1418].

DAWSON, Mary. See "John Dawson," q.v.

DAWSON, Medford. See "John Dawson," q.v.

DAWSON, Richard. See "John Dawson," q.v.

DAWSON, Ritta. See "John Dawson," q.v.

DAWSON, Sarah. See "John Dawson," q.v.

DAWSON, Sovren. See "John Dawson," q.v.

DAWSON, William. Private, Militia, 14th Battalion, Capt. Richard Andrew's Company, by August 13, 1777 [Ref: M-156]. See "John Dawson," q.v.

DAWSON, Zaccheus. See "John Dawson," q.v.

DAY, Richard. Private, Militia, Capt. Shadrack Liden's Company, 14th Battalion, by August 13, 1777 [Ref: M-155]. Rendered patriotic service by providing wheat for the use of the military in August, 1782, as verified by Giles Hicks 3rd, Commissary for Caroline County [Ref: V-6636].

DEAN, Elijah (1740 - after 1798). Private, Militia, Capt. Joseph Douglass' Company, 14th Battalion, by August 13, 1777 [Ref: M-156]. Private, 5th Maryland Line, enlisted May 15, 1778 [Ref: D-199]. Aged 57 in a 1797 deposition, aged 57 in a 1798 deposition, and noted as the son of Francis Dean in a 1798 deposition [Ref: T-18, T-19].

DEAN, Elizabeth. See "John Stevens," q.v.

DEAN, Ezekiel. On June 29, 1778, he filed a petition in Caroline County stating that he was a "hired and contracted servant" for Nathan Faris and his indenture expired in February, 1779. He was "taken up as a vagrant" for not enlisting and desired Gov. Thomas Johnson to grant him relief. Certifications were made by Lawrence Hale and John Downes, in their handwriting, that Ezekiel Dean was "incapable for duty." [Ref: O-105]. Ezekiel Dean married Diana Bell by license dated November 15, 1780 [Ref: X-12].

DEAN, Francis. See "Elijah Dean," q.v.

DEAN, Joshua. Private, Militia, Capt. Nehemiah Andrew's Company, 14th Battalion, by August 13, 1777 [Ref: M-155].

DEAN, Mary. See "Isaac Nichols," q.v.

DEAN, Moses. Private, Militia, Capt. Nehemiah Andrew's Company, 14th Battalion, by August 13, 1777 [Ref: M-155].

DEAN, Nancy. See "John Stevens," q.v.

DEAN, Rhoda. See "James Gray," q.v.

DEAN, Robert. Private, Militia, 14th Battalion, Capt. Joseph Richardson's Company, by August 13, 1777 [Ref: M-154].

DEAN, Solomon. See "John Stevens," q.v.

DEAN, William. Private, Militia, Capt. Andrew Fountain's Company, 14th Battalion, by August 13, 1777 [Ref: M-157].

DEAN, William. Private, Militia, Capt. Joseph Douglass' Company, 14th Battalion, by August 13, 1777 [Ref: M-156].

DEFORD, Jesse. Private, 5th Maryland Line, enlisted June 24, 1777 and served to January, 1780 [Ref: D-198].

DEFORD, John. Private, Militia, Capt. Samuel Jackson's Company, 28th Battalion, by August 13, 1777 [Ref: M-153]. Private, 5th Maryland Line, enlisted March 8, 1778 and died on October 10, 1779 [Ref: D-199].

DEFORD, Joseph. Private, 5th Maryland Line, enlisted March 8, 1778 and corporal by October, 1780 [Ref: D-199].

DEFORD, Thomas. Private, Maryland Line, who applied for pension (S2514) in Delaware County, Ohio on November 19, 1832, stating he was born on December 9, 1736 on the Eastern Shore of Maryland [probably in Dorchester, now Caroline, County] and lived near Taneytown in Frederick County, Maryland at the time of his enlistment. In 1810 he moved to Pickaway County, Ohio and in 1824 he moved to Delaware County, Ohio [Ref: W-936].

DELAHAY, John. Private, Militia, Capt. Nehemiah Andrew's Company, 14th Battalion, by August 13, 1777 [Ref: M-155].
DELANY, Thomas. Private, Militia, Capt. William Chipley's Company, 28th Battalion, by August 13, 1777 [Ref: M-153].
DENNY, Richard. Private, Militia, Capt. John Mitchell's Company, 14th Battalion, by August 13, 1777 [Ref: M-154].
DERICKSON, James. See "John Dawson," q.v.
DERICKSON, Mary. See "John Dawson," q.v.
DEROACHBRUNE, Jacob. See "John Deroachbrune," q.v.
DEROACHBRUNE (DEROACHBROOM), John. Private, Militia, Capt. William Hopper's Company, 28th Battalion, by August 13, 1777 [Ref: M-151]. Private (recruit), Maryland Troops, enrolled in Caroline County by William Whiteley, County Lieutenant, on August 14, 1781 to serve in the Maryland Line until December 10, 1781 [Ref: D-385]. In an 1807 land commission record "John Deroachbrune" was noted as having died (date not given) seized of a tract called "Vaughan's Kindness" and leaving the following children: Ann Martindale (wife of Henry Martindale), Jacob Deroachbrune (minor), Philemon Deroachbrune (minor), Peregrine Deroachbrune (minor), and Sarah Deroachbrune (minor). [Ref: T-23]. "John Derochbound" married Mary Boone by license dated July 16, 1782 [Ref: X-14].
DEROACHBRUNE (DEROCHBROOM), Matthew (c1761-1804). Private, Militia, Capt. William Hopper's Company, 28th Battalion, by August 13, 1777 [Ref: M-151]. "Mathew Derochbonne" married Sarah Wootters by license dated July 17, 1780 [Ref: X-12]. "Matthew Derochbrune" was born circa 1761 in Maryland, married "Sarah Wooters" and died on October 10, 1804 [Ref: Y-821].
DEROACHBRUNE, Peregrine. See "John Deroachbrune," q.v.
DEROACHBRUNE, Philemon. See "John Deroachbrune," q.v.
DEROACHBRUNE, Sarah. See "John Deroachbrune," q.v.
DEVILISH, John. Private, Militia, Capt. John Fauntleroy's Company, 28th Battalion, by August 13, 1777 [Ref: M-154].
DIAL, Araminta. See "Gallient Lane," q.v.
DICKINSON, --?--. See "Philip Walker," q.v.
DICKINSON, Charles. Court Justice, 1775-1776 [Ref: Z-1, Z-26]. Served on the Committee of Observation in 1776 [Ref: A-480, A-481]. Justice who administered the Oath of Allegiance and Fidelity in 1778 [Ref: J-1814]. Commissioned a Justice of the Orphans' Court on June 19, 1778 [Ref: E-140]. "Charles Dickinson (Magistrate)" subscribed to the Oath of Allegiance and Fidelity before the Hon. Nathaniel Potter on March 2, 1778 [Ref: J-1814]. He may have been the Charles Dickinson who died in 1779 [Ref: R-268]. See "Henry Dickinson" and "Philip Walker" and "Thomas Wynn Loockerman," q.v.
DICKINSON, Henry. Son of Charles Dickinson (died in 1779) and Sophia Richardson, Henry married three times: first to Elizabeth Walker by 1774, second to Ann Walker (widow of both Andrew Mein and Edward Hindman or Hirdman)

by license dated January 17, 1784 (she and Elizabeth were daughters of Rev. Philip Walker, rector of St. Mary's Whitechapel Parish in Caroline County), and third to Deborah Perry by license dated March 15, 1787. Henry's children were Charles Dickinson, Philip Dickinson, Henry Dickinson, Elizabeth Richardson, and Rebecca Daffin, and his stepson was Andrew Mein. Henry attended the Maryland Conventions from 1774 to 1776, served in the Lower House in 1777 and 1778, and was Treasurer of the Eastern Shore from 1779 to 1789. He also served on the Committee of Observation in 1776 and was Loan Officer for the Continental Loan Office in 1777. He was a County Court Justice from 1779 to at least 1782, Justice of the Orphans' Court in 1782 and 1783 ("will not qualify" in 1785), Justice of the Peace in 1782 and 1783, and Judge of the Court of Appeals for Tax Assessment in 1786. [Ref: R-268, R-269, R-70, R-71, R-72, R-74, R-76, R-78, O-1, O-4, O-28, A-10, I-45, I-341, X-15, X-18]. Appointed a Collector of Gold and Silver in Caroline County on February 1, 1776 [Ref: A-132]. "Henry Dickinson (Assemblyman)" subscribed to the Oath of Allegiance and Fidelity before the Hon. Charles Dickinson on March 1, 1778 [Ref: J-1418]. Lieutenant Colonel, 14th Battalion, January 12, 1776, and succeeded on June 24, 1777 [Ref: M-70, G-475]. He died in November, 1789 [Ref: R-269].

DICKINSON, Henry. Private, Militia, 14th Battalion, Capt. Joseph Richardson's Company, by August 13, 1777 [Ref: M-154]. Captain, Company of Light Horse Troops, June 12, 1781 [Ref: M-157].

DICKINSON, James. See "Philip Walker," q.v.

DICKINSON, John. See "Philip Walker," q.v.

DICKINSON, Margaret. See "Philip Walker," q.v.

DICKINSON, Philip. See "Henry Dickinson," q.v.

DICKINSON, Sidney. See "Thomas Wynn Loockerman," q.v.

DICKINSON, Sousana. See "Jonathan Garey," q.v.

DICKINSON, William. Private, Militia, Capt. Vincent Price's Company, 28th Battalion, by August 13, 1777 [Ref: M-151]. Ensign, Militia, Capt. Joseph Reynolds' Company, 28th Battalion, April 9, 1778. First Lieutenant, Capt. David Robertson's Company, August 14, 1779 [Ref: M-70, E-23, E-493]. Subscribed to the Oath of Allegiance and Fidelity before the Hon. Henry Downes, Jr. on March 2, 1778 [Ref: J-1814, which spelled the name "Dickenson"]. See "Philip Walker," q.v.

DICKINSON, William Jr. Private, Militia, Capt. Vincent Price's Company, 28th Battalion, by August 13, 1777 [Ref: M-151].

DIETT, Adam. Private, Militia, Capt. William Hopper's Company, 28th Battalion, by August 13, 1777 [Ref: M-151].

DIGGANS (DIGGINS, DIGGIN), John. Private, Militia, Capt. Vincent Price's Company, 28th Battalion, by August 13, 1777 [Ref: M-151]. Subscribed to the Oath of Allegiance and Fidelity (made his "+" mark) before the Hon. Henry Downes, Jr. on March 2, 1778 [Ref: J-1814]. Rendered patriotic service by providing wheat for the use of the military in September, 1782, as verified by

Giles Hicks 3rd, Commissary for Caroline County [Ref: V-6636]. "John Diggin" married Tamsey Thomas by license dated April 19, 1784 [Ref: X-15].

DIGGOR, John. Subscribed to the Oath of Allegiance and Fidelity (made his mark that somewhat resembled a fat "P") before the Hon. Henry Downes, Jr. on March 2, 1778 [Ref: J-1814].

DILL, Abner. See "William Adams," q.v.

DILL, Chaney. See "William Adams," q.v.

DILL, Price. Private, Militia, Capt. Andrew Fountain's Company, 14th Battalion, by August 13, 1777 [Ref: M-157].

DILLAHAY, William. Rendered patriotic service by providing wheat for the use of the military in August, 1782, as verified by Giles Hicks 3rd, Commissary for Caroline County [Ref: V-6636].

DILLEN, Ann. See "John Dillen," q.v.

DILLEN (DILLING), James. Private, Militia, Capt. Nehemiah Andrew's Company, 14th Battalion, by August 13, 1777 [Ref: M-155]. Rendered patriotic service by providing wheat for the use of the military in August, 1782, as verified by Giles Hicks 3rd, Commissary for Caroline County [Ref: V-6636]. James Dilling married Tilley Blades by license dated August 12, 1778 [Ref: X-9].

DILLEN (DILLIN), John. Private, Militia, Capt. Shadrack Liden's Company, 14th Battalion, by August 13, 1777 [Ref: M-155]. John Dillen married Ann --?-- and their daughter Mary Dillen (born in 1769) married James Stevens. John died by 1809 [Ref: T-25].

DILLEN (DILLING), Joshua. Private, Militia, Capt. Nehemiah Andrew's Company, 14th Battalion, by August 13, 1777 [Ref: M-155]. Rendered patriotic service by providing wheat for the use of the military in August, 1782, as verified by Giles Hicks 3rd, Commissary for Caroline County [Ref: V-6636].

DILLEN, Mary. See "John Dillen," q.v.

DIXON, Benjamin. Ensign, Militia, Capt. Andrew Fountain's Company, 14th Battalion, by August 13, 1777 [Ref: M-156]. First Lieutenant, Militia, Capt. Peter Rich's Company, April 9, 1778 [Ref: M-70, E-23]. Subscribed to the Oath of Allegiance and Fidelity before the Hon. Benson Stainton on February 23, 1778 [Ref: J-1814].

DIXON, China. See "John Merrick," q.v.

DIXON, Garrad. Subscribed to the Oath of Allegiance and Fidelity (made his "X" mark) before the Hon. Benson Stainton on February 2, 1778 [Ref: J-1814].

DIXON, Joseph. Private, Militia, Capt. William Haslett's Company, 28th Battalion, by August 13, 1777 [Ref: M-152]. Ensign, Militia, Capt. Postlewait's Company, 28th [8th?] Battalion, April 18, 1780 [Ref: M-70, F-144]. "Joseph Dixon, lately arrived to the age prescribed by law, took the Oath of Allegiance and Fidelity on August 21, 1778." [Ref: N-25]. Joseph Dixon married Ann With by license dated May 3, 1791 [Ref: X-23].

DIXON, Obed (Obediah). Subscribed to the Oath of Allegiance and Fidelity (made his "O" mark) before the Hon. Benson Stainton on February 2, 1778 [Ref: J-

1814]. See "Thomas Hughlett," q.v.

DIXON, Sarah. See "Thomas Hughlett" and "Christopher Wilson," q.v.

DOBSON, Edward. Private, Militia, Capt. John Fauntleroy's Company, 28th Battalion, by August 13, 1777 [Ref: M-154]. See "Edward Dabson," q.v.

DODD, Katharine. See "James Harris," q.v.

DOFFIN, Charles. See "Charles Daffin," q.v.

DOPSON, James. Private, Militia, Capt. Joseph Douglass' Company, 14th Battalion, by August 13, 1777 [Ref: M-156].

DORMAN, William. Private, Maryland Troops, enrolled by Lieut. Levin Handy in Caroline County and passed by Col. William Hopewell on August 4, 1776 [Ref: D-69].

DOUGLASS (DOUGLAS), Elizabeth. See "Joseph Douglass," q.v.

DOUGLASS (DOUGLAS), James. Private, Militia, Capt. Joseph Douglass' Company, 14th Battalion, by August 13, 1777 [Ref: M-156]. Captain, Militia, 14th Battalion, April 9, 1778, and succeeded on June 28, 1780 [Ref: M-71, E-23, F-207]. See "William Douglass," q.v.

DOUGLASS (DOUGLAS), Jane. See "Nathaniel Potter," q.v.

DOUGLASS (DOUGLAS), Jeremiah. See "Joseph Douglass," q.v.

DOUGLASS (DOUGLAS), John. See "John Douglass," q.v.

DOUGLASS (DOUGLAS), Joseph (1747-1816). Son of Capt. Joseph Douglas (died in 1756) and Catharine (Musgrove) Harris (died in 1768), of Charles County. Joseph married Rebecca Lee Nichols (of age in 1766, and died in March, 1812), daughter of Isaac and Mary Nichols of Caroline County. Their children were as follows: Mary Nichols Douglas (married Amasa Robinson or Robertson), Elizabeth Douglas (born October 20, 1779, married John T. Smoot in 1799, and their daughter Arrietta C. Smoot was born in 1802, married Charles Turpin Smith in 1822, and died in 1866; Elizabeth died in 1849), Thomas H. Douglas (married Janet or Jennet Smoot in 1800), Joseph Douglas (born in 1784 and married first to Celia Wright and second to Charlotte Wilson), John Douglas (married Nancy or Ann Turpin in 1812, and died in 1832), and Jeremiah Douglas (born in 1791, went to Kentucky, married Susan Thompson in 1817 in Scott County, and migrated to Pike County, Missouri where he died in 1864). Capt. Joseph Douglass died on January 1, 1816 [Ref: DAR No. 487889, approved application of Mary Douglass Osburn, of St. Helena, California (1968), based on the service of Capt. Joseph Douglas; DAR No. 670175, approved application of Veronica Clarke Peden (1983), based on the service of Capt. John Smoot; Layton Genealogical Collection G5077 (Box 19), Maryland Historical Society Library; Harry Wright Newman's *The Smoots of Maryland and Virginia*, p. 30]. Captain, Militia, 14th Battalion, May 14, 1776 and succeeded on August 27, 1780 or December 17, 1781, both dates were given in the records [Ref: M-71, M-156, A-424, E-23, E-493, F-207]. Subscribed to the Oath of Allegiance and Fidelity before the Hon. Nathaniel Potter on March 2, 1778 [Ref: J-1814]. On December 7, 1780, "Joseph Dugless" was recommended for appointment as one of the magistrates in Caroline County [Ref: G-200]. Justice of the Peace from 1782 to at least 1784 [Ref: I-45, I-341, I-503].

DOUGLASS (DOUGLAS), Joseph. Private, Light Horse Troops, Capt. Henry Dickinson's Company, June 12, 1781 [Ref: M-157].

DOUGLASS (DOUGLAS), Mary. See "Joseph Douglass," q.v.

DOUGLASS (DOUGLAS), Sarah. See "William Douglass," q.v.

DOUGLASS (DOUGLAS), William. Private, Militia, Capt. William Haslett's Company, 28th Battalion, by August 13, 1777 [Ref: M-152].

DOUGLASS (DOUGLAS), William. Probably born in Pennsylvania (of age by 1763), resided in Caernarvon Township, Lancaster County, Pennsylvania and possibly Kent County, Delaware. Immigrated to Worcester County, Maryland by 1763 and was in Great Choptank Hundred, Dorchester County in 1771, which part became Caroline County in 1773. Co-owner of the Nanticoke Forge and Deep Creek Furnace, the first of its kind in Worcester County. Represented Caroline County in the Lower House of the Maryland General Assembly, 1777-1778, Commissary of Horses, and Commissioner of Tax, 1779. Rendered patriotic service by providing wheat for the use of the military in August, 1782, as verified by Giles Hicks 3rd, Commissary for Caroline County. William died in 1782 and his widow Sarah Douglass married William Carpenter, Sr., of Kent County, Delaware by March, 1785, which was where his son James Douglass died circa 1799 [Ref: V-6636, R-76, R-78, R-280].

DOWLING, George. Private, 6th Company, Capt. Peter Adams, 1st Maryland Line, enlisted May 7, 1776 [Ref: D-15].

DOWLING, Roger. Private, 5th Maryland Line, enlisted June 16, 1779 and still in service on November 1, 1780 [Ref: D-199].

DOWNES, Aaron (1734 - after 1788). Served on the Committee of Observation for Caroline County on August 2, 1775 [Ref: A-48]. Subscribed to the Oath of Allegiance and Fidelity before the Hon. Henry Downes, Jr. on March 2, 1778 [Ref: J-1814]. Aged 48 in a 1782 deposition, aged 54 in a 1788 deposition, and noted in a 1799 deposition as the son of Hawkins Downes (probably the Hawkins who was buried on May 1, 1756 at St. John's P. E. Church). [Ref: T-5, T-13, T-21, K-27]. Aaron Downes married Elizabeth Oxenham on November 11, 1756 [Ref: K-26]. An Aaron Downes was a private in the militia, Capt. Vincent Price's Company, 28th Battalion, by August 13, 1777; Ensign, Militia, Capt. David Robertson's Company, August 14, 1779; Second Lieutenant, December 17, 1781 [Ref: M-151, M-71, E-493, I-27]. See "William Downes" and "Aaron Downes, Jr.," q.v.

DOWNES, Aaron Jr. (1760 -   ). Private, Militia, Capt. Vincent Price's Company, 28th Battalion, by August 13, 1777 [Ref: M-151]. Aaron Downes, son of Aaron and Elizabeth Downes, was born April 14, 1760 [Ref: K-25].

DOWNES, Deborah. See "Robert Jones," q.v.

DOWNES, Elizabeth. See "Aaron Downes," q.v.

DOWNES, Esther. See "Bartholomew Feddeman," q.v.

DOWNES, Hawkins (1757-1831). Subscribed to the Oath of Allegiance and Fidelity before the Hon. Henry Downes, Jr. on March 2, 1778 [Ref: J-1814]. Hawkins Downes, son of Solomon and Nancy Downes, was born May 13, 1757, married Mrs. Sarah Hall Vanderford, and died on October 29, 1831 [Ref: K-25, Y-871]. See "Aaron Downes," q.v.

DOWNES, Henrietta. See "John Hardcastle" and "Thomas Hardcastle" and "Aaron Hardcastle," q.v.

DOWNES, Henry (1747-1816). Son of Henry Downes (died by 1772) and Frances Noble, of Queen Anne's County, Henry was born May 15, 1747, married first to Margaret Baynard, of Talbot County, by 1769, and second to Margaret Green by license dated November 8, 1788 in Caroline County. His known daughters were Elizabeth Sellers (wife of Francis Sellers) and --?-- Nichols, wife of Henry Nichols. There may have been other children, but none survived him at the time of his death in 1816. Henry served in the Lower House in 1777, 1784, 1785, 1787, 1788, and 1790 and was Sheriff of Caroline County, 1778-1779. He was a County Court Justice in 1777, 1778, 1783 ("will not qualify"), 1785, 1786; Purchasing Agent and Subscription Officer, Continental Loan Office, 1779; Collector for Caroline County, 1780; Justice of the Orphans' Court in 1783 ("will not qualify") and 1785 ("did not qualify"); Commissioner of the Tax, 1783; Judge of the Court of Appeals for Taxation, 1786; Associate Justice, Fourth District, 1791-1793 [Ref: R-280, R-281, R-76, R-78, R-89, R-90, R-92, F-9, F-245, X-19, Y-871]. "Henry Downes, Jr." was a Justice who administered the Oath of Allegiance and Fidelity in 1778 [Ref: J-1814, E-249]. "Henry Downes" was a Captain, Militia, August 2, 1775; Second Major, 28th Battalion, January 12, 1776; Adjutant, 28th Battalion, August 30, 1776; Major, April 9, 1778, but resigned on September 29, 1778 to become Adjutant under Col. Federman (Feddeman?); Lieutenant Colonel, December 17, 1781 [Ref: M-152, A-48, B-248, E-23, I-27, Y-871]. Took the Oath of Sheriff on March 21, 1780 [Ref: N-70]. Aged 37 in a 1784 deposition [Ref: T-8]. Henry Downes was President of Hillsborough School in Caroline County at the time of his death on December 4, 1816, which position passed to his grandson Henry Downes Sellers [Ref: R-281]. See "Philemon Downes" and "James Reed," q.v.

DOWNES, Henry (1757-1831). First Lieutenant, Maryland Troops, 1776 [Ref: D-68]. Captain, Militia, 28th Battalion, by August 13, 1777 [Ref: M-71]. Born in Maryland on March 4, 1757, he married Rebecca Morton, served in Maryland during the war, and died in Delaware on September 24, 1831 [Ref: Y-871].

DOWNES, Jacob, of Queen Anne's County. On January 6, 1781, he filed a certificate in Caroline County Court that he had subscribed to the Oath of Allegiance and Fidelity [Ref: N-03].

DOWNES, John. See "Ezekiel Dean," q.v.

DOWNES (DOWNS), Lodman. Corporal, 5th Maryland Line, enlisted on January 28, 1777, demoted to private on January 11, 1778, promoted to sergeant on January 1, 1779, and discharged on February 5, 1780 [Ref: D-198].

DOWNES, Nancy. See "Hawkins Downes," q.v.

DOWNES, Nathan. Subscribed to the Oath of Allegiance and Fidelity before the Hon. Henry Downes, Jr. on March 2, 1778 [Ref: J-1814]. Nathan Downes married Ann Cooper by license dated June 1, 1774 [Ref: X-3].

DOWNES, Philemon. Son of Henry Downes (died by 1772) and Frances Noble, Philemon married first to Mary Seth, widow of Jacob Seth (Mary died in 1808), and second to Elizabeth Tillotson (widow of John Tillotson, Jr. and daughter of Thomas Baynard) by license dated August 31, 1780. Philemon's children were Philemon Downes, Henry Downes, and Mary Downes, and his stepsons were Thomas Baynard Tillotson and John Tillotson. He was elected to the Lower House in 1782 (did not attend) and served in 1795. Philemon held offices in Queen Anne's County, 1773-1778 (including Sheriff), lived in Baltimore County in 1778-1779, moved back to Queen Anne's County in 1779, and then to Caroline County in 1780, where he was a Justice of the Peace from 1782 to at least 1784, and Justice of the Orphans' Court from 1782 to at least 1792 [Ref: I-341, I-371, I-503, I-45 (which spelled the name "Downs"), R-87, R-281]. Captain, Militia, 28th Battalion, December 17, 1781 [Ref: M-71, I-27, X-12]. His will was probated in Caroline County on January 23, 1796 [Ref: R-282].

DOWNES, Solomon. See "Hawkins Downes," q.v.

DOWNES, William (1758 -   ). Private, Militia, Capt. Vincent Price's Company, 28th Battalion, by August 13, 1777 [Ref: M-151]. Subscribed to the Oath of Allegiance and Fidelity before the Hon. Henry Downes, Jr. on March 2, 1778 [Ref: J-1814]. William Downes, son of Aaron and Elizabeth Downes, was born June 7, 1758 [Ref: K-25].

DOWNES, Zachariah. Born in Maryland circa 1748, married Elizabeth Ann Mason, served as a private in the Revolutionary War, and died before February 15, 1837 [Ref: Y-871].

DRAPER, Ephraim. Private, Militia, Capt. William Haslett's Company, 28th Battalion, by August 13, 1777 [Ref: M-152].

DRAPER, John. Private, Militia, Capt. William Haslett's Company, 28th Battalion, by August 13, 1777 [Ref: M-152].

DRAPER, Judrek (Judal?). "Judrek Draper" rendered patriotic service by providing wheat for the use of the military in August, 1782, as verified by Giles Hicks 3rd, Commissary for Caroline County [Ref: V-6636]. "Judal Draper" was aged 58 in a 1782 deposition [Ref: T-5].

DRAPER, Nehemiah. Private, Militia, Capt. Andrew Fountain's Company, 14th Battalion, by August 13, 1777 [Ref: M-157]. Nehemiah Draper married Sidney Barwick by license dated June 26, 1792 [Ref: X-24].

DRAPER, Samuel. Private, Militia, Capt. William Haslett's Company, 28th Battalion, by August 13, 1777 [Ref: M-152]. Rendered patriotic service by providing wheat for the use of the military in August, 1782, as verified by Giles Hicks 3rd, Commissary for Caroline County [Ref: V-6636].

DRISKELL, Lawrence. Private, Militia, Capt. John Stafford's Company, 14th

Battalion, by August 13, 1777 [Ref: M-156].

DRIVER, Christopher. Constable, Bridgetown Hundred, 1775-1776 [Ref: Z-2, Z-27]. Ensign, Militia, Capt. William Haslett's Company, before March 9, 1776 and First Lieutenant from April 10, 1776 to at least by August 13, 1777 [Ref: M-71, M-152, A-230, A-320, J-1814]. Brother of Matthew Driver, Christopher married Sarah Ringgold in 1775 [Ref: R-282]. See "Matthew Driver," q.v.

DRIVER, Esther. See "Matthew Driver," q.v.

DRIVER, Henry. See "Matthew Driver," q.v.

DRIVER, Joshua. See "Thomas Lecompte" and "Matthew Driver," q.v.

DRIVER, Margaret. See "William Robinson," q.v.

DRIVER, Matthew (1740-1798). Son of Matthew and Renness Driver, he was born on August 30, 1740 in Dorchester County and resided in Bridgetown Hundred of Caroline County in 1776. Matthew married first to Margaret Casson (widow of John Casson and daughter of John Pratt Baynard) on January 12, 1762, and second to Esther Casson (daughter of Henry Casson) on January 21, 1777. His children were Joshua Driver, Henry Driver, Matthew Driver, Margaret Robinson (wife of William Robinson), Elizabeth Edmondson (wife of Peter Edmondson), Anne Broome (wife of James M. Broome), and Esther Driver. His stepchildren were Robert Casson, John Casson, Ferdinando Casson, Myers Casson, and Elizabeth Casson. Matthew represented Caroline County in the Lower House of the Maryland General Assembly, 1778-1781, 1785, and attended the Constitution Ratification Convention in 1788. He also served on the Committee of Observation, 1775-1776, Commissioner of Tax, 1777, 1782-1785, Court Justice, 1774-1796, Justice of the Peace, 1778-1784, and Justice of the Orphans' Court, 1778-1797. He was a Captain in the Militia, 14th Battalion, 1775, Second Major, January 12, 1776, Lieutenant Colonel, June 24, 1777, and Colonel, April 9, 1778 [Ref: R-80, R-82, R-84, R-90, R-282, R-283, M-71, M-72, M-154 (which styled him as "Sr."), C-299, E-23, E-140, E-249, Z-1, Z-26 (which styled him as "Jr."), N-70, A-481, I-45, I-341, I-371, I-503]. Justice who administered the Oath of Allegiance and Fidelity in 1778 [Ref: J-1814]. He died on July 23, 1798 in Caroline County [Ref: R-283]. "Mrs. Esther Driver, relict of the late Col. Matthew Driver, died in Caroline County on October 13, 1807, in her 62nd year." [Ref: *Republican Star* newspaper, October 20, 1807]. See "Christopher Driver," q.v.

DRIVER, Renness. See "Matthew Driver," q.v.

DUDLEY, Ann. See "Timothy Price," q.v.

DUDLEY, Juliet. See "Mathias Freeman," q.v.

DUE, Enock. See "James Due," q.v.

DUE, James. Private, Maryland Line, who applied for pension (S34771) on November 4, 1818 in Queen Anne's County, but was living in Caroline County. In 1821 he resided at Hillsborough in Caroline County with two sons, Enock (aged 26) and John (aged 17), and two daughters, Rachel (aged 17) and Surrena (aged 12). James died on February 4, 1832 [Ref: W-1032].

DUE, John. See "James Due," q.v.
DUE, Rachel. See "James Due," q.v.
DUE, Surrena. See "James Due," q.v.
DUKES, Ann. See "William Satterfield," q.v.
DUKES (DUKE), Isaac (c1761-1835). Private, Militia, Capt. Shadrack Liden's Company, 14th Battalion, by August 13, 1777 [Ref: M-155]. Rendered patriotic service by providing wheat for the use of the military in August, 1782, as verified by Giles Hicks 3rd, Commissary for Caroline County [Ref: V-6636]. Isaac Duke or Dukes was born circa 1761 in Maryland, married Elizabeth King, and died on April 17, 1835 in Indiana [Ref: Y-887].
DUKES (DUKE), Thomas. Private, Militia, Capt. Shadrack Liden's Company, 14th Battalion, by August 13, 1777 [Ref: M-155]. Thomas Duke or Dukes married Sarah --?-- and died after December 11, 1792 [Ref: Y-887].
DUKES (DUKE), Zebelun (Zebulun). Private, Militia, Capt. Shadrack Liden's Company, 14th Battalion, by August 13, 1777 [Ref: M-155]. Rendered patriotic service by providing wheat for the use of the military in August, 1782, as verified by Giles Hicks 3rd, Commissary for Caroline County [Ref: V-6636].
DULANEY, Ann. See "William Dulaney," q.v.
DULANEY, Mary. See "William Dulaney," q.v.
DULANEY, Thomas. Private, Militia, Capt. William Chipley's Company, 28th Battalion, by August 13, 1777 [Ref: M-153, which spelled the name "Dulany"].
DULANEY, William. Private, Militia, Capt. William Hopper's Company, 28th Battalion, by August 13, 1777 [Ref: M-151]. One William Dulaney married Mary --?-- and their daughter Ann Dulaney was born December 15, 1763 [Ref: K-25].
DUNCAN, Isaac. Private, Maryland Troops, enrolled by Lieut. Levin Handy in Caroline County and passed by Col. William Hopewell on August 4, 1776 [Ref: D-69].
DUNKER, Aaron. Private, Militia, Capt. Joseph Douglass' Company, 14th Battalion, by August 13, 1777 [Ref: M-156].
DUNN, Nancy. See "Batchelor Chance," q.v.
DURGAN (DURGINS), James. Private, 5th Maryland Line, enlisted June 16, 1779; Fifer, August 1, 1779; still in service on November 1, 1780 [Ref: D-199]. Subscribed to the Oath of Allegiance and Fidelity before the Hon. Henry Downes, Jr. on March 2, 1778 [Ref: J-1814].
DURGAN (DIRAGIN, DUREGIN), John. Private, Maryland Troops, enlisted by Capt. Joseph Richardson in Caroline County and passed by Col. William Richardson on August 31, 1776 [Ref: D-69]. Private, Militia, 14th Battalion, Capt. Joseph Richardson's Company, by August 13, 1777 [Ref: M-154].
DURGAN, Patrick. Private, 5th Maryland Line, enlisted June 13, 1779 and died November 21, 1779 [Ref: D-199].
DWIGANS (DWIGENS), Daniel. Corporal, 6th Company, Capt. Peter Adams, 1st Maryland Line, enlisted January 22, 1776 [Ref: D-14].
DWIGANS (DWIGGANS, DWIGONS), James. On December 27, 1776 he joined

a company of men in Caroline County who marched to Talbot County to obtain a supply of salt [Ref: B-564, B-565]. Ensign, promoted to Second Lieutenant, Militia, Capt. Vincent Price's Company, 28th Battalion, June 19, 1777 [Ref: J-1814, M-151]. First Lieutenant, Militia, Capt. John Reynolds' Company, April 9, 1778 [Ref: M-72, E-23].

DWIGANS (DWIGGANS), James Jr. Private, Militia, Capt. Vincent Price's Company, 28th Battalion, by August 13, 1777 [Ref: M-151].

DWIGANS (DWIGINS), James Sr. Subscribed to the Oath of Allegiance and Fidelity (made his "X" mark) before the Hon. Henry Downes, Jr. on March 2, 1778 [Ref: J-1814].

DWIGANS (DWIGGANS), John (1735 - after 1784). Private, Militia, Capt. Vincent Price's Company, 28th Battalion, by August 13, 1777 [Ref: M-151]. Rendered patriotic service by providing wheat for the use of the military in August, 1782, as verified by Giles Hicks 3rd, Commissary for Caroline County [Ref: V-6636]. Aged 48 in a 1783 deposition and aged 49 in a 1784 deposition [Ref: T-6, T-12].

DWIGANS (DWIGGANS), Nathan. Private, Militia, Capt. Henry Downes' Company, 28th Battalion, by August 13, 1777 [Ref: M-152].

DWIGANS (DWIGGINS), Robert. Born in Maryland circa 1740-1745, married Lydia --?--, served as a second lieutenant and rendered patriotic service in Maryland during the Revolutionary War, and died before May, 1789 in North Carolina [Ref: Y-907].

DWIGANS (DWIGENS), Samuel. Corporal, 6th Company, Capt. Peter Adams, 1st Maryland Line, enlisted January 22, 1776 [Ref: D-14].

DWYER, Thomas. Sergeant, 6th Company, Capt. Peter Adams, 1st Maryland Line, enlisted January 30, 1776 [Ref: D-13].

DYRS, Abram. Private, Militia, Capt. John Fauntleroy's Company, 28th Battalion, by August 13, 1777 [Ref: M-154].

DYRS, Symon (Lymon?). Private, Militia, Capt. John Fauntleroy's Company, 28th Battalion, by August 13, 1777 [Ref: M-154].

EAGLE, Solomon (1722 - after 1786). On December 27, 1776 he joined a company of men in Caroline County who marched to Talbot County to obtain a supply of salt [Ref: B-564, B-565]. On May 26, 1780, he filed a certificate in Caroline County Court that he had subscribed to the Oath of Allegiance and Fidelity before the Hon. Richard Mason [Ref: N-78]. Aged 60 in a 1782 deposition and aged 64 in a 1786 deposition [Ref: T-4, T-11].

EAGLE, William. Private, Militia, Capt. Vincent Price's Company, 28th Battalion, by August 13, 1777 [Ref: M-151]. Private (draft), Maryland Troops, enrolled in Caroline County by William Whiteley, County Lieutenant, on August 14, 1781 to serve in the Maryland Line until December 10, 1781 [Ref: D-385].

EATON, Anderton. Private, Militia, 14th Battalion, Capt. Joseph Richardson's Company, by August 13, 1777 [Ref: M-154].

EATON, Edward. Private, Militia, 14th Battalion, Capt. Joseph Richardson's

Company, by August 13, 1777 [Ref: M-154].
EATON, Jonathan. Private, Militia, Capt. Joseph Douglass' Company, 14th Battalion, by August 13, 1777 [Ref: M-156].
EATON, Levi. Private, Militia, 14th Battalion, Capt. Joseph Richardson's Company, by August 13, 1777 [Ref: M-154].
EATON, Mary. See "Roger Fountain," q.v.
EATON, Peter. Rendered patriotic service by providing wheat for the use of the military in May, 1782, as verified by Giles Hicks 3rd, Commissary for Caroline County [Ref: V-6636].
EATON, Rebecca. See "Henry Turner," q.v.
EATON, Richard. Private, Militia, 14th Battalion, Capt. Joseph Richardson's Company, by August 13, 1777 [Ref: M-154].
EATON, Thomas. First Lieutenant, Militia, 14th Battalion, May 14, 1776. First Lieutenant, Militia, Capt. Joseph Douglass' Company, by August 13, 1777, and Capt. Hugh McBride's Company, April 9, 1778. Captain, December 17, 1781 [Ref: M-73, M-156, A-424, E-23, I-27]. Rendered patriotic service by providing wheat for the use of the military in June and August, 1782, as verified by Giles Hicks 3rd, Commissary for Caroline County [Ref: V-6636]. Subscribed to the Oath of Allegiance and Fidelity before the Hon. Matthew Driver on February 1, 1778 [Ref: J-1814].
EATON, William. Private, Militia, 14th Battalion, Capt. Joseph Richardson's Company, by August 13, 1777 [Ref: M-154].
ECCLESTON, Rachel. See "John Stevens," q.v.
EDGE, Jesse. Rendered patriotic service by providing wheat for the use of the military in August, 1782, as verified by Giles Hicks 3rd, Commissary for Caroline County [Ref: V-6636].
EDGELL, Abram. Private, Militia, 14th Battalion, Capt. Joseph Richardson's Company, by August 13, 1777 [Ref: M-154].
EDGELL, Benjamin (1750-c1791). Born in Maryland in 1750, married Rebecca --?--, served as a private during the Revolutionary War, and died before July 7, 1791 [Ref: Y-927]. See the other two men named "Benjamin Edgell," q.v.
EDGELL, Benjamin, of James. Private, Militia, Capt. John Mitchell's Company, 14th Battalion, by August 13, 1777 [Ref: M-154].
EDGELL, Benjamin, of John. Private, Militia, 14th Battalion, Capt. Joseph Richardson's Company, by August 13, 1777 [Ref: M-154]. Subscribed to the Oath of Allegiance and Fidelity (made his "+" mark) before the Hon. Peter Richardson on February 28, 1778 [Ref: J-1814].
EDGELL, Daniel. Private, Militia, 14th Battalion, Capt. Joseph Richardson's Company, by August 13, 1777 [Ref: M-154]. Rendered patriotic service by providing wheat for the use of the military in August, 1782, as verified by Giles Hicks 3rd, Commissary for Caroline County [Ref: V-6636]. "Daniel Edgall" married Mary Lowe by license dated November 3, 1778 [Ref: X-9].
EDGELL, Henry (1751 -   ). Private, Militia, 14th Battalion, Capt. Joseph

Richardson's Company, by August 13, 1777 [Ref: M-154]. Aged 38 in a 1789 deposition and aged 43 in a 1794 deposition [Ref: T-13, T-17].

EDGELL, James. Born in Maryland circa 1724, married Mary --?--, and died before May 7, 1782 in Maryland [Ref: Y-927].

EDGELL, Walter. Private, Militia, 14th Battalion, Capt. Joseph Richardson's Company, by August 13, 1777 [Ref: M-154]. Private (draft), Maryland Troops, enrolled in Caroline County by William Whiteley, County Lieutenant, on August 14, 1781 to serve in the Maryland Line until December 10, 1781 [Ref: D-385].

EDGELL, William. Private, Militia, 14th Battalion, Capt. Joseph Richardson's Company, by August 13, 1777 [Ref: M-154].

EDGERLY, Edward. Sergeant, 6th Company, Capt. Peter Adams, 1st Maryland Line, enlisted February 15, 1776 [Ref: D-13].

EDGERLY, William. Private, 5th Maryland Line, enlisted May 29, 1778 and served to at least March, 1779 [Ref: D-203].

EDMONDSON, Elizabeth. See "Matthew Driver," q.v.

EDMONDSON, James. Private, Militia, Capt. John Mitchell's Company, 14th Battalion, by August 13, 1777 [Ref: M-154]. "James Edmondson, Quaker" was aged 55 in a 1792 deposition [Ref: T-16].

EDMONDSON, Peter (Sub-Sheriff). Subscribed to the Oath of Allegiance and Fidelity before the Hon. Charles Dickinson on March 1, 1778 [Ref: J-1418]. He was elected Sheriff and commissioned on October 25, 1782 [Ref: I-292]. See "Matthew Driver," q.v.

EDMONDSON, Peter. Subscribed to the Oath of Allegiance and Fidelity before the Hon. Charles Dickinson on March 1, 1778 [Ref: J-1418]. "Peter Edmondson" was a brother of William Edmondson (deceased). In 1780 "Peter Sharpe Edmondson" was aged 78 (born 1702) and in 1785 "Peter Edmondson" was aged 83 (born 1702), as noted in depositions taken in Caroline County [Ref: T-2, T-3, T-10]. "Peter Edmordson" married Elizabeth Driver by license dated May 5, 1791 [Ref: X-23].

EDMONDSON, Samuel. Quartermaster, 5th Maryland Line, enlisted on December 10, 1776 and resigned on October 14, 1777 [Ref: D-203].

EDMONDSON, William. See "Peter Edmondson," q.v.

ELLERS, Mary. See "John Stant," q.v.

ELLIOTT, Ann. See "Parrish Garner," q.v.

ELLIOTT, Benjamin. See "Richard Mason," q.v.

ELLIOTT, Joseph. Sergeant, 6th Company, Capt. Peter Adams, 1st Maryland Line, enlisted January 30, 1776 [Ref: D-13].

ELLIOTT, William. Private, Militia, Capt. Thomas Hughlett's Company, 28th Battalion, by August 13, 1777 [Ref: M-152]. William Elliott married Sarah Robinson by license dated December 10, 1779 [Ref: X-11].

EMERSON, William. See "John Spurrey," q.v.

EMMERTON, Henry. Private (draft), Maryland Troops, enrolled in Caroline County by William Whiteley, County Lieutenant, on August 14, 1781 to serve in the Maryland Line until December 10, 1781 [Ref: D-385]. Honorably discharged from the service on November 29, 1781 [Ref: I-7, which spelled the name "Emerten"].

EMORY, Arthur. Private, Militia, Capt. Samuel Jackson's Company, 28th Battalion, by August 13, 1777 [Ref: M-153, which spelled the name "Emmory"]. Subscribed to the Oath of Allegiance and Fidelity before the Hon. Richard Mason on March 2, 1778 [Ref: J-1814].

EMORY, John. Private, Militia, Capt. Samuel Jackson's Company, 28th Battalion, by August 13, 1777 [Ref: M-153]. Subscribed to the Oath of Allegiance and Fidelity in 1780 [Ref: L-110].

EMORY, Sally. See "John Spurrey," q.v.

ERWIN, John. There were two men with this name who were privates in the militia in Capt. Thomas Hughlett's Company, 28th Battalion, by August 13, 1777 [Ref: M-153].

ERWIN, Robert. Private, Militia, Capt. Thomas Hughlett's Company, 28th Battalion, by August 13, 1777 [Ref: M-153, which listed the name twice].

EUBANKS (EWBANKS), Edward. Private, Militia, Capt. William Chipley's Company, 28th Battalion, by August 13, 1777 [Ref: M-153].

EUBANKS (EWBANKS), George. Private, Militia, Capt. Samuel Jackson's Company, 28th Battalion, by August 13, 1777 [Ref: M-153]. George Euberts [Eubanks?] married Rebecca Herrington, and James Eubanks married Margaret Herrington, both by licenses dated October 17, 1780 [Ref: X-12].

EUBANKS (EWBANKS), James. Private, Militia, Capt. Samuel Jackson's Company, 28th Battalion, by August 13, 1777 [Ref: M-153]. James Eubanks married Margaret Herrington by license dated October 17, 1780 [Ref: X-12]. See "George Eubanks," q.v.

EUBANKS (EWBANKS), John. Private, Militia, Capt. Samuel Jackson's Company, 28th Battalion, by August 13, 1777 [Ref: M-153]. Rendered patriotic service by providing wheat for the use of the military in August, 1782, as verified by Giles Hicks 3rd, Commissary for Caroline County [Ref: V-6636].

EUBANKS (EWBANKS), Jonathan. Private, 5th Maryland Line, enlisted May 13, 1778 and reportedly "deserted" on July 2, 1778 [Ref: D-203].

EUBANKS (EXBANKS), Mary. See "James Lemarr," q.v.

EUBANKS (EWBANKS), Thomas. Private, 5th Maryland Line, enlisted on May 9, 1778 and reportedly "deserted" on July 2, 1778 [Ref: D-203].

EUBANKS (EWBANKS), William (1736 -   ). Private, Militia, Capt. Samuel Jackson's Company, 28th Battalion, by August 13, 1777 [Ref: M-153]. Aged 46 in a 1782 deposition [Ref: T-11, which spelled the name "Eubancks"].

EVANS, Ann. See "John Ryall," q.v.

EVANS, H. See "Purnell Sylvester," q.v.

EVANS (EVINS), Nancy. See "James Fisher," q.v.

EVANS (EVINS), Warrington. Private, Militia, Capt. Joseph Douglass' Company, 14th Battalion, by August 13, 1777 [Ref: M-156]. Rendered patriotic service by providing wheat for the use of the military in August, 1782, as verified by Giles Hicks 3rd, Commissary for Caroline County [Ref: V-6636].

EVERETT (EVERITT), Elizabeth. See "John Spurrey," q.v.

EVERETT (EVERITT), Laurance (1720 - after 1779). Subscribed to the Oath of Allegiance and Fidelity (made his mark that resembled an "A" with a short horizontal line under each leg) before the Hon. Richard Mason on March 2, 1778 [Ref: J-1814]. Aged 59 in a 1779 deposition [Ref: T-2].

EVERETT (EVERITT), Joseph. Private, Militia, Capt. William Haslett's Company, 28th Battalion, by August 13, 1777 [Ref: M-152]. Second Lieutenant, Militia, Capt. Postlethwait's Company, April 9, 1778 [Ref: M-73, E-23]. Subscribed to the Oath of Allegiance and Fidelity before the Hon. Thomas Hardcastle on February 13, 1778 [Ref: J-1814, which spelled the name "Evertt"].

EVITT, Abram. Private, Militia, Capt. John Stafford's Company, 14th Battalion, by August 13, 1777 [Ref: M-156]. Abram Evitt married Mary Stevens by license dated September 20, 1779 [Ref: X-11].

EVITT, Seth Hill. Ensign, Militia, Capt. Shadrack Liden's Company, 14th Battalion, June 24, 1777, and Capt. John Hooper's Company, July 24, 1780 [Ref: M-73, M-155, E-23 (which listed the name as "Seth Evitts"), G-27 (which listed the name as "Seth Hill Evett"), C-299]. Subscribed to the Oath of Allegiance and Fidelity before the Hon. Nathaniel Potter on March 2, 1778 [Ref: J-1814, which listed the name as "Seth Hill Evett (Ensign)"].

EWEN, James (1734 - after 1794). Subscribed to the Oath of Allegiance and Fidelity before the Hon. Matthew Driver on February 1, 1778 [Ref: J-1814]. Aged 60 in a 1794 deposition [Ref: T-16].

EWIN, William. Private, Militia, Capt. Thomas Hughlett's Company, 28th Battalion, by August 13, 1777 [Ref: M-152].

EWING, James. Private, Militia, Capt. John Stafford's Company, 14th Battalion, by August 13, 1777 [Ref: M-156]. Ensign, Militia, Capt. Jesse Greyless' Company, June 28, 1780 [Ref: M-73, F-207]. Rendered patriotic service by providing wheat for the use of the military in August, 1782, as verified by Giles Hicks 3rd, Commissary for Caroline County [Ref: V-6636]. James Ewing married Elizabeth Griffith by license dated February 15, 1792 [Ref: X-23].

EWING, Nathaniel. First Lieutenant, 6th Company, Capt. Peter Adams, 1st Maryland Line, commissioned January 3, 1776 [Ref: D-13].

EYLOR(?), Henry. Private, Militia, Capt. William Chipley's Company, 28th Battalion, by August 13, 1777 [Ref: M-153].

FAISTON, Levi. Private, Militia, Capt. John Mitchell's Company, 14th Battalion, by August 13, 1777 [Ref: M-154].

FARIS, Nathan. See "Ezekiel Dean," q.v.

FARMER, Benjamin. See "James Fisher," q.v.

FARROW, Samuel. Seaman, enlisted June 4, 1782 to serve on the barge "Fearnaught" under Capt. Edward Spedden, and was paid £3 bounty for enlisting; physical description given as 5' 8" tall with a fair complexion [Ref: D-612].

FASTON, Elizabeth. See "Zadock Harvey," q.v.

FAULKENOR (FALKNER), Asa. Private, Militia, Capt. Joseph Douglass' Company, 14th Battalion, by August 13, 1777 [Ref: M-156].

FAULKENOR (FALKNER), Benjamin. Private, Militia, Capt. Joseph Douglass' Company, 14th Battalion, by August 13, 1777 [Ref: M-156]. "Benjamin Faulker" married Elizabeth Narvell by license dated January 18, 1779 [Ref: X-9].

FAULKENOR (FALKNER, FAUKENOR), Greenbury. Private, Militia, Capt. Nehemiah Andrew's Company, 14th Battalion, by August 13, 1777 [Ref: M-155].

FAULKENOR (FALKNER), Jacob. Private, Militia, Capt. Joseph Douglass' Company, 14th Battalion, by August 13, 1777 [Ref: M-156]. Aged 33 in a 1792 deposition, noting he was a brother of Salathiel "Falkner" [Ref: T-15].

FAULKENOR (FALKNER), Salathiel. Private, Militia, Capt. Joseph Douglass' Company, 14th Battalion, by August 13, 1777 [Ref: M-156]. See "Jacob Faulkenor," q.v.

FAUNTLEROY, Catherine. See "Thomas Goldsborough," q.v.

FAUNTLEROY, Griffin. See "William Keene" and "Thomas Goldsborough," q.v.

FAUNTLEROY, John. Captain, Militia, 28th Battalion, September 17, 1776 to at least August 13, 1777 [Ref: M-153 (which spelled the name as "John Fountleroy"), M-75, J-1814 (which listed the name as "John FtLeroy"), B-505]. Subscribed to the Oath of Allegiance and Fidelity before the Hon. Henry Downes, Jr. on March 2, 1778 [Ref: J-1814]. See "William Keene," q.v.

FEDDEMAN, Bartholomew. Private, Militia, Capt. Andrew Fountain's Company, 14th Battalion, by August 13, 1777 [Ref: M-156]. Rendered patriotic service by providing wheat for the use of the military in September, 1782, as verified by Giles Hicks 3rd, Commissary for Caroline County [Ref: V-6636]. Bartholomew Feddeman married Esther Downes on November 11, 1756 [Ref: K-27].

FEDDEMAN, Harkins. Private, Militia, Capt. Andrew Fountain's Company, 14th Battalion, by August 13, 1777 [Ref: M-156].

FENDAL, John. Subscribed to the Oath of Allegiance and Fidelity before the Hon. Henry Downes, Jr. on March 2, 1778 [Ref: J-1814].

FERRISS, Nathan. Private, Militia, 14th Battalion, Capt. Joseph Richardson's Company, by August 13, 1777 [Ref: M-154].

FIDDEMAN, Philip. Colonel, Militia, 28th Battalion, January 12, 1776 [Ref: M-75]. Captain, Maryland Troops, 1776 [Ref: D-68]. "No enlistments of Capt. Philip Fiddeman's Company found. The company was raised, however, and marched to Philadelphia" later in 1776 [Ref: D-69, B-225, B-234, B-251, B-258].

FIELDS, Tabatha. See "James Kirkman," q.v.

FISHER, Dudley. Private, Militia, Capt. William Hopper's Company, 28th Battalion, by August 13, 1777 [Ref: M-151].

FISHER, Esther. See "Richard Fisher," q.v.

FISHER, Henry. Private, Militia, Capt. William Hopper's Company, 28th Battalion, by August 13, 1777 [Ref: M-151]. Private (substitute), Maryland Troops, furnished in Caroline County by William Whiteley, County Lieutenant, on April

16, 1781 [Ref: D-368].

FISHER, James (1749-1832). Private, Militia, Capt. William Chipley's Company, 28th Battalion, by August 13, 1777 [Ref: M-153]. Private (substitute), Maryland Troops, furnished in Caroline County by William Whiteley, County Lieutenant, on April 16, 1781 [Ref: D-368]. Born in 1749 in Caroline County, where he lived at the time of his enlistment, James was in Lincoln County, North Carolina by 1783 where "he raised a crop." He married Nancy Evins or Evans on February 2, 1804. In 1824 he had 4 daughters (not named) living at home, the oldest being aged 15. James applied for a pension on November 13, 1824, aged 73 (75?), in Spartanburg District, South Carolina and died on March 4, 1832 in Jackson County, South Carolina. His widow applied for a pension (W7271) on July 5, 1853, aged 81. Benjamin Farmer, of Greenville District, South Carolina, stated he was at their wedding, and John Reeves, aged 50 in 1853, stated he knew them from boyhood. Nancy Fisher died on July 1, 1855 [Ref: W-1199]. It must be noted also, in Caroline County, that a James Fisher married Mary Holson by license dated July 21, 1777, and a James Fisher married Nice Turner by license dated February 4, 1778 [Ref: X-7, X-8].

FISHER, John. Private, Militia, 14th Battalion, Capt. Richard Andrew's Company, by August 13, 1777 [Ref: M-156].

See "Richard Fisher," q.v.

FISHER, Nancy. See "James Fisher," q.v.

FISHER, Rachel. See "Richard Fisher," q.v.

FISHER, Richard (1734-1794). Private, Militia, Capt. William Chipley's Company, 28th Battalion, by August 13, 1777 [Ref: M-153]. Aged 50 in a 1784 deposition and aged 56 in a 1790 deposition, noting he was a brother of Thomas Fisher [Ref: T-9, T-15]. In an 1805 land commission record, "Richard Fisher, Jr." was noted as having died intestate in 1794, seized of a tract called "Fisher's Meadows" and leaving heirs as follows: John Fisher (over 21), William Fisher (over 21). Lydia Blunt (over 21, wife of Levi Blunt), Elizabeth Teat (over 21), Rachel Fisher (over 21), Esther Fisher (under 21), and Susannah Fisher (under 21). [Ref: T-22].

FISHER, Risdon. Private, Militia, Capt. William Chipley's Company, 28th Battalion, by August 13, 1777 [Ref: M-153]. Risdon Fisher married Mary Parker by license recorded January 28, 1775 [Ref: X-5].

FISHER, Susannah. See "Richard Fisher," q.v.

FISHER, Thomas. Private, 6th Company, Capt. Peter Adams, 1st Maryland Line, enlisted January 30, 1776 [Ref: D-14].

FISHER, William. See "Richard Fisher," q.v.

FITZGERALD (FITZGARREL), Charles (1761-1836). Private, Maryland Troops, recruited in Caroline County by William Whiteley, County Lieutenant, on October 17, 1780 [Ref: D-340]. Applied for pension (S17950) in Knox County, Indiana on August 2, 1828, aged 67, stating he lived in Caroline County, Maryland at the time of his enlistment in the Maryland Line. He died about July 2, 1836 and his son James Fitzgerald was administrator of his estate. He lived in

Knox County, Indiana in 1839 [Ref: W-1205].
FITZGERALD, James. See "Charles Fitzgerald," q.v.
FITZGERALD (FITZGARREL), William. Private, Maryland Troops, recruited in Caroline County by William Whiteley, County Lieutenant, on October 17, 1780 [Ref: D-340].
FITZHUGH, George. Clerk of the County Court, 1775-1776 [Ref: Z-1, Z-26].
FLEHARTY, Stephen. Private, Militia, 14th Battalion, Capt. Joseph Richardson's Company, by August 13, 1777 [Ref: M-154]. Subscribed to the Oath of Allegiance and Fidelity before the Hon. Peter Richardson on February 28, 1778 [Ref: J-1814].
FLOWERS, Edmond. Private, Militia, Capt. Nehemiah Andrew's Company, 14th Battalion, by August 13, 1777 [Ref: M-155].
FLOYD, Aaron. Private, Militia, Capt. Vincent Price's Company, 28th Battalion, by August 13, 1777 [Ref: M-151]. Rendered patriotic service by providing wheat for the use of the military in August, 1782, as verified by Giles Hicks 3rd, Commissary for Caroline County [Ref: V-6636].
FLOYD, Daniel. Corporal, 6th Company, Capt. Peter Adams, 1st Maryland Line, enlisted January 23, 1776 [Ref: D-14].
FLOYD, Elijah. Private, 6th Company, Capt. Peter Adams, 1st Maryland Line, enlisted January 23, 1776 [Ref: D-14].
FLOYD, John. Private, 6th Company, Capt. Peter Adams, 1st Maryland Line, enlisted January 23, 1776 [Ref: D-14].
FLOYD, Moses. Private, 6th Company, Capt. Peter Adams, 1st Maryland Line, enlisted January 23, 1776 [Ref: D-14]. Moses Floyd married Drucilla Rumbly by license recorded October 30, 1775 [Ref: X-6].
FOGWELL, Rebeckah. See "Shadrack Liden," q.v.
FORD, John. Private, Maryland Troops, enlisted by Capt. Joseph Richardson in Caroline County and passed by Col. William Richardson on August 31, 1776 [Ref: D-69].
FORREST, Colonel. See "Christopher Parrott" and "James Bright," q.v.
FOSTER, Joseph (1737 -   ). Private, Militia, Capt. John Stafford's Company, 14th Battalion, by August 13, 1777 [Ref: M-156]. Aged 47 in a 1784 deposition, noting he was a son of Thomas Foster of Dorchester County [Ref: T-8].
FOSTER, Rigby. Private, Militia, 14th Battalion, Capt. Joseph Richardson's Company, by August 13, 1777 [Ref: M-154].
FOSTER, Thomas. Private, Militia, Capt. John Stafford's Company, 14th Battalion, by August 13, 1777 [Ref: M-156]. See "Joseph Foster," q.v.
FOSTER, William. Private, Maryland Troops, enrolled by Lieut. Levin Handy in Caroline County and passed by Col. William Hopewell on August 4, 1776 [Ref: D-69].
FOUNTAIN, --?--. See "Samuel Fountain," q.v.
FOUNTAIN, Andrew. Captain, Militia, 14th Battalion, by August 13, 1777 [Ref: M-156]. Rendered patriotic service by providing wheat for the use of the military

in August, 1782, as verified by Giles Hicks 3rd, Commissary for Caroline County [Ref: V-6636].

FOUNTAIN, David. See "James McQuality," q.v.

FOUNTAIN, Deborah. See "John Fountain, Jr.," q.v.

FOUNTAIN, Elizabeth. See "Edward White," q.v.

FOUNTAIN, James. Rendered patriotic service by providing wheat for the use of the military in August, 1782, as verified by Giles Hicks 3rd, Commissary for Caroline County [Ref: V-6636]. James Fountain married Elenor Bell by license dated October 19, 1780, and James Fountain married Margaret Saulsbury by license dated September 8, 1789 [Ref: X-12, X-20].

FOUNTAIN, John. Private, Militia, Capt. Andrew Fountain's Company, 14th Battalion, by August 13, 1777 [Ref: M-157].

FOUNTAIN, John. Private, Militia, Capt. Vincent Price's Company, 28th Battalion, by August 13, 1777 [Ref: M-151].

FOUNTAIN, John. Subscribed to the Oath of Allegiance and Fidelity before the Hon. Henry Downes, Jr. on March 2, 1778 [Ref: J-1814].

FOUNTAIN, John Jr. Private, Militia, Capt. Vincent Price's Company, 28th Battalion, by August 13, 1777 [Ref: M-151]. John Fountain, Jr. married Deborah Fountain by license dated February 15, 1791 [Ref: X-22].

FOUNTAIN, Mary. See "Robert Bell," q.v.

FOUNTAIN, Massey (Massy). Private, Maryland Troops, enlisted by Capt. Joseph Richardson in Caroline County and passed by Col. William Richardson on August 31, 1776 [Ref: D-69]. Private, Militia, Capt. Vincent Price's Company, 28th Battalion, by August 13, 1777 [Ref: M-151]. Massey Fountain married Henrietta Hicks by license dated August 9, 1780 [Ref: X-12].

FOUNTAIN, Roger (1759 - after 1809). Private, Militia, Capt. Shadrack Liden's Company, 14th Battalion, by August 13, 1777 [Ref: M-155]. Aged 50 in an 1809 deposition [Ref: T-26]. Roger Fountain married Mary Eaton by license dated June 21, 1780 [Ref: X-12].

FOUNTAIN, Samuel. Private, Militia, Capt. Shadrack Liden's Company, 14th Battalion, by August 13, 1777 [Ref: M-155]. One Samuel Fountain married --?-- Fountain by license dated August 17, 1774, and a Samuel Fountain married Sarah Lawrence by license dated August 9, 1793 [Ref: X-4, X-25].

FOUNTAIN, Thomas. Rendered patriotic service by providing wheat for the use of the military in August, 1782, as verified by Giles Hicks 3rd, Commissary for Caroline County [Ref: V-6636].

FOUNTAIN, Thomas Sr. Rendered patriotic service by providing wheat for the use of the military in August, 1782, as verified by Giles Hicks 3rd, Commissary for Caroline County [Ref: V-6636].

FOUNTAIN, William. Private, Militia, Capt. Andrew Fountain's Company, 14th Battalion, by August 13, 1777 [Ref: M-157]. One William Fountain was a private in the 5th Maryland Line who enlisted on June 13, 1778 and died in October, 1778 [Ref: D-205].

FOUNTAIN, William. Private, Militia, Capt. Shadrack Liden's Company, 14th Battalion, by August 13, 1777 [Ref: M-155].

FOUNTAIN, William. Rendered patriotic service by providing wheat for the use of the military in June, 1782, as verified by Giles Hicks 3rd, Commissary for Caroline County [Ref: V-6636]. One William Fountain married Elizabeth Satterfield by license dated June 20, 1781, and a William Fountain married Margaret Morgan by license dated June 25, 1783 [Ref: X-13, X-15].

FOURACRES, William. Private, Militia, Capt. John Fauntleroy's Company, 28th Battalion, by August 13, 1777 [Ref: M-154].

FOWLER, John. Private (draft), Maryland Troops, enrolled in Caroline County by William Whiteley, County Lieutenant, on August 14, 1781 to serve in the Maryland Line until December 10, 1781 [Ref: D-385].

FOWLER, Thomas. Private, Militia, Capt. Nehemiah Andrew's Company, 14th Battalion, by August 13, 1777 [Ref: M-155]. Rendered patriotic service by providing wheat for the use of the military in August, 1782, as verified by Giles Hicks 3rd, Commissary for Caroline County [Ref: V-6636].

FOXWELL, Rebecca. See "Shadrack Liden," q.v.

FRAMPTON, Richard. Ensign, Militia, 14th Battalion, Capt. Joseph Richardson's Company, 1777 [Ref: M-154]. Second Lieutenant, Militia, Capt. Thomas Loockerman's Company, June 24, 1777; commissioned again on April 9, 1778; resigned on July 24, 1780 [Ref: E-23, G-27, M-76, C-299, which latter two sources spelled the name "Frantum"].

FRAMPTON, William. Private, Militia, 14th Battalion, Capt. Joseph Richardson's Company, by August 13, 1777 [Ref: M-154]. "William Frantham" married Ann Newman on January 6, 1755 [Ref: K-27].

FRAZIER, Charles. Private, Militia, Capt. John Mitchell's Company, 14th Battalion, by August 13, 1777 [Ref: M-154].

FRAZIER, James. Rendered patriotic service by providing wheat for the use of the military in August, 1782, as verified by Giles Hicks 3rd, Commissary for Caroline County [Ref: V-6636].

FRAZIER, Solomon, of Dorchester County. "Marriner, belonging to Capt. Thomas Noel's sloop now lying at his wharf," subscribed to the Oath of Allegiance and Fidelity before the Hon. Peter Richardson on March 1, 1778 [Ref: J-1814].

FRAZIER, William (1757 -   ). In Caroline County Court on November 17, 1778, William Frazier reported that he had taken the Oath of Allegiance and Fidelity before the Hon. Charles Dickinson on July 24, 1778 [Ref: N-39]. Justice of the Peace from 1782 to at least 1784, and Justice of the Orphans' Court, 1783-1784 [Ref: I-45, I-341, I-371, I-503]. Aged 35 in a 1792 deposition [Ref: T-16]. William Frazier married Henrietta Johnson by license dated February 9, 1779 [Ref: X-10]. One William Frazier was a first lieutenant in the 5th Maryland Line on December 10, 1776 [Ref: D-204].

FREEMAN, John (1760 -   ). Private, Militia, Capt. Vincent Price's Company, 28th Battalion, by August 13, 1777 [Ref: M-151]. Rendered patriotic service by providing wheat for the use of the military in September, 1782, as verified by Giles Hicks 3rd, Commissary for Caroline County [Ref: V-6636]. Aged 31 in a 1791 deposition [Ref: T-15]. John Freeman married Margaret Clark by license dated January 16, 1787 [Ref: X-17].

FREEMAN, Mathias (Mathyas). Private, Militia, Capt. Vincent Price's Company, 28th Battalion, by August 13, 1777 [Ref: M-151]. Mathias Freeman married Juliet Dudley by license dated October 5, 1785 [Ref: X-17].

FRENCH, Abisha. See "James Summers," q.v.

FRENCH, Thomas. Private, Militia, Capt. Andrew Fountain's Company, 14th Battalion, by August 13, 1777 [Ref: M-157].

FRIEND, Cornish. Private (recruit), Maryland Troops, enrolled in Caroline County by William Whiteley, County Lieutenant, on August 14, 1781 to serve in the Maryland Line for 3 years [Ref: D-385].

FROUME, John. Private, Maryland Troops, enrolled by Lieut. Levin Handy in Caroline County and passed by Col. William Hopewell on August 4, 1776, although reported sick at the time [Ref: D-69].

FULTON, Alexander. Private, 6th Company, Capt. Peter Adams, 1st Maryland Line, enlisted February 22, 1776 [Ref: D-14].

GADD, Robert. Private, Militia, Capt. William Chipley's Company, 28th Battalion, by August 13, 1777 [Ref: M-153]. Subscribed to the Oath of Allegiance and Fidelity before the Hon. Henry Downes, Jr. on March 2, 1778 [Ref: J-1814].

GALWAY, Hugh. Private, 6th Company, Capt. Peter Adams, 1st Maryland Line, enlisted May 7, 1776 [Ref: D-15].

GAMBLE, Isaac. Private, Militia, 14th Battalion, Capt. Joseph Richardson's Company, by August 13, 1777 [Ref: M-154].

GAMBREL, Gideon. Seaman, enlisted June 15, 1782 to serve on the barge "Fearnaught" under Capt. Edward Spedden, and was paid £3 bounty for enlisting; physical description given as 5' 7" tall with a fair complexion [Ref: D-612].

GANNON, Mary. See "Hynson Glanden (Glanding)," q.v.

GANNON, Perry. Private, Maryland Troops, enlisted by Capt. Joseph Richardson in Caroline County and passed by Col. William Richardson on August 31, 1776 [Ref: D-69]. Private, Militia, Capt. Vincent Price's Company, 28th Battalion, by August 13, 1777 [Ref: M-151]. Rendered patriotic service by providing wheat for the use of the military in August, 1782, as verified by Giles Hicks 3rd, Commissary for Caroline County [Ref: V-6636].

GAREY, Elizabeth. See "Vincent Price," q.v.

GAREY, Jonathan. Subscribed to the Oath of Allegiance and Fidelity before the Hon. Henry Downes, Jr. on March 2, 1778 [Ref: J-1814]. "Jonathan Gary" married "Sousana Dickinson" by license dated February 2, 1785 [Ref: X-16].

GAREY, Susannah. See "Robert Hardcastle," q.v.

GARNER (GARNOR), Joseph. Private, Militia, Capt. William Haslett's Company, 28th Battalion, by August 13, 1777 [Ref: M-152].

GARNER, Parrish. Subscribed to the Oath of Allegiance and Fidelity before the

Hon. Benson Stainton on February 2, 1778 [Ref: J-1814]. Parish Garner married Ann Elliott by license dated December 10, 1779 [Ref: X-11].

GARNER, Sheverall(?). Private, Militia, Capt. William Chipley's Company, 28th Battalion, by August 13, 1777 [Ref: M-153].

GARNETT, William. Private, Militia, Capt. Thomas Hughlett's Company, 28th Battalion, by August 13, 1777 [Ref: M-153].

GARRETT, Job. Private, Militia, Capt. Samuel Jackson's Company, 28th Battalion, by August 13, 1777 [Ref: M-153]. Job Garrett married Priscilla Hignett by license dated November 9, 1780 [Ref: X-12].

GARRETT, John. Private, Militia, Capt. William Haslett's Company, 28th Battalion, by August 13, 1777 [Ref: M-152]. Subscribed to the Oath of Allegiance and Fidelity in 1780 [Ref: L-111, which spelled the name "Garrat"].

GARY, Jonathan. See "Jonathan Garey," q.v.

GASHFORD, James. Private, Militia, Capt. John Fauntleroy's Company, 28th Battalion, by August 13, 1777 [Ref: M-154].

GAUDEN, Prestin. See "Preiston Godwin," q.v.

GENN, Ann. See "Baptist Davis," q.v.

GENN, Elizabeth. See "John Genn," q.v.

GENN (GINN), James. Subscribed to the Oath of Allegiance and Fidelity before the Hon. Benson Stainton on February 26, 1778 [Ref: J-1814]. Appointed as the Inspector of Tobacco at Choptank Bridge in Caroline County by the Council of Maryland on August 30, 1780 [Ref: F-271].

GENN (GINN), John. Subscribed to the Oath of Allegiance and Fidelity before the Hon. Richard Mason on March 2, 1778 [Ref: J-1814]. Rendered patriotic service by providing wheat for the use of the military in August, 1782, as verified by Giles Hicks 3rd, Commissary for Caroline County [Ref: V-6636]. In an 1808 land commission record it stated that John Genn had died (date not given) owning tracts called "Merrick's Delight," "Bank's Delight" and "Bank's Addition" and leaving heirs as follows: Elizabeth Jarmon (wife of Robert Jarmon), Thomas Genn (of age), William Genn (minor), Nancy Genn (minor), John Genn (minor), and "one grandchild Margaret Genn, daughter of a son now deceased." [Ref: T-24].

GENN (GINN), Josiah (1750 -   ). Private, Militia, Capt. John Stafford's Company, 14th Battalion, by August 13, 1777 [Ref: M-156]. Subscribed to the Oath of Allegiance and Fidelity before the Hon. Nathaniel Potter on March 2, 1778 [Ref: J-1814]. Aged 32 in a 1782 deposition [Ref: T-10].

GENN (GINN), Margaret. See "John Genn," q.v.

GENN (GINN), Nancy. See "John Genn," q.v.

GENN (GINN), Thomas. See "John Genn," q.v.

GENN (GINN), William. See "John Genn," q.v.

GIBSON, Elizabeth. See "John Thomas," q.v.

GIBSON, James. Private, 6th Company, Capt. Peter Adams, 1st Maryland Line, enlisted February 24, 1776 [Ref: D-15].

GIBSON, John. Private, Militia, 14th Battalion, Capt. Joseph Richardson's Company, by August 13, 1777 [Ref: M-154]. John Gibson married Mary Massey by license dated October 26, 1782 [Ref: X-14].

GIBSON, Rebecca. See "John Thomas," q.v.

GILCHRIST, Robert. On December 10, 1779, he filed a certificate in Caroline County Court that he had subscribed to the Oath of Allegiance and Fidelity before the Hon. Solomon Wright in Queen Anne's County [Ref: N-67]. On December 7, 1781, Robert Gilchrist of Caroline County filed a petition to the Governor and Council of Maryland stating, in part, that he was "a native of Britain and came early into this country where he carried on a very extensive and successful trade, both upon his own account, and conjunct with some gentlemen of London, until this war put a total stop thereto, which, your petitioner has suffered so severely by the Tender Law's being in force so long, and by many and heavy losses by sea, that he is now reduced from a state of genteel and independent affluence to that of great, if not ridiculous, distress, which moved him to beg, more from necessity, than choice." The petition continues with his plea that "your Excellency and honours would give him liberty to move into the city of New York, that he may remove from thence to Great Britain or unto the Island of Jamaica, at both which places he has many friends and relations in very affluent circumstances, who have long wished him among them. He begs leave to prefer this method of removing hence, at least, to that of touching at any of the Neuter Islands." The petition closed with his statement that "his conduct and behaviour has been steady, regular and uniform during this contest, early taking the Oaths prescribed by law and behaving in all respects as a peaceable and dutiful subject, which he will always endeavour to do remove where he will, nor will any rewards, threats or promises, ever make him forfeit his declared Allegiance to these States, to whom he wishes all success and will leave with regret." [Ref: H-565]. On February 18, 1782, the Council of Maryland granted Robert Gilchrist permission "to solicit His Excellency General Washington or the Commanding Officer at the Out Posts of the American Army for license to go into the City of New York for the purpose of obtaining passage from thence to Scotland, not to return to this State during the present war between America and Great Britain without the leave of the Governor and Council for the time being, first had and obtained." [Ref: I-79, I-80].

GILL, Hepsebeath. Private, Militia, Capt. Henry Downes' Company, 28th Battalion, by August 13, 1777 [Ref: M-152]. See "Hephzebah Guild," q.v.

GLADSON (GLADSTON), Nathan. Private, Militia, Capt. John Stafford's Company, 14th Battalion, by August 13, 1777 [Ref: M-156]. Nathan Gladston married Ann Hobbs by license dated September 27, 1780 [Ref: X-12].

GLAND, Jonas. Private, Militia, Capt. Samuel Jackson's Company, 28th Battalion, by August 13, 1777 [Ref: M-153].

GLANDEN (GLANDON), Cloudsberry. Private, Militia, Capt. William Haslett's Company, 28th Battalion, by August 13, 1777 [Ref: M-152].

GLANDEN (GLANDON), Herrington. Private, Militia, Capt. William Haslett's Company, 28th Battalion, by August 13, 1777 [Ref: M-152].
GLANDEN (GLANDON, GLANDING), Hynson (Hinson). Private, Militia, Capt. William Chipley's Company, 28th Battalion, by August 13, 1777 [Ref: M-153]. Subscribed to the Oath of Allegiance and Fidelity (made his "+" mark) before the Hon. Richard Mason on March 2, 1778 [Ref: J-1814]. Hynson Glanding married Mary Gannon by license dated January 8, 1780 [Ref: X-11].
GLANDEN (GLANDON), Laban. Private, Militia, Capt. John Fauntleroy's Company, 28th Battalion, by August 13, 1777 [Ref: M-153].
GLANDEN (GLANDING), Sally. See "Richard Roe," q.v.
GLANDEN (GLANDON), Sidney. See "William Whitley," q.v.
GLANDEN (GLANDON), William. Private, Militia, Capt. John Fauntleroy's Company, 28th Battalion, by August 13, 1777 [Ref: M-153].
GLENN, Joannes. Subscribed to the Oath of Allegiance and Fidelity before the Hon. Henry Downes, Jr. on March 2, 1778 [Ref: J-1814].
GLOVER, William. Private, 6th Company, Capt. Peter Adams, 1st Maryland Line, enlisted February 15, 1776 [Ref: D-14].
GODWIN, Preiston. Ensign, Militia, Capt. John Stafford's Company, 14th Battalion, June 24, 1777 [Ref: C-299 (which spelled the name "Prestin Gauden"), M-78, M-156].
GOLDSBOROUGH, Foster. Attended the Maryland Convention on July 3, 1776 for the "express purpose of forming a new government." [Ref: O-35]. Appointed a Judge of Elections for Caroline County at the Maryland Convention on November 8, 1776 [Ref: O-55]. Foster Goldsborough, son of Nicholas Goldsborough and Sarah Jolly Turbutt (widow of Samuel Turbutt and daughter of Peter Jolly), was born circa 1730 and married Rachel Bruff of Caroline County. They had a son Foster Goldsborough who married a Miss Potter (daughter of Col. William Potter) and had children Thomas and Sophia [Ref: S-223, S-224].
GOLDSBOROUGH, Griffin. See "Thomas Goldsborough," q.v.
GOLDSBOROUGH, John. See "Benson Stainton," q.v.
GOLDSBOROUGH, Nicholas. See "Foster Goldsborough" and "Thomas Goldsborough," q.v.
GOLDSBOROUGH, Rachel. Rendered patriotic service by providing wheat for the use of the military in August, 1782, as verified by Giles Hicks 3rd, Commissary for Caroline County [Ref: V-6636]. See "Foster Goldsborough," q.v.
GOLDSBOROUGH, Sophia. See "Foster Goldsborough," q.v.
GOLDSBOROUGH, Thomas (c1728-1793). Son of Nicholas Goldsborough and Sarah Turbutt, he married after 1775 to Catherine Fauntleroy (daughter of Griffin Fauntleroy and Judith Swan, of Northumberland County, Virginia, and niece of President George Washington). Their children were Thomas Goldsborough, Griffin Goldsborough, Sarah Fauntleroy Barnett, and Catherine Potter. Thomas attended the Maryland Conventions in 1774 and 1775, and although elected to

serve in the Lower House in 1786, did not attend. He served as Commissioner of the Tax from 1777 to at least 1782, Justice of the Orphans' Court in 1781, and Judge of the Court of Appeals for Tax Assessment in Caroline County in 1786. He died testate on March 9, 1793 in Talbot County [Ref: R-364, R-70, O-1]. Also, during the revolution, he stored grain for the use of the State of Maryland, as certified by Richard Keene, Commissary for Caroline County, on June 21, 1780, and rendered patriotic service by providing wheat for the use of the military in August, 1782, as verified by Giles Hicks 3rd, Commissary for Caroline County [Ref: P-297, V-6636].

GOLDSBOROUGH, Thomas. Private, Militia, Capt. Samuel Jackson's Company, 28th Battalion, by August 13, 1777 [Ref: M-153]. See "Foster Goldsborough," q.v.

GOLLERTHEM (GOLLERTHERM), Edward Pinder (1746 -   ). Private, Militia, Capt. John Mitchell's Company, 14th Battalion, by August 13, 1777 [Ref: M-154, which spelled the name "Galonthon"]. Subscribed to the Oath of Allegiance and Fidelity before the Hon. Charles Dickinson on March 1, 1778 [Ref: J-1418, which spelled the name "Golothim"]. Aged 47 in a 1793 deposition and aged 51 in a 1798 deposition [Ref: T-17, T-20].

GORDON, William (1753 -   ). Private, Militia, Capt. Henry Downes' Company, 28th Battalion, by August 13, 1777 [Ref: M-152]. Aged 46 in a 1799 deposition [Ref: T-24].

GOUTEE (GOUTY), John (c1740-1818). Private, Militia, Capt. Nehemiah Andrew's Company, 14th Battalion, by August 13, 1777 [Ref: M-155, Y-1201].

GOW, William. Private, Militia, Capt. John Mitchell's Company, 14th Battalion, by August 13, 1777 [Ref: M-154]. Private, 5th Maryland Line, enlisted May 29, 1778, promoted to corporal on April 1, 1779 and reported missing on August 16, 1780 at the Battle of Camden in South Carolina [Ref: D-209].

GRACE, George. Private, Militia, Capt. Shadrack Liden's Company, 14th Battalion, by August 13, 1777 [Ref: M-155].

GRACE, James. Private, Militia, Capt. Shadrack Liden's Company, 14th Battalion, by August 13, 1777 [Ref: M-155].

GRACE, Solomon. Private, Militia, Capt. Shadrack Liden's Company, 14th Battalion, by August 13, 1777 [Ref: M-155]. Rendered patriotic service by providing wheat for the use of the military in August, 1782, as verified by Giles Hicks 3rd, Commissary for Caroline County [Ref: V-6636].

GRACE, Thomas. Private, Militia, Capt. Shadrack Liden's Company, 14th Battalion, by August 13, 1777 [Ref: M-155].

GRAHAM, Charles. Private, Militia, Capt. John Mitchell's Company, 14th Battalion, by August 13, 1777 [Ref: M-154].

GRAHAM, John. Subscribed to the Oath of Allegiance and Fidelity before the Hon. Nathaniel Potter on March 2, 1778 [Ref: J-1814]. See "John Dawson," q.v.

GRAHAM, Ritta. See "John Dawson," q.v.

GRAHAM, William (Taylor). Subscribed to the Oath of Allegiance and Fidelity

before the Hon. Peter Richardson on February 23, 1778 [Ref: J-1814].
GRAY, James. Private, Militia, Capt. Nehemiah Andrew's Company, 14th Battalion, by August 13, 1777 [Ref: M-155]. James Gray married Rhoda Dean by license dated February 18, 1779 [Ref: X-10].
GRAY, Mary Ann. See "Thomas Wynn Loockerman," q.v.
GRAY, William. Private, Militia, Capt. Nehemiah Andrew's Company, 14th Battalion, by August 13, 1777 [Ref: M-155].
GRAY, William Jr. Private, Militia, Capt. Nehemiah Andrew's Company, 14th Battalion, by August 13, 1777 [Ref: M-155].
GRAYDOCK, William. Private, Militia, Capt. William Chipley's Company, 28th Battalion, by August 13, 1777 [Ref: M-153].
GRAYLESS (GREYLESS), Jesse (1738 - after 1790). Second Lieutenant, Militia, Capt. John Stafford's Company, 14th Battalion, by August 13, 1777 [Ref: M-156]. First Lieutenant, Militia, Capt. Joseph Douglass' Company, April 9, 1778. Captain, June 28, 1780 to at least December 17, 1781 [Ref: M-80, E-23 (which spelled the name "Greyless"), I-28 (which spelled the name "Guyless"), F-207]. Subscribed to the Oath of Allegiance and Fidelity before the Hon. Nathaniel Potter on March 2, 1778 [Ref: J-1814]. Rendered patriotic service by providing wheat for the use of the military in August, 1782, as verified by Giles Hicks 3rd, Commissary for Caroline County [Ref: V-6636]. Aged 47 in a 1785 deposition and aged 52 in a 1790 deposition [Ref: T-9, T-14]. One Jesse Grayless married Sarah Andrew by license dated May 3, 1790 [Ref: X-21].
GRAYLESS, Nathan. See "Levin Johnson," q.v.
GRAYLESS, William. Private, Militia, Capt. John Stafford's Company, 14th Battalion, by August 13, 1777 [Ref: M-156].
GREEN, Ann. See "William Smith" and "Valentine Green," q.v.
GREEN, Elizabeth. See "William Richardson" and William Walker," q.v.
GREEN, John. Private, Militia, Capt. William Chipley's Company, 28th Battalion, by August 13, 1777 [Ref: M-153].
GREEN, John. Private, Militia, 14th Battalion, Capt. Joseph Richardson's Company, by August 13, 1777 [Ref: M-154].
GREEN, John. Ensign, Militia, 28th Battalion, August 14, 1779 [Ref: E-493]. Subscribed to the Oath of Allegiance and Fidelity before the Hon. Richard Mason on March 2, 1778 [Ref: J-1814]. One John Green married Elizabeth Phillips by license dated May 21, 1783, and a John Green married Sarah Smith by license dated May 12, 1790 [Ref: X-21]. [Ref: X-15]. John Green, son of Valentine and Sarah Green, was born April 7, 1758 [Ref: K-25]. Since there was more then one man named John Green, additional research will be necessary before drawing conclusions. See "Valentine Green," q.v.
GREEN, Margaret. See "Henry Downes," q.v.
GREEN, Rachel. See "Valentine Green," q.v.
GREEN. Sarah. See "Valentine Green," q.v.
GREEN, Valentine. On February 12, 1778, Valentine Green, of Choptank

Hundred, wrote to Gov. Thomas Johnson and offered pork, beef, and corn for the Army, stating "3,000 weight could be found, desires to know prices." [Ref: O-88]. Subscribed to the Oath of Allegiance and Fidelity before the Hon. Henry Downes, Jr. on March 2, 1778 [Ref: J-1814]. Rendered patriotic service by providing wheat for the use of the military in August, 1782, as verified by Giles Hicks 3rd, Commissary for Caroline County [Ref: V-6636]. Valentine Green married Sarah --?-- and had these children: Valentine Green (born October 25, 1755), John Green (born April 7, 1758), Ann Green (born December 17, 1759), and Rachel Green (born February 23, 1762). [Ref: K-25]. One Valentine Green married Jane Sylvester by license dated June 9, 1781 [Ref: X-13].

GREEN, Zachariah. Private, Militia, Capt. William Haslett's Company, 28th Battalion, by August 13, 1777 [Ref: M-152].

GREEN, Zebulon. Private, Militia, Capt. William Haslett's Company, 28th Battalion, by August 13, 1777 [Ref: M-152].

GREENBAUGH, Elizabeth. See "Richard Willis," q.v.

GREENBERGH (GREENBURGH), Jonathan. Private, Militia, Capt. Andrew Fountain's Company, 14th Battalion, by August 13, 1777 [Ref: M-157]. Private (draft), Maryland Troops, furnished in Caroline County by William Whiteley, County Lieutenant, on April 16, 1781 [Ref: D-368, which spelled the name "Greenhugh"].

GREENHAWK (GREEHAWK), Deborah. See "Joshua Willis," q.v.

GREENHAWK, Jonathan. Rendered patriotic service by providing wheat for the use of the military in August, 1782, as verified by Giles Hicks 3rd, Commissary for Caroline County [Ref: V-6636].

GREENHAWK, William (1720 - after 1786). Subscribed to the Oath of Allegiance and Fidelity (made his "X" mark) before the Hon. Peter Richardson on February 23, 1778 [Ref: J-1814]. Aged 66 in a 1786 deposition [Ref: T-12].

GREENWELL, Henry. Subscribed to the Oath of Allegiance and Fidelity before the Hon. Matthew Driver on February 1, 1778 [Ref: J-1814].

GREGG, John. Private, Militia, Capt. Samuel Jackson's Company, 28th Battalion, by August 13, 1777 [Ref: M-153].

GREYLESS, Jesse. See "Jesse Grayless," q.v.

GRIFFITH, Abraham. See "Charles Manship, Jr.," q.v.

GRIFFITH, Alexander. Private, Militia, Capt. Joseph Douglass' Company, 14th Battalion, by August 13, 1777 [Ref: M-156].

GRIFFITH, Elizabeth. See "James Ewing," q.v.

GRIFFITH, George. Private, Militia, Capt. Joseph Douglass' Company, 14th Battalion, by August 13, 1777 [Ref: M-156].

GRIFFITH, Henry. Private, Militia, Capt. John Fauntleroy's Company, 28th Battalion, by August 13, 1777 [Ref: M-154].

GRIFFITH, John. First Lieutenant, Militia, Capt. James Andrew's Company, December 17, 1781 [Ref: M-81, I-27].

GRIFFITH, Mary. See "Charles Manship," q.v.

GRIFFITH, Saunders. Rendered patriotic service by providing wheat for the use of the military in August, 1782, as verified by Giles Hicks 3rd, Commissary for Caroline County [Ref: V-6636].
GRIMES, George. Subscribed to the Oath of Allegiance and Fidelity before the Hon. Richard Mason on March 2, 1778 [Ref: J-1814].
GUILD, Hephzebah. Subscribed to the Oath of Allegiance and Fidelity before the Hon. Henry Downes, Jr. on March 2, 1778 [Ref: J-1814]. This may be the "Hebijah --?--" who married "--?-- Walker, of Queen Ann Co." by license dated July 7, 1774 in Caroline County [Ref: X-3]. See "Hepsebeath Gill," q.v.
GWINN, John. See "Henry Willis," q.v.
HACKETT, Oliver. Private, Militia, Capt. John Stafford's Company, 14th Battalion, by August 13, 1777 [Ref: M-156].
HACKETT, Oliver Jr. Rendered patriotic service by providing wheat for the use of the military in June, 1782, as verified by Giles Hicks 3rd, Commissary for Caroline County [Ref: V-6636]. Oliver Hackett, Jr. married Ann Wilson by license dated July 18, 1777 [Ref: X-7].
HACKETT, Oliver Sr. Rendered patriotic service by providing wheat for the use of the military in August, 1782, as verified by Giles Hicks 3rd, Commissary for Caroline County [Ref: V-6636].
HALE, Lawrence. See "Ezekiel Dean," q.v.
HALL, James. See "Thomas Hall," q.v.
HALL, Sarah. See "Thomas Hall," q.v.
HALL, Thomas. Subscribed to the Oath of Allegiance and Fidelity before the Hon. Henry Downes, Jr. on March 2, 1778 [Ref: J-1814]. Thomas Hall married Elizabeth Meeds on June 18, 1752 and had at least two children: James Hall (born October 30, 1759) and Sarah Hall (born March 19, 1762). [Ref: K-25, K-27]. One Thomas Hall married Naomi Hammond by license dated October 18, 1780 [Ref: X-12].
HALL, Tyler. Private, Militia, Capt. Nehemiah Andrew's Company, 14th Battalion, by August 13, 1777 [Ref: M-155].
HAMBLETON, James. Private, Militia, Capt. Vincent Price's Company, 28th Battalion, by August 13, 1777 [Ref: M-151].
HAMBLETON, James. Private, Militia, Capt. John Stafford's Company, 14th Battalion, by August 13, 1777 [Ref: M-156]. James Hambleton married Dorothy Ozwell by license dated April 28, 1784 [Ref: X-15].
HAMILTON, James. Subscribed to the Oath of Allegiance and Fidelity before the Hon. Henry Downes, Jr. on March 2, 1778 [Ref: J-1814].
HAMMOND, Naomi. See "Thomas Hall," q.v.
HANCOCK, John. Private, Militia, Capt. William Chipley's Company, 28th Battalion, by August 13, 1777 [Ref: M-153, which listed the name as "Hancock(?)]. John Hancock married Cleia [Celia?] Morris by license recorded January 28, 1775 [Ref: X-5].
HAND, John. Private, Militia, Capt. Thomas Hughlett's Company, 28th Battalion,

by August 13, 1777 [Ref: M-152].
HANDLY, Handy. Private (substitute), Maryland Troops, furnished in Caroline County by William Whiteley, County Lieutenant, on April 16, 1781 [Ref: D-368].
HANDY, George. Private, Maryland Troops, enrolled by Lieut. Levin Handy in Caroline County and passed by Col. William Hopewell on August 4, 1776 [Ref: D-69].
HANDY, John. See "Isaac Nichols," q.v.
HANDY, Levin. Second Lieutenant, Maryland Troops, 1776 [Ref: D-68].
HANDY, Rebecca. See "Isaac Handy," q.v.
HANEY(?), John. Rendered patriotic service by providing wheat for the use of the military in August, 1782, as verified by Giles Hicks 3rd, Commissary for Caroline County [Ref: V-6636].
HANNINGTON, Philip. See "Philip Harrington," q.v.
HARDCASTLE, Aaron (1759-1795). Son of Thomas Hardcastle and Henrietta Downes, Aaron married Arabella Stokely by license dated June 10, 1788 [Ref: R-410, X-18]. Private, Militia, Capt. Henry Downes' Company, 28th Battalion, by August 13, 1777 [Ref: M-152]. Subscribed to the Oath of Allegiance and Fidelity before the Hon. Thomas Hardcastle on February 27, 1778 [Ref: J-1814]. See "Thomas Hardcastle," q.v.
HARDCASTLE, Ann. See "William Bell," q.v.
HARDCASTLE, Edward. See "Thomas Hardcastle," q.v.
HARDCASTLE, Elizabeth. See "James Wilson," q.v.
HARDCASTLE, Henrietta. See "Thomas Hardcastle," q.v.
HARDCASTLE, James (c1755-c1816). Private, Militia, Capt. Thomas Hughlett's Company, 28th Battalion, by August 13, 1777 [Ref: M-153]. One James Hardcastle married Sarah Parratt by license dated June 11, 1784, and a James Hardcastle married Elizabeth Baggs by license dated June 20, 1787 [Ref: X-15, X-18]. James Hardcastle was born circa 1755, married Mrs. Elizabeth (Clarke) Baggs, and died before June 11, 1816 [Ref: Y-1305].
HARDCASTLE, Jane. See "Nathaniel Potter," q.v.
HARDCASTLE, John (1757-1810). Son of Thomas Hardcastle and Henrietta Downes, John married first to Jane Potter (1750-1786), widow of Nathaniel Potter, by license dated June 11, 1781, and second to Polly Costen (1774-1854) in 1790 [Ref: R-410, R-657, X-13]. Private, Militia, Capt. Henry Downes' Company, 28th Battalion, by August 13, 1777 [Ref: M-152]. Second Lieutenant, Militia, Capt. Thomas Burk's Company, April 9, 1778 [Ref: M-84, E-23]. Subscribed to the Oath of Allegiance and Fidelity before the Hon. Richard Mason on March 2, 1778 [Ref: J-1814]. In an 1816 land commission record it stated that John Hardcastle died on February 10, 1810, leaving a widow Mary (who married William Orrell) and the following children: Samuel Hardcastle, Ann Culbreth (wife of Thomas Culbreth), Susan Hardcastle (minor), Philip Hardcastle (minor), John Hardcastle (minor), Robert Hardcastle (minor), and William H. C.

Hardcastle (minor). [Ref: T-32]. See "Nathaniel Potter," q.v.

HARDCASTLE, John. Private, Light Horse Troops, Capt. Henry Dickinson's Company, June 12, 1781 [Ref: M-157]. Rendered patriotic service by providing wheat for the use of the military in August, 1782, as verified by Giles Hicks 3rd, Commissary for Caroline County [Ref: V-6636]. See the other "John Hardcastle," q.v.

HARDCASTLE, Mary. See "John Hardcastle," q.v.

HARDCASTLE, Matthew. See "Thomas Hardcastle," q.v.

HARDCASTLE, Nancy. See "Allemby Jump," q.v.

HARDCASTLE, Peter. See "Thomas Hardcastle," q.v.

HARDCASTLE, Philip. See "John Hardcastle" and "Thomas Hardcastle," q.v.

HARDCASTLE, Rebekah. See "Richard Mason, Jr.," q.v.

HARDCASTLE, Robert (1739-1831). Son of Robert Hardcastle who immigrated from Yorkshire, England, he settled in Queen Anne's County, then in Caroline County, married Jane Pratt, and subsequently migrated to Wheeling, (West) Virginia [Ref: R-410]. Served on the Committee of Observation for Caroline County on August 2, 1775 [Ref: A-48]. Second Lieutenant, promoted to First Lieutenant, Militia, Capt. Thomas Hughlett's Company, 28th Battalion, June 19, 1777. Captain, December 17, 1781 [Ref: M-152, M-84, C-294, E-23, I-27, J-1814]. Subscribed to the Oath of Allegiance and Fidelity before the Hon. Thomas Hardcastle on February 13, 1778 [Ref: J-1814]. Aged 47 in a 1786 deposition [Ref: T-12]. See "Thomas Hardcastle" and "Solomon Hardcastle" and the other "Robert Hardcastle," q.v.

HARDCASTLE, Robert. Stored grain for the use of the State of Maryland, as certified by Richard Keene, Commissary for Caroline County, on June 5, 1780 [Ref: P-294]. Robert Hardcastle married Susannah Garey by license dated December 1, 1787 in Caroline County [Ref: X-18]. There was also a Robert Hardcastle who married Tamson --?-- and had a son William Hardcastle born December 25, 1756. [Ref: K-26]. Since there was more then one man named Robert Hardcastle, additional research will be necessary before drawing conclusions. See the other "Robert Hardcastle," q.v.

HARDCASTLE, Samuel. See "John Hardcastle," q.v.

HARDCASTLE, Solomon. Son of Robert Hardcastle who immigrated from Yorkshire, England and settled in Queen Anne's County and then in Caroline County [Ref: R-410]. Private, Militia, Capt. Thomas Hughlett's Company, 28th Battalion, June 19, 1777 [Ref: M-153]. Rendered patriotic service by providing wheat for the use of the military in August, 1782, as verified by Giles Hicks 3rd, Commissary for Caroline County [Ref: V-6636]. Subscribed to the Oath of Allegiance and Fidelity (made his "C" mark) before the Hon. Henry Downes, Jr. on March 2, 1778 [Ref: J-1814].

HARDCASTLE, Susan. See "John Hardcastle," q.v.

HARDCASTLE, Tamson. See "Robert Hardcastle," q.v.

HARDCASTLE, Thomas (1736/7-1808). Son of Robert Hardcastle of Yorkshire,

England. Thomas married Henrietta Downes, daughter of John Downes, Sr., of Queen Anne's County, on November 8, 1756 and their children were: John Hardcastle (1757-1810, married first to Jane Potter, widow, and second to Polly Costen), Aaron Hardcastle (1759-1795, married Arabella Stokely), Thomas Hardcastle (1763-1824), Henrietta Hardcastle (married James Pearce), Robert Hardcastle (1768-1852, married Sarah Baynard), Philip Hardcastle (1776-1815), William Molleston Hardcastle (1779-1874, married Anne Colston), Matthew Hardcastle (1786-1835), and Peter Hardcastle (married Mary Baynard in 1797). [Ref: R-410, Y-1305]. Thomas represented Caroline County in the Lower House of the Maryland General Assembly between 1783 and 1787. He also served as County Court Justice from 1777 to at least 1787, Justice of the Peace, 1778-1784, Justice of the Orphans' Court from 1779 to at least 1787, and was appointed Commissioner of Tax in 1777 and 1779 [Ref: R-411, R-88, R-89, R-91, N-70, E-249, I-45, I-341, I-503]. Quartermaster, Militia, 28th Battalion, January 12, 1776, and Second Lieutenant, Militia, Capt. Henry Downes' Company, 28th Battalion, by August 13, 1777 [Ref: M-84, M-152]. Served on the Committee of Observation for Caroline County on August 2, 1775 [Ref: A-48]. Justice who administered the Oath of Allegiance and Fidelity in 1778 [Ref: J-1814]. Rendered patriotic service by providing corn for the use of the military in February, 1780, and wheat in August, 1782, as verified by Richard Keene and Giles Hicks 3rd, Commissaries for Caroline County, respectively [Ref: P-269, V-6636]. Stored corn for the use of the State of Maryland, as certified by Richard Keene, Commissary for Caroline County, on June 18, 1780 [Ref: P-296]. Aged 40 in a 1776 deposition [Ref: T-1]. "Thomas Hardcastle was a son of Robert Hardcastle who moved circa 1740 to that part of Queen Anne's County which became Caroline County in 1773, settling at the head of navigation on the Choptank River [at "Castle Hall"]. He was a major in the Revolutionary War and furnished supplies and recruits to the Army at Brandywine. A younger brother Peter Hardcastle was a lieutenant in the Maryland Line in the command in the south. Aaron Hardcastle, eldest son of Thomas, was a farmer and died early in manhood, leaving a widow [not named], a son [Edward B. Hardcastle], and a daughter [not named]. [Ref: S-13, S-14]. Thomas Hardcastle, of Caroline County, aged 71, died on September 29, 1808 in Dorchester County "at the house of Mathew Hardcastle, after a painful illness which he had borne for 8 months with great resignation, cutting off this valuable man; agriculture was the pursuit of his life." [Ref: R-411, and the *Republican Star* newspaper, October 25, 1808]. See "John Hardcastle" and "Nathaniel Potter," q.v.

HARDCASTLE, William. See "John Hardcastle" and "Robert Hardcastle" and "Thomas Hardcastle," q.v.

HARDING (HARDIN), Edward. Private, Maryland Troops, enlisted by Capt. Joseph Richardson in Caroline County and passed by Col. William Richardson on August 31, 1776 [Ref: D-69, which spelled the name "Hardin"]. Private, Militia, Capt. Nehemiah Andrew's Company, 14th Battalion, by August 13, 1777

[Ref: M-155].

HARDING (HARDEN), Thomas. Private, Militia, Capt. Shadrack Liden's Company, 14th Battalion, by August 13, 1777 [Ref: M-155]. Rendered patriotic service by providing wheat for the use of the military in August, 1782, as verified by Giles Hicks 3rd, Commissary for Caroline County [Ref: V-6636, which spelled the name "Harden"].

HARGIDINE, Katharine. See "Thomas Purnell," q.v.

HARKINGS (HUCKINGS, HUCHINGS), John. Private, Militia, Capt. Samuel Jackson's Company, 28th Battalion, by August 13, 1777 [Ref: M-153].

HARNAMAN, Henry. Private (draft), Maryland Troops, enrolled in Caroline County by William Whiteley, County Lieutenant, on August 14, 1781 to serve in the Maryland Line until December 10, 1781 [Ref: D-385].

HARNEY, Joseph. Private, Militia, Capt. Andrew Fountain's Company, 14th Battalion, by August 13, 1777 [Ref: M-157].

HARNEY, Philip. Private, Militia, Capt. Andrew Fountain's Company, 14th Battalion, by August 13, 1777 [Ref: M-157].

HARPER, Anthony. Private, Militia, Capt. Andrew Fountain's Company, 14th Battalion, by August 13, 1777 [Ref: M-157].

HARPER, John. Private, Militia, Capt. Vincent Price's Company, 28th Battalion, by August 13, 1777 [Ref: M-151].

HARPER, John. Private, Militia, Capt. Shadrack Liden's Company, 14th Battalion, by August 13, 1777 [Ref: M-155].

HARPER, William. Private, Militia, Capt. Andrew Fountain's Company, 14th Battalion, by August 13, 1777 [Ref: M-157].

HARPER, William. Private, Militia, Capt. John Fauntleroy's Company, 28th Battalion, by August 13, 1777 [Ref: M-154].

HARPER, William. Second Lieutenant, Militia, Capt. Richard Keene's Company, April 9, 1778. First Lieutenant, December 17, 1781 [Ref: M-84, E-23, I-27]. Subscribed to the Oath of Allegiance and Fidelity before the Hon. Richard Mason on March 2, 1778 [Ref: J-1814]. Rendered patriotic service by providing wheat for the use of the military in August, 1782, as verified by Giles Hicks 3rd, Commissary for Caroline County [Ref: V-6636]. One William Harper married Amelia Holden by license dated June 27, 1788 [Ref: X-19].

HARRINGTON, Abigail. Rendered patriotic service by providing wheat for the use of the military in August, 1782, as verified by Giles Hicks 3rd, Commissary for Caroline County [Ref: V-6636].

HARRINGTON, Ann. See "Thomas Strawhan," q.v.

HARRINGTON, John. See "John Herrington," q.v.

HARRINGTON, Peter. Ensign, Militia, Capt. Thomas Hughlett's Company, 28th Battalion, June 19, 1777. Second Lieutenant, April 9, 1778 [Ref: M-152, M-84, E-23, and C-294, J-1814, which latter two sources spelled the name "Herrington"]. Appointed to be Constable of Bridgetown Hundred on December 15, 1778 [Ref: N-45]. Rendered patriotic service by providing wheat for the use of the military in September, 1782, as verified by Giles Hicks III, Commissary for Caroline County [Ref: P-552].

HARRINGTON, Philip. Private, Militia, Capt. Samuel Jackson's Company, 28th Battalion, by August 13, 1777 [Ref: M-153].

HARRINGTON, Philip (1718 - after 1780). Subscribed to the Oath of Allegiance and Fidelity in 1780 [Ref: L-112, which listed the name as "Philip Hannington"]. Aged 58 in a 1776 deposition, noting he was a son of Richard Harrington [Ref: T-1].

HARRINGTON, Priscilla. See "James Slaughter," q.v.

HARRINGTON, Rebecca. Rendered patriotic service by providing wheat for the use of the military in August, 1782, as verified by Giles Hicks 3rd, Commissary for Caroline County [Ref: V-6636, which spelled the name "Harington"].

HARRINGTON, Richard. See "Philip Harrington," q.v.

HARRINGTON, Thomas. Private, Militia, Capt. Thomas Hughlett's Company, 28th Battalion, by August 13, 1777 [Ref: M-153]. Subscribed to the Oath of Allegiance and Fidelity before the Hon. Thomas Hardcastle on February 27, 1778 [Ref: J-1814]. Thomas Harrington married Rebekah Slaughter by license dated April 6, 1784 [Ref: X-15].

HARRINGTON, William (1733 -   ). Appointed to be Constable of Choptank Hundred on December 15, 1778 [Ref: N-45]. Rendered patriotic service by providing wheat for the use of the military in August, 1782, as verified by Giles Hicks 3rd, Commissary for Caroline County [Ref: V-6636, which spelled the name "Herrington"]. Aged 49 in a 1782 deposition [Ref: T-10].

HARRIS, Benjamin. Private, Militia, Capt. John Stafford's Company, 14th Battalion, by August 13, 1777 [Ref: M-156].

HARRIS, Catharine. See "Joseph Douglass," q.v.

HARRIS, Celia. See "James Anderson," q.v.

HARRIS, Elizabeth. See "Michael Smith," q.v.

HARRIS, James. Private, Militia, Capt. John Stafford's Company, 14th Battalion, by August 13, 1777 [Ref: M-156]. James Harris married Katharine Dodd by license dated February 24, 1778 [Ref: X-8].

HARRIS, John. Private, Militia, 14th Battalion, Capt. Richard Andrew's Company, by August 13, 1777 [Ref: M-156].

HARRIS, John. Private, Militia, Capt. John Mitchell's Company, 14th Battalion, by August 13, 1777 [Ref: M-154]. Rendered patriotic service by providing wheat for the use of the military in June, 1782, as verified by Giles Hicks 3rd, Commissary for Caroline County [Ref: V-6636].

HARRIS, Mary. See "Ellis Thomas," q.v.

HARRIS, Nicholas. Private, Militia, Capt. John Mitchell's Company, 14th Battalion, by August 13, 1777 [Ref: M-154].

HARRIS, William. Private, Militia, Capt. John Stafford's Company, 14th Battalion, by August 13, 1777 [Ref: M-156]. This soldier is represented in the Sons of the American Revolution by Robert Henry Taylor, P. O. Box 100, Greensboro,

Maryland 21639 [Ref: National Society No. 113362 and Maryland State Society No. 2363, approved and elected to membership in October, 1977].

HARRISON, William. Private, Militia, Capt. Joseph Douglass' Company, 14th Battalion, by August 13, 1777 [Ref: M-156]. William Harrison married Penelope Collison by license dated March 13, 1790 [Ref: X-21].

HARVEY, John. Private, Militia, Capt. Shadrack Liden's Company, 14th Battalion, by August 13, 1777 [Ref: M-155]. Rendered patriotic service by providing wheat for the use of the military in August, 1782, as verified by Giles Hicks 3rd, Commissary for Caroline County [Ref: V-6636]. A chancery sale of the real estate of John Harvey, deceased, Caroline County, was announced in the *Republican Star* newspaper on April 14, 1812, by James Chaplain, trustee.

HARVEY, Samuel. Rendered patriotic service by providing wheat for the use of the military in June, 1782, as verified by Giles Hicks 3rd, Commissary for Caroline County [Ref: V-6636].

HARVEY, Thomas. Private, Militia, Capt. William Chipley's Company, 28th Battalion, by August 13, 1777 [Ref: M-153]. Rendered patriotic service by providing wheat for the use of the military in August, 1782, as verified by Giles Hicks 3rd, Commissary for Caroline County [Ref: V-6636]. Thomas Harvey married Nelly Beadley by license dated July 24, 1792 [Ref: X-24].

HARVEY, Zadock. Private, Maryland Troops, enlisted by Capt. Joseph Richardson in Caroline County and passed by Col. William Richardson on August 31, 1776 [Ref: D-69]. Private, Militia, Capt. John Mitchell's Company, 14th Battalion, by August 13, 1777 [Ref: M-154]. Private, 5th Maryland Line, enlisted on May 5, 1778 [Ref: D-213]. Seaman, enlisted on May 29, 1782 to serve on the barge "Fearnaught" under Capt. Edward Spedden, and was paid £3 bounty for enlisting; physical description given as 5' 10" tall with a dark complexion [Ref: D-611]. "Zadoc Harvey" married Elizabeth Faston by license dated June 27, 1784 [Ref: X-15].

HASKINS, William. Subscribed to the Oath of Allegiance and Fidelity before the Hon. Charles Dickinson on March 1, 1778 [Ref: J-1418].

HASLETT (HASLET, HASSLETT), William. Served on the Committee of Observation for Caroline County on August 2, 1775 [Ref: A-48]. Captain, Militia, 28th Battalion, March 9, 1776. Colonel, April 9, 1778, and succeeded on December 17, 1781 [Ref: M-152, J-1814, P-170, P-187, M-85, A-230, I-27, E-23]. Subscribed to the Oath of Allegiance and Fidelity before the Hon. Benson Stainton on January 23, 1778 [Ref: J-1814]. He owned a granary used for the storage of wheat for the use of the State of Maryland in April, 1780 [Ref: P-287]. See "George Hutton," q.v.

HATTON, John. Private, 6th Company, Capt. Peter Adams, 1st Maryland Line, enlisted January 23, 1776 [Ref: D-14].

HAWKINS, Deborah. See "William Banckes," q.v.

HEATH, Charles. Private, Militia, Capt. John Fauntleroy's Company, 28th Battalion, by August 13, 1777 [Ref: M-154].

HEFFERSON, Robert. Rendered patriotic service by providing wheat for the use of the military in August, 1782, as verified by Giles Hicks 3rd, Commissary for Caroline County [Ref: V-6636].

HEIRS, Abraham. Rendered patriotic service by providing wheat for the use of the military in August, 1782, as verified by Giles Hicks 3rd, Commissary for Caroline County [Ref: V-6636].

HENDERSON, James (1760 - after 1834). Private, Maryland Line, who applied for pension (S8708) in Guilford County, North Carolina on February 21, 1834, stating he was born in (now) Caroline County, Maryland on February 18, 1760 and lived there at the time of his enlistment. In 1778 he moved to North Carolina and also enlisted there. He married on August 11, 1779, but the name of his wife was not stated [Ref: W-1600].

HENDRICKS (HENRICK), Henry. Private, Militia, Capt. Thomas Hughlett's Company, 28th Battalion, by August 13, 1777 [Ref: M-153]. See "James Kirkman," q.v.

HENDRICKS (HENRICK), William. Private, Militia, Capt. Thomas Hughlett's Company, 28th Battalion, by August 13, 1777 [Ref: M-153].

HENNECY, Perry. Private, Militia, 14th Battalion, Capt. Richard Andrew's Company, by August 13, 1777 [Ref: M-156].

HENRY, John Jr. See "Benson Stainton," q.v.

HENRY (HENREY), Thomas. Subscribed to the Oath of Allegiance and Fidelity (made his "x" mark) before the Hon. Henry Downes, Jr. on March 2, 1778 [Ref: J-1814].

HENRY, William. See "Hugh McBryde," q.v.

HERD, Joseph. See "Joseph Hurd," q.v.

HERRICK, William, of Choptank Hundred. Subscribed to the Oath of Allegiance and Fidelity before the Hon. Benson Stainton on February 2, 1778 [Ref: J-1814].

HERRINGTON, John. Rendered patriotic service by providing wheat for the use of the military in August, 1782, as verified by Giles Hicks 3rd, Commissary for Caroline County [Ref: V-6636].

HERRINGTON, Margaret. See "James Eubanks," q.v.

HERRINGTON, Peter. See "Peter Harrington," q.v.

HERRINGTON, Rebecca. See "George Eubanks," q.v.

HICKS, Giles (1719 - after 1782). Served on the Committee of Observation for Caroline County on August 2, 1775 [Ref: A-48]. Subscribed to the Oath of Allegiance and Fidelity before the Hon. Henry Downes, Jr. on March 2, 1778 [Ref: J-1814]. Rendered patriotic service by providing wheat for the use of the military in September, 1782, as verified by Giles Hicks III, Commissary for Caroline County [Ref: P-552, which listed the name as "Sr."]. Aged 56 in a 1775 deposition, aged 57 in a 1776 deposition, and aged 63 in a 1782 deposition [Ref: T-1, T-3]. Giles Hicks married Mary Oxenham on December 3, 1759 [Ref: K-27].

HICKS, Giles Jr. Private, Militia, Capt. Vincent Price's Company, 28th Battalion, by August 13, 1777 [Ref: M-151]. "Giles Hicks" married Margaret Chalmers by license dated March 18, 1785, and "Giles Hiche" married Mary Colston by license dated December 27, 1786 [Ref: X-16, X-17]. Additional research will be necessary before drawing conclusions.

HICKS, Giles 3rd (or III). Commissary for Caroline County in 1782 [Ref: P-527, P-533, V-6636]. It is interesting to note that a Giles Hicks was a captain in the 10th Maryland Regiment in August, 1780, but there were only eight regiments in the Maryland Continental Line [Ref: P-310].

HICKS, Henrietta. See "Massey Fountain," q.v.

HICKS, James Jr. On December 27, 1776 he joined a company of men in Caroline County who marched to Talbot County to obtain a supply of salt [Ref: B-564, B-565, which listed the name as "James Hix, son of James"]. Private, Militia, Capt. Vincent Price's Company, 28th Battalion, by August 13, 1777 [Ref: M-151].

HICKS, James Sr. (1715 - after 1788). Rendered patriotic service by providing wheat for the use of the military in August, 1782, as verified by Giles Hicks 3rd, Commissary for Caroline County [Ref: V-6636]. Aged 62 in a 1776 deposition, aged 67 in a 1782 deposition and aged 73 in a 1788 deposition [Ref: T-1, T-5, T-13].

HICKS, Levin. Private, Militia, Capt. Vincent Price's Company, 28th Battalion, by August 13, 1777 [Ref: M-151]. Levin Hicks married Elizabeth Stewart by license dated November 17, 1791 [Ref: X-23].

HICKS, Thomas. Private, Militia, Capt. Henry Downes' Company, 28th Battalion, by August 13, 1777 [Ref: M-152].

HIGGNUTT (HIGNUT), Daniel (1746-1808). Private, Militia, Capt. John Stafford's Company, 14th Battalion, by August 13, 1777 [Ref: M-156]. Aged 49 in a 1795 deposition [Ref: T-16]. Daniel Higgnutt married Sarah H. --?-- and died in 1808 [Ref: Y-1417].

HIGNUT (HIGNETT), Priscilla. See "Job Garrett," q.v.

HIGNUT, Thomas. Rendered patriotic service by providing wheat for the use of the military in August, 1782, as verified by Giles Hicks 3rd, Commissary for Caroline County [Ref: V-6636].

HILL, Eliza. See "John Chilcutt," q.v.

HILL, John. Private, Militia, Capt. Henry Downes' Company, 28th Battalion, by August 13, 1777 [Ref: M-152].

HILL, Nathan. Private, Militia, Capt. John Stafford's Company, 14th Battalion, by August 13, 1777 [Ref: M-156]. Nathan Hill married Rachel Lewis by license dated December 30, 1783 [Ref: X-15].

HILL, William. Private, Militia, Capt. Henry Downes' Company, 28th Battalion, by August 13, 1777 [Ref: M-152].

HILL, William Earl. Private, Maryland Troops, recruited in Caroline County by William Whiteley, County Lieutenant, on October 17, 1780 [Ref: D-340].

HINDMAN, Doctor. See "William Richardson," q.v.

HINDMAN, Edward. See "Henry Dickinson," q.v.

HINES, Daniel. Private, Militia, Capt. William Haslett's Company, 28th Battalion, by August 13, 1777 [Ref: M-152].

HINSON, John. Private, Militia, Capt. Thomas Hughlett's Company, 28th Battalion, by August 13, 1777 [Ref: M-153].

HIRDMAN, Edward. See "Henry Dickinson," q.v.

HOBBS, Ann. See "Nathan Gladson" and "John Spurrey," q.v.

HOBBS, Elizabeth. See "John Spurrey," q.v.

HOBBS, Gary. Private, Militia, Capt. Andrew Fountain's Company, 14th Battalion, by August 13, 1777 [Ref: M-157].

HOBBS, Jacob. Private, Militia, Capt. Vincent Price's Company, 28th Battalion, by August 13, 1777 [Ref: M-151].

HOBBS, John. Private, Maryland Troops, enlisted by Capt. Joseph Richardson in Caroline County and passed by Col. William Richardson on August 31, 1776 [Ref: D-69]. Subscribed to the Oath of Allegiance and Fidelity before the Hon. Charles Dickinson on March 1, 1778 [Ref: J-1418]. One John Hobbs was aged 52 in a 1783 deposition and aged 58 in a 1788 deposition [Ref: T-6, T-12]. See "John Spurrey," q.v.

HOBBS, John. Private, Militia, Capt. John Mitchell's Company, 14th Battalion, by August 13, 1777 [Ref: M-154].

HOBBS, John. Private, Militia, Capt. Vincent Price's Company, 28th Battalion, by August 13, 1777 [Ref: M-151].

HOBBS, John Jr. Private, Militia, Capt. Vincent Price's Company, 28th Battalion, by August 13, 1777 [Ref: M-151].

HOBBS, Joshua. Private, Militia, Capt. Shadrack Liden's Company, 14th Battalion, by August 13, 1777 [Ref: M-155]. Rendered patriotic service by providing wheat for the use of the military in August, 1782, as verified by Giles Hicks 3rd, Commissary for Caroline County [Ref: V-6636]. In 1783 he gave his age as 51 and 54 in two different depositions, and stated he was a son of Robert Hobbs [Ref: T-6, T-7, T-8]. One Joshua Hobbs married Rhody Cranmer by license dated July 21, 1791 [Ref: X-23].

HOBBS, Joy. Private, Militia, Capt. John Stafford's Company, 14th Battalion, by August 13, 1777 [Ref: M-156]. Rendered patriotic service by providing wheat for the use of the military in August, 1782, as verified by Giles Hicks 3rd, Commissary for Caroline County [Ref: V-6636].

HOBBS, Mary. See "James Towers," q.v.

HOBBS, Mathias. Private, Militia, Capt. John Stafford's Company, 14th Battalion, by August 13, 1777 [Ref: M-156].

HOBBS, Peter. Private, Militia, Capt. Andrew Fountain's Company, 14th Battalion, by August 13, 1777 [Ref: M-157].

HOBBS, Robert. Private (draft), Maryland Troops, enrolled in Caroline County by William Whiteley, County Lieutenant, on August 14, 1781 (although reported "run" at the time) to serve in the Maryland Line until December 10, 1781 [Ref: D-385]. See "Joshua Hobbs," q.v.

HOBBS, Solomon. Private, Militia, Capt. Samuel Jackson's Company, 28th Battalion, by August 13, 1777 [Ref: M-153].
HOBBS, Solomon. Private, Militia, 14th Battalion, Capt. Joseph Richardson's Company, by August 13, 1777 [Ref: M-154].
HOBBS, Thomas. Private, Militia, Capt. William Chipley's Company, 28th Battalion, by August 13, 1777 [Ref: M-153].
HOBBS, William. Private, Maryland Troops, enlisted by Capt. Joseph Richardson in Caroline County and passed by Col. William Richardson on August 31, 1776 [Ref: D-69]. Private, Militia, Capt. John Stafford's Company, 14th Battalion, by August 13, 1777 [Ref: M-156].
HOBBS, Zebulon. Private, Militia, Capt. John Stafford's Company, 14th Battalion, by August 13, 1777 [Ref: M-156].
HODSON, John. Private, Militia, Capt. John Stafford's Company, 14th Battalion, by August 13, 1777 [Ref: M-156].
HOLDBROOK, Alice. See "Solomon Morgan," q.v.
HOLDEN, Amelia. See "William Harper," q.v.
HOLDING, Caleb. Subscribed to the Oath of Allegiance and Fidelity before the Hon. Richard Mason on March 2, 1778 [Ref: J-1814].
HOLDING, John. Subscribed to the Oath of Allegiance and Fidelity before the Hon. Richard Mason on March 2, 1778 [Ref: J-1814].
HOLDING, William. Private, Militia, Capt. John Fauntleroy's Company, 28th Battalion, by August 13, 1777 [Ref: M-154]. Subscribed to the Oath of Allegiance and Fidelity before the Hon. Richard Mason on March 2, 1778 [Ref: J-1814].
HOLLAND, Andrew and C. C. See "William Holland," q.v.
HOLLAND, Dorothy. See "Henry Powell," q.v.
HOLLAND, Elizabeth. See "William Holland," q.v.
HOLLAND, Jeanes. See "William Holland," q.v.
HOLLAND, John. See "William Holland," q.v.
HOLLAND, Laban. Private, Militia, Capt. Nehemiah Andrew's Company, 14th Battalion, by August 13, 1777 [Ref: M-155].
HOLLAND, Leven. See "William Holland," q.v.
HOLLAND, Levi. Private, Militia, Capt. Nehemiah Andrew's Company, 14th Battalion, by August 13, 1777 [Ref: M-155].
HOLLAND, Lovina. See "William Holland," q.v.
HOLLAND, Mahalah. See "William Holland," q.v.
HOLLAND, Mary. See "William Holland," q.v.
HOLLAND, Niminah. See "William Holland," q.v.
HOLLAND, Pleasant. See "William Holland," q.v.
HOLLAND, Rebeccah. See "William Holland," q.v.
HOLLAND, Richard. Private, Militia, Capt. Nehemiah Andrew's Company, 14th Battalion, by August 13, 1777 [Ref: M-155].
HOLLAND (HOLLIN), William (1763-1839). Private, Maryland Line, who was

born in (now) Caroline County on September 21, 1763 and lived there at the time of his enlistment. After the war he moved to Guilford County, North Carolina where he married on August 25, 1788 or 1789 to Lovina (Lovey or Lovele) Lewis (born August 31, 1771). Their children were: Leven Holland (born June 25, 1790), William Holland (born September 7, 1792), Mary Holland (born November 22, 1794), Niminah Holland (born February 2, 1797), Elizabeth Holland (born August 14, 1799), Rebeccah Holland (born June 17, 1801), Mahalah Holland (born December 20, 1803), Mary Ambley Holland (born January 8, 1807), John Holland (born October 24, 1809), Pleasant Holland (born June 25, 1812), and Andrew Jackson Holland (born April 25, 1815). William later moved to Kentucky and then to Tennessee. He applied for a pension in Morgan County on October 23, 1833 and died on February 19, 1839. His widow applied for a pension (W-9065) in Morgan County, Tennessee on December 16, 1839 and also applied for bounty land (warrant #28628-160-55) in Barren County, Kentucky on May 8, 1855. Witnesses were John Holland and C. C. Holland. Also mentioned in the family records were William Holland's uncle Charles Ross and the following: William Holland, son of Leven and Lewcey (born January 8, 1810), Jeanes Holland (born August 17, 1812), Lovey Holland (born September 13, 1814), Tiry Adcock (born December 23, 1829), Niminah Adcock (born February 9, 1797), Lovy Adcock (born August 18, 1816), Agga Adcock (born December 9, 1816), and William Adcock (born September 7, --?--). [Ref: W-1682, Y-1459, and Harry Wright Newman's *Maryland Revolutionary Records*, p. 116].

HOLLIS (HOLLINS), Clark. Subscribed to the Oath of Allegiance and Fidelity in 1780 [Ref: L-113, which spelled the name "Hollis"]. Rendered patriotic service by providing wheat for the use of the military in August, 1782, as verified by Giles Hicks 3rd, Commissary for Caroline County [Ref: V-6636, which spelled the name "Hollins"].

HOLMS, William. Private, 6th Company, Capt. Peter Adams, 1st Maryland Line, enlisted February 15, 1776 [Ref: D-14].

HOLSON, Hanson. Private, Militia, Capt. Henry Downes' Company, 28th Battalion, by August 13, 1777 [Ref: M-152].

HOLSON, Mary. See "James Fisher," q.v.

HOLSON, William. Rendered patriotic service by providing wheat for the use of the military in August, 1782, as verified by Giles Hicks 3rd, Commissary for Caroline County [Ref: V-6636].

HOOD, Lillie. See "Stephen Chance," q.v.

HOOPER, Foster. Private, Militia, Capt. Andrew Fountain's Company, 14th Battalion, by August 13, 1777 [Ref: M-157].

HOOPER, Henry. See "William Richardson," q.v.

HOOPER, John. First Lieutenant, Militia, Capt. Shadrack Liden's Company, 14th Battalion, June 24, 1777; commissioned again on April 9, 1778; Captain, June 28, 1780, who either resigned on June 12, 1781 or succeeded on December 17, 1781, both dates and events were given in the records [Ref: M-88, M-155, C-299 (which listed the name as "John Ascum Hooper"), E-23, F-207, I-492, C-27, G-27].

HOOPER, Martha. See "Richard Liden," q.v.

HOOPER, Thomas. Private, Militia, Capt. Shadrack Liden's Company, 14th Battalion, by August 13, 1777 [Ref: M-155].

HOOPER, William. Collector of Tax in Caroline County, 1779-1780 [Ref: F-49].

HOPKINS, Samuel. Private, Maryland Troops, enrolled by Lieut. Thomas Wynn Loockerman in Caroline County in July, 1776 [Ref: D-69].

HOPKINS, Thomas. Private, Militia, Capt. John Fauntleroy's Company, 28th Battalion, by August 13, 1777 [Ref: M-154].

HOPKINS, Thomas. Private, Militia, Capt. John Mitchell's Company, 14th Battalion, by August 13, 1777 [Ref: M-154].

HOPKINS, William. Private, Militia, Capt. William Hopper's Company, 28th Battalion, by August 13, 1777 [Ref: M-151].

HOPPER, Anna. See "William Hopper," q.v.

HOPPER, Daniel. See "William Hopper," q.v.

HOPPER, Mary. See "William Hopper," q.v.

HOPPER, Philemon. See "William Hopper," q.v.

HOPPER, Sarah. See "William Hopper," q.v.

HOPPER, Thomas. See "William Hopper," q.v.

HOPPER, William. Son of William Hooper (died in 1772) and Mary Anne Wright (died in 1747), William married first to Elizabeth Oldham (his first cousin, she being the daughter of Edward Oldham and Ann Wright) and second to Ann Cox (daughter of Daniel Cox) in 1776. His children were William Hopper (died 1793), Daniel Cox Hopper, Thomas Wright Hopper, Philemon Blake Hopper, William Hopper, Sarah Hopper, Mary Hopper, and Anna Maria Hopper. William attended the Maryland Convention in 1775 and served in the Lower House from 1781 to 1783 (also elected in 1780, but did not attend, and resigned on November 1, 1780). He was also elected to the Committee of Correspondence in 1774 and was Sheriff of Caroline County from 1774 until he resigned on February 19, 1778. Captain, Militia, 28th Battalion, by August 13, 1777, he was criticized by Col. Mordecai Gist in a letter to Gov. Thomas Johnson after the Battle of Germantown in 1777 in which Hopper was said to have been attacked with "qualms of sickness" that forced him to leave his regiment when under attack [Ref: R-461, R-462, A-8, A-9, O-4, C-520, M-89, M-151, P-146, J-1814, Z-1, Z-26]. William died in late November, 1806, in Queen Anne's County [Ref: R-462].

HOPPER, William. Private, Light Horse Troops, Capt. Henry Dickinson's Company, June 12, 1781 [Ref: M-157].

HORNEY, Lydia. See "John Salisberry (Salisbury)," q.v.

HOSIER, William. Private, Maryland Troops, enrolled by Lieut. Levin Handy in Caroline County and passed by Col. William Hopewell on August 4, 1776 [Ref: D-69].

HOUSTON, James. See "Hugh McBryde (McBride)," q.v.
HOWARD, Amelia. See "Samuel Willoughby," q.v.
HOWARD, James. Subscribed to the Oath of Allegiance and Fidelity (made his "+" mark) before the Hon. Henry Downes, Jr. on March 2, 1778 [Ref: J-1814].
HOWELL, Thomas. Private, Militia, Capt. Henry Downes' Company, 28th Battalion, by August 13, 1777 [Ref: M-152].
HUBBERT (HUBBERD), Jesse. Private, Militia, Capt. Nehemiah Andrew's Company, 14th Battalion, by August 13, 1777 [Ref: M-155]. Rendered patriotic service by providing wheat for the use of the military in August, 1782, as verified by Giles Hicks 3rd, Commissary for Caroline County [Ref: V-6636]. See "William Kelly," q.v.
HUBBERT, Lydia. See "John Carter," q.v.
HUBBERT, Solomon. Rendered patriotic service by providing wheat for the use of the military in August, 1782, as verified by Giles Hicks 3rd, Commissary for Caroline County [Ref: V-6636].
HUBBERT, Thomas. Private, Militia, 14th Battalion, Capt. Richard Andrew's Company, by August 13, 1777 [Ref: M-156]. Rendered patriotic service by providing wheat for the use of the military in August, 1782, as verified by Giles Hicks 3rd, Commissary for Caroline County [Ref: V-6636].
HUGHES (HEWS), Daniel (1746 -   ). Private, Militia, Capt. William Haslett's Company, 28th Battalion, by August 13, 1777 [Ref: M-152]. Rendered patriotic service by providing wheat for the use of the military in August, 1782, as verified by Giles Hicks 3rd, Commissary for Caroline County [Ref: V-6636, which spelled the name "Hews"]. Aged 36 in a 1782 deposition [Ref: T-11].
HUGHES (HUGHS), John. Private, Maryland Troops, enlisted by Capt. Joseph Richardson in Caroline County and passed by Col. William Richardson on August 31, 1776 [Ref: D-69]. Private, Militia, Capt. John Mitchell's Company, 14th Battalion, by August 13, 1777 [Ref: M-154].
HUGHLETT, Mary. See "Thomas Hughlett," q.v.
HUGHLETT, Rebecca. See "Richard Mason," q.v.
HUGHLETT, Richard. See "Thomas Hughlett," q.v.
HUGHLETT, Thomas (c1739-c1803). Son of William and Mary Hughlett who immigrated from St. Stephen's Parish in Northumberland County, Virginia circa 1749 to Queen Anne's County, Maryland (part which became Caroline County in 1773). Thomas married first to Sarah Dixon (daughter of Obediah Dixon) in 1767 and married second to Rebeckah Mason (daughter of Richard Mason) in 1778 (license dated January 2, 1778). His children were William Hughlett, Richard Hughlett, Mary Adams (wife of Charles Adams), and Ann Caldwell (wife of Dr. Timothy Caldwell; she died February 15, 1806). Thomas represented Caroline County in the Maryland General Assembly between 1783 and 1798, County Coroner in 1778 and 1792, County Court Justice between 1782 and 1800, Justice of the Peace from 1782 to at least 1784, and Maryland State Elector in 1786. He also served as Tobacco Inspector at Choptank Bridge in 1786, Sheriff

of Caroline County between 1787 and 1791, and Commissioner of Tax in 1798 [Ref: R-471, R-472, R-88, R-89, R-90, R-92, N-36, T-23, E-172, I-223, I-341, I-503, X-7]. Captain, Militia, 28th Battalion, June 19, 1777, and Major, December 17, 1781 [Ref: M-152, E-23, C-294, I-27, J-1814]. Subscribed to the Oath of Allegiance and Fidelity before the Hon. Richard Mason on March 2, 1778 [Ref: J-1814]. Rendered patriotic service by providing wheat and corn for the use of the military in February, 1780 [Ref: P-270]. On November 25, 1780 he and Joseph Richardson were appointed by the Council of Maryland "to carry the Act to prohibit for a limited time the Exportation of Indian Corn, &tc., by land" into execution in Caroline County [Ref: G-251]. See "Richard Mason," q.v.

HUGHLETT, William. See "Thomas Hughlett," q.v.

HUNT, John. Private, Militia, Capt. Henry Downes' Company, 28th Battalion, by August 13, 1777 [Ref: M-152].

HUNTER, Ezekiel (1729 - after 1792). Served on the Committee of Observation for Caroline County on August 2, 1775 [Ref: A-48]. Subscribed to the Oath of Allegiance and Fidelity before the Hon. Richard Mason on March 2, 1778 [Ref: J-1814]. Aged 63 in a 1792 deposition [Ref: T-15].

HUNTER, Ezekiel Jr. Private, Militia, Capt. Thomas Hughlett's Company, 28th Battalion, by August 13, 1777 [Ref: M-153, which listed the name without the "Jr."]. Subscribed to the Oath of Allegiance and Fidelity before the Hon. Richard Mason on March 2, 1778 [Ref: J-1814]. "Ezekel Hunter, Jr." married Prudence Boone by license dated February 22, 1785 [Ref: X-16]. "Ezekel Hunter" married Sarah Sylvester by license dated July 25, 1790 [Ref: X-21].

HUNTER, Izabel. See "Noah Mason," q.v.

HUNTER, Nathan. Private, Militia, Capt. William Chipley's Company, 28th Battalion, by August 13, 1777 [Ref: M-153]. Rendered patriotic service by providing wheat for the use of the military in August, 1782, as verified by Giles Hicks 3rd, Commissary for Caroline County [Ref: V-6636].

HUNTER, Samuel. Subscribed to the Oath of Allegiance and Fidelity before the Hon. Richard Mason on March 2, 1778 [Ref: J-1814].

HURD (HERD), Joseph. Private, Militia, Capt. William Haslett's Company, 28th Battalion, by August 13, 1777 [Ref: M-152]. Rendered patriotic service by providing wheat for the use of the military in August, 1782, as verified by Giles Hicks 3rd, Commissary for Caroline County [Ref: V-6636]. In an 1808 land commission record it stated that Joseph Hurd had died on December 6, 1807 seized of tracts called "Golden Grove," "Hardship," "Addition to Hardship," "Maiden's Forrest," "Exchange," "Whitesborough Divided," and "Partnership" (originally called "Loockerman's Delight"), leaving a widow Mary Hurd and four children: Major Hurd, Araminta Rich (wife of James Rich), William Hurd (minor), and Robert Hurd (minor). [Ref: T-24].

HURD, Major. See "Joseph Hurd," q.v.

HURD, Mary. See "Joseph Hurd," q.v.

HURD, Robert. See "Joseph Hurd," q.v.

HURD (HERD), William. Private, Militia, Capt. William Haslett's Company, 28th Battalion, by August 13, 1777 [Ref: M-152]. See "Joseph Hurd," q.v.

HURLEY, Abraham. Rendered patriotic service by providing wheat for the use of the military in August, 1782, as verified by Giles Hicks 3rd, Commissary for Caroline County [Ref: V-6636].

HURLEY, Joshua. Subscribed to the Oath of Allegiance and Fidelity (made his "D" mark) before the Hon. Henry Downes, Jr. on March 2, 1778 [Ref: J-1814].

HURT, Thomas. See "Levin Noble," q.v.

HUTCHINS, Aquilla. Rendered patriotic service by providing wheat for the use of the military in August, 1782, as verified by Giles Hicks 3rd, Commissary for Caroline County [Ref: V-6636].

HUTCHINSON, John. Rendered patriotic service by providing wheat for the use of the military in August, 1782, as verified by Giles Hicks 3rd, Commissary for Caroline County [Ref: V-6636].

HUTSON, Hooper. Private (draft), Maryland Troops, enrolled in Caroline County by William Whiteley, County Lieutenant, on August 14, 1781 to serve in the Maryland Line until December 10, 1781 [Ref: D-385].

HUTSON, John. Private (draft), Maryland Troops, enrolled in Caroline County by William Whiteley, County Lieutenant, on August 14, 1781 to serve in the Maryland Line until December 10, 1781 [Ref: D-385].

HUTSON, Thomas. Rendered patriotic service by providing wheat for the use of the military in August, 1782, as verified by Giles Hicks 3rd, Commissary for Caroline County [Ref: V-6636].

HUTSON, William. Private (draft), Maryland Troops, enrolled in Caroline County by William Whiteley, County Lieutenant, on August 14, 1781 (although reported "run" at the time) to serve in the Maryland Line until December 10, 1781 [Ref: D-385].

HUTTON, George. Private, Militia, Capt. Thomas Hughlett's Company, 28th Battalion, by August 13, 1777 [Ref: M-153]. On September 3, 1778, the Council of Maryland wrote a letter to William Whiteley, County Lieutenant of Caroline County, stating, in part, that "George Hutton was, in April last, adjudged a vagrant, by Col. Haslet; he thinks himself aggrieved by the adjudication and appeals to the Governor and Council. We must request you to enquire of Col. Haslet upon what grounds he formed his opinion ..." [Ref: E-193].

HUTTON, Mary. Rendered patriotic service by providing wheat for the use of the military in June, 1782, as verified by Giles Hicks 3rd, Commissary for Caroline County [Ref: V-6636].

HUTTON, William. Private, Militia, Capt. Thomas Hughlett's Company, 28th Battalion, by August 13, 1777 [Ref: M-153]. William Hutton, Jr. married Catharine Jackson by license dated December 3, 1780 [Ref: X-12].

HUTTON, William Sr. Rendered patriotic service by providing wheat for the use of the military in August, 1782, as verified by Giles Hicks 3rd, Commissary for Caroline County [Ref: V-6636].

HYNSON, Charles. Subscribed to the Oath of Allegiance and Fidelity before the Hon. Nathaniel Potter on March 2, 1778 [Ref: J-1814].
HYNSON, Cordelia. See "James Barwick," q.v.
HYNSON, Elizabeth. See "John Slaughter," q.v.
HYNSON, Henrietta. See "Jadwin Monticue," q.v.
HYNSON, John. Ensign, Militia, 28th Battalion, January 3, 1776 [Ref: M-91]. Subscribed to the Oath of Allegiance and Fidelity before the Hon. Thomas Hardcastle on February 27, 1778 [Ref: J-1814].
INGRAHAM, John, of Choptank Hundred. Subscribed to the Oath of Allegiance and Fidelity (made his mark that resembled a large "a") before the Hon. Benson Stainton on February 2, 1778 [Ref: J-1814].
IRELAND, John. Private, Militia, Capt. Shadrack Liden's Company, 14th Battalion, by August 13, 1777 [Ref: M-155]. John Ireland married Ann Alford by license dated January 4, 1778 [Ref: X-7].
IRELAND, Jonathan (1724 - after 1785). Rendered patriotic service by providing wheat for the use of the military in May, 1782, as verified by Giles Hicks 3rd, Commissary for Caroline County [Ref: V-6636]. Aged 51 in a 1775 deposition and aged 61 in a 1785 deposition [Ref: T-1, T-10].
IRELAND, Samuel. Private, Militia, Capt. Shadrack Liden's Company, 14th Battalion, by August 13, 1777 [Ref: M-155].
IRELAND, Samuel Jr. Private, Militia, Capt. Shadrack Liden's Company, 14th Battalion, by August 13, 1777 [Ref: M-155].
JACKSON, Catharine. See "William Hutton," q.v.
JACKSON, George. Private, 6th Company, Capt. Peter Adams, 1st Maryland Line, enlisted January 22, 1776 [Ref: D-14]. Private, Militia, Capt. Andrew Fountain's Company, 14th Battalion, by August 13, 1777 [Ref: M-157].
JACKSON, James. Private, Militia, Capt. Samuel Jackson's Company, 28th Battalion, by August 13, 1777 [Ref: M-153]. Rendered patriotic service by providing wheat for the use of the military in August, 1782, as verified by Giles Hicks 3rd, Commissary for Caroline County [Ref: V-6636]. Subscribed to the Oath of Allegiance and Fidelity in 1780 [Ref: L-114].
JACKSON, James Jr. Private, Militia, Capt. Samuel Jackson's Company, 28th Battalion, by August 13, 1777 [Ref: M-153].
JACKSON, John. Private, Militia, Capt. Samuel Jackson's Company, 28th Battalion, by August 13, 1777 [Ref: M-153]. Subscribed to the Oath of Allegiance and Fidelity in 1780 [Ref: L-114].
JACKSON, Nancy. See "Noah Mason," q.v.
JACKSON, Peter. Private, Militia, Capt. Samuel Jackson's Company, 28th Battalion, by August 13, 1777 [Ref: M-153]. Second Lieutenant, Militia, Capt. Alexander Robertson's Company, December 17, 1781 [Ref: M-91, I-27]. Subscribed to the Oath of Allegiance and Fidelity before the Hon. Richard Mason on March 2, 1778 [Ref: J-1814].
JACKSON, Samuel (1725/6 - after 1784). Captain, Militia, 28th Battalion, June 19,

1777, and succeeded on December 17, 1781 [Ref: M-91, M-153, E-23, I-27, J-1814]. Subscribed to the Oath of Allegiance and Fidelity before the Hon. Richard Mason on March 2, 1778 [Ref: J-1814]. "Samuel Jackson" gave his age as 56 in a 1782 deposition and "Capt. Samuel Jackson" gave his age as 59 in a 1784 deposition [Ref: T-9, T-11].

JACKSON, Samuel Jr. Private, Militia, Capt. Samuel Jackson's Company, 28th Battalion, by August 13, 1777 [Ref: M-153]. Subscribed to the Oath of Allegiance and Fidelity before the Hon. Richard Mason on March 2, 1778 [Ref: J-1814, which listed the name without the "Jr."].

JACKSON, Susannah. See "William Causey," q.v.

JACKSON, Thomas. Private (draft), Maryland Troops, enrolled in Caroline County by William Whiteley, County Lieutenant, on August 14, 1781 (although reported "run" at the time) to serve in the Maryland Line until December 10, 1781 [Ref: D-385].

JACKSON, William. Ensign, Militia, Capt. Samuel Jackson's Company, 28th Battalion, by August 13, 1777 to at least April 9, 1778 [Ref: M-153, M-91, E-23].

JACKSON, William. First Lieutenant, Militia, Capt. Henry Downes' Company, 28th Battalion, by August 13, 1777 to at least December 17, 1781 [Ref: M-91, M-152, I-27].

JACKSON, William. Private, Militia, Capt. Nehemiah Andrew's Company, 14th Battalion, by August 13, 1777 [Ref: M-155].

JACKSON, William. Rendered patriotic service by providing wheat for the use of the military in August, 1782, as verified by Giles Hicks 3rd, Commissary for Caroline County [Ref: V-6636].

JACKSON, William. Subscribed to the Oath of Allegiance and Fidelity before the Hon. Richard Mason on March 2, 1778 [Ref: J-1814]. One William Jackson married Tryphenia Garrett by license dated September 2, 1780 [Ref: X-12]. Since there was more the one man named William Jackson, additional research will be necessary before drawing conclusions.

JADWIN, Bartholomew. Private, Militia, Capt. Thomas Hughlett's Company, 28th Battalion, by August 13, 1777 [Ref: M-152]. Private (draft), Maryland Troops, enrolled in Caroline County by William Whiteley, County Lieutenant, on August 14, 1781 (although reported sick at the time) to serve in the Maryland Line until December 10, 1781 [Ref: D-385].

JADWIN, Davis. Private, Militia, Capt. John Fauntleroy's Company, 28th Battalion, by August 13, 1777 [Ref: M-154].

JAMES, Henry. Private, Militia, 14th Battalion, Capt. Joseph Richardson's Company, by August 13, 1777 [Ref: M-154]. Henry James married Jane Clark by license dated December 31, 1778 [Ref: X-9].

JAMES, John. Private, Militia, Capt. Andrew Fountain's Company, 14th Battalion, by August 13, 1777 [Ref: M-157]. Subscribed to the Oath of Allegiance and Fidelity before the Hon. Matthew Driver on February 1, 1778 [Ref: J-1814].

JARMAN, Elizabeth. See "Thomson Wootters," q.v.

JARMAN, Stephen, of Queen Anne's County. On December 10, 1779, he filed a certificate in Caroline County Court that he had subscribed to the Oath of Allegiance and Fidelity [Ref: N-67].

JARMON, Robert. See "John Genn," q.v.

JENKINS, Richard. Private, Militia, Capt. Nehemiah Andrew's Company, 14th Battalion, by August 13, 1777 [Ref: M-155]. Rendered patriotic service by providing wheat for the use of the military in June, 1782, as verified by Giles Hicks 3rd, Commissary for Caroline County [Ref: V-6636].

JENKINS, Thomas. Private, Militia, Capt. Nehemiah Andrew's Company, 14th Battalion, by August 13, 1777 [Ref: M-155].

JERBOROUGH, Clement. Private, Militia, Capt. Vincent Price's Company, 28th Battalion, by August 13, 1777 [Ref: M-151].

JERLAND, Samuel. Rendered patriotic service by providing wheat for the use of the military in August, 1782, as verified by Giles Hicks 3rd, Commissary for Caroline County [Ref: V-6636].

JESTER, Nancy. See "Beacham Causey," q.v.

JESTER, William. See "Beacham Causey," q.v.

JEWELL, George. Private (draft), Maryland Troops, enrolled in Caroline County by William Whiteley, County Lieutenant, on August 14, 1781 (although reported sick at the time) to serve in the Maryland Line until December 10, 1781 [Ref: D-385].

JEWELL, William. Private, Militia, Capt. William Haslett's Company, 28th Battalion, by August 13, 1777 [Ref: M-152]. Subscribed to the Oath of Allegiance and Fidelity (made his "U" mark) before the Hon. Benson Stainton on February 2, 1778 [Ref: J-1814].

JOHNSON, Charlotte. See "Levin Johnson," q.v.

JOHNSON, Cornelius (1740 -   ). First Lieutenant, Militia, 14th Battalion, Capt. Joseph Richardson's Company, July 24, 1780. Captain, December 17, 1781 [Ref: M-92, F-230, G-27, I-27]. Rendered patriotic service by providing wheat for the use of the military in August, 1782, as verified by Giles Hicks 3rd, Commissary for Caroline County [Ref: V-6636]. Subscribed to the Oath of Allegiance and Fidelity before the Hon. Nathaniel Potter on March 2, 1778 [Ref: J-1814]. Aged 43 in a 1783 deposition [Ref: T-7]. Cornelius Johnson married Sarah Brannock by license dated December 21, 1793 [Ref: X-25].

JOHNSON, Ezekiel. Private, Militia, Capt. John Mitchell's Company, 14th Battalion, by August 13, 1777 [Ref: M-154].

JOHNSON, Henrietta. See "William Frazier," q.v.

JOHNSON, Henry. Rendered patriotic service by providing wheat for the use of the military in August, 1782, as verified by Giles Hicks 3rd, Commissary for Caroline County [Ref: V-6636]. See "Levin Johnson," q.v.

JOHNSON, James. Private, Militia, Capt. Henry Downes' Company, 28th Battalion, by August 13, 1777 [Ref: M-152].

JOHNSON, James. Private, Militia, Capt. Shadrack Liden's Company, 14th

Battalion, by August 13, 1777 [Ref: M-155].
JOHNSON, James. Subscribed to the Oath of Allegiance and Fidelity before the Hon. Thomas Hardcastle on January 29, 1778 [Ref: J-1814, which listed the name as "Jonson"]. One James Johnson married Elizabeth Russum by license dated October 11, 1785 [Ref: X-17].
JOHNSON, John. Private, 6th Company, Capt. Peter Adams, 1st Maryland Line, enlisted January 25, 1776 [Ref: D-14]. Private, Militia, Capt. Andrew Fountain's Company, 14th Battalion, by August 13, 1777 [Ref: M-157].
JOHNSON, Leveniah. See "Benjamin Kelly," q.v.
JOHNSON, Levin. Private, Militia, Capt. Shadrack Liden's Company, 14th Battalion, by August 13, 1777 [Ref: M-155]. In an 1812 land commission record it stated that Levin Johnson had died on September 1, 1808, possessed of tracts called "Johnson's Delight," "Johnson's Entrance," and "Hardship," and leaving these children: Margaret Johnson (who married Eli Connelly), Charlotte Johnson (who married Nathan Grayless), Tilghman Johnson (minor), and Henry John (minor). [Ref: T-27, T-28].
JOHNSON, Margaret. See "Levin Johnson," q.v.
JOHNSON, Sarah. See "Peter Collison," q.v.
JOHNSON, Thomas. Attended the Maryland Convention in 1776 [Ref: R-74]. See "Valentine Green" and "Ezekiel Dean" and "William Hopper," q.v.
JOHNSON, Tilghman. See "Levin Johnson," q.v.
JOHNSON, William. Private, Militia, Capt. Shadrack Liden's Company, 14th Battalion, by August 13, 1777 [Ref: M-155]. Rendered patriotic service by providing wheat for the use of the military in August, 1782, as verified by Giles Hicks 3rd, Commissary for Caroline County [Ref: V-6636].
JOHNSON, William, of Talbot County. "Marriner, belonging to Capt. Thomas Noel's sloop now lying at his wharf," subscribed to the Oath of Allegiance and Fidelity (made his mark that resembled a "J") before the Hon. Peter Richardson on March 1, 1778 [Ref: J-1814].
JOHNSTON, James. Rendered patriotic service by providing wheat for the use of the military in August, 1782, as verified by Giles Hicks 3rd, Commissary for Caroline County [Ref: V-6636].
JOLLY, Peter. See "Foster Goldsborough," q.v.
JOLLY, Sarah. See "Foster Goldsborough," q.v.
JONES, Eber. Private, Militia, Capt. Joseph Douglass' Company, 14th Battalion, by August 13, 1777 [Ref: M-156].
JONES, Edward. Private, Militia, Capt. John Fauntleroy's Company, 28th Battalion, by August 13, 1777 [Ref: M-154].
JONES, Henry. Private, Militia, Capt. Henry Downes' Company, 28th Battalion, by August 13, 1777 [Ref: M-152]. Rendered patriotic service by providing wheat for the use of the military in August, 1782, as verified by Giles Hicks 3rd, Commissary for Caroline County [Ref: V-6636].
JONES, James. Private, Militia, Capt. Henry Downes' Company, 28th Battalion,

by August 13, 1777 [Ref: M-152]. James Jones married Susannah Jones by license dated December 16, 1781 [Ref: X-14].

JONES, James, of Handcock. Subscribed to the Oath of Allegiance and Fidelity (made his "+" mark) before the Hon. Henry Downes, Jr. on March 2, 1778 [Ref: J-1814].

JONES, James, of James. Private, Militia, Capt. Henry Downes' Company, 28th Battalion, by August 13, 1777 [Ref: M-152].

JONES, John. Private, Militia, Capt. Vincent Price's Company, 28th Battalion, by August 13, 1777 [Ref: M-151]. Private (draft), Maryland Troops, furnished in Caroline County by William Whiteley, County Lieutenant, on April 16, 1781 [Ref: D-368]. One John Jones married Elizabeth Roberts by license dated June 3, 1778, and a John Jones married Sarah Caulk by license dated October 27, 1792 [Ref: X-8, X-24]. Since there was more then one mane named John Jones, additional research will be necessary before drawing conclusions.

JONES, John, of James. Private, Militia, Capt. Henry Downes' Company, 28th Battalion, by August 13, 1777 [Ref: M-152].

JONES, John (Tanner). Subscribed to the Oath of Allegiance and Fidelity before the Hon. Henry Downes, Jr. on March 2, 1778 [Ref: J-1814].

JONES, Joshua. Private, Militia, Capt. Andrew Fountain's Company, 14th Battalion, by August 13, 1777 [Ref: M-157].

JONES, McMurdy. Private, Militia, Capt. Henry Downes' Company, 28th Battalion, by August 13, 1777 [Ref: M-152].

JONES, Robert. Private, Militia, Capt. Henry Downes' Company, 28th Battalion, by August 13, 1777 [Ref: M-152]. Subscribed to the Oath of Allegiance and Fidelity (made his "x" mark) before the Hon. Henry Downes, Jr. on March 2, 1778 [Ref: J-1814]. Robert Jones married Deborah Downes by license dated January 30, 1778 [Ref: X-8].

JONES, Susannah. See "James Jones," q.v.

JONES, William (1732 - after 1793). Subscribed to the Oath of Allegiance and Fidelity in 1780 [Ref: L-114]. Aged 61 in a 1793 deposition [Ref: T-17].

JONES, William (1746-1844). Private, Militia, Capt. John Mitchell's Company, 14th Battalion, by August 13, 1777 [Ref: M-154]. Private (recruit), Maryland Troops, enrolled in Caroline County by William Whiteley, County Lieutenant, on August 14, 1781 to serve in the Maryland Line until December 10, 1781 [Ref: D-385]. "William Jones, aged about 98, died at Denton in Caroline County on October 2, 1844, a patriot of the Revolution." [Ref: Q-6:3 (1965), p. 52, citing the *Baltimore Sun*, October 9, 1844].

JONES, William (1756 - after 1836). Applied for a pension (R5756) on December 27, 1836 in Caroline County, stating he was born on October 16, 1756 in Caroline County and lived there at the time of his enlistment; however, his application was rejected, probably due to lack of proof of service [Ref: W-1884].

JORDAN, Dickinson, of Choptank Hundred. Subscribed to the Oath of Allegiance and Fidelity before the Hon. Benson Stainton on February 2, 1778 [Ref: J-1814].

JORDAN, John. Private, Militia, Capt. John Mitchell's Company, 14th Battalion, by August 13, 1777 [Ref: M-154].
JORDAN, John. Ensign, 6th Company, Capt. Peter Adams, 1st Maryland Line, commissioned January 3, 1776 [Ref: D-13].
JORDAN, Sidney. See "James Blades," q.v.
JUMP, Allemby (Allenby, Allensby). Subscribed to the Oath of Allegiance and Fidelity before the Hon. Henry Downes, Jr. on March 2, 1778 [Ref: J-1814]. Private, Militia, Capt. William Hopper's Company, 28th Battalion, by August 13, 1777. First Lieutenant, Militia, Capt. Thomas Casson's Company, April 9, 1778. Captain, July 24, 1780 [Ref: M-151, M-94, F-230 (which spelled his name "Allensby"), E-23, G-28]. "Allemby Jump" married Nancy Hardcastle by license dated September 12, 1782 [Ref: X-14]. See "Andrew Jump," q.v.
JUMP, Andrew. Rendered patriotic service by providing wheat for the use of the military in August, 1782, as verified by Giles Hicks 3rd, Commissary for Caroline County [Ref: V-6636]. In an 1815 land commission record it stated that Andrew Jump had died in 1811, seized of tracts called "Horse Pasture," "Jump's Lot," "Richard and Mary's Forest," and "William's Neglect," and leaving the following heirs: William Jump, Elizabeth Jump (who married Isaac Morgan), and the children of his daughter Margaret Jump who had married Kendall Latchum, viz., Sarah Latchum, Nodera Latchum, Eliza Ann Latchum, Maria Latchum, and Winlock Latchum. It also noted that Allemby Jump had purchased William Jump's part [Ref: T-29]. One Andrew Jump married Letitia Boon by license dated May 16, 1786 [Ref: X-17].
JUMP, Benjamin (1743 -   ). Private, Militia, Capt. William Hopper's Company, 28th Battalion, by August 13, 1777 [Ref: M-151]. Aged 40 in 1782 and 1783 depositions (noting he was a grandson of Thomas Jump) and aged 51 in a 1794 deposition [Ref: T-4, T-5, T-16]. One Benjamin Jump married Sidney Carter by license dated August 3, 1791 [Ref: X-23].
JUMP, Christopher. Private, Militia, Capt. William Hopper's Company, 28th Battalion, by August 13, 1777 [Ref: M-151]. Christopher Jump married Hannah Wootters by license dated April 29, 1778 [Ref: X-8].
JUMP, Elijah (1750 -   ). Private, Militia, Capt. William Hopper's Company, 28th Battalion, by August 13, 1777 [Ref: M-151]. Private (draft), Maryland Troops, furnished in Caroline County by William Whiteley, County Lieutenant, on April 16, 1781 [Ref: D-368]. Aged 32 in a 1782 deposition [Ref: T-4].
JUMP, Elizabeth. See "Andrew Jump," q.v.
JUMP, Isaac. Private, Militia, Capt. William Hopper's Company, 28th Battalion, by August 13, 1777 [Ref: M-151]. Isaac Jump married Sarah Leverton by license dated January 14, 1778 [Ref: X-7].
JUMP, Jacob. On May 10, 1780, he filed a certificate in Caroline County Court that he had subscribed to the Oath of Allegiance and Fidelity [Ref: N-77]. Rendered patriotic service by providing wheat for the use of the military in August, 1782, as verified by Giles Hicks 3rd, Commissary for Caroline County [Ref: V-6636].

One Jacob Jump married Mary Leverton by license dated February 11, 1778, and a Jacob Jump married Lucretia Reed by license dated June 19, 1782 [Ref: X-8, X-14].

JUMP, Margaret. See "Andrew Jump," q.v.

JUMP, Mary. See "Charles Lemarr," q.v.

JUMP, Peter (1729 or 1730 - after 1786). Press Master, appointed by the County Court on November 27, 1775 [Ref: Z-24]. Private, Militia, Capt. William Hopper's Company, 28th Battalion, by August 13, 1777 [Ref: M-151]. Subscribed to the Oath of Allegiance and Fidelity before the Hon. Henry Downes, Jr. on March 2, 1778 [Ref: J-1814]. Aged 53 in a 1782 deposition, noting he was a son of Thomas Jump; aged 54 in 1783 and 1784 depositions, noting he was a brother of Thomas Jump, and mentioning his aunt Susanna Jump and her son Thomas Jump, and cousin Vaughn Jump; and, aged 55 in a 1786 deposition [Ref: T-4, T-5, T-7, T-9].

JUMP, Solomon. Private, Militia, Capt. William Hopper's Company, 28th Battalion, by August 13, 1777 [Ref: M-151]. Rendered patriotic service by providing wheat for the use of the military in August, 1782, as verified by Giles Hicks 3rd, Commissary for Caroline County [Ref: V-6636]. Solomon Jump married Sarah Cannon by license dated November 19, 1784 [Ref: X-16].

JUMP, Susanna. See "Peter Jump," q.v.

JUMP, Thomas. Private, Militia, Capt. William Hopper's Company, 28th Battalion, by August 13, 1777 [Ref: M-151]. See "Peter Jump" and "Benjamin Jump," q.v.

JUMP, Vaughn. See "Peter Jump," q.v.

JUMP, William (1745 -   ). Private, Militia, Capt. William Hopper's Company, 28th Battalion, by August 13, 1777 [Ref: M-151]. Rendered patriotic service by providing wheat for the use of the military in August, 1782, as verified by Giles Hicks 3rd, Commissary for Caroline County [Ref: V-6636]. Aged 38 in a 1783 deposition [Ref: T-5]. See "Andrew Jump," q.v.

KANAHAN, John. Private, Maryland Troops, enlisted by Capt. Joseph Richardson in Caroline County and passed by Col. William Richardson on August 31, 1776 [Ref: D-69].

KEENE (KEEN), Charles. Private, Militia, Capt. John Fauntleroy's Company, 28th Battalion, by August 13, 1777 [Ref: M-154]. Rendered patriotic service by providing corn for the use of the military in February, 1780 [Ref: P-273]. The State of Maryland employed the use of Charles Keene's cart and driver, as certified by Richard Keene, Commissary for Caroline County, on June 27, 1780 [Ref: P-298].

KEENE (KEEN), Edmond. Subscribed to the Oath of Allegiance and Fidelity before the Hon. Richard Mason on March 2, 1778 [Ref: J-1814]. Employed by the State of Maryland to transport public stores, as certified by Richard Keene, Commissary for Caroline County, on May 10, 1780 [Ref: P-290].

KEENE (KEEN), Edward. Private, Militia, Capt. John Fauntleroy's Company, 28th Battalion, by August 13, 1777 [Ref: M-154].

KEENE (KEEN), Elizabeth. See "Nathan Smith," q.v.
KEENE (KEEN), John. Rendered patriotic service by providing wheat for the use of the military in August, 1782, as verified by Giles Hicks 3rd, Commissary for Caroline County [Ref: V-6636]. John Keene, of Queen Anne's County, filed a certificate in Caroline County Court on June 16, 1779, stating he had taken the Oath of Allegiance and Fidelity [Ref: N-58].
KEENE (KEEN), Marcellus. Rendered patriotic service by providing corn for the use of the military in February, 1780, as verified by Richard Keene, Commissary for Caroline County [Ref: P-269].
KEENE (KEEN), Pollard. Rendered patriotic service by providing wheat for the use of the military in August, 1782, as verified by Giles Hicks 3rd, Commissary for Caroline County [Ref: V-6636].
KEENE (KEEN), Richard. Ensign, Militia, Capt. John Fauntleroy's Company, 28th Battalion, May 16, 1776 [Ref: M-153, M-84, J-1814 (which listed the name as "Ricard Keene, Jr.") and A-428 (which listed the name as "Richard Keene, son of Wm."), E-23]. Subscribed to the Oath of Allegiance and Fidelity before the Hon. Richard Mason on March 2, 1778 [Ref: J-1814]. "Richard Keene, of William" was captain in the militia on April 9, 1778 [Ref: A-428]. Richard Keene was Commissary for Caroline County in 1780 [Ref: P-268, P-269, F-98, F-130]. Rendered patriotic service by providing corn for the use of the military in March, 1780, as verified by Richard Keene, Commissary for Caroline County [Ref: P-277]. "Col. Richard Keene" died in September, 1819, at an advanced age, "on Thursday last." [Ref: *Republican Star*, September 7, 1819]. See "William Keene," q.v.
KEENE (KEEN), Samuel. Subscribed to the Oath of Allegiance and Fidelity before the Hon. Richard Mason on March 2, 1778 [Ref: J-1814].
KEENE, Sarah. See "William Keene," q.v.
KEENE (KEEN), Thomas. Private, Militia, Capt. John Fauntleroy's Company, 28th Battalion, by August 13, 1777 [Ref: M-154]. "T. Keene" subscribed to the Oath of Allegiance and Fidelity before the Hon. Richard Mason on March 2, 1778 [Ref: J-1814].
KEENE (KEEN), Thomas B. Rendered patriotic service by providing wheat for the use of the military in August, 1782, as verified by Giles Hicks 3rd, Commissary for Caroline County [Ref: V-6636]. Subscribed to the Oath of Allegiance and Fidelity before the Hon. Richard Mason on March 2, 1778 [Ref: J-1814].
KEENE (KEEN), William. Represented Caroline County in the Lower House of the Maryland General Assembly, 1778-1783. Served as County Commissioner in 1774, and Judge of the Court of Appeals, appointed under the Act to Procure Troops for the American Army, 1778 [Ref: R-503, R-80, R-82, R-87, R-88]. Rendered patriotic service by providing corn for the use of the military in February, 1780, as verified by Richard Keene, Commissary for Caroline County [Ref: P-268]. He married first to Sarah --?--, and second to Ann Colston (widow) in 1774, daughter of Griffin Fauntleroy, of Northumberland County, Virginia.

William's children were Richard Keene, Mary Watkins Stevens (widowed by 1774), and --?-- Fauntleroy (wife of John Fauntleroy). William was a brother of Richard Keene and resided in Queen Anne's County by 1761. In 1774 he went to Northumberland County, Virginia and in 1775 he returned to Caroline County. By 1785 he had moved to Kentucky and still lived there in 1797 [Ref: R-502].

KEENE (KEEN), Young. Second Lieutenant, Militia, Capt. John Fauntleroy's Company, 28th Battalion, by August 13, 1777. First Lieutenant, Militia, Capt. Richard Keene's Company, April 9, 1778 [Ref: M-153, M-94, E-23, J-1814]. Subscribed to the Oath of Allegiance and Fidelity before the Hon. Richard Mason on March 2, 1778 [Ref: J-1814]. Rendered patriotic service by providing wheat for the use of the military in August, 1782, as verified by Giles Hicks 3rd, Commissary for Caroline County [Ref: V-6636].

KEETS, Thomas. Private, Militia, Capt. William Hopper's Company, 28th Battalion, by August 13, 1777 [Ref: M-151].

KELL, Nathan. Rendered patriotic service by providing wheat for the use of the military in August, 1782, as verified by Giles Hicks 3rd, Commissary for Caroline County [Ref: V-6636].

KELLY, Ann. See "William Kelly," q.v.

KELLY, Benjamin (Ben). Private, Militia, 14th Battalion, Capt. Richard Andrew's Company, by August 13, 1777 [Ref: M-156]. Rendered patriotic service by providing wheat for the use of the military in August, 1782, as verified by Giles Hicks 3rd, Commissary for Caroline County [Ref: V-6636]. Benjamin Kelly married Leveniah Johnson by license dated July 16, 1778 [Ref: X-8].

KELLY, Deliza. See "William Kelly," q.v.

KELLY, Dennis. Private, Militia, 14th Battalion, Capt. Joseph Richardson's Company, by August 13, 1777 [Ref: M-154].

KELLY, Elizabeth. See "William Kelly," q.v.

KELLY, James. Private, 6th Company, Capt. Peter Adams, 1st Maryland Line, enlisted January 26, 1776 [Ref: D-14].

KELLY, Joseph. Private, Militia, Capt. Shadrack Liden's Company, 14th Battalion, by August 13, 1777 [Ref: M-155].

KELLY, Paulson. See "William Kelly," q.v.

KELLY (KELLEY), Sarah. See "Edwin Lunceford," q.v.

KELLY, William. Private, Militia, 14th Battalion, Capt. Joseph Richardson's Company, by August 13, 1777 [Ref: M-154]. See the other "William Kelly," q.v.

KELLY, William. Private, Militia, Capt. William Haslett's Company, 28th Battalion, by August 13, 1777 [Ref: M-152]. One William Kelly was a Nicholite living in Caroline County in 1785 [Ref: T-12]. One William Kelly is noted in a land commission record in 1819 has having died on January 1, 1815, possessed of tracts called "Out Range," "Waddell's Venture," and "Potter's Hazard" (or "Henry's Hazard"), and left the following children: Elizabeth Kelly (who married Jesse Hubbard), Ann Kelly (who died without issue), Deliza Kelly (who married Andrew Barton), William Kelly (minor), and Paulson Kelly (minor). [Ref: T-32].

One "William Kelley" married Roxanna Wing by license dated January 9, 1786 [Ref: X-17]. Since there was more then one man named William Kelly, additional research will be necessary before drawing conclusions.

KEMP, Henry. Private, Militia, Capt. Henry Downes' Company, 28th Battalion, by August 13, 1777 [Ref: M-152]. Henry Kemp married Mary Layton by license dated March 13, 1789 [Ref: X-19].

KENDERDINE, Cooper. Private, Militia, Capt. Thomas Hughlett's Company, 28th Battalion, by August 13, 1777 [Ref: M-152]. Ensign, August 14, 1779 [Ref: M-95, E-493]. Rendered patriotic service by providing wheat for the use of the military in August, 1782, as verified by Giles Hicks 3rd, Commissary for Caroline County [Ref: V-6636]. "Cooper Kenderdine, of Choptank Hundred" subscribed to the Oath of Allegiance and Fidelity before the Hon. Benson Stainton on February 2, 1778 [Ref: J-1814].

KENNARD (KENARD), John. Rendered patriotic service by providing corn for the use of the military in February, 1780 [Ref: P-273].

KENNARD (KINNARD), Richard. Private, Militia, Capt. Andrew Fountain's Company, 14th Battalion, by August 13, 1777 [Ref: M-157]. Richard Kennard married Anne Carroll by license recorded August 9, 1775 [Ref: X-6]. Richard Kinnard married Elizabeth Stanton by license dated December 22, 1783 [Ref: X-15]. See "Benson Stainton," q.v.

KENT, Solomon. See "Solomon Kenton, Jr.," q.v.

KENTON (KENTING), Howell. Private, Militia, Capt. Henry Downes' Company, 28th Battalion, by August 13, 1777 [Ref: M-152]. Subscribed to the Oath of Allegiance and Fidelity before the Hon. Henry Downes, Jr. on March 2, 1778 [Ref: J-1814]. Howell Kenton married Elizabeth Downes by license dated January 20, 1783 [Ref: X-14].

KENTON (KENTING), James. Private, Militia, Capt. William Hopper's Company, 28th Battalion, by August 13, 1777 [Ref: M-151]. James Kenton married Sarah Micton by license dated August 15, 1789 [Ref: X-20].

KENTON, Nancy. See "Robert Postlethwaite," q.v.

KENTON (KENTING), Solomon. Private, Militia, Capt. Henry Downes' Company, 28th Battalion, by August 13, 1777 [Ref: M-152]. Ensign, Militia, Capt. Thomas Casson's Company, April 9, 1778. Second Lieutenant, Militia, Capt. Allenby Jump's Company, July 26, 1780 to at least December 17, 1781 in Capt. Philemon Downes' Company [Ref: M-95, E-23, F-230, I-27]. Subscribed to the Oath of Allegiance and Fidelity before the Hon. Henry Downes, Jr. on March 2, 1778 [Ref: J-1814]. See "Solomon Kenton, Jr.," q.v.

KENTON (KENTING), Solomon Jr. Subscribed to the Oath of Allegiance and Fidelity before the Hon. Thomas Hardcastle on February 27, 1778 [Ref: J-1814]. "Solomon Kenton (Quaker)" was aged 60 in a 1775 deposition [Ref: T-3]. "Solomon Kent (Quaker)" was aged 50 in an 1800 deposition [Ref: T-21]. Additional research will be necessary before drawing conclusions. See the other "Solomon Kenton," q.v.

KENTON (KENTING), Solomon (Taylor). Ensign, Militia, Capt. William Hopper's Company, 28th Battalion, June 19, 1777. First Lieutenant, Militia, Capt. Thomas Burk's Company, April 9, 1778 [Ref: M-95, M-151, C-294 (which spelled the name "Kinton"), E-23]. "Solomon Kenton (Taylor)" subscribed to the Oath of Allegiance and Fidelity before the Hon. Henry Downes, Jr. on March 2, 1778 [Ref: J-1814]. "Solomon Kenton (Taylor), son of James" became an ensign in Capt. William Hopper's Company upon the death of Ensign John Tillotson in 1777 [Ref: J-1814]. "Solomon Kinton T." was second lieutenant in Capt. Allenby Jump's Company on July 24, 1780 [Ref: G-28].

KERAP, Lydia. See "Samuel Ball," q.v.

KERN, Nathan. Private, Militia, Capt. Thomas Hughlett's Company, 28th Battalion, by August 13, 1777 [Ref: M-152].

KERR, David. On August 20, 1778, David Kerr of Talbot County filed a certificate in Caroline County Court relating to his having taken the Oath of Allegiance and Fidelity [Ref: N-35].

KIDD, William. Private, Militia, Capt. William Haslett's Company, 28th Battalion, by August 13, 1777 [Ref: M-152].

KILLMAN, John. Private, Militia, Capt. John Mitchell's Company, 14th Battalion, by August 13, 1777 [Ref: M-154].

KING, Alexander. Private, Militia, Capt. Henry Downes' Company, 28th Battalion, by August 13, 1777 [Ref: M-152]. Subscribed to the Oath of Allegiance and Fidelity before the Hon. Henry Downes, Jr. on March 2, 1778 [Ref: J-1814].

KING, Elizabeth. See "Isaac Dukes," q.v.

KING, John. Private, Militia, Capt. Vincent Price's Company, 28th Battalion, by August 13, 1777 [Ref: M-152]. John King married Ann Smith by license dated December 13, 1783 [Ref: X-15].

KINIMONT (KINEMONT), Benjamin. Private, Militia, Capt. Henry Downes' Company, 28th Battalion, by August 13, 1777 [Ref: M-152].

KINIMONT (KINEMONT), Phillip. Private, Militia, Capt. William Chipley's Company, 28th Battalion, by August 13, 1777 [Ref: M-153].

KINIMONT (KINNEMON), Samuel (1750 -   ). Private, Militia, Capt. Vincent Price's Company, 28th Battalion, by August 13, 1777 [Ref: M-151]. Aged 49 in a 1799 deposition [Ref: T-20].

KINNARD, Richard. See "Richard Kennard," q.v.

KIRBY (KERBY), John. Private, 6th Company, Capt. Peter Adams, 1st Maryland Line, enlisted February 24, 1776 [Ref: D-15]. John Kirby married Sarah Kirby by license recorded January 28, 1775 [Ref: X-5].

KIRBY, Sarah. See "John Kirby," q.v.

KIRK, James. Private, 6th Company, Capt. Peter Adams, 1st Maryland Line, enlisted February 15, 1776 [Ref: D-14].

KIRKMAN, Donna. See "George Kirkman," q.v.

KIRKMAN, Elijah. See "James Kirkman," q.v.

KIRKMAN, Elisha. See "James Kirkman," q.v.

KIRKMAN, Elizabeth. See "George Kirkman," q.v.

KIRKMAN, George (c1735-1820). Son of James Kirkman and Mary Sherwood (or White) of Dorchester County (now Caroline County), George was born circa 1735, married Elizabeth --?--, and died in Guilford County, North Carolina on October 3, 1820 [Ref: Research compiled prior to 1995 by Donna Kirkman, of Pinellas Park, Florida, and Dora W. Mitchell, of Preston, Maryland, which is on file at the Maryland Historical Society Library]. George Kirkman was a private in the militia, Capt. John Stafford's Company, 14th Battalion, by August 13, 1777 [Ref: M-156]. He also rendered patriotic service by providing wheat for the use of the military in May, 1782, as verified by Giles Hicks 3rd, Commissary for Caroline County [Ref: V-6636]. See "James Kirkman," q.v.

KIRKMAN, James (c1713-1791). Son of George Kirkman or Kirkmon (died testate in 1749), James was born circa 1713 in Dorchester County, married Mary Sherwood (or White), migrated from Caroline County to Pleasant Garden on Beaver Creek in Guilford County, North Carolina circa 1787, and died testate in 1791. His children were as follows: George Kirkman (c1735-1820, married Elizabeth --?--), William Kirkman (married Rhoda Sullivan), Elisha Kirkman, Elijah Kirkman, Mary Kirkman (married Henry Hendricks), Thomas Sherwood Kirkman (1771-1850, married Tabatha Fields), and Roger Kirkman (1774-1862, married Sarah Wood). [Ref: *Maryland Calendar of Wills, Volume 10 (1748-1753)*, page 75; Guilford County, North Carolina, Will Book A, page 205; and information by researchers cited under "George Kirkman" above]. James Kirkman rendered patriotic service by providing wheat for the use of the military in August, 1782, as verified by Giles Hicks 3rd, Commissary for Caroline County [Ref: V-6636]. See "George Kirkman," q.v.

KIRKMAN, Mary. See "James Kirkman," q.v.

KIRKMAN, Roger. See "James Kirkman," q.v.

KIRKMAN, Thomas. See "James Kirkman," q.v.

KIRKMAN, William. See "John Spurrey" and "James Kirkman," q.v.

KITE, John. Rendered patriotic service by providing wheat for the use of the military in August, 1782, as verified by Giles Hicks 3rd, Commissary for Caroline County [Ref: V-6636].

KNOTTS, Nathaniel. Private, Militia, Capt. William Chipley's Company, 28th Battalion, by August 13, 1777 [Ref: M-153].

KNOTTS, Thomas. Second Lieutenant, Militia, Capt. William Chipley's Company, 28th Battalion, by August 13, 1777. Captain, December 17, 1781 [Ref: M-153, M-96, E-493 (which spelled the name "Noots"), I-27]. Subscribed to the Oath of Allegiance and Fidelity before the Hon. Thomas Hardcastle on February 6, 1778 [Ref: J-1814].

KNOTTS, William. Private, Militia, Capt. William Chipley's Company, 28th Battalion, by August 13, 1777 [Ref: M-153].

KOPES, John. Private, Militia, Capt. Samuel Jackson's Company, 28th Battalion, by August 13, 1777 [Ref: M-153]. See "John Coupes," q.v.

LAFFY, Thomas. Private, 6th Company, Capt. Peter Adams, 1st Maryland Line, enlisted February 15, 1776 [Ref: D-14].
LAIGHTON, William. Private, 6th Company, Capt. Peter Adams, 1st Maryland Line, enlisted January 22, 1776 [Ref: D-14].
LAMARR, John. See "John Lemarr," q.v.
LAMBDIN (LAMBDEN), Daniel (1759-1809). Private, Militia, Capt. Vincent Price's Company, 28th Battalion, by August 13, 1777 [Ref: M-152]. Subscribed to the Oath of Allegiance and Fidelity before the Hon. Henry Downes, Jr. on March 2, 1778 [Ref: J-1814]. Daniel Lambdin was born in Maryland on May 16, 1759, married Mary Spry, and died on September 7, 1809 [Ref: Y-1730].
LAMBDIN (LAMBDEN), John. Private, Militia, Capt. Samuel Jackson's Company, 28th Battalion, by August 13, 1777 [Ref: M-153].
LANE (LAYNE), Anthony. Private, Militia, Capt. Andrew Fountain's Company, 14th Battalion, by August 13, 1777 [Ref: M-157].
LANE (LAYNE), Gallient. Private, Militia, Capt. William Haslett's Company, 28th Battalion, by August 13, 1777 [Ref: M-152]. "Gally Lane" married Araminta Dial by license dated September 14, 1774 [Ref: X-4].
LANE (LAYNE), James. Private, Militia, Capt. Andrew Fountain's Company, 14th Battalion, by August 13, 1777 [Ref: M-157].
LANE (LAYN), John. Private, Militia, Capt. John Fauntleroy's Company, 28th Battalion, by August 13, 1777 [Ref: M-154, which listed the name twice].
LANE (LAYNE), Owen (1755 - after 1832). Private, Militia, Capt. Nehemiah Andrew's Company, 14th Battalion, by August 13, 1777 [Ref: M-155]. Applied for pension (R6131) in Davidson County, Tennessee on October 17, 1832, aged 77, stating he was born in (now) Caroline County, Maryland and lived there at the time of his enlistment; however, his application was rejected because he "did not serve six months in person." After the war he moved to Guilford County, North Carolina and then to Nashville in Davidson County, Tennessee [Ref: W-2009, and *Rejected or Suspended Applications for Revolutionary War Pensions* (Originally published in Washington, D. C., 1852), p. 383].
LANE (LAYNE), Richard. Private, Militia, Capt. Nehemiah Andrew's Company, 14th Battalion, by August 13, 1777 [Ref: M-155].
LANE, Thomas. Private (draft), Maryland Troops, enrolled in Caroline County by William Whiteley, County Lieutenant, on August 14, 1781 to serve in the Maryland Line until December 10, 1781 [Ref: D-385].
LANE (LAYNE), Walter. Private, Militia, Capt. Thomas Hughlett's Company, 28th Battalion, by August 13, 1777 [Ref: M-153].
LANGRELL, James. Private, Militia, 14th Battalion, Capt. Richard Andrew's Company, by August 13, 1777 [Ref: M-156].
LAREY, James. On December 27, 1776 he joined a company of men in Caroline County who marched to Talbot County to obtain a supply of salt [Ref: B-564, B-565]. Rendered patriotic service by providing wheat for the use of the military in September, 1782, as verified by Giles Hicks 3rd, Commissary for Caroline

County [Ref: V-6636]. James Larey married Elizabeth Morgan by license dated February 23, 1778 [Ref: X-8].

LATCHUM, Margaret and family. See "Andrew Jump," q.v.

LAVINGTON, Garey. See "Garey Leverton," q.v.

LAWFULL, Ann. See "Tilghman Blades," q.v.

LAWRENCE, Elizabeth. See "Richard Willoughby," q.v.

LAWRENCE (LAURENCE), James. On July 31, 1778, the Treasurer of Maryland's Western Shore was directed to pay Nathaniel Potter, Esquire, for the purchase of provisions, "and the further sum of four pounds ten shillings for the use of James Laurence as per account passed by the Auditor General." [Ref: E-171].

LAWRENCE, Mary. See "John Malcolm," q.v.

LAWRENCE, Sarah. See "Samuel Fountain," q.v.

LAYTON, Charles. Private, Militia, 14th Battalion, Capt. Richard Andrew's Company, by August 13, 1777 [Ref: M-156].

LAYTON, John. Private, Militia, Capt. Joseph Douglass' Company, 14th Battalion, by August 13, 1777 [Ref: M-156].

LAYTON, Mary. See "Henry Kemp," q.v.

LEA, John. See "John Lee" and "John Legh," q.v.

LEATH (LEETH), Alexander. A substitute who was to serve in the Maryland Line until December 10, 1781, "Alexander Leath" was deemed to be "unfit for the service for which he was intended and hereby discharged" on October 30, 1781 [Ref: G-657]. "Alexander Leeth" rendered patriotic service by providing wheat for the use of the military in August, 1782, as verified by Giles Hicks 3rd, Commissary for Caroline County [Ref: V-6636].

LEAVERTON, Elisabeth. Rendered patriotic service by providing wheat for the use of the military in September, 1782, as verified by Giles Hicks 3rd, Commissary for Caroline County [Ref: V-6636].

LECOMPTE, Anthony. See "James Lecompte," q.v.

LECOMPTE, Charles. Private, Militia, Capt. William Haslett's Company, 28th Battalion, by August 13, 1777 [Ref: M-152]. Second Lieutenant, Militia, Capt. Robert Postlewait's Company, April 18, 1780 [Ref: M-97, F-144]. See "James Lecompte," q.v.

LECOMPTE, Elizabeth. See "Thomas Lecompte" and "Richard Ozmont, Jr.," q.v.

LECOMPTE, Fanny. See "Thomas Lecompte," q.v.

LECOMPTE, James (1727 - after 1797). Rendered patriotic service by providing wheat for the use of the military in August, 1782, as verified by Giles Hicks 3rd, Commissary for Caroline County [Ref: V-6636, which spelled the name "Lecompt"]. "James LeCompte, son of John and grandson of Anthony, was the ancestor of the LeComptes in Caroline County, Maryland. He married --?-- Mallet, and had issue: James, Philemon, Anthony, Charles and Nathan." [Ref: U-12 (1917), p. 53]. Aged 70 in a 1797 deposition [Ref: T-19]. See "Thomas Lecompte," q.v.

LECOMPTE, James Jr. Press Master, appointed by the County Court on November 27, 1775 [Ref: Z-24].
LECOMPTE, John. Private, Militia, 14th Battalion, Capt. Richard Andrew's Company, by August 13, 1777 [Ref: M-156]. See "James Lecompte," q.v.
LECOMPTE, Nathan. Private, Militia, Capt. William Haslett's Company, 28th Battalion, by August 13, 1777 [Ref: M-152]. See "James Lecompte," q.v.
LECOMPTE, Philemon (Phillemon). Private, Militia, 14th Battalion, Capt. Richard Andrew's Company, by August 13, 1777 [Ref: M-156]. See "James Lecompte," q.v.
LECOMPTE, Priscilla. See "Thomas Lecompte," q.v.
LECOMPTE, Sarah. See "Thomas Lecompte," q.v.
LECOMPTE, Thomas. Private, Militia, Capt. William Haslett's Company, 28th Battalion, by August 13, 1777 [Ref: M-152]. Rendered patriotic service by providing wheat for the use of the military in August, 1782, as verified by Giles Hicks 3rd, Commissary for Caroline County [Ref: V-6636, which spelled the name "Lecompt"]. In an 1815 land commission record it stated that Thomas Lecompte had died intestate in 1812, owning a tract called "Lecompte's Regulation" and leaving the following heirs: Elizabeth Lecompte (over 21, who married James Lecompte), Fanny Lecompte (almost 21, who married Joseph Bell), Sarah Lecompte (over 21 and single), Priscilla Lecompte (under 21 and single; her guardian is Joshua Driver). [Ref: T-28].
LECOMPTE, William. Private, Militia, Capt. Andrew Fountain's Company, 14th Battalion, by August 13, 1777 [Ref: M-157]. Rendered patriotic service by providing wheat for the use of the military in August, 1782, as verified by Giles Hicks 3rd, Commissary for Caroline County [Ref: V-6636, which spelled the name "Lecompt"].
LEE, John. Ensign, Militia, Capt. Richard Keene's Company, April 9, 1778. Second Lieutenant, December 17, 1781 [Ref: M-97, E-23, I-27]. Subscribed to the Oath of Allegiance and Fidelity before the Hon. Richard Mason on March 2, 1778 [Ref: J-1814, which spelled the name "Lea"].
LEE, Thomas Sim. See "Peter Adams," q.v.
LEESON, William. Private, 6th Company, Capt. Peter Adams, 1st Maryland Line, enlisted February 15, 1776 [Ref: D-14].
LEETH, Alexander. See "Alexander Leath," q.v.
LEGG, Richard. See "Purnell Sylvester," q.v.
LEGH, John. Private, Militia, Capt. John Fauntleroy's Company, 28th Battalion, by August 13, 1777 [Ref: M-154].
LEGH, William. Private, Militia, Capt. John Fauntleroy's Company, 28th Battalion, by August 13, 1777 [Ref: M-154].
LEMARR (LAMARR, LEMAR), Charles. Private, Militia, Capt. William Chipley's Company, 28th Battalion, by August 13, 1777 [Ref: M-153]. Rendered patriotic service by providing wheat for the use of the military in August, 1782, as verified

by Giles Hicks 3rd, Commissary for Caroline County [Ref: V-6636]. Charles Lemarr married Mary Jump by license dated November 26, 1781 [Ref: X-14].

LEMARR (LAMARR), Galee. Rendered patriotic service by providing wheat for the use of the military in August, 1782, as verified by Giles Hicks 3rd, Commissary for Caroline County [Ref: V-6636].

LEMARR (LAMARR), Garland. Private, Militia, Capt. Samuel Jackson's Company, 28th Battalion, by August 13, 1777 [Ref: M-153].

LEMARR (LAMARR), James. Private, Militia, Capt. William Chipley's Company, 28th Battalion, by August 13, 1777 [Ref: M-153]. It is interesting to note that a "James Slemarr" [James Lemarr?] married "Mary Exbanks" [Eubanks?] by license dated February 23, 1778 [Ref: X-8].

LEMARR (LAMARR), John. Private, Militia, Capt. William Chipley's Company, 28th Battalion, by August 13, 1777 [Ref: M-153]. Rendered patriotic service by providing wheat for the use of the military in August, 1782, as verified by Giles Hicks 3rd, Commissary for Caroline County [Ref: V-6636].

LEMARR (LAMARR), Lemuel. Private, Militia, Capt. Samuel Jackson's Company, 28th Battalion, by August 13, 1777 [Ref: M-153].

LEMARR (LAMARR), Nancy. See "Harrison Monticue," q.v.

LEMARR (LAMARR), Samuel. Rendered patriotic service by providing wheat for the use of the military in August, 1782, as verified by Giles Hicks 3rd, Commissary for Caroline County [Ref: V-6636].

LEVERTON, Elizabeth. See "Elisabeth Leaverton," q.v.

LEVERTON, Garey. Private, Militia, Capt. William Hopper's Company, 28th Battalion, by August 13, 1777 [Ref: M-151]. Private (draft), Maryland Troops, enrolled in Caroline County by William Whiteley, County Lieutenant, on August 14, 1781 to serve in the Maryland Line until December 10, 1781 [Ref: D-385]. However, the proceedings of the Council of Maryland indicate that "Garey Lavington" [among others] was "deemed unfit for the service and hereby discharged therefrom" on November 12, 1781 [Ref: G-666]. "Garcy Leverton" married Mary Spencer (Spemcer?) by license dated October 6, 1783 [Ref: X-15].

LEVERTON, James. Private, Militia, Capt. John Stafford's Company, 14th Battalion, by August 13, 1777 [Ref: M-156]. James Leverton married Lydia Kenton by license dated December 8, 1787 [Ref: X-18].

LEVERTON, Mary. See "Jacob Jump," q.v.

LEVERTON, Moses. Private, Militia, Capt. Joseph Douglass' Company, 14th Battalion, by August 13, 1777 [Ref: M-156].

LEVERTON, Sarah. See "Isaac Jump," q.v.

LEVERTON, Thomas (1758 -   ). Private, Militia, Capt. Vincent Price's Company, 28th Battalion, by August 13, 1777 [Ref: M-152]. Aged 24 in a 1782 deposition [Ref: T-4]. Thomas Leverton married Lydia Calston [Colston] by license dated March 29, 1780 [Ref: X-11].

LEWIS, Aaron. Private, Militia, Capt. Joseph Douglass' Company, 14th Battalion, by August 13, 1777 [Ref: M-156]. First Lieutenant, Militia, Capt. Thomas Eaton's

Company, December 17, 1781 [Ref: M-97, I-27]. Aaron Lewis married Sapphira Griffith by license dated August 17, 1785 [Ref: X-16].

LEWIS, Abraham (Abram). Private, Militia, Capt. Joseph Douglass' Company, 14th Battalion, by August 13, 1777 [Ref: M-156]. On December 10, 1779, he filed a certificate in Caroline County Court that he had subscribed to the Oath of Allegiance and Fidelity before the Hon. Nathaniel Potter [Ref: N-67].

LEWIS, Lovina. See "William Holland," q.v.

LEWIS, Rachel. See "Nathan Hill," q.v.

LEWIS, Rebecca. See "Joseph Stack," q.v.

LIDEN (LYDEN), Richard. Second Lieutenant, Militia, Capt. John Hooper's Company, July 24, 1780. First Lieutenant, Militia, Capt. Cornelius Johnson's Company, December 17, 1781 [Ref: M-97, F-230, I-27, E-23, G-27]. Subscribed to the Oath of Allegiance and Fidelity before the Hon. Nathaniel Potter on March 2, 1778 [Ref: J-1814]. Richard Lyden married Martha Hooper by license dated July 19, 1780 [Ref: X-12].

LIDEN, Shadrack or Shadrach (c1750-c1811). Private, Militia, Capt. Shadrack Liden's Company, 14th Battalion, June 24, 1777 to at least April 9, 1778 [Ref: M-155, C-299 (which listed the name "Shadrick Lighton"), I-27, F-230, E-23]. Rendered patriotic service by providing wheat for the use of the military in August, 1782, as verified by Giles Hicks 3rd, Commissary for Caroline County [Ref: V-6636]. Shadrach Liden was born circa 1750 in Maryland, married "Rebecca Foxwell" and died after February 9, 1811 [Ref: Y-1800]. Shadrach Liden married "Rebeckah Fogwell" by license recorded October 30, 1775 [Ref: X-7].

LISTER (LYSTER), John (1752 -   ). Private, Militia, Capt. Nehemiah Andrew's Company, 14th Battalion, by August 13, 1777 [Ref: M-155]. Aged 40 in a 1792 deposition [Ref: T-15].

LISTER (LYSTER), Joshua. Private, Militia, Capt. Andrew Fountain's Company, 14th Battalion, by August 13, 1777 [Ref: M-157]. Rendered patriotic service by providing wheat for the use of the military in August, 1782, as verified by Giles Hicks 3rd, Commissary for Caroline County [Ref: V-6636].

LISTER (LYSTER), William (1760-1848). Private, Militia, Capt. Joseph Douglass' Company, 14th Battalion, by August 13, 1777 [Ref: M-156]. Although there was a William Lister in the militia of Somerset County, Maryland in 1780, the above William Lister is probably the one who was born in Kent County, Maryland in 1760. At the age of 12 he moved with his father (name not given) to "Carlisle" County, Maryland and, since there is no such county in Maryland, the reference is most likely to "Caroline" County. He served in the Revolutionary War, as noted, and also served as a substitute for his father. After the war William moved to Guilford County, North Carolina, where he lived for three and a half years before moving to Marlborough District, South Carolina. He applied for a pension (S32377) on March 12, 1833 [Ref: W-2092]. William Lister was born in Maryland on April 10, 1760, married Mary Ann --?--, and died before April 26,

1848 in Alabama [Ref: Y-1812].

LOCKE, William. Private, 6th Company, Capt. Peter Adams, 1st Maryland Line, enlisted February 24, 1776 [Ref: D-15].

LONEY, Thomas. Rendered patriotic service by providing wheat for the use of the military in August, 1782, as verified by Giles Hicks 3rd, Commissary for Caroline County [Ref: V-6636].

LONG, Elizabeth. See "Beacham Causey," q.v.

LONG, John. Private, Militia, Capt. William Haslett's Company, 28th Battalion, by August 13, 1777 [Ref: M-152].

LONG, Samuel. See "Beacham Causey," q.v.

LONG, William. Private, Militia, Capt. William Haslett's Company, 28th Battalion, by August 13, 1777 [Ref: M-152].

LONGFELLOW, Gidian (Gideon). Private (recruit), Maryland Troops, enrolled in Caroline County by William Whiteley, County Lieutenant, on August 14, 1781 to serve in the Maryland Line until December 10, 1781 [Ref: D-385]. The Council was informed that "there is a man by the name of Gideon Longfellow who is a recruit for this [Caroline] county and has since gone to Queen Ann's County and there entered as a substitute for a class, therefore beg you'll please to have him entered for this county." [Ref: D-385].

LONGFELLOW, John (1740 -   ). Private, Militia, Capt. William Chipley's Company, 28th Battalion, by August 13, 1777 [Ref: M-153]. Aged 50 in a 1790 deposition [Ref: T-15].

LONGFELLOW, Thomas. Private, 5th Maryland Line, enlisted June 4, 1778 and reported missing on August 16, 1780 at the Battle of Camden in South Carolina [Ref: D-224].

LOOCKERMAN, Jacob (1759 -   ). Private, Militia, Capt. Vincent Price's Company, 28th Battalion, by August 13, 1777 [Ref: M-152]. Subscribed to the Oath of Allegiance and Fidelity before the Hon. Henry Downes, Jr. on March 2, 1778 [Ref: J-1814]. Jacob Loockerman, son of John and Mary Loockerman, was born January 22, 1759 [Ref: K-26]. "Jacob Lockerman" married Elizabeth Clark by license dated July 17, 1784 [Ref: X-15].

LOOCKERMAN, John. See "Jacob Loockerman," q.v.

LOOCKERMAN, Mary. See "Jacob Loockerman," q.v.

LOOCKERMAN, Richard. Private, Militia, Capt. Vincent Price's Company, 28th Battalion, by August 13, 1777 [Ref: M-152]. Subscribed to the Oath of Allegiance and Fidelity before the Hon. Henry Downes, Jr. on March 2, 1778 [Ref: J-1814]. Rendered patriotic service by providing wheat for the use of the military in August, 1782, as verified by Giles Hicks 3rd, Commissary for Caroline County [Ref: V-6636]. One Richard Loockerman married Mary Darden by license recorded August 9, 1775, and a Richard Loockerman married Ann Wood by license dated November 22, 1779 [Ref: X-6, X-11]. See "Thomas Wynn Loockerman," q.v.

LOOCKERMAN, Thomas Wynn (1752-1801). Son of Thomas Loockerman (died in 1753) and Sidney Dickinson, daughter of Charles Dickinson. "If Loockerman had a wife, her name is not known. His grandfather's will, probated in 1779, stated that Mary Ann Gray was Loockerman's mistress and that she had borne him a bastard child." His sons were Thomas Wynn Loockerman (died in 1829) and Richard Loockerman. [Ref: R-545, R-546]. Second Lieutenant, May 24, 1776, and then First Lieutenant [Ref: A-442, which spelled the name "Thomas Wynn Lockerman," D-68, which spelled the name "Thomas Wyer Lockerman" and D-69, which spelled the name "Thomas Wynn Loockerman" and M-98, which spelled the name "Thomas Lockerman"]. First Lieutenant, Militia, 14th Battalion, Capt. Joseph Richardson's Company, by August 13, 1777. Captain, April 9, 1778, and resigned on July 24, 1780 [Ref: E-23, F-230 (which listed the name as "Thomas Lockerman"), G-27, M-98, M-154]. "Thomas Loockerman (Constable)" subscribed to the Oath of Allegiance and Fidelity before the Hon. Charles Dickinson on March 1, 1778 [Ref: J-1418]. Captain, Militia, 14th Battalion, June 24, 1777 [Ref: C-299 (which listed the name "Thomas Wm. Lockerman"), M-98]. Appointed to be Constable of Great Choptank Hundred on December 15, 1778 [Ref: N-45]. Aged 46 in a 1798 deposition [Ref: T-20]. He represented Caroline County in the Lower House of the Maryland General Assembly, 1786-1792, and was a Court Justice, 1791-1801. He died by September 28, 1801 (date of administration bond) in Caroline County [Ref: R-546].

LORD (LOARD), Able. Private, Militia, 14th Battalion, Capt. Richard Andrew's Company, by August 13, 1777 [Ref: M-156].

LORD, Elizabeth. See "Richard Kennard," q.v.

LOVE, William. Rendered patriotic service by providing wheat for the use of the military in August, 1782, as verified by Giles Hicks 3rd, Commissary for Caroline County [Ref: V-6636]. William Love married Elizabeth Parratt by license dated February 2, 1780 [Ref: X-11].

LOWE, Mary. See "Daniel Edgell," q.v.

LOWREY, Elizabeth. See "John Vallient," q.v.

LOWRY, John. Private, 6th Company, Capt. Peter Adams, 1st Maryland Line, enlisted February 22, 1776 [Ref: D-14].

LUCAS, Eliza. See "John Cooper," q.v.

LUCAS, John. Private, Militia, Capt. Andrew Fountain's Company, 14th Battalion, by August 13, 1777 [Ref: M-157]. Private, 5th Maryland Line, enlisted on May 13, 1777, promoted to corporal, and discharged on May 8, 1780 [Ref: D-223]. One John Lucas married --?-- Morgan by license dated April 27, 1774, and a John Lucas married Rebecca Cooper by license dated April 22, 1790, and a John Lucas married Caroline Scott by license dated September 3, 1790 [Ref: X-3, X-21]. Additional research will be necessary before drawing conclusions.

LUCAS, Joshua. Private, Militia, Capt. Henry Downes' Company, 28th Battalion, by August 13, 1777 [Ref: M-152]. Joshua Lucas married Deborah Willis by license dated December 28, 1789 [Ref: X-20].

LUCAS, Maria. See "Charles Manship," q.v.

LUCAS, Michael (Michal). Private, Militia, Capt. Andrew Fountain's Company, 14th Battalion, by August 13, 1777 [Ref: M-157]. Rendered patriotic service by providing wheat for the use of the military in August, 1782, as verified by Giles Hicks 3rd, Commissary for Caroline County [Ref: V-6636].

LUCAS, Samuel. See "Charles Manship, Jr.," q.v.

LUCAS, William. Private, Militia, Capt. Andrew Fountain's Company, 14th Battalion, by August 13, 1777 [Ref: M-157].

LUNCEFORD, Edwin (Edmond). "Edwin Luneiford(?)" was a private in the militia, Capt. Vincent Price's Company, 28th Battalion, by August 13, 1777 [Ref: M-152]. "Edmond Lunceford" was a private (draft), Maryland Troops, furnished in Caroline County by William Whiteley, County Lieutenant, on April 16, 1781 [Ref: D-368]. "Edwin Lunceford" married Sarah Kelley by license dated July 16, 1785 [Ref: X-16].

LYDEN, Martha. See "John Clark," q.v.

LYDEN, Richard. See "Richard Liden," q.v.

LYNCH, James. Private, Militia, 14th Battalion, Capt. Joseph Richardson's Company, by August 13, 1777 [Ref: M-154].

LYNCH, John. Private, 6th Company, Capt. Peter Adams, 1st Maryland Line, enlisted February 24, 1776 [Ref: D-15].

LYSTER, Joshua. See "Joshua Lister," q.v.

MABERRY, Aaron. Rendered patriotic service by providing wheat for the use of the military in August, 1782, as verified by Giles Hicks 3rd, Commissary for Caroline County [Ref: V-6636].

MALCOLM, John. Subscribed to the Oath of Allegiance and Fidelity before the Hon. Richard Mason on March 2, 1778 [Ref: J-1814]. John Malcolm married Mary Lawrence by license dated August 22, 1777 [Ref: X-7].

MALLET, --?--. See "James Lecompte," q.v.

MAN, Robert. Private, 6th Company, Capt. Peter Adams, 1st Maryland Line, enlisted February 15, 1776 [Ref: D-14].

MANNING, Ann. See "Mark Andrew," q.v.

MANNING, John. Private (draft), Maryland Troops, enrolled in Caroline County by William Whiteley, County Lieutenant, on August 14, 1781 to serve in the Maryland Line until December 10, 1781 [Ref: D-385]. Honorably discharged from the service on November 29, 1781 [Ref: I-7]. One John Manning, who served in Maryland during the war, died in Missouri in 1814 or 1815 [Ref: Y-1887].

MANSFIELD, John. Private, Militia, Capt. John Fauntleroy's Company, 28th Battalion, by August 13, 1777 [Ref: M-153].

MANSHIP (MAINSHIP), Aaron (Aron). Second Lieutenant, Militia, Capt. Nehemiah Andrew's Company, 14th Battalion, by August 13, 1777 [Ref: M-155]. First Lieutenant, April 9, 1778 [Ref: M-100, E-23, which spelled the name "Mainship"]. Subscribed to the Oath of Allegiance and Fidelity before the Hon.

Nathaniel Potter on March 2, 1778 [Ref: J-1814]. Aaron Manship married Sarah Bland, and Charles Manship married Ann Bland, both by licenses dated July 28, 1778 [Ref: X-8]. Also, an Aaron Manship married Nancy Matthews by license dated May 20, 1793 [Ref: X-25]. See "Charles Manship, Jr.," q.v.

MANSHIP, Ann. See "Charles Manship, Jr." and "Aaron Manship," q.v.

MANSHIP (MAINSHIP), Charles (1707 - after 1783). Subscribed to the Oath of Allegiance and Fidelity (made his mark that resembled a large "A" with the left leg missing) before the Hon. Nathaniel Potter on March 2, 1778 [Ref: J-1814]. Rendered patriotic service by providing wheat for the use of the military in August, 1782, as verified by Giles Hicks 3rd, Commissary for Caroline County [Ref: V-6636]. Aged 76 in a 1783 deposition [Ref: T-6].

MANSHIP (MAINSHIP), Charles Jr. (c1755-1812). On February 18, 1780, he filed a certificate in Caroline County Court that he had subscribed to the Oath of Allegiance and Fidelity before the Clerk of Queen Anne's County [Ref: N-67, which listed the name without the "Jr."]. In an 1815 land commission record it stated that Charles Manship had died in 1812, seized of tracts called "Revival" and "Perry's Grove" and leaving a widow Ann Manship (now married to Samuel Talbott) and the following heirs: Mary Manship (who married Abraham Griffith), Maria Manship (who married Samuel Lucas), and Elizabeth Manship (under 21). [Ref: T-29]. "Charles Manship" married Ann Bland, and Aaron Manship married Sarah Bland, both by licenses dated July 28, 1778; also, "Charles Manship" married Mary Keene by license dated December 22, 1786 [Ref: X-8, X-17]. "Charles Mainship, Jr." rendered patriotic service by providing wheat for the use of the military in August, 1782, as verified by Giles Hicks 3rd, Commissary for Caroline County [Ref: V-6636]. See "Aaron Manship," q.v.

MANSHIP (MAINSHIP), Elijah. Private, Militia, Capt. Nehemiah Andrew's Company, 14th Battalion, by August 13, 1777 [Ref: M-155]. Subscribed to the Oath of Allegiance and Fidelity before the Hon. Nathaniel Potter on March 2, 1778 [Ref: J-1814].

MANSHIP, Elizabeth. See "Charles Manship, Jr.," q.v.

MANSHIP, Maria. See "Charles Manship, Jr.," q.v.

MANSHIP, Mary. See "Charles Manship, Jr.," q.v.

MANSHIP (MAINSHIP), Nathan. Private, Militia, Capt. Nehemiah Andrew's Company, 14th Battalion, by August 13, 1777 [Ref: M-155]. Subscribed to the Oath of Allegiance and Fidelity before the Hon. Nathaniel Potter on March 2, 1778 [Ref: J-1814]. Second Lieutenant, April 9, 1778 [Ref: E-23, which spelled the name "Mainship"]. Nathan Manship married Eleanora Andrews by license dated May 17, 1779 [Ref: X-10].

MANSHIP, Sarah. See "Charles Manship, Jr.," q.v.

MARPHEY, John. Subscribed to the Oath of Allegiance and Fidelity before the Hon. Richard Mason on March 2, 1778 [Ref: J-1814].

MARSH, Charles Hynson. Rendered patriotic service by providing wheat for the use of the military in August, 1782, as verified by Giles Hicks 3rd, Commissary

for Caroline County [Ref: V-6636].
MARSHALL, Benjamin 7th. Lieutenant, Militia, July 1, 1777, and resigned on October 2, 1780 [Ref: M-101].
MARSHALL, Hugh. Private, Militia, Capt. Shadrack Liden's Company, 14th Battalion, by August 13, 1777 [Ref: M-155].
MARSHALL, Mary. See "John Oram," q.v.
MARSHALL, Ralph. Private, Militia, Capt. Shadrack Liden's Company, 14th Battalion, by August 13, 1777 [Ref: M-155].
MARTIN, George. Private, Maryland Troops, enrolled by Lieut. Levin Handy in Caroline County and passed by Col. William Hopewell on August 4, 1776 [Ref: D-69]. George Martin married Elizabeth Nicols (Nichols) by license dated November 19, 1789 [Ref: X-20].
MARTIN, John Selby. Private, Maryland Troops, enrolled by Lieut. Levin Handy in Caroline County and passed by Col. William Hopewell on August 4, 1776 [Ref: D-69].
MARTINDALE, Ann. See "John Deroachbrune," q.v.
MARTINDALE, Daniel. Private, Militia, Capt. Vincent Price's Company, 28th Battalion, by August 13, 1777 [Ref: M-152].
MARTINDALE, Henry. Private, Militia, Capt. Henry Downes' Company, 28th Battalion, by August 13, 1777 [Ref: M-152]. Henry Martindale married Nancy Nicols by license dated October 17, 1780 [Ref: X-12]. See "John Deroachbrune," q.v.
MARTINDALE, Lemuel. Private, Militia, Capt. Henry Downes' Company, 28th Battalion, by August 13, 1777 [Ref: M-152].
MARTINDALE, Levin. On December 27, 1776 he joined a company of men in Caroline County who marched to Talbot County to obtain a supply of salt [Ref: B-564, B-565, which spelled the name "Martingale"].
MARTINDALE, Samuel. On December 27, 1776 he joined a company of men in Caroline County who marched to Talbot County to obtain a supply of salt [Ref: B-564, B-565, which spelled the name "Martingale"]. Private, Militia, Capt. Henry Downes' Company, 28th Battalion, by August 13, 1777 [Ref: M-152]. Samuel Martindale was born in Maryland, married Mary --?--, and died after December 29, 1801 [Ref: Y-1911].
MARTINDALE, Stephen. Private, Militia, Capt. Henry Downes' Company, 28th Battalion, by August 13, 1777 [Ref: M-152].
MASON, Abram. Private, Militia, Capt. John Stafford's Company, ru14th Battalion, by August 13, 1777 [Ref: M-156].
MASON, Ann. See "James Baggs," q.v.
MASON, Elizabeth. See "Zachariah Downes," q.v.
MASON, Hannah. Rendered patriotic service by providing wheat for the use of the military in August, 1782, as verified by Giles Hicks 3rd, Commissary for Caroline County [Ref: V-6636].
MASON, Henry. Private, Militia, Capt. John Fauntleroy's Company, 28th

Battalion, by August 13, 1777 [Ref: M-153]. Rendered patriotic service by providing wheat for the use of the military in August, 1782, as verified by Giles Hicks 3rd, Commissary for Caroline County [Ref: V-6636]. Subscribed to the Oath of Allegiance and Fidelity before the Hon. Richard Mason on March 2, 1778 [Ref: J-1814]. One Henry Mason married Esther Baggs by license recorded October 30, 1775, and a Henry Mason married Mary Clark by license dated January 4, 1791 [Ref: X-6, X-22].

MASON, James. Private, Militia, Capt. William Hopper's Company, 28th Battalion, by August 13, 1777 [Ref: M-151].

MASON, Margaret. See "Richard Mason," q.v.

MASON, Nancy. See "James Baggs," q.v.

MASON, Noah. Subscribed to the Oath of Allegiance and Fidelity (made his mark that resembled a large "+") before the Hon. Richard Mason on March 2, 1778 [Ref: J-1814]. Noah Mason married Izabel Hunter by license dated November 19, 1784, and Noah Mason married Nancy Jackson by license dated August 5, 1788 [Ref: X-16, X-19].

MASON, Rebeckah. See "Thomas Hughlett," q.v.

MASON, Richard. Born in Queen Anne's County (of age by 1754), son of Richard Mason (died in 1748), and resided in that part which became Caroline County in 1773. He married first to --?-- Baggs, daughter of Thomas Baggs, and second to Sarah --?-- (name unknown) who subsequently married Benjamin Elliott by 1784. His children were Thomas Mason, Rebecca Hughlett (wife of Thomas Hughlett), Sarah Swiff (or Swift; husband's name unknown), and Margaret Mason. Richard attended the Maryland Conventions in 1775 and 1776, and represented Caroline County in the Lower House of the Maryland General Assembly between 1777 and 1781. He was a Justice of Queen Anne's County from 1763 to 1773, Commissioner of Caroline County in 1774, Court Justice (Quorum) of Caroline County and Justice of the Orphans' Court from 1774 to at least March 21, 1780. He also served on the Committee of Correspondence in 1774 and on the Committee of Observation in 1776 [Ref: R-579, R-580, R-71, R-72, R-74, R-76, R-78, R-80, R-86, A-481, Z-1, Z-26 (which also spelled the name as "Masson"), A-4, O-4, O-28, N-70, E-140]. First Major, Militia, 28th Battalion, January 12, 1776 [Ref: M-101]. Justice who administered the Oath of Allegiance and Fidelity in 1778 [Ref: J-1814]. He died intestate in December, 1781 (administration bond dated January 1, 1782) in Caroline County [Ref: R-580]. See "Thomas Hughlett," q.v.

MASON, Richard. First Lieutenant, Militia, Capt. William Chipley's Company, 28th Battalion, by August 13, 1777 to at least April 14, 1779 [Ref: M-153, M-101, E-493].

MASON, Richard. Private, Militia, Capt. Vincent Price's Company, 28th Battalion, by August 13, 1777 [Ref: M-152]. Private, Light Horse Troops, Capt. Henry Dickinson's Company, June 12, 1781 [Ref: M-157].

MASON, Richard Jr. Subscribed to the Oath of Allegiance and Fidelity before the

Hon. Henry Downes, Jr. on March 2, 1778 [Ref: J-1814]. Richard Mason, Jr. married Rebekah Hardcastle by license dated February 26, 1783 [Ref: X-15].

MASON, Richard (Taylor). Private, Militia, Capt. William Chipley's Company, 28th Battalion, by August 13, 1777 [Ref: M-153].

MASON, Sarah. See "Richard Mason" and "Thomas Swift," q.v.

MASON, Solomon. Constable, 1775 [Ref: Z-2]. Served on the Committee of Observation for Caroline County on August 2, 1775 [Ref: A-48]. Ensign, promoted to Second Lieutenant, Militia, Capt. Samuel Jackson's Company, 28th Battalion, June 19, 1777 [Ref: M-153, M-101, C-294, J-1814].

MASON, Sophia. See "Herrington Sylvester," q.v.

MASON, Thomas. Ensign, Maryland Troops, 1776 [Ref: D-68].

MASON, Thomas. Constable, Choptank Hundred, 1776 [Ref: Z-27]. Private, Militia, Capt. John Fauntleroy's Company, 28th Battalion, by August 13, 1777 [Ref: M-154]. Subscribed to the Oath of Allegiance and Fidelity before the Hon. Richard Mason on March 2, 1778 [Ref: J-1814]. One Thomas Mason married Eliza Saven by license dated September 27, 1793 [Ref: X-25]. See "Richard Mason" and "James Roe," q.v.

MASON, William. "William Wr. Mason" subscribed to the Oath of Allegiance and Fidelity before the Hon. Richard Mason on March 2, 1778 [Ref: J-1814]. "William Mason" married Nancy Baggs by license dated January 3, 1785 [Ref: X-16].

MASON, Winchester. Private, Militia, Capt. John Fauntleroy's Company, 28th Battalion, by August 13, 1777 [Ref: M-154].

MASSEY, Mary. See "John Gibson," q.v.

MATTHEWS, Ann. See "Thomas Roe," q.v.

MATTHEWS, Cloudsberry. Private, Militia, Capt. John Fauntleroy's Company, 28th Battalion, by August 13, 1777 [Ref: M-154]. On May 20, 1778, Col. William Haslett acknowledged payment to Matthews for his service and that he had been discharged. On September 2, 1778 Matthews gave a deposition pertaining to "the purchase of a substitute." [Ref: P-170, P-187]. "Clousberry Matthews" married Mary Slaughter by license dated January 3, 1781 [Ref: X-13].

MATTHEWS, Greenbury (Greenberry). Private, Militia, Capt. William Chipley's Company, 28th Battalion, by August 13, 1777 [Ref: M-153]. Rendered patriotic service by providing wheat for the use of the military in August, 1782, as verified by Giles Hicks 3rd, Commissary for Caroline County [Ref: V-6636]. "Greenberry Mathews" married Ann Monticue by license dated January 19, 1780, and "Greenbury Mathews" married Sarah Pratt by license dated November 12, 1780 [Ref: X-11, X-12].

MATTHEWS, John. Private, Militia, Capt. John Fauntleroy's Company, 28th Battalion, by August 13, 1777 [Ref: M-154].

MATTHEWS, Joseph. Private, Militia, Capt. William Chipley's Company, 28th Battalion, by August 13, 1777 [Ref: M-153].

MATTHEWS, Nancy. See "Aaron Manship," q.v.

MATTHEWS, Samuel. See "Thomas Roe," q.v.

MATTHEWS, Thomas. Private (draft), Maryland Troops, enrolled in Caroline County by William Whiteley, County Lieutenant, on August 14, 1781 (although reported "run" at the time) to serve in the Maryland Line until December 10, 1781 [Ref: D-385]. One Thomas Matthews married Mary Ann Jackson by license dated August 8, 1780 [Ref: X-12]. See the other "Thomas Matthews," q.v.

MATTHEWS, Thomas. Private, Militia, Capt. John Fauntleroy's Company, 28th Battalion, by August 13, 1777 [Ref: M-153]. Rendered patriotic service by providing wheat for the use of the military in August, 1782, as verified by Giles Hicks 3rd, Commissary for Caroline County [Ref: V-6636]. See the other "Thomas Matthews," q.v.

MATTHEWS, Thomas, of John. Private, Militia, Capt. John Fauntleroy's Company, 28th Battalion, by August 13, 1777 [Ref: M-154].

MAXWELL, Alexander. See "John Allen Sangston," q.v.

MAYER, Charles (Doctor). On February 18, 1780, he filed a certificate in Caroline County Court that he had subscribed to the Oath of Allegiance and Fidelity before the Clerk of Queen Anne's County [Ref: N-67].

McAFEE(?), George. Private, Militia, Capt. John Fauntleroy's Company, 28th Battalion, by August 13, 1777 [Ref: M-154].

McBEATH (MACBETH), Elizabeth. See "William Whitely," q.v.

McBEATH (MACBETH), John. See "William Whitely," q.v.

McBRIDE, Hugh. Private, Militia, Capt. Joseph Douglass' Company, 14th Battalion, by August 13, 1777 [Ref: M-156].

McBRYDE (McBRIDE), Hugh. First Lieutenant, Vienna Company, 3rd Battalion, Dorchester County, by January, 1776, and Captain, by July, 1777. "Hugh McBride" was a Captain, Militia, 14th Battalion, April 9, 1778, and succeeded on August 14, 1779 [Ref: M-102, E-23, E-493, R-586]. "Hugh McBryde (Justice)" subscribed to the Oath of Allegiance and Fidelity before the Hon. Charles Dickinson on March 1, 1778 [Ref: J-1418]. "Hugh McBryde" resided in Charles County by 1770, in Dorchester County by 1773, in Caroline County by 1777, and in Baltimore Town by 1783. He married Sarah --?-- and apparently had no children. Hugh represented Caroline County in the Lower House of the Maryland General Assembly between 1779 and 1783. He also served as a Court Justice, 1777-1782, Justice of the Peace, 1778-1783, and Justice of the Orphans' Court, 1780-1782 [Ref: R-586, R-82, R-86, R-87, E-249, I-45, I-341]. Hugh McBryde was a merchant on the Eastern Shore and in Baltimore Town. In June, 1778, letters of marque and reprisal were issued to the captain of the schooner *Beggars Benison* belonging to Hugh McBryde, John Craig, William McBryde, and Charles Phillysill. Letters of marque and reprisal were also issued in December, 1778, to the master of the schooner *Nelly and Polly*, which was owned by Hugh and William McBryde, James Houston, and William Henry [Ref: R-586]. Hugh died by July 25, 1787 (date of administration bond) in Baltimore County [Ref: R-586, R-587].

McBRYDE, Sarah. See "Hugh McBryde," q.v.

McBRYDE, William. See "Hugh McBryde," q.v.

McCAN, Margaret. See "William Batchelor," q.v.

McCLAIN, Hugh. Private, 6th Company, Capt. Peter Adams, 1st Maryland Line, enlisted February 24, 1776 [Ref: D-15].

McCLAIN, John. Private, 6th Company, Capt. Peter Adams, 1st Maryland Line, enlisted January 23, 1776 [Ref: D-14].

McCOMB, John. Subscribed to the Oath of Allegiance and Fidelity before the Hon. Richard Mason on March 2, 1778 [Ref: J-1814].

McCOMBS, Jacob. Private, Militia, Capt. John Fauntleroy's Company, 28th Battalion, by August 13, 1777 [Ref: M-154]. Rendered patriotic service by providing wheat for the use of the military in August, 1782, as verified by Giles Hicks 3rd, Commissary for Caroline County [Ref: V-6636]. Subscribed to the Oath of Allegiance and Fidelity (made his "X" mark) before the Hon. Richard Mason on March 2, 1778 [Ref: J-1814].

McCUBBIN, Samuel. Private, 6th Company, Capt. Peter Adams, 1st Maryland Line, enlisted February 15, 1776 [Ref: D-14].

McDANIEL, William. Private, 6th Company, Capt. Peter Adams, 1st Maryland Line, enlisted January 22, 1776 [Ref: D-14].

McDANIEL, William 2nd. Private, 6th Company, Capt. Peter Adams, 1st Maryland Line, enlisted January 30, 1776 [Ref: D-14].

McFADON, John. Private, 6th Company, Capt. Peter Adams, 1st Maryland Line, enlisted January 23, 1776 [Ref: D-14].

McGREGOR, William. Private, 6th Company, Capt. Peter Adams, 1st Maryland Line, enlisted January 30, 1776 [Ref: D-14].

McGUINES (McGINES), Daniel. Rendered patriotic service by providing wheat for the use of the military in August, 1782, as verified by Giles Hicks 3rd, Commissary for Caroline County [Ref: V-6636]. Subscribed to the Oath of Allegiance and Fidelity in 1780 [Ref: L-117, which listed the name as "Daniel McGuines"].

McGUINNEY, Daniel. Private, Militia, Capt. Samuel Jackson's Company, 28th Battalion, by August 13, 1777 [Ref: M-153, which spelled the name "MaGuinney"].

McHARD, Isaac. See "James Seth," q.v.

McKEEL, Charles. Fifer, 6th Company, 1st Maryland Line, enlisted January 22, 1776 and discharged June 7, 1776 [Ref: D-14]. Private, Militia, Capt. Shadrack Liden's Company, 14th Battalion, by August 13, 1777 [Ref: M-155].

McKEEL, Thomas (1759 - after 1828). Sergeant, 6th Company, 1st Maryland Line, enlisted January 30, 1776 [Ref: D-13]. Ensign, 1st Maryland Line, enlisted December 10, 1776, but never served [Ref: D-136]. Applied for pension (S37977) in Talbot County on May 23, 1818, stating he lived in Caroline County at the time of his enlistment and in 1789 he moved to Easton, Maryland. In 1828 he was aged 69 with a wife Eglanline, aged about 50 [Ref: W-2287].

McKIMMEY, Elijah. Private, Militia, Capt. Joseph Douglass' Company, 14th Battalion, by August 13, 1777 [Ref: M-156].

McKIMMEY (McKIMMY), Gideon. Private, Militia, Capt. Shadrack Liden's Company, 14th Battalion, by August 13, 1777 [Ref: M-155]. Rendered patriotic service by providing wheat for the use of the military in June, 1782, as verified by Giles Hicks 3rd, Commissary for Caroline County [Ref: V-6636].

McKINNEY, John. Private, Maryland Troops, enlisted by Capt. Joseph Richardson in Caroline County and passed by Col. William Richardson on August 31, 1776 [Ref: D-69].

McMAHAN (McMAHON), William. Private, Militia, Capt. Andrew Fountain's Company, 14th Battalion, by August 13, 1777 [Ref: M-157]. William McMahon married Catharine Mifflin by license recorded January 28, 1775 [Ref: X-5].

McNEERE, --?--. On July 26, 1782, the Council of Maryland sent a letter to General Smallwood stating they had received a "petition from Mrs. McNeere setting forth that her son, an apprentice, has been enlisted by a Recruiting Sergeant to Captain Wright; we also enclose a certificate from the Clerk of Caroline County, that the lad was bound apprentice by the County Court in 1775, by which it appears that his time of service is not yet expired." [Ref: I-224, which indexed the name as "Mrs. McNeeve"].

McQUALITY, Catharine. See "James McQuality," q.v.

McQUALITY, Elizabeth. See "James McQuality," q.v.

McQUALITY (McQUALLITY), James. Private, Maryland Troops, enrolled by Lieut. Thomas Wynn Loockerman in Caroline County in July, 1776 [Ref: D-69]. In an 1818 land commission record it stated that James McQuality had died in June, 1806, owning tracts called "Harris'es Outlet," "Vaux's Addition" and "Friendship Regulated," and leaving a widow Margaret McQuality (now married to David Fountain) and the following children: Joseph McQuality, Catharine McQuality (of age and married to Bennett Tomlinson of Talbot County), and Elizabeth McQuality (a minor, living in Talbot County). [Ref: T-31].

McQUALITY, Joseph. See "James McQuality," q.v.

McQUALITY, Margaret. See "James McQuality," q.v.

McRYON, Michal. Private, Militia, Capt. William Haslett's Company, 28th Battalion, by August 13, 1777 [Ref: M-152].

MEANS, Henry. Private, Militia, Capt. Joseph Douglass' Company, 14th Battalion, by August 13, 1777 [Ref: M-156].

MEARS, John, of Talbot County. "Marriner, belonging to Capt. Thomas Noel's sloop now lying at his wharf," subscribed to the Oath of Allegiance and Fidelity before the Hon. Peter Richardson on March 1, 1778 [Ref: J-1814].

MEARS, Zadock (Zedok). Private, Militia, 14th Battalion, Capt. Joseph Richardson's Company, by August 13, 1777 [Ref: M-154]. Ensign, Militia, Capt. Vincent Price's Company, July 24, 1780 [Ref: M-103, F-230, G-27].

MEEDS, Elizabeth. See "Thomas Hall" and Rachel Meeds," q.v.

MEEDS, Lydia. See "Rachel Meeds," q.v.

MEEDS, Peggy. See "Rachel Meeds," q.v.

MEEDS, Rachel. Rendered patriotic service by providing wheat for the use of the military in August, 1782, as verified by Giles Hicks 3rd, Commissary for Caroline County [Ref: V-6636]. Thomas Meeds married Rachel --?-- and had these children: Rebeccah Meeds (born February 22, 1748), Peggy Meeds (born December 17, 1751), Lydia Meeds (born May 4, 1754), Elisabeth Meeds (born July 20, 1756), Rachel Meeds (born October 12, 1758), and Thomas Whittington Meeds (born August 9, 1762). [Ref: K-26]. "Thomas White Meeds" married Mary Cooper by license dated May 12, 1783 [Ref: X-15].

MEEDS, Rebeccah. See "Rachel Meeds," q.v.

MEEDS (MEADS), Thomas. Ensign, Militia, Capt. Philemon Downes' Company, 28th Battalion, December 17, 1781 [Ref: M-103, I-27]. Recommended as Second Lieutenant in Capt. Thomas Burk's Company, June 12, 1781 [Ref: M-103]. See "Rachel Meeds," q.v.

MEFFIN, Elizabeth. See "William Owens," q.v.

MEIN, Andrew. See "Henry Dickinson," q.v.

MELVILL, David. Private, Militia, Capt. William Haslett's Company, 28th Battalion, by August 13, 1777 [Ref: M-152]. David Melvill married Sarah Medford by license dated March 16, 1781 [Ref: X-13].

MELVILL, John. Private, Militia, Capt. Shadrack Liden's Company, 14th Battalion, by August 13, 1777 [Ref: M-155]. Rendered patriotic service by providing wheat for the use of the military in June, 1782, as verified by Giles Hicks 3rd, Commissary for Caroline County [Ref: V-6636].

MERRICK, --?--. See "William Williams," q.v.

MERRICK, Isaac. Private, Militia, Capt. William Haslett's Company, 28th Battalion, by August 13, 1777 [Ref: M-152]. On May 20, 1778, he gave a promissory note to William Haslett for payment of a substitute and Haslett subsequently certified that Merrick had furnished a substitute [Ref: P-170]. Rendered patriotic service by providing wheat for the use of the military in August, 1782, as verified by Giles Hicks 3rd, Commissary for Caroline County [Ref: V-6636]. Isaac Merrick married Rachel Sylvester by license dated August 21, 1792 [Ref: X-24].

MERRICK, Israel (Ezerail). Private, Militia, Capt. Thomas Hughlett's Company, 28th Battalion, by August 13, 1777 [Ref: M-153]. Rendered patriotic service by providing wheat for the use of the military in August, 1782, as verified by Giles Hicks 3rd, Commissary for Caroline County [Ref: V-6636].

MERRICK, James. Private, Militia, Capt. John Fauntleroy's Company, 28th Battalion, by August 13, 1777 [Ref: M-154]. James Merrick married Tilpha [Zilpha?] Quarternnis by license dated January 29, 1775 [Ref: X-5].

MERRICK, John. Rendered patriotic service by providing wheat for the use of the military in May, 1782, as verified by Giles Hicks 3rd, Commissary for Caroline County [Ref: V-6636]. John Merrick married China Dixon by license dated July 24, 1778 [Ref: X-8].

MERRICK, Lambert. Private, Militia, Capt. William Haslett's Company, 28th Battalion, by August 13, 1777 [Ref: M-152].

MERRILL, Thomas. Private, Maryland Troops, enrolled by Lieut. Levin Handy in Caroline County and passed by Col. William Hopewell on August 4, 1776 [Ref: D-69].

MICTON, Sarah. See "James Kenton," q.v.

MIDDLETON, Major. Private, Militia, 14th Battalion, Capt. Richard Andrew's Company, by August 13, 1777 [Ref: M-156].

MIERS, William. Private (substitute), Maryland Troops, furnished in Caroline County by William Whiteley, County Lieutenant, on April 16, 1781 [Ref: D-368].

MIFFLIN, Catharine. See "William McMahan," q.v.

MILLINGTON, Allemby. Private (draft), Maryland Troops, furnished in Caroline County by William Whiteley, County Lieutenant, on April 16, 1781 [Ref: D-368]. Private (draft), Maryland Troops, enrolled in Caroline County by William Whiteley, County Lieutenant, on August 14, 1781 (although reported "run" at the time) to serve in the Maryland Line until December 10, 1781 [Ref: D-385]. However, the proceedings of the Council of Maryland on September 10, 1781 contained the following clarification: "It appearing to this Board that Allemby Millington is an inhabitant of Talbot County and that he has stood his draught in that county and that the said Millington was draughted as an inhabitant of Caroline County to serve till the 10th of December next, the said Allemby Millington is hereby discharged from the said draught in Caroline County." [Ref: G-618, H-485]. A report in September, 1781, from the Talbot County Lieutenant stated, in part, that Millington has "attended constantly at the muster field and does his duty as a good soldier. He has also been classed and stood all the draughts in the county." [Ref: H-476].

MILLIS, James. On May 30, 1780, he filed a certificate in Caroline County Court that he had subscribed to the Oath of Allegiance and Fidelity before the Hon. Nathaniel Potter [Ref: N-78].

MILLS, James. Private, Militia, Capt. Nehemiah Andrew's Company, 14th Battalion, by August 13, 1777 [Ref: M-155]. Rendered patriotic service by providing wheat for the use of the military in August, 1782, as verified by Giles Hicks 3rd, Commissary for Caroline County [Ref: V-6636].

MILSON, James. Private, Militia, Capt. John Fauntleroy's Company, 28th Battalion, by August 13, 1777 [Ref: M-154].

MILSON, Samuel. Rendered patriotic service by providing wheat for the use of the military in August, 1782, as verified by Giles Hicks 3rd, Commissary for Caroline County [Ref: V-6636].

MINNER, Edward. Private, Militia, 14th Battalion, Capt. Richard Andrew's Company, by August 13, 1777 [Ref: M-156].

MINNER, Elisha. Private, Militia, 14th Battalion, Capt. Richard Andrew's Company, by August 13, 1777 [Ref: M-156].

MINNER, Leven. Private (recruit), Maryland Troops, enrolled in Caroline County by William Whiteley, County Lieutenant, on August 14, 1781 to serve in the Maryland Line until December 10, 1781 [Ref: D-385].

MINNER, Priscilla. See "Edward Pritchett," q.v.

MINNER, William. Private, Militia, 14th Battalion, Capt. Joseph Richardson's Company, by August 13, 1777 [Ref: M-154].

MITCHELL, Ambrose (Ambros). Private, Militia, Capt. John Mitchell's Company, 14th Battalion, by August 13, 1777 [Ref: M-154]. Private, Light Horse Troops, Capt. Henry Dickinson's Company, June 12, 1781 [Ref: M-157]. See "John Mitchell," q.v.

MITCHELL, Dora. See "George Kirkman," q.v.

MITCHELL, John. Captain, Militia, 14th Battalion, November 16, 1776 to at least April 9, 1778 [Ref: M-104, M-154, E-23]. Subscribed to the Oath of Allegiance and Fidelity before the Hon. Peter Richardson on February 28, 1778 [Ref: J-1814]. John Mitchell married Sarah Scott by license dated January 16, 1778 [Ref: X-7]. "John Mitchell, son of Ambrose" was aged 35 in a 1785 deposition [Ref: T-10].

MITCHELL, Richard. Private, Militia, Capt. John Mitchell's Company, 14th Battalion, by August 13, 1777 [Ref: M-154]. Subscribed to the Oath of Allegiance and Fidelity before the Hon. Peter Richardson on February 28, 1778 [Ref: J-1814]. Richard Mitchell married Sarah Carter by license dated February 26, 1781 [Ref: X-13].

MOLLESTON, Elizabeth Ann. See "William Molleston," q.v.

MOLLESTON, William. Served on the Committee of Correspondence in Queen Anne's County in 1774 and represented Caroline County at the Maryland Conventions in 1774 and 1775. He married Elizabeth Ann --?-- and was a first cousin of Samuel Skidmore of Kent County, Delaware. A physician by 1774, William was the founding incorporator of the Delaware Medical Society in 1789. He died in October, 1790 at Dover, Delaware [Ref: R-71, R-602, O-5, A-4].

MONTICUE, Ann. See "Greenbury Matthews," q.v.

MONTICUE (MONTIGUE, MONTEGUE), Harrison. Private, Militia, Capt. Thomas Hughlett's Company, 28th Battalion, by August 13, 1777 [Ref: M-153]. Harrison Monticue married Nancy Lemarr by license dated October 19, 1780 [Ref: X-12].

MONTICUE (MONTIGUE, MONTAGUE), Jadwin. Private, Militia, Capt. Samuel Jackson's Company, 28th Battalion, by August 13, 1777 [Ref: M-153]. Jadwin Montague married Henrietta Hynson by license dated November 12, 1777 [Ref: X-7].

MONTICUE (MONTEGUE, MONTIGUE), Jeremiah. Private, Militia, Capt. Thomas Hughlett's Company, 28th Battalion, by August 13, 1777 [Ref: M-153]. Jeremiah Monticue was aged 46 or 47 in a 1779 deposition, noting he was a son of William Monticue, and Jeremiah Monticue was aged 45 in a 1782 deposition, noting he was a cousin of William Monticue [Ref: T-2, T-11]. Jeremiah Montigue

married Elizabeth Clough by license dated March 2, 1790 [Ref: X-20].
MONTICUE (MONTIGUE, MONTEGUE, MOUNTICUE), John. Private, Militia, Capt. Samuel Jackson's Company, 28th Battalion, by August 13, 1777 [Ref: M-153]. Rendered patriotic service by providing wheat for the use of the military in August, 1782, as verified by Giles Hicks 3rd, Commissary for Caroline County [Ref: V-6636].
MONTICUE, William. See "Jeremiah Monticue," q.v.
MOORE (MORE), John Irons. Rendered patriotic service by providing wheat for the use of the military in August, 1782, as verified by Giles Hicks 3rd, Commissary for Caroline County [Ref: V-6636].
MOORE, Thomas. Seaman, enlisted May 27, 1782 to serve on the barge "Fearnaught" under Capt. Edward Spedden, and was paid £3 bounty for enlisting; physical description given as 5' 11" tall with a fair complexion [Ref: D-611].
MOORE, William. Private, Militia, Capt. Samuel Jackson's Company, 28th Battalion, by August 13, 1777 [Ref: M-153].
MORGAN, --?--. See "John Lucas," q.v.
MORGAN, Benjamin (Ben). Private, Militia, Capt. Nehemiah Andrew's Company, 14th Battalion, by August 13, 1777 [Ref: M-155]. Rendered patriotic service by providing wheat for the use of the military in August, 1782, as verified by Giles Hicks 3rd, Commissary for Caroline County [Ref: V-6636].
MORGAN, David. Private, Militia, Capt. Henry Downes' Company, 28th Battalion, by August 13, 1777 [Ref: M-152].
MORGAN, David. Private, Militia, Capt. Vincent Price's Company, 28th Battalion, by August 13, 1777 [Ref: M-152].
MORGAN, David. On December 27, 1776 he joined a company of men in Caroline County who marched to Talbot County to obtain a supply of salt [Ref: B-564, B-565]. Rendered patriotic service by providing wheat for the use of the military in August, 1782, as verified by Giles Hicks 3rd, Commissary for Caroline County [Ref: V-6636].
MORGAN, Elizabeth. See "James Larey" and "Nehemiah Cooper," q.v.
MORGAN, George. Private, Militia, Capt. John Stafford's Company, 14th Battalion, by August 13, 1777 [Ref: M-156]. George Morgan married Africa Towers by license dated October 28, 1780 [Ref: X-12].
MORGAN, Hal(?). Rendered patriotic service by providing wheat for the use of the military in August, 1782, as verified by Giles Hicks 3rd, Commissary for Caroline County [Ref: V-6636].
MORGAN, James. Private, Militia, Capt. Andrew Fountain's Company, 14th Battalion, by August 13, 1777 [Ref: M-157]. James Morgan married Justina Cromeen [Cremeen?] by license dated March 20, 1781 [Ref: X-13].
MORGAN, John. Private, Militia, Capt. Shadrack Liden's Company, 14th Battalion, by August 13, 1777 [Ref: M-155].
MORGAN, John. Private, Militia, Capt. Nehemiah Andrew's Company, 14th Battalion, by August 13, 1777 [Ref: M-155].

MORGAN, John. Rendered patriotic service by providing wheat for the use of the military in August and September, 1782, as verified by Giles Hicks 3rd, Commissary for Caroline County [Ref: V-6636]. One John Morgan was aged 44 in a 1783 deposition and another John Morgan was aged 40 in an 1800 deposition [Ref: T-6, T-21]. One John Morgan married Sarah Chaffinch by license dated December 4, 1780, and a John Morgan married Sarah Clift by license dated January 27, 1791 [Ref: X-13, X-22]. Since there was more then one man named John Morgan, additional research will be necessary before drawing conclusions.

MORGAN, Margaret. See "Abner Clements" and "William Fountain," q.v.

MORGAN, Solomon. Two men with this name were privates in the militia, Capt. John Stafford's Company, 14th Battalion, by August 13, 1777 [Ref: M-156]. One Solomon Morgan married Alice Holdbrook by license dated March 6, 1781 [Ref: X-13].

MORGAN, Solomon. Private, Militia, Capt. Shadrack Liden's Company, 14th Battalion, by August 13, 1777 [Ref: M-155].

MORGAN, William. Private, Militia, Capt. John Stafford's Company, 14th Battalion, by August 13, 1777 [Ref: M-156].

MORINE, Thomas. Private, Militia, 14th Battalion, Capt. Richard Andrew's Company, by August 13, 1777 [Ref: M-156].

MORRIS, Cleia (Celia?). See "John Hancock," q.v.

MORRIS, Cornelius. Private, Maryland Troops, enlisted by Capt. Joseph Richardson in Caroline County and passed by Col. William Richardson on August 31, 1776 [Ref: D-69]. Rendered patriotic service by providing wheat for the use of the military in August, 1782, as verified by Giles Hicks 3rd, Commissary for Caroline County [Ref: V-6636].

MORRIS, John. Private, Militia, Capt. Shadrack Liden's Company, 14th Battalion, by August 13, 1777 [Ref: M-155].

MORROW, John. Private, 6th Company, Capt. Peter Adams, 1st Maryland Line, enlisted May 7, 1776 [Ref: D-15].

MORTON, Rebecca. See "Henry Downes," q.v.

MOUN, Jaclevin (Jadwin?). Subscribed to the Oath of Allegiance and Fidelity in 1780 [Ref: L-116].

MOUNTAIN, Thomas. Subscribed to the Oath of Allegiance and Fidelity in 1780 [Ref: L-116].

MOWBREY, Aaron. Private, Militia, Capt. John Stafford's Company, 14th Battalion, by August 13, 1777 [Ref: M-156].

MULLIKIN, Joseph (1750 -   ). Private, Militia, Capt. John Mitchell's Company, 14th Battalion, by August 13, 1777 [Ref: M-154]. Second Lieutenant, August 14, 1779 [Ref: M-106 (which spelled the name "Mullikan"), E-493]. Subscribed to the Oath of Allegiance and Fidelity before the Hon. Charles Dickinson on March 1, 1778 [Ref: J-1418]. Aged 35 in a 1785 deposition [Ref: T-11].

MUNNETT, Abram. Private, Militia, Capt. John Stafford's Company, 14th Battalion, by August 13, 1777 [Ref: M-156].

MUNNETT, William. Private, Militia, Capt. Joseph Richardson's Company, 14th Battalion, by August 13, 1777 [Ref: M-154].

MUNNETT, William. Private, Militia, Capt. John Stafford's Company, 14th Battalion, by August 13, 1777 [Ref: M-156].

MURPHEY, John. Subscribed to the Oath of Allegiance and Fidelity (made his mark that resembled a small backwards "C") before the Hon. Richard Mason on March 2, 1778 [Ref: J-1814].

MURPHY, William. Private, Militia, Capt. Joseph Douglass' Company, 14th Battalion, by August 13, 1777 [Ref: M-156]. Seaman, enlisted June 12, 1782 to serve on the barge "Fearnaught" under Capt. Edward Spedden, and was paid £3 bounty for enlisting; physical description given as 5' 9" tall with a dark complexion [Ref: D-612].

MURRAY, Alexander. Second Lieutenant, 6th Company, Capt. Peter Adams, 1st Maryland Line, commissioned January 3, 1776 [Ref: D-13].

MUSGROVE, Catharine. See "Joseph Douglass," q.v.

NABB, Polly. See "Henry Casson, Jr.," q.v.

NAGLE, William. Private, 6th Company, Capt. Peter Adams, 1st Maryland Line, enlisted February 24, 1776 [Ref: D-15].

NECESSARY, Thomas. Rendered patriotic service by providing wheat for the use of the military in August, 1782, as verified by Giles Hicks 3rd, Commissary for Caroline County [Ref: V-6636].

NEEDLES, John. Private, Maryland Troops, enlisted by Capt. Joseph Richardson in Caroline County and passed by Col. William Richardson on August 31, 1776 [Ref: D-69].

NEGRO DICK. Private (recruit), Maryland Troops, enrolled in Caroline County by William Whiteley, County Lieutenant, on August 14, 1781 to serve in the Maryland Line until December 10, 1781 [Ref: D-385].

NEILE, Samuel. Rendered patriotic service by providing wheat for the use of the military in August, 1782, as verified by Giles Hicks 3rd, Commissary for Caroline County [Ref: V-6636].

NELSON, John. Private, Militia, Capt. William Hopper's Company, 28th Battalion, by August 13, 1777 [Ref: M-151].

NEVELL (NERVILLE), Robert. Private, 5th Maryland Line, enlisted on May 18, 1778 [Ref: D-234]. Rendered patriotic service by providing wheat for the use of the military in August, 1782, as verified by Giles Hicks 3rd, Commissary for Caroline County [Ref: V-6636].

NEWCOMB, John. Private, Militia, Capt. Samuel Jackson's Company, 28th Battalion, by August 13, 1777 [Ref: M-153]. "John Nucomb" married Mary Swift by license dated October 16, 1779 [Ref: X-11].

NEWELLS, Mary. See "Bentol Stevens," q.v.

NEWMAN, Ann. See "William Frampton," q.v.

NEWMAN, Betsey. See "Levin Blades," q.v.

NEWMAN, Harry Wright. See "William Holland" and "Joseph Douglass," q.v.

NEWNAM, Joseph. Private, Militia, 14th Battalion, Capt. Joseph Richardson's Company, by August 13, 1777 [Ref: M-154].

NEWNAM, Nixon Sylvester. Private, Militia, Capt. William Haslett's Company, 28th Battalion, by August 13, 1777 [Ref: M-152].

NICHOLS, --?--. See "Henry Downes," q.v.

NICHOLS (NICOLS), Charles. Subscribed to the Oath of Allegiance and Fidelity before the Hon. Henry Downes, Jr. on March 2, 1778 [Ref: J-1814]. Charles Nicols married Mary Smith on July 23, 1754 and a daughter Margarett Nicols was born November 20, 1755 [Ref: K-26, K-27].

NICHOLS, Edward. See "Isaac Nichols," q.v.

NICHOLS, Henry. See "Henry Downes," q.v.

NICHOLS (NICOLS), Iky. Private, Militia, Capt. Joseph Douglass' Company, 14th Battalion, by August 13, 1777 [Ref: M-156].

NICHOLS (NICOLS), Isaac. Private, Militia, Capt. Joseph Douglass' Company, 14th Battalion, by August 13, 1777 [Ref: M-156]. Land commission records in 1815 and 1816 state that Isaac Nicols had died in 1810 seized of tracts called "The Grove," "Plain Dealing," and "Bartlett's Meadows," plus a sawmill, which descended to the following heirs: Edward Nicols (of full age), William Nicols (of full age), Rebecca Nicols (wife of John Handy), Tilghman Nicols (minor), Mary Nicols (minor), and Washington Nicols (minor). [Ref: T-29, I-30]. One Isaac Nicols married Mary Dean by license dated January 19, 1779, and an Isaac Nicols married Celia Wright by license dated November 24, 1787 [Ref: X-9, X-18]. See "Joseph Douglass," q.v.

NICHOLS (NICOLS), John. Private, Militia, Capt. Joseph Douglass' Company, 14th Battalion, by August 13, 1777 [Ref: M-156].

NICHOLS (NICOLS), Joseph. Private, Light Horse Troops, Capt. Henry Dickinson's Company, June 12, 1781 [Ref: M-157].

NICHOLS (NICOLS), Joseph. Second Lieutenant, Militia, Capt. Joseph Douglass' Company, 14th Battalion, May 14, 1776 to at least by August 13, 1777 [Ref: M-107 (which spelled the name "Nicholls"), A-424 (which spelled the name "Nicolls"), M-156].

NICHOLS (NICOLS), Margarett. See "Charles Nichols," q.v.

NICHOLS, Mary. See "Isaac Nichols" and "Joseph Douglass," q.v.

NICHOLS, Rebecca. See "Joseph Douglass" and "Isaac Nichols," q.v.

NICHOLS (NICOLS), Thomas. Private, Militia, Capt. Joseph Douglass' Company, 14th Battalion, by August 13, 1777 [Ref: M-156].

NICHOLS, Tilghman. See "Isaac Nichols," q.v.

NICHOLS, Washington and William. See "Isaac Nichols," q.v.

NICHOLSON, Zachariah. Private, 6th Company, Capt. Peter Adams, 1st Maryland Line, enlisted January 22, 1776 [Ref: D-14].

NOBLE, Caleb. See "Levin Noble," q.v.

NOBLE, Charity. See "Levin Noble," q.v.

NOBLE, Frances. See "Henry Downes" and "Philemon Downes," q.v.

NOBLE, Levin. Private, Militia, Capt. Joseph Douglass' Company, 14th Battalion, by August 13, 1777 [Ref: M-156]. Rendered patriotic service by providing wheat for the use of the military in August, 1782, as verified by Giles Hicks 3rd, Commissary for Caroline County [Ref: V-6636]. In an 1816 land commission record it stated that Levin Noble had died intestate (date not given), seized of tracts called "Mt. Andrew," "Nabb's Ceasant" and "Double Purchase" and leaving a widow (then living, but name not given) and the following children: Nancy Noble (married William Williams), Tamsey Noble (married Thomas Hurt and died leaving issue), Charity Noble, Levin Noble, Caleb Noble, Nathan Noble, Summers Noble, and William Noble (the petitioner), all of Ross County, Ohio. It also noted that "William Noble, an uncle, occupies the farm." [Ref: T-32, and a notice in the *Republican Star* newspaper on April 6, 1819]. Levin Noble married first to Ann Ward by license dated December 31, 1779, second to Mary White Ward by license dated March 30, 1789, and died before August 6, 1805 in Ohio [Ref: X-11, X-19, Y-2154, which latter source stated he rendered patriotic service in Virginia].

NOBLE, Nancy. See "Levin Noble," q.v.

NOBLE, Nathan. See "Levin Noble," q.v.

NOBLE, Rhoda. Rendered patriotic service by providing wheat for the use of the military in August, 1782, as verified by Giles Hicks 3rd, Commissary for Caroline County [Ref: V-6636].

NOBLE, Richard. Private, Militia, Capt. Joseph Douglass' Company, 14th Battalion, by August 13, 1777 [Ref: M-156].

NOBLE, Summers. See "Levin Noble," q.v.

NOBLE, Tamsey. See "Levin Noble," q.v.

NOBLE, William. See "Levin Noble," q.v.

NOEL, Thomas. Captain of a sloop (name not given) "lying at his wharf" on March 1, 1778, at which time the Hon. Peter Richardson administered the Oath of Allegiance and Fidelity to his crew [Ref: J-1814].

NOELL, Thomas. Private, Militia, 14th Battalion, Capt. Joseph Richardson's Company, by August 13, 1777 [Ref: M-154]. Subscribed to the Oath of Allegiance and Fidelity before the Hon. Charles Dickinson on March 1, 1778 [Ref: J-1418]. On December 7, 1780 "Thomas Nowell" was recommended for an appointment as one of the magistrates for Caroline County [Ref: G-200].

NOLAND (NOWLAND), Matthias. Private (draft), Maryland Troops, furnished in Caroline County by William Whiteley, County Lieutenant, on April 16, 1781 [Ref: D-368]. Rendered patriotic service by providing wheat for the use of the military in August, 1782, as verified by Giles Hicks 3rd, Commissary for Caroline County [Ref: V-6636]. Subscribed to the Oath of Allegiance and Fidelity before the Hon. Richard Mason on March 2, 1778 [Ref: J-1814].

NOLEE, William. Rendered patriotic service by providing wheat for the use of the military in August, 1782, as verified by Giles Hicks 3rd, Commissary for Caroline County [Ref: V-6636].

NOOTS, Thomas. See "Thomas Knotts," q.v.

NUNAR, Jacob. Rendered patriotic service by providing wheat for the use of the military in August, 1782, as verified by Giles Hicks 3rd, Commissary for Caroline County [Ref: V-6636].

OLDFIELD, Henry. Private, Militia, Capt. Thomas Hughlett's Company, 28th Battalion, by August 13, 1777 [Ref: M-153].

OLDFIELD, Tacy. See "James Black," q.v.

OLDHAM, Anne. See "Joshua Clark," q.v.

OLDHAM, Edward. See "William Hopper," q.v.

OLDHAM, Elizabeth. See "William Hopper," q.v.

OPENHAM, Peter. See "Peter Oxenham," q.v.

ORAM, John. Private, Militia, Capt. John Mitchell's Company, 14th Battalion, by August 13, 1777 [Ref: M-154]. John Oram married Mary Marshall by license dated October 30, 1775 [Ref: X-6].

ORRELL, Alice. Rendered patriotic service by providing wheat for the use of the military in August, 1782, as verified by Giles Hicks 3rd, Commissary for Caroline County [Ref: V-6636].

ORRELL, Durdin. Private, Militia, Capt. William Chipley's Company, 28th Battalion, by August 13, 1777 [Ref: M-153].

ORRELL, Francis (1721 - after 1788). Subscribed to the Oath of Allegiance and Fidelity before the Hon. Thomas Hardcastle on February 20, 1778 [Ref: J-1814, which spelled the name "Orrill"]. Rendered patriotic service by providing wheat for the use of the military in August, 1782, as verified by Giles Hicks 3rd, Commissary for Caroline County [Ref: V-6636]. Aged 67 in a 1788 deposition [Ref: T-13].

ORRELL, John. Subscribed to the Oath of Allegiance and Fidelity before the Hon. Benson Stainton on January 29, 1779 [Ref: N-46].

ORRELL, Mary. See "John Hardcastle," q.v.

ORRELL, Robert. Rendered patriotic service by providing wheat for the use of the military in August, 1782, as verified by Giles Hicks 3rd, Commissary for Caroline County [Ref: V-6636]. Robert Orrell married Margaret Bayley by license dated June 21, 1781 [Ref: X-13].

ORRELL, Thomas. Private, Militia, Capt. John Stafford's Company, 14th Battalion, by August 13, 1777 [Ref: M-156]. Subscribed to the Oath of Allegiance and Fidelity in 1781 [Ref: L-117]. Rendered patriotic service by providing wheat for the use of the military in August, 1782, as verified by Giles Hicks 3rd, Commissary for Caroline County [Ref: V-6636]. One Thomas Orrell married Sarah Sommers [Summers] by license dated June 1, 1774, and a Thomas Orrell married Elizabeth Rumbley by license dated February 19, 1779 [Ref: X-3, X-10].

ORRELL, Thomas, of Francis. Subscribed to the Oath of Allegiance and Fidelity before the Hon. Matthew Driver on February 1, 1778 [Ref: J-1814, which spelled the name "Orrill"]. See the other "Thomas Orrell," q.v.

ORRELL, William. See "John Hardcastle," q.v.
OSBURN, Mary Douglass. See "Joseph Douglass," q.v.
OUTERBRIDGE, James. Private, Militia, Capt. Joseph Douglass' Company, 14th Battalion, by August 13, 1777 [Ref: M-156].
OUTERBRIDGE, Leonard. Private, Militia, Capt. Joseph Douglass' Company, 14th Battalion, by August 13, 1777 [Ref: M-156]. Private, 2nd Maryland Line, enlisted May 1, 1778, and discharged April 25, 1781 [Ref: D-148, D-550].
OUTERBRIDGE, Stephen. Private, 5th Maryland Line, enlisted May 15, 1778 and reportedly "deserted" in September, 1780 [Ref: D-236].
OVERSTOCK (OVERSTOCKS), James. Private, Militia, Capt. William Hopper's Company, 28th Battalion, by August 13, 1777 [Ref: M-151]. James Overstock married Elizabeth Perry by license dated October 10, 1783 [Ref: X-15].
OWENS, William. Private, Militia, Capt. Andrew Fountain's Company, 14th Battalion, by August 13, 1777 [Ref: M-157]. William Owens married Elizabeth Meffin by license recorded January 28, 1775 [Ref: X-5].
OXENHAM, Elizabeth. See "Aaron Downes," q.v.
OXENHAM, Mary. See "Giles Hicks" and "Peter Oxenham," q.v.
OXENHAM, Peter (1756 -   ). Private, Militia, Capt. Henry Downes' Company, 28th Battalion, by August 13, 1777 [Ref: M-152]. Rendered patriotic service by providing wheat for the use of the military in September, 1782, as verified by Giles Hicks 3rd, Commissary for Caroline County [Ref: V-6636, where the name looked like "Peter Openham"]. Peter Oxenham, son of William and Mary Oxenham, was born February 8, 1756 [Ref: K-26].
OXENHAM, William. See "Peter Oxenham," q.v.
OZMONT, Richard. Private, Militia, Capt. Joseph Douglass' Company, 14th Battalion, by August 13, 1777 [Ref: M-156]. Ensign, Militia, Capt. Hugh McBride's Company, April 9, 1778 [Ref: M-109 (which spelled the name "Ozment"), E-23]. Rendered patriotic service by providing wheat for the use of the military in August, 1782, as verified by Giles Hicks 3rd, Commissary for Caroline County [Ref: V-6636, which spelled the name "Ozmant" and also "Ozman"].
OZMONT, Richard Jr. Private, Militia, Capt. Joseph Douglass' Company, 14th Battalion, by August 13, 1777 [Ref: M-156]. Richard Ozmont, Jr. married Elizabeth Lecompte (Lacompte) by license dated July 16, 1778 [Ref: X-8].
OZMONT, Samuel. Private, Militia, Capt. Nehemiah Andrew's Company, 14th Battalion, by August 13, 1777 [Ref: M-155].
OZMONT, Thomas. Private, Militia, 14th Battalion, Capt. Joseph Richardson's Company, by August 13, 1777 [Ref: M-154]. Thomas Ozment married Rachel Sylvester by license dated November 26, 1778 [Ref: X-9].
OZWELL, Dorothy. See "James Hambleton," q.v.
PADGETT, William. Private, Militia, Capt. Samuel Jackson's Company, 28th Battalion, by August 13, 1777 [Ref: M-153].
PAINE, John. See "John Payne," q.v.

123

PARKER, Allen. Private, Militia, Capt. John Mitchell's Company, 14th Battalion, by August 13, 1777 [Ref: M-155].

PARKER, Elizabeth. See "John Payne," q.v.

PARKER, Jesse. Private, Maryland Troops, enrolled by Lieut. Levin Handy in Caroline County and passed by Col. William Hopewell on August 4, 1776 [Ref: D-69].

PARKER, Mary. See "Risdon Fisher," q.v.

PARMARR (PARMER), James. Private, Militia, Capt. Andrew Fountain's Company, 14th Battalion, by August 13, 1777. Ensign, Militia, Capt. Peter Rich's Company, April 9, 1778 [Ref: M-157 (which listed the name as "Parnarr?"), E-23 (which spelled the name "Parmer"), M-110].

PARMARR, Sophia. See "James Porter," q.v.

PARMARR (PERMARR), William. Private, Militia, Capt. Thomas Hughlett's Company, 28th Battalion, by August 13, 1777 [Ref: M-153, which listed the name as "Parnarr"]. Rendered patriotic service by providing wheat for the use of the military in September, 1782, as verified by Giles Hicks 3rd, Commissary for Caroline County [Ref: V-6636].

PARROTT (PARROT), Christopher. Sergeant, 2nd Maryland Line, 1777, who was discharged January 10, 1780, but was reenlisted by Col. Forrest "to take up deserts till August, 1780." [Ref: D-150].

PARROTT (PARRATT), Elizabeth. See "William Love," q.v.

PARROTT (PARRATT), Sarah. See "James Hardcastle" and "Timothy Price," q.v.

PARROTT, Silah. Private, Maryland Troops, enlisted by Capt. Joseph Richardson in Caroline County and passed by Col. William Richardson on August 31, 1776 [Ref: D-69].

PARROTT, William. Private, Militia, Capt. Thomas Hughlett's Company, 28th Battalion, by August 13, 1777 [Ref: M-153]. Rendered patriotic service by providing wheat for the use of the military in August, 1782, as verified by Giles Hicks 3rd, Commissary for Caroline County [Ref: V-6636].

PAULSON (PAWSON), Matthew. Private, Militia, Capt. Vincent Price's Company, 28th Battalion, by August 13, 1777 [Ref: M-152, which misspelled the name as "Paulon"]. Matthew Pawson married Mary Caulk by license recorded August 9, 1775 [Ref: X-6].

PAYNE (PAINE), Isaac. Private, Militia, Capt. John Stafford's Company, 14th Battalion, by August 13, 1777 [Ref: M-156]. Rendered patriotic service by providing wheat for the use of the military in August, 1782, as verified by Giles Hicks 3rd, Commissary for Caroline County [Ref: V-6636].

PAYNE (PAINE), John. Private, Militia, Capt. John Stafford's Company, 14th Battalion, by August 13, 1777 [Ref: M-156]. Rendered patriotic service by providing wheat for the use of the military in August, 1782, as verified by Giles Hicks 3rd, Commissary for Caroline County [Ref: V-6636]. John Payne married Elizabeth Parker by license dated July 6, 1778 [Ref: X-8].

PEARCE, Henrietta. See "Thomas Hardcastle," q.v.

PEARCE, James. See "Thomas Hardcastle," q.v.
PEARSON, Richard. Private, Militia, 14th Battalion, Capt. Richard Andrew's Company, by August 13, 1777 [Ref: M-156].
PEARSON, William. Private, Militia, Capt. Andrew Fountain's Company, 14th Battalion, by August 13, 1777 [Ref: M-157].
PEDEN, Veronica Clarke. See "Joseph Douglass," q.v.
PENDLETON, Serena and family. See "Benjamin Sylvester," q.v.
PENKEND (PENKIND, PINKIND), Vinson or Vincent. Subscribed to the Oath of Allegiance and Fidelity in 1780 [Ref: L-118]. Rendered patriotic service by providing wheat for the use of the military in August, 1782, as verified by Giles Hicks 3rd, Commissary for Caroline County [Ref: V-6636]. "Vincent Pinkind" married Rebekah Young by license dated May 11, 1778, and "Vincent Pinkine" married Catharine Cooper by license dated September 3, 1790 [Ref: X-8, X-21].
PENNINGTON, Elizabeth. See "John Reynolds," q.v.
PENNINGTON, Thomas. Served on the Committee of Observation for Caroline County on August 2, 1775 [Ref: A-48].
PERRY, Deborah. See "Henry Dickinson," q.v.
PERRY, Elizabeth. See "James Overstock," q.v.
PERRY, Henry. Seaman, enlisted June 1, 1782 to serve on the barge "Fearnaught" under Capt. Edward Spedden, and was paid £3 bounty for enlisting; physical description given as 5' 6" tall with a fair complexion [Ref: D-611].
PERRY, James. Private, Militia, Capt. Shadrack Liden's Company, 14th Battalion, by August 13, 1777 [Ref: M-155].
PERRY, Sarah. See "James Collins," q.v.
PERRY, Thomas. Private, Militia, Capt. John Mitchell's Company, 14th Battalion, by August 13, 1777 [Ref: M-155]. Seaman, enlisted June 1, 1782 to serve on the barge "Fearnaught" under Capt. Edward Spedden, and was paid £3 bounty for enlisting; physical description given as 5' 6" tall with a fair complexion [Ref: D-611].
PERRY, William. Private, Militia, Capt. Henry Downes' Company, 28th Battalion, by August 13, 1777 [Ref: M-152]. A William Perry married Elizabeth Porter by license dated December 3, 1779 [Ref: X-11]. "William Perry, son of Richard" was aged 45 in a 1785 deposition [Ref: T-10].
PERRY, William. Private, Militia, Capt. John Mitchell's Company, 14th Battalion, by August 13, 1777 [Ref: M-154]. See the other "William Perry," q.v.
PERT, John. Private, Militia, Capt. Shadrack Liden's Company, 14th Battalion, by August 13, 1777 [Ref: M-155]. "John Pert, ship carpenter" was aged 45 in a 1776 deposition [Ref: T-8].
PETERS, William. Private, Militia, 14th Battalion, Capt. Richard Andrew's Company, by August 13, 1777 [Ref: M-156].
PHELPS, John. Private, 6th Company, Capt. Peter Adams, 1st Maryland Line, enlisted May 20, 1776 [Ref: D-15].
PHILLIPS, Elizabeth. Rendered patriotic service by providing wheat for the use of

the military in August, 1782, as verified by Giles Hicks 3rd, Commissary for Caroline County [Ref: V-6636, which listed the name as "Elisabeth Philips"]. See "John Green," q.v.

PHILLIPS, Stephen Sr. In the 1840 census of Maryland, Stephen Phillips, Sr., age 77, a Revolutionary War pensioner, was head of household and lived in the 2nd Division of Caroline County [Ref: Q-28:4 (1987), p. 445].

PHILLYSILL, Charles. See "Hugh McBryde," q.v.

PIKE, Philip. Private, Militia, Capt. Vincent Price's Company, 28th Battalion, by August 13, 1777 [Ref: M-152].

PINDER (PINDAR), Thomas. Private, Militia, Capt. Thomas Hughlett's Company, 28th Battalion, by August 13, 1777 [Ref: M-153]. Rendered patriotic service by providing wheat for the use of the military in August, 1782, as verified by Giles Hicks 3rd, Commissary for Caroline County [Ref: V-6636].

PINFIELD, James. Private, Militia, Capt. William Haslett's Company, 28th Battalion, by August 13, 1777 [Ref: M-152].

PINKIND, Vincent. See "Vincent Penkend," q.v.

PIPPIN, Robert. Private, Militia, Capt. John Fauntleroy's Company, 28th Battalion, by August 13, 1777 [Ref: M-154].

PIPPIN (PIPIN), Uriah. Private, Militia, Capt. John Fauntleroy's Company, 28th Battalion, by August 13, 1777 [Ref: M-154].

PIPPIN, William. Private, Militia, Capt. John Fauntleroy's Company, 28th Battalion, by August 13, 1777 [Ref: M-154].

PIRKENS, Joseph. Private, 6th Company, Capt. Peter Adams, 1st Maryland Line, enlisted January 30, 1776 [Ref: D-14].

PLOUGHMAN, Philip. Private, Militia, Capt. Nehemiah Andrew's Company, 14th Battalion, by August 13, 1777 [Ref: M-155].

POLK, William. Court Justice, 1775 [Ref: Z-1].

POOLE (POOL), John. Private, Militia, Capt. Joseph Douglass' Company, 14th Battalion, by August 13, 1777 [Ref: M-156]. Rendered patriotic service by providing wheat for the use of the military in August, 1782, as verified by Giles Hicks 3rd, Commissary for Caroline County [Ref: V-6636].

POOR, Henry. Private, Militia, Capt. John Fauntleroy's Company, 28th Battalion, by August 13, 1777 [Ref: M-154].

PORTER, Elizabeth. See "William Perry," q.v.

PORTER, Francis. Private, Militia, Capt. William Hopper's Company, 28th Battalion, by August 13, 1777 [Ref: M-151].

PORTER, George. Rendered patriotic service by providing wheat for the use of the military in August, 1782, as verified by Giles Hicks 3rd, Commissary for Caroline County [Ref: V-6636].

PORTER, James. Private, Militia, Capt. William Chipley's Company, 28th Battalion, by August 13, 1777 [Ref: M-153]. Rendered patriotic service by providing wheat for the use of the military in August, 1782, as verified by Giles Hicks 3rd, Commissary for Caroline County [Ref: V-6636]. James Porter married

Sophia Parmarr by license recorded August 9, 1775 [Ref: X-5].
PORTER, Lawrence. Private, Militia, Capt. Andrew Fountain's Company, 14th Battalion, by August 13, 1777 [Ref: M-157].
PORTER, Mary. Rendered patriotic service by providing wheat for the use of the military in August, 1782, as verified by Giles Hicks 3rd, Commissary for Caroline County [Ref: V-6636].
PORTER, Rhoda. See "Richard Thomas," q.v.
PORTER, Robert. Private, Militia, Capt. Andrew Fountain's Company, 14th Battalion, by August 13, 1777 [Ref: M-157].
PORTER, Tilly. See "Thomas Roe," q.v.
POSTLETHWAITE (POSTLEWAIT)), Robert. Private, Militia, Capt. William Haslett's Company, 28th Battalion, by March 9, 1776, and Ensign on April 10, 1776; Captain, April 9, 1778 [Ref: M-152 (which spelled the name "Poslethwaite"), M-112, A-230, A-320, E-23, J-1814]. Subscribed to the Oath of Allegiance and Fidelity before the Hon. Matthew Driver on February 1, 1778 [Ref: J-1814]. Robert Postlethwaite married Nancy Kenton by license dated July 14, 1789 [Ref: X-19].
POTTER, Ann Webb. See "William Richardson," q.v.
POTTER, Catherine. See "Thomas Goldsborough," q.v.
POTTER, Jane. See "John Hardcastle" and "Thomas Hardcastle" and "Nathaniel Potter," q.v.
POTTER, Miss. See "Foster Goldsborough," q.v.
POTTER, Nathaniel. Son of Capt. Zabdiel Potter who was a mariner who came to Maryland from Rhode Island as early as 1730, resided at "Potter's Hall" five miles south of Denton, founded Potter's Landing (a commercial center on the Choptank River) in Dorchester County, and died at sea in 1761. Nathaniel married Jane Douglass on March 22, 1778 and died between November 25 and December 7, 1780 in Caroline County, probably without issue. Jane Potter, widow (1759-1786), married John Hardcastle (1757-1810), son of Thomas Hardcastle, on June 11, 1781 [Ref: R-657]. Nathaniel Potter attended the Maryland Conventions from 1774 to 1776 and represented Caroline County in the Lower House, 1778-1779 [Ref: R-70, R-71, R-74, R-80, O-1, O-4, O-28, G-200]. Court Justice, 1773-1780; Justice of the Orphans' Court, 1777-1780; Commissioner of Tax, 1777-1778; Sheriff, commissioned February 24, 1778, resigned March 9, 1778; Purchasing Agent for the Army of the Unites States, 1778-1780; Subscription Officer, Continental Loan Office, 1779 [Ref: R-657, P-147, N-70, C-520, C-551, A-4, E-140, E-518, F-215, G-200, Z-1]. Subscribed to the Oath of Allegiance and Fidelity before the Hon. Charles Dickinson on March 1, 1778 [Ref: J-1418]. Captain, Militia, 14th Battalion, May 24, 1776; First Major, June 24, 1777; Lieutenant Colonel, April 9, 1778 [Ref: M-154, M-112, A-442, C-299, E-23]. Justice who administered the Oath of Allegiance and Fidelity in 1778 [Ref: J-1814, E-249]. On October 26, 1779, Nathaniel Potter wrote to the Governor of Maryland and informed him of his inability to fulfill his

commission as purchaser of wheat and flour [Ref: P-246]. See "John Hardcastle" and "Thomas Hardcastle" and "James Seth" and "James Lawrence," q.v.

POTTER, William. See "Foster Goldsborough" and "William Richardson," q.v.

POTTER, Zebdial. Private, Militia, Capt. John Stafford's Company, 14th Battalion, by August 13, 1777 [Ref: M-156].

POTTER, Zebdiel (Zebdiah, Zabdiel). Son of Zabdiel Potter (died 1761) who came to Maryland from Rhode Island as early as 1730 [Ref: R-657]. Ensign, Militia, Capt. Joseph Richardson's Company, 14th Battalion, resigned May 15, 1776; mentioned as "Surgeon, 14th Battalion" on same date [Ref: M-112 (which misspelled the name as "Libdial"), E-427]. In 1776, "Capt. Zabdiel Potter, unable to raise a company, resigned and was appointed Surgeon's Mate by the Council of Safety. As his successor the Council of Safety appointed Joseph Richardson." [Ref: D-68]. "Zabdiel Potter (MDD)" subscribed to the Oath of Allegiance and Fidelity before the Hon. Nathaniel Potter on March 2, 1778 [Ref: J-1814]. "Dr. Zebdiel Potter" rendered patriotic service by providing wheat for the use of the military in September, 1782, as verified by Giles Hicks, Deputy Commissary for Caroline County [Ref: P-549]. "Zabdiel Potter" was aged 33 in a 1780 deposition [Ref: T-3]. On December 7, 1780, "Zebulon Potter" was recommended for an appointment as one of the magistrates in Caroline County [Ref: G-200]. "Zebdiel Potter" was a Justice of the Peace from 1782 to at least 1784, and Justice of the Orphans' Court in 1783 and 1784 [Ref: I-45, I-341, I-504 (which spelled the name "Zabdiel Potter"), I-371]. See "Nathaniel Potter," q.v.

POTTS, John. Two men with this name were privates in the militia in Capt. William Chipley's Company, 28th Battalion, by August 13, 1777 [Ref: M-153]. "John Potts, taylor" was aged 36 in a 1782 deposition [Ref: T-11].

POTTS, Thomas (Tom). Private (substitute), Maryland Troops, furnished in Caroline County by William Whiteley, County Lieutenant, on April 16, 1781 [Ref: D-368].

POWELL, George. Private, Militia, Capt. Samuel Jackson's Company, 28th Battalion, by August 13, 1777 [Ref: M-153]. Rendered patriotic service by providing wheat for the use of the military in August, 1782, as verified by Giles Hicks 3rd, Commissary for Caroline County [Ref: V-6636].

POWELL (POWEL), Henry. Seaman, enlisted June 4, 1782 to serve on the barge "Fearnaught" under Capt. Edward Spedden, and was paid £3 bounty for enlisting; physical description given as 5' 8 1/2" tall with a dark complexion [Ref: D-612]. Henry Powell married Dorothy Holland by license dated December 28, 1779 [Ref: X-11].

POWELL, James. Private, Militia, Capt. Samuel Jackson's Company, 28th Battalion, by August 13, 1777 [Ref: M-153].

POWELL, John. Private, 6th Company, Capt. Peter Adams, 1st Maryland Line, enlisted January 30, 1776 [Ref: D-14]. Private, Militia, Capt. Samuel Jackson's Company, 28th Battalion, by August 13, 1777 [Ref: M-153]. There were two men named John Powell who were privates in the 5th Maryland Line: one enlisted on March 2, 1778 and the other enlisted on June 19, 1778 [Ref: D-237].

PRATT, Jacob (1758 -   ). Private, Militia, Capt. Henry Downes' Company, 28th Battalion, by August 13, 1777 [Ref: M-152]. Aged 28 in a 1786 deposition [Ref: T-21].

PRATT, Jane. See "Robert Hardcastle" and "Thomas Hardcastle," q.v.

PRATT, Nathaniel. Private, Militia, Capt. Henry Downes' Company, 28th Battalion, by August 13, 1777 [Ref: M-152].

PRATT, Sarah. See "Greenbury Matthews," q.v.

PRICE, Andrew. Private, Maryland Troops, enlisted by Capt. Joseph Richardson in Caroline County and passed by Col. William Richardson on August 31, 1776 [Ref: D-69]. Private, Militia, Capt. Vincent Price's Company, 28th Battalion, by August 13, 1777 [Ref: M-152]. Subscribed to the Oath of Allegiance and Fidelity before the Hon. Henry Downes, Jr. on March 2, 1778 [Ref: J-1814]. Rendered patriotic service by providing beef for the use of the military in December, 1782, as verified by Giles Hicks III, Commissary for Caroline County [Ref: P-573]. Andrew Price married Prudence White by license dated January 23, 1778 [Ref: X-7].

PRICE, James. Rendered patriotic service by providing wheat for the use of the military in August, 1782, as verified by Giles Hicks 3rd, Commissary for Caroline County [Ref: V-6636]. See "William Richardson," q.v.

PRICE, Katharine. See "Thomas Smith," q.v.

PRICE, Mary. See "William Richardson" and "Richard Wootters," q.v.

PRICE, Morgan. On February 18, 1780, he filed a certificate in Caroline County Court that he had subscribed to the Oath of Allegiance and Fidelity before the Clerk of Queen Anne's County [Ref: N-67].

PRICE, Neale (Neal). Appointed to be Constable of Tuckahoe Hundred on December 15, 1778 [Ref: N-45]. First Lieutenant, Militia, Capt. Philemon Downes' Company, December 17, 1781 [Ref: M-112, I-27].

PRICE, Nicholas. Private, Militia, Capt. John Stafford's Company, 14th Battalion, by August 13, 1777 [Ref: M-156]. "Nicholas Price" was aged 52 in a 1782 deposition and "Capt. Nicholas Price" was aged 52 in a 1783 deposition [Ref: T-5, T-6].

PRICE, O'Neal (Oneal). Private, Militia, Capt. Henry Downes' Company, 28th Battalion, by August 13, 1777 [Ref: M-152].

PRICE, Rebecca. See "Thomas Chance," q.v.

PRICE, Susanna. See "Charles Walker," q.v.

PRICE, Timothy. Private, Light Horse Troops, Capt. Henry Dickinson's Company, June 12, 1781 [Ref: M-157]. Timothy Price married Ann Dudley, of Talbot County, by license dated October 29, 1774 in Caroline County, and Timothy Lane Price married Sarah Parratt by license dated August 19, 1780 [Ref: X-4, X-12].

PRICE, Vincent (c1718 - after 1786). Captain, Militia, 28th Battalion, by August 13, 1777. Lieutenant Colonel, April 9, 1778. Colonel, December 17, 1781 [Ref:

M-112, M-113, M-151, E-23, I-27, J-1814]. Subscribed to the Oath of Allegiance and Fidelity before the Hon. Henry Downes, Jr. on March 2, 1778 [Ref: J-1814]. "Vinson Price" was aged 56 in a 1774 deposition and "Col. Vincent Price" was aged 63 in a 1780 deposition, aged 63 in a 1782 deposition, aged 64 in a 1783 deposition, and 68 in a 1786 deposition [Ref: T-3, T-5, T-6, T-11].

PRICE, Vincent. Adjutant to the 14th Battalion of Militia by June 8, 1776 [Ref: A-481, which record referred to him as "Mr. Vincent Price" and yet his deposition was signed "Vincent Price, Jr."]. Captain, Militia, 14th Battalion, July 24, 1780 [Ref: M-112, F-230, G-27]. A "Vincent Lowe Price" married Elizabeth Garey by license dated September 16, 1779 [Ref: X-11]. See "Vincent Price, Jr.," q.v.

PRICE, Vincent Jr. Private, Militia, Capt. Vincent Price's Company, 28th Battalion, by August 13, 1777 [Ref: M-152]. Lieutenant, Light Horse Troops, Capt. Henry Dickinson's Company, June 12, 1781 [Ref: M-157, G-475 (which listed the name without the "Jr."), M-113]. Subscribed to the Oath of Allegiance and Fidelity before the Hon. Henry Downes, Jr. on March 2, 1778 [Ref: J-1814]. See "Vincent Price," q.v.

PRIEST, Elizabeth. See "James Swiggate," q.v.

PRIEST, Richard. Private, Militia, Capt. William Hopper's Company, 28th Battalion, by August 13, 1777 [Ref: M-151].

PRITCHARD, Edward. Private, Militia, 14th Battalion, Capt. Richard Andrew's Company, by August 13, 1777 [Ref: M-156].

PRITCHARD, Henry. Private, Militia, Capt. Joseph Douglass' Company, 14th Battalion, by August 13, 1777 [Ref: M-156].

PRITCHARD, John. Private, Militia, 14th Battalion, Capt. Richard Andrew's Company, by August 13, 1777 [Ref: M-156].

PRITCHETT, Edward. Rendered patriotic service by providing wheat for the use of the military in August, 1782, as verified by Giles Hicks 3rd, Commissary for Caroline County [Ref: V-6636]. Edward Pritchett married Priscilla Minner by license dated February 15, 1779 [Ref: X-10].

PRITCHETT, Elizabeth. See "Robert Wilson," q.v.

PRITCHETT, Rebekah. See "Reubin Connerly," q.v.

PROGHARVE (PROGHAWE?), Sylvinus. Private, Militia, Capt. John Fauntleroy's Company, 28th Battalion, by August 13, 1777 [Ref: M-154].

PROTHELO, Sylvanus. Rendered patriotic service by providing wheat for the use of the military in August, 1782, as verified by Giles Hicks 3rd, Commissary for Caroline County [Ref: V-6636].

PROUCE, John. Private, Militia, Capt. John Mitchell's Company, 14th Battalion, by August 13, 1777 [Ref: M-155]. Private (draft), Maryland Troops, enrolled in Caroline County by William Whiteley, County Lieutenant, on August 14, 1781 to serve in the Maryland Line until December 10, 1781 [Ref: D-385].

PROUCE (PRONCE?), Rachel. See "William Andrew," q.v.

PROUCE (PROUS), Thomas. Private, Militia, Capt. John Mitchell's Company, 14th Battalion, by August 13, 1777 [Ref: M-154]. Subscribed to the Oath of

Allegiance and Fidelity before the Hon. Charles Dickinson on March 1, 1778 [Ref: J-1418].

PURNELL, Adeline. See "Benjamin Sylvester," q.v.

PURNELL, Clarissa. See "Benjamin Sylvester," q.v.

PURNELL, Frederick. See "Benjamin Sylvester," q.v.

PURNELL, Isaac. See "Benjamin Sylvester," q.v.

PURNELL (PURNAL, PURNALL), John (1739 -   ). Private, Militia, Capt. William Chipley's Company, 28th Battalion, by August 13, 1777 [Ref: M-153]. Subscribed to the Oath of Allegiance and Fidelity before the Hon. Henry Downes, Jr. on March 2, 1778 [Ref: J-1814]. "John Purnell" was aged 40 in a 1779 deposition and "John Purnall" was aged 43 in a 1782 deposition [Ref: T-2, T-4].

PURNELL, Martha. See "Benjamin Sylvester," q.v.

PURNELL, Mary. See "Benjamin Sylvester," q.v.

PURNELL (PURNAL, PURNALL), Richard. Private, Militia, Capt. William Chipley's Company, 28th Battalion, by August 13, 1777 [Ref: M-153].

PURNELL, Serena. See "Benjamin Sylvester," q.v.

PURNELL (PURNALL), Thomas. Private, Militia, Capt. William Hopper's Company, 28th Battalion, by August 13, 1777 [Ref: M-151]. Second Lieutenant, Militia, Capt. Thomas Knotts' Company, December 17, 1781 [Ref: M-113, I-27]. Thomas Purnell married Katharine Hargidine by license dated June 7, 1785 [Ref: X-16].

PURNELL (PURNAL, PURNALL), William. Private, Militia, Capt. William Hopper's Company, 28th Battalion, by August 13, 1777 [Ref: M-151]. Subscribed to the Oath of Allegiance and Fidelity before the Hon. Matthew Driver on February 1, 1778 [Ref: J-1814]. Rendered patriotic service by providing wheat for the use of the military in August, 1782, as verified by Giles Hicks 3rd, Commissary for Caroline County [Ref: V-6636].

PURNELL (PURNALL), William Jr. Private, Militia, Capt. William Hopper's Company, 28th Battalion, by August 13, 1777 [Ref: M-151]. William Purnell, Jr. married Elizabeth Cooper by license dated December 9, 1785 [Ref: X-17].

QUARTERNNIS, Tilpha (Zilpha?). See "James Merrick," q.v.

QUIGLEY, Patrick. Private, 6th Company, Capt. Peter Adams, 1st Maryland Line, enlisted February 22, 1776 [Ref: D-15].

QUINNELY, William. Private, Militia, Capt. Andrew Fountain's Company, 14th Battalion, by August 13, 1777 [Ref: M-157].

RAKES, James. Subscribed to the Oath of Allegiance and Fidelity on May 6, 1778 [Ref: P-165].

RATHALL, Thomas. Private, Militia, Capt. John Stafford's Company, 14th Battalion, by August 13, 1777 [Ref: M-156].

RAY, William. Private, 6th Company, Capt. Peter Adams, 1st Maryland Line, enlisted February 15, 1776 [Ref: D-14].

REECE (REES), David. Private, Militia, Capt. Shadrack Liden's Company, 14th

Battalion, by August 13, 1777 [Ref: M-155]. Subscribed to the Oath of Allegiance and Fidelity before the Hon. Nathaniel Potter on March 2, 1778 [Ref: J-1814].

REED, Andrew. See "Beacham Causey," q.v.

REED, Charles, of Choptank Hundred. Subscribed to the Oath of Allegiance and Fidelity before the Hon. Benson Stainton on February 2, 1778 [Ref: J-1814].

REED, Eleanor. See "Beacham Causey," q.v.

REED, Elizabeth. See "James Reed," q.v.

REED, Ezekiel. Private, Militia, 14th Battalion, Capt. Richard Andrew's Company, by August 13, 1777 [Ref: M-156].

REED, James. Private, Militia, Capt. William Chipley's Company, 28th Battalion, by August 13, 1777 [Ref: M-153]. In an 1806 (or 1808?) land commission record it stated that James Reed had died (date not given), seized of a tract called "New Nottingham Rectified" and leaving the following children: William Reed, Elizabeth Reed (minor), James Reed (minor), Thomas Reed (minor), and Samuel Reed (minor), with Henry Downes as their guardian [Ref: T-24].

REED, John. Private, Maryland Troops, enrolled by Lieut. Levin Handy in Caroline County and passed by Col. William Hopewell on August 4, 1776 [Ref: D-69].

REED, Lucretia. See "Jacob Jump," q.v.

REED, Samuel. See "James Reed," q.v.

REED, Thomas. Private, Militia, Capt. William Chipley's Company, 28th Battalion, by August 13, 1777 [Ref: M-153]. Subscribed to the Oath of Allegiance and Fidelity before the Hon. Henry Downes, Jr. on March 2, 1778 [Ref: J-1814]. See "James Reed," q.v.

REED, William. See "James Reed," q.v.

REEVES, John. Private, Militia, Capt. John Mitchell's Company, 14th Battalion, by August 13, 1777 [Ref: M-155]. Subscribed to the Oath of Allegiance and Fidelity before the Hon. Peter Richardson on February 28, 1778 [Ref: J-1814]. See "James Fisher," q.v.

REYNOLDS, John. Second Lieutenant, Maryland Troops, June 25, 1776. First Lieutenant, Militia, Capt. Vincent Price's Company, 28th Battalion, June 19, 1777. Captain, April 9, 1778, and succeeded August 14, 1779 [Ref: M-151, M-115, C-294, E-23, D-68, J-1814]. "John Reynolds, of Choptank Hundred" subscribed to the Oath of Allegiance and Fidelity before the Hon. Benson Stainton on February 2, 1778 [Ref: J-1814]. John Reynolds married Elizabeth Pennington by license recorded August 9, 1775 [Ref: X-6].

REYNOLDS, Sarah. See "Richard Swift," q.v.

RHODES (ROADS), Jeremiah. Private, Militia, Capt. John Stafford's Company, 14th Battalion, by August 13, 1777 [Ref: M-156]. Subscribed to the Oath of Allegiance and Fidelity before the Hon. Matthew Driver on February 1, 1778 [Ref: J-1814].

RICH, Araminta. See "Joseph Hurd," q.v.

RICH, James. See "Joseph Hurd," q.v.

RICH, Peter. Captain, Militia, 14th Battalion, April 9, 1778 [Ref: M-115, E-23]. Recruiting Officer, 1779-1780 [Ref: F-49].

RICH, Peter. Private, Militia, Capt. William Haslett's Company, 28th Battalion, by August 13, 1777 [Ref: M-152]. Subscribed to the Oath of Allegiance and Fidelity before the Hon. Benson Stainton on January 23, 1778 [Ref: J-1814].

RICH, William. Served on the Committee of Observation for Caroline County on August 2, 1775 [Ref: A-48]. Second Lieutenant, Militia, Capt. William Haslett's Company, 28th Battalion, by August 13, 1777 [Ref: M-152]. A list of officers in 1777 noted that William Rich was "about 4 miles out of the province, but willing to continue, and a good officer." [Ref: J-1814].

RICHARDS, Henry (Harry). First Lieutenant, Militia, Capt. Andrews' Company, 14th Battalion, March 29, 1776 [Ref: M-115, A-424]. First Lieutenant, Militia, 14th Battalion, Capt. Richard Andrew's [sic] Company, August 13, 1777 [Ref: M-156]. Rendered patriotic service by providing wheat for the use of the military in August, 1782, as verified by Giles Hicks 3rd, Commissary for Caroline County [Ref: V-6636].

RICHARDSON, Anthony. See "Philip Walker," q.v.

RICHARDSON, Charles. Private, Maryland Troops, enrolled by Lieut. Levin Handy in Caroline County and passed by Col. William Hopewell on August 2, 1776 [Ref: D-69]. Rendered patriotic service by providing wheat for the use of the military in August, 1782, as verified by Giles Hicks 3rd, Commissary for Caroline County [Ref: V-6636].

RICHARDSON, Daniel. Private, Militia, 14th Battalion, Capt. Joseph Richardson's Company, by August 13, 1777 [Ref: M-154]. Ensign, Militia, Capt. John Hooper's Company, July 24, 1780. Second Lieutenant, Militia, Capt. Cornelius Johnson's Company, December 17, 1781 [Ref: M-115, F-230, G-27, I-27]. Rendered patriotic service by providing wheat for the use of the military in August, 1782, as verified by Giles Hicks 3rd, Commissary for Caroline County [Ref: V-6636]. See "William Richardson," q.v.

RICHARDSON, Elizabeth. See "William Richardson" and "Henry Dickinson" and "Philip Walker," q.v.

RICHARDSON, John (1705 - after 1782). Subscribed to the Oath of Allegiance and Fidelity before the Hon. Charles Dickinson on March 1, 1778 [Ref: J-1418]. Aged 75 in a 1780 deposition and aged 77 in a 1782 deposition [Ref: T-3, T-4]. See "Ellis Thomas," q.v.

RICHARDSON, John (1740 -   ). Private, Militia, Capt. John Stafford's Company, 14th Battalion, by August 13, 1777 [Ref: M-156]. Rendered patriotic service by providing wheat for the use of the military in August, 1782, as verified by Giles Hicks 3rd, Commissary for Caroline County [Ref: V-6636]. Aged 45 in a 1785 deposition [Ref: T-10].

RICHARDSON, Joseph. Captain, Maryland Troops, 1776. Captain, Militia, 14th Battalion, November 16, 1776. Second Major, June 24, 1777. Major, April 9,

1778 [Ref: M-115, M-154, C-299, D-68, E-23]. "Joseph Richardson, Register of Wills" subscribed to the Oath of Allegiance and Fidelity before the Hon. Charles Dickinson on March 1, 1778 [Ref: J-1418]. On November 25, 1780, he and Thomas Hughlett were appointed by the Council of Maryland "to carry the Act to prohibit for a limited time the Exportation of Indian, &tc., by land" into execution in Caroline County [Ref: G-251]. On March 2, 1781 he was appointed County Auctioneer [Ref: G-334]. Justice of the Peace in 1783 and 1784 [Ref: I-341, I-503]. See "Joseph Richardson, Jr." and "William Richardson," q.v.

RICHARDSON, Joseph Jr. (1745 -   ). Private, Light Horse Troops, Capt. Henry Dickinson's Company, June 12, 1781 [Ref: M-157]. "Joseph Richardson, Jr." was aged 40 in a 1785 deposition and "Joseph Richardson" was aged 52 in a 1797 deposition [Ref: T-12, T-19].

RICHARDSON, Mary. See "Thomas Chance," q.v.

RICHARDSON, Perry. Private, Militia, Capt. Thomas Hughlett's Company, 28th Battalion, by August 13, 1777 [Ref: M-153].

RICHARDSON, Peter. First Lieutenant, Militia, Capt. John Mitchell's Company, 14th Battalion, by August 13, 1777 to at least April 4, 1778, and may have died thereafter [Ref: M-115, M-154, E-23]. Justice who administered the Oath of Allegiance and Fidelity in January, February, and March, 1778 [Ref: J-1814, E-249].

RICHARDSON, Philemon. Rendered patriotic service by providing wheat for the use of the military in August, 1782, as verified by Giles Hicks 3rd, Commissary for Caroline County [Ref: V-6636].

RICHARDSON, Philip. Private, Militia, Capt. Thomas Hughlett's Company, 28th Battalion, by August 13, 1777 [Ref: M-153].

RICHARDSON, Sophia. See "Henry Dickinson," q.v.

RICHARDSON, Thomas. See "William Richardson," q.v.

RICHARDSON, William (1735-1825). Son of William Richardson (a Quaker of Talbot County) and Ann Webb, William was born August 17, 1735 in Talbot County and resided at "Gilpin's Point" in that part of Dorchester County which became the Great Choptank Hundred in Caroline County after 1773. He married Elizabeth Green by 1765 and had these children: William Richardson, Jr. (became a captain), Daniel Peter Richardson, Joseph Richardson (became Clerk of Caroline County in 1818 and 1824), Thomas Richardson, Ann Webb Potter (wife of Gen. William Potter), Mary Price (wife of James Price), and Elizabeth Richardson [Ref: R-679]. William attended the Maryland Conventions in 1775 and 1776, and served in many subsequent offices: Lower House of the Maryland General Assembly from 1771 to 1776; Deputy Treasurer of the Eastern Shore in 1780; Constitution Ratification Committee in 1788; Treasurer of the Eastern Shore, 1789-1801, 1813-1825; Associate Justice, Fourth Judicial District, 1791-1793; County Court Justice, 1774; Deputy Commissary, 1774-1777; Deputy Clerk, 1774-1776, and County Clerk, from 1777 to at least 1790; Maryland State Elector, 1791 [Ref: R-679, R-71, R-72, R-74, O-4, O-28, A-10, X-5, Y-2460].

Appointed as Collector of Gold and Silver in Caroline County on February 1, 1776 [Ref: A-132]. Colonel, Militia, 14th Battalion, January 12, 1776; first active service was at the Battle of Harlem Heights in New York in 1776; assisted Gen. Henry Hooper in quelling insurrection of Tories in Somerset and Worcester Counties in 1777 [Ref: R-679, M-115]. The proceedings of the Maryland Council on September 6, 1777 indicate, in part, that "an insurrection of Tories on the borders of Queen Ann's and Caroline Counties [were] headed by some scoundrel Methodist preachers ... Col. Richardson remains in Caroline County to suppress those that are there assembled." [Ref: C-364]. "William Richardson, of Choptank Hundred" subscribed to the Oath of Allegiance and Fidelity before the Hon. Benson Stainton on February 2, 1778 [Ref: J-1814]. "When the British attacked Philadelphia in 1777, Richardson was commissioned to remove the Continental Treasury from there to Baltimore. Richardson was in the Army and was away from Maryland from June, 1780 until the end of March, 1782. During part of this time he was held captive in England. Richardson was apparently on a merchant vessel in 1781 when it was captured by the British. He hired a privateer to transport him and a Dr. Hindman to France, where they were again captured. Both Richardson and Hindman were later released, no charges having been proven against them." [Ref: R-679]. Rendered patriotic service by providing wheat for the use of the military in August, 1782, as verified by Giles Hicks 3rd, Commissary for Caroline County [Ref: V-6636]. He died in Caroline County on June 25, 1825, after being ill for several weeks [Ref: R-680].

RICHARDSON, William. Private, Militia, Capt. Thomas Hughlett's Company, 28th Battalion, by August 13, 1777 [Ref: M-153].

RIDGAWAY, Henrietta. See "Benjamin Townshend," q.v.

RIDGAWAY, Richard. See "Benjamin Townshend," q.v.

RIDGEWAY, Samuel. See "Joseph Boone," q.v.

RIDGERS, John. Rendered patriotic service by providing wheat for the use of the military in August, 1782, as verified by Giles Hicks 3rd, Commissary for Caroline County [Ref: V-6636].

RIDGERS, Joshua. Rendered patriotic service by providing wheat for the use of the military in August, 1782, as verified by Giles Hicks 3rd, Commissary for Caroline County [Ref: V-6636].

RIDGWAY, --?--. See "Charles Daffin," q.v.

RIDGWAY, Susannah. See "Charles Daffin," q.v.

RIDGWAY, William. See "Charles Daffin," q.v.

RIGGING, Solomon. Private, Militia, Capt. Joseph Douglass' Company, 14th Battalion, by August 13, 1777 [Ref: M-156].

RINGGOLD, Sarah. See "Christopher Driver," q.v.

RITCHEE (RICHEE), John. Private, Maryland Troops, enrolled by Lieut. Thomas Wynn Loockerman in Caroline County in July, 1776 [Ref: D-69].

RITCHIE, Robert. Private, 6th Company, Capt. Peter Adams, 1st Maryland Line, enlisted February 24, 1776 [Ref: D-15].

ROACH, Charles. Private, Maryland Troops, enrolled by Lieut. Levin Handy in Caroline County and passed by Col. William Hopewell on August 4, 1776 [Ref: D-69].

ROADS, Jeremiah. See "Jeremiah Rhodes," q.v.

ROBBS, Alexander. Private, Maryland Troops, enlisted by Capt. Joseph Richardson in Caroline County and passed by Col. William Richardson on August 31, 1776 [Ref: D-69].

ROBERTS, Elizabeth. See "John Jones," q.v.

ROBERTS, Hugh. Private, Militia, Capt. Thomas Hughlett's Company, 28th Battalion, by August 13, 1777 [Ref: M-152]. "Hugh Roberts, of Choptank Hundred" subscribed to the Oath of Allegiance and Fidelity before the Hon. Benson Stainton on February 2, 1778 [Ref: J-1814].

ROBERTSON, John. See "John Robinson," q.v.

ROBERTSON, David. See "David Robinson," q.v.

ROBERTSON, William. See "William Robinson," q.v.

ROBINSON (ROBERTSON), Alexander. Second Lieutenant, promoted to First Lieutenant, Militia, Capt. Samuel Jackson's Company, June 19, 1777 [Ref: M-117, C-294, J-1814]. Captain, 1781 [Ref: M-70, I-27, which spelled the name "Robertson"].

ROBINSON, Alexander. Private, Militia, Capt. Samuel Jackson's Company, 28th Battalion, by August 13, 1777 [Ref: M-153]. Subscribed to the Oath of Allegiance and Fidelity before the Hon. Richard Mason on March 2, 1778 [Ref: J-1814].

ROBINSON (ROBERTSON), Amasa. See "Joseph Douglass," q.v.

ROBINSON (ROBERTSON), Daniel. Private, Militia, Capt. Samuel Jackson's Company, 28th Battalion, by August 13, 1777 [Ref: M-153, which spelled the name "Robertson"]. Rendered patriotic service by providing wheat for the use of the military in August, 1782, as verified by Giles Hicks 3rd, Commissary for Caroline County [Ref: V-6636, which spelled the name "Robinson"].

ROBINSON (ROBERTSON), David (1733 -   ). Constable, Tuckahoe Hundred, 1775-1776 [Ref: Z-2, Z-27]. Served on the Committee of Observation for Caroline County on August 2, 1775 [Ref: A-48]. Ensign, Militia, Capt. Vincent Price's Company, 28th Battalion, June 19, 1777 [Ref: J-1814 and M-117 (which spelled the name "Robinson"), C-294 and M-151, which spelled the name "Robertson"]. Captain, Militia, August 14, 1779 [Ref: E-493 (which spelled the name "Robertson"), M-116]. Subscribed to the Oath of Allegiance and Fidelity before the Hon. Henry Downes, Jr. on March 2, 1778 [Ref: J-1814, which spelled the name "Robinson"]. David Robinson was aged 49 in a 1782 deposition [Ref: T-5].

ROBINSON, Elizabeth. See "Elijah Clark," q.v.

ROBINSON, Ezekiel (Ezekial). First Lieutenant, Militia, Capt. Samuel Jackson's Company, 28th Battalion, by August 13, 1777 to at least April 9, 1778 [Ref: M-153, M-117, E-23].

ROBINSON, John. Private, Militia, 14th Battalion, Capt. Richard Andrew's Company, by August 13, 1777 [Ref: M-156]. Rendered patriotic service by providing wheat for the use of the military in August, 1782, as verified by Giles Hicks 3rd, Commissary for Caroline County [Ref: V-6636]. One John Robinson married Amelia Sullivane by license dated September 29, 1778, a John Robinson married Elizabeth Thorman by license dated February 8, 1780, and a John Robertson married Margaret Stevens by license dated June 19, 1786 [Ref: X-9, X-11, X-17].

ROBINSON, Luke. Rendered patriotic service by providing wheat for the use of the military in August, 1782, as verified by Giles Hicks 3rd, Commissary for Caroline County [Ref: V-6636].

ROBINSON, Sarah. See "William Elliott," q.v.

ROBINSON, William. Private, Militia, Capt. Henry Downes' Company, 28th Battalion, by August 13, 1777 [Ref: M-152].

ROBINSON, William. Private, Light Horse Troops, Capt. Henry Dickinson's Company, June 12, 1781 [Ref: M-157].

ROBINSON (ROBERTSON), William. Second Lieutenant, Militia, 28th Battalion, August 14, 1779 [Ref: E-493, which spelled the name "Robertson"]. Subscribed to the Oath of Allegiance and Fidelity before the Hon. Henry Downes, Jr. on March 2, 1778 [Ref: J-1814]. One William Robinson married Margaret Driver by license dated May 22, 1782 [Ref: X-14]. Since there was more then one man named William Robinson or Robertson, additional research will be necessary before drawing conclusions. See "Matthew Driver," q.v.

ROBINSON, William Jr. Private, Militia, Capt. Vincent Price's Company, 28th Battalion, by August 13, 1777 [Ref: M-152].

ROE, Abner. Rendered patriotic service by providing wheat for the use of the military in August, 1782, as verified by Giles Hicks 3rd, Commissary for Caroline County [Ref: V-6636]. Abner (Abnor) Roe was a son of Thomas Roe, Jr. and Ann Cooper. He married Julia Sylvester by license recorded August 9, 1775 and their children were as follows: Richard Roe, Abner Roe, David Sylvester Roe, Thomas Cooper Roe, Rachel Roe, Ann Roe, Mary Roe (married --?-- Bartlett), and Priscella Roe (married Joseph Cox). [Ref: X-5, and Q-32:2 (Spring, 1991, p. 139), which mistakenly indicated Abner Roe married Juley Sylvester in 1755]. See "Thomas Roe," q.v.

ROE, Ann. See "Thomas Roe" and "Abner Roe," q.v.

ROE, Anthony. Private, Militia, Capt. Henry Downes' Company, 28th Battalion, by August 13, 1777 [Ref: M-152].

ROE, David. See "James Roe" and "Abner Roe," q.v.

ROE, Deborah. See "Thomas Roe," q.v.

ROE, Elizabeth. See "James Roe" and "Thomas Roe," q.v.

ROE, Edward. See "Edward Rowe," q.v.

ROE, James (1744-1789). Private, Militia, Capt. John Fauntleroy's Company, 28th Battalion, by August 13, 1777 [Ref: M-154]. Subscribed to the Oath of

Allegiance and Fidelity before the Hon. Richard Mason on March 2, 1778 [Ref: J-1814]. In an 1816 land commission record it stated that "James Roe, the Elder" had died in September, 1789, seized of a tract called "Roe's Addition" and leaving the following heirs: Elizabeth Roe (married Henry Baggs), David Roe (who died in May, 1815, leaving Wilson Roe, James Roe, Sarah Roe, and Elizabeth Roe, all minors, under the guardianship of Thomas Mason), Sarah Roe (married first to Abram Baggs and second to Samuel Milburn), Margaret Clements (married Joel Clements), Parrott Roe (married Rebecca Roe), Ann (Nancy) Wilson (married Peter Wilson), Samuel Roe, and James Roe (plus a son Isaac Roe who died before 1816). [Ref: T-30, Q-32:2 (Spring, 1991), pp. 139-140]. See "Thomas Roe," q.v.

ROE, Jane. See "Thomas Roe," q.v.

ROE, John. Private, Militia, Capt. William Hopper's Company, 28th Battalion, by August 13, 1777 [Ref: M-151]. See "Thomas Roe," q.v.

ROE, John. Private, Militia, Capt. Andrew Fountain's Company, 14th Battalion, by August 13, 1777 [Ref: M-157].

ROE, Mary. See "Abner Roe," q.v.

ROE, Obediah. Private, Militia, Capt. Andrew Fountain's Company, 14th Battalion, by August 13, 1777 [Ref: M-157].

ROE, Parrott. See "James Roe" and "Thomas Roe," q.v.

ROE, Priscella. See "Abner Roe," q.v.

ROE, Rachel. See "Abner Roe," q.v.

ROE, Rebecca. See "Thomas Roe" and "James Roe," q.v.

ROE, Richard. Private, Militia, Capt. Vincent Price's Company, 28th Battalion, by August 13, 1777 [Ref: M-152]. Subscribed to the Oath of Allegiance and Fidelity before the Hon. Richard Mason on March 2, 1778 [Ref: J-1814]. Richard Roe married Sally Glanding by license dated February 24, 1781 [Ref: X-13]. See "Abner Roe," q.v.

ROE, Samuel. See "James Roe" and "Thomas Roe," q.v.

ROE, Sarah. See "Thomas Roe" and "James Roe," q.v.

ROE, Thomas. Private, Militia, Capt. Andrew Fountain's Company, 14th Battalion, by August 13, 1777 [Ref: M-157]. Subscribed to the Oath of Allegiance and Fidelity before the Hon. Richard Mason on March 2, 1778 [Ref: J-1814]. There appears to have been three men named Thomas Roe in Caroline County, so additional research will be necessary before drawing conclusions: (1) In an 1814 land commission record it stated that one Thomas Roe died circa 1798 seized of a tract called "Lane's Ridge" and leaving these children: William Roe, Rebecca Caperoon (wife of William Caperoon), Mary Caldwell (wife of James Caldwell), Ann Roe (minor), Jane Roe (minor), Sarah Roe (minor); (2) In another 1814 land commission record it stated that a Thomas Roe died in 1799 and owned a tract called "Lloyd's Regulation" and leaving these heirs: William Roe, Samuel Roe, Thomas Roe, John Roe, Deborah Roe (minor), and Abner Roe (minor); (3) In an 1818 land commission record it stated that a Thomas Roe died intestate on

January 1, 1807, seized of tracts called "Abner's Park," "Wooter's Choice Resurveyed," and "Susanna's Right" and leaving a widow Mary Roe and the following children: Thomas Roe, Ann Matthews (wife of Samuel Matthews), Mary Sylvester (wife of David Sylvester), Rebecca Roe (wife of Parrott Roe), Sarah Chance (wife of Levi Chance), Elizabeth Roe (minor, aged between 15 or 16 years), and James Roe (minor, aged above 14 years). [Ref: T-28, T-28, T-29, T-30]. One Thomas Roe married Mary Baggs by license dated February 10, 1778, and a Thomas Roe married Tilly Porter by license dated March 16, 1785 [Ref: X-16]. [Ref: X-8]. See "Abner Roe," q.v.

ROE, William (1732 - after 1782). Private, Militia, Capt. Henry Downes' Company, 28th Battalion, by August 13, 1777 [Ref: M-152]. Aged 50 in a 1782 deposition [Ref: T-4]. See "Thomas Roe," q.v.

ROE, Wilson. See "James Roe," q.v.

ROGAN, James. Corporal, 6th Company, Capt. Peter Adams, 1st Maryland Line, enlisted January 30, 1776 [Ref: D-14].

ROGERS, Elizabeth. See "John Smith," q.v.

ROGERS, Frances. See "John Smith," q.v.

ROGERS, John. Private, Militia, Capt. William Haslett's Company, 28th Battalion, by August 13, 1777 [Ref: M-152].

ROGERS, Joseph. See "John Smith," q.v.

ROGERS, Rebekah. See "John Clements," q.v.

ROGERS, William. Private, Militia, Capt. William Haslett's Company, 28th Battalion, by August 13, 1777 [Ref: M-152].

ROSS, Anthony. Private, Militia, 14th Battalion, Capt. Richard Andrew's Company, by August 13, 1777 [Ref: M-156]. Rendered patriotic service by providing wheat for the use of the military in August, 1782, as verified by Giles Hicks 3rd, Commissary for Caroline County [Ref: V-6636].

ROSS, Bartholomew. Private, 5th Maryland Line, enlisted June 30, 1777 and was in the service until May, 1779 [Ref: D-240].

ROSS, Charles. See "William Holland," q.v.

ROSS, Edward. Private, Militia, 14th Battalion, Capt. Richard Andrew's Company, by August 13, 1777 [Ref: M-156].

ROSS, James Jr. Private, Militia, Capt. John Stafford's Company, 14th Battalion, by August 13, 1777 [Ref: M-156, which listed the name without the "Jr."]. Rendered patriotic service by providing wheat for the use of the military in August, 1782, as verified by Giles Hicks 3rd, Commissary for Caroline County [Ref: V-6636].

ROSS, James Sr. (1703 - after 1782). Rendered patriotic service by providing wheat for the use of the military in August, 1782, as verified by Giles Hicks 3rd, Commissary for Caroline County [Ref: V-6636]. Aged 71 in a 1774 deposition [Ref: T-1].

ROSS, Lewis. Private, Militia, Capt. Joseph Douglass' Company, 14th Battalion, by August 13, 1777 [Ref: M-156]. Rendered patriotic service by providing wheat for the use of the military in August, 1782, as verified by Giles Hicks 3rd, Commissary for Caroline County [Ref: V-6636].

ROSS, Peggy. Rendered patriotic service by providing wheat for the use of the military in August, 1782, as verified by Giles Hicks 3rd, Commissary for Caroline County [Ref: V-6636].

ROSS, Robert. Drummer, 6th Company, Capt. Peter Adams, 1st Maryland Line, enlisted February 15, 1776 [Ref: D-14].

ROSS, Rubin. Private, Militia, Capt. John Stafford's Company, 14th Battalion, by August 13, 1777 [Ref: M-156].

ROSS, Thomas. Private, 5th Maryland Line, 1777 [Ref: D-241].

ROSS, William. Private, Militia, 14th Battalion, Capt. Richard Andrew's Company, by August 13, 1777 [Ref: M-156].

ROUSE, Benjamin. Private, Militia, Capt. Thomas Hughlett's Company, 28th Battalion, by August 13, 1777 [Ref: M-152].

ROUSE, Edward. Private, Militia, Capt. Thomas Hughlett's Company, 28th Battalion, by August 13, 1777 [Ref: M-152].

ROUSE, Joseph. Private, Militia, Capt. Thomas Hughlett's Company, 28th Battalion, by August 13, 1777 [Ref: M-152]. He may have been the son of "Joseph Rouse, Sr." who was aged 64 in a 1784 deposition [Ref: T-9].

ROUSE, Samuel. Private, Militia, Capt. Thomas Hughlett's Company, 28th Battalion, by August 13, 1777 [Ref: M-152].

ROUSE, Solomon. Private, Militia, Capt. Thomas Hughlett's Company, 28th Battalion, by August 13, 1777 [Ref: M-152]. See "John Spurrey," q.v.

ROWE, Edward. Private, Militia, Capt. Nehemiah Andrew's Company, 14th Battalion, by August 13, 1777 [Ref: M-155].

ROWENS, Francis. Private, Militia, Capt. Nehemiah Andrew's Company, 14th Battalion, by August 13, 1777 [Ref: M-155]. Francis Rowins married Elizabeth Lord by license dated December 16, 1783 [Ref: X-15].

ROWENS, Joseph. Private, Militia, Capt. Nehemiah Andrew's Company, 14th Battalion, by August 13, 1777 [Ref: M-155]. Rendered patriotic service by providing wheat for the use of the military in August, 1782, as verified by Giles Hicks 3rd, Commissary for Caroline County [Ref: V-6636, which spelled the name "Roens"].

ROWENS, Mary. See "Luke Andrew," q.v.

ROWENS, William. Private, Militia, Capt. Nehemiah Andrew's Company, 14th Battalion, by August 13, 1777 [Ref: M-155].

ROYALL, John. See "John Ryall," q.v.

RUMBLE, William. Seaman, enlisted June 15, 1782 to serve on the barge "Fearnaught" under Capt. Edward Spedden, and was paid £3 bounty for enlisting; physical description given as 5' 9" tall with a dark complexion [Ref: D-612].

RUMBLY, Drucilla. See "Moses Floyd," q.v.

RUMBLY, Edgar (Edger). Private, Militia, Capt. William Haslett's Company, 28th Battalion, by August 13, 1777 [Ref: M-152]. Subscribed to the Oath of

Allegiance and Fidelity before the Hon. Matthew Driver on February 1, 1778 [Ref: J-1814].
RUMBLY (RUMBLEY), Elizabeth. See "Thomas Orrell," q.v.
RUMBLY (RUMBLEY), Edward. Subscribed to the Oath of Allegiance and Fidelity before the Hon. Nathaniel Potter on March 2, 1778 [Ref: J-1814].
RUMBLY, Henry. Private, Militia, Capt. Shadrack Liden's Company, 14th Battalion, by August 13, 1777 [Ref: M-155].
RUMBLY, Jacob. Private, Militia, Capt. William Haslett's Company, 28th Battalion, by August 13, 1777 [Ref: M-152]. Subscribed to the Oath of Allegiance and Fidelity before the Hon. Matthew Driver on February 1, 1778 [Ref: J-1814].
RUMBLY, James. Private, Militia, Capt. Shadrack Liden's Company, 14th Battalion, by August 13, 1777 [Ref: M-155].
RUMBLY, John. Private, Militia, Capt. Shadrack Liden's Company, 14th Battalion, by August 13, 1777 [Ref: M-155].
RUMBLY (RUMBLEY), Lavinia. See "John Carter," q.v.
RUMBLY, Shadrack. Private, Militia, Capt. Shadrack Liden's Company, 14th Battalion, by August 13, 1777 [Ref: M-155].
RUMBLY, William. See "William Rumble," q.v.
RUMBOLD, Thomas. Private, Militia, Capt. John Mitchell's Company, 14th Battalion, by August 13, 1777 [Ref: M-155].
RUMBOLD, William. Private, Militia, Capt. John Mitchell's Company, 14th Battalion, by August 13, 1777 [Ref: M-155].
RUMNEY, Edgar. Ensign, Militia, Capt. Postlethwait's Company, 28th Battalion, April 9, 1778. First Lieutenant, 28th [8th?] Battalion, April 18, 1780 [Ref: M-118, E-23, F-144].
RUSSEL, Andrew. See "William Whitely," q.v.
RUSSEL, Kitty. See "William Whitely," q.v.
RUSSUM, Edward. Private, Militia, 14th Battalion, Capt. Richard Andrew's Company, by August 13, 1777 [Ref: M-156].
RUSSUM, Elizabeth. See "James Johnson," q.v.
RUSSUM (RUSSOM), John (c1729 - after 1786). On December 27, 1776 he joined a company of men in Caroline County who marched to Talbot County to obtain a supply of salt [Ref: B-564, B-565]. On May 26, 1780, he filed a certificate in Caroline County Court that he had subscribed to the Oath of Allegiance and Fidelity before the Hon. Nathaniel Potter [Ref: N-78]. John Russom was aged 50 in a 1776 deposition and aged 50 in a 1779 deposition, and John Russom, son of John, was aged 56 in a 1786 deposition [Ref: T-2, T-3, T-11]. One John Russum married Tryphena Sylvester by license dated July 13, 1783 [Ref: X-15].
RUSSUM (RUSSOM), William. Rendered patriotic service by providing wheat for the use of the military in August, 1782, as verified by Giles Hicks 3rd, Commissary for Caroline County [Ref: V-6636].

RYALL, Betty. See "Thomas Swan," q.v.
RYALL, James. See "Thomas Swan," q.v.
RYALL, John. Private, Militia, Capt. Henry Downes' Company, 28th Battalion, by August 13, 1777 [Ref: M-152]. Private, 5th Maryland Line, enlisted June 6, 1778 and discharged March 20, 1779 [Ref: D-241]. "John Ryall" married Mary Davis by license dated July 24, 1781, and "John Royall" married Ann Evans by license dated March 19, 1787 [Ref: X-14, X-18].
RYAN, John. Private, Maryland Troops, enrolled by Lieut. Thomas Wynn Loockerman in Caroline County in July, 1776 [Ref: D-69].
RYON, William. Private, Militia, 14th Battalion, Capt. Joseph Richardson's Company, by August 13, 1777 [Ref: M-154]. Subscribed to the Oath of Allegiance and Fidelity (made his "R" mark) before the Hon. Peter Richardson on February 28, 1778 [Ref: J-1814]. William Ryon married Sarah Alford by license dated September 26, 1787 [Ref: X-18].
SAFFORD, John. Captain, Militia, 14th Battalion, June 10, 1776 [Ref: M-118, A-481, A-481]. Appointed to be Constable of Bridgetown Hundred on July 17, 1779 [Ref: N-58]. See "John Stafford," q.v.
SALISBERRY, James. Private, Militia, Capt. Andrew Fountain's Company, 14th Battalion, by August 13, 1777 [Ref: M-157]. Rendered patriotic service by providing wheat for the use of the military in May, 1782, as verified by Giles Hicks 3rd, Commissary for Caroline County [Ref: V-6636].
SALISBERRY, John. Private, Militia, Capt. John Stafford's Company, 14th Battalion, by August 13, 1777 [Ref: M-156].
SALISBERRY, John. Private, Militia, Capt. Andrew Fountain's Company, 14th Battalion, by August 13, 1777 [Ref: M-157].
SALISBERRY (SALISBURY), John. Rendered patriotic service by providing wheat for the use of the military in May, 1782, as verified by Giles Hicks 3rd, Commissary for Caroline County [Ref: V-6636]. One John Salisbury married Lydia Horney by license dated January 23, 1781 [Ref: X-13].
SALISBERRY (SALISBURY), John Jr. Rendered patriotic service by providing wheat for the use of the military in May, 1782, as verified by Giles Hicks 3rd, Commissary for Caroline County [Ref: V-6636].
SALISBERRY (SALSBERRY), Nehemiah. Rendered patriotic service by providing wheat for the use of the military in August, 1782, as verified by Giles Hicks 3rd, Commissary for Caroline County [Ref: V-6636].
SALISBERRY, Olivi(?). Private, Militia, Capt. John Stafford's Company, 14th Battalion, by August 13, 1777 [Ref: M-156].
SALISBERRY (SALSBERRY), William. Private, Militia, Capt. Thomas Hughlett's Company, 28th Battalion, by August 13, 1777 [Ref: M-153]. Rendered patriotic service by providing wheat for the use of the military in August, 1782, as verified by Giles Hicks 3rd, Commissary for Caroline County [Ref: V-6636].
SANGSTON, Allen. See "John Allen Sangston," q.v.
SANGSTON, James. See "John Allen Sangston," q.v.

SANGSTON, John Allen. Subscribed to the Oath of Allegiance and Fidelity before the Hon. Nathaniel Potter on March 2, 1778 [Ref: J-1814]. In an 1816 land commission record it stated that John Allen Sangston had died on December 1, 1802, leaving a widow Rachel and children, viz., Elizabeth Maxwell (wife of Alexander Maxwell, Jr.), Susan Wright (wife of Solomon Wright), James Sangston, and Allen Sangston (minor); also grandchildren, all born of Rebecca Baynard, daughter of John Allen Sangston, who died before him, viz., John Baynard, Thomas Baynard, Henry Baynard, Eliza Baynard (who married William Whiteley), and Mary Baynard (who married Samuel Slaughter). [Ref: T-30].

SANGSTON, Rachel. See "John Allen Sangston," q.v.

SANGSTON, Rebekah. See "Thomas Baynard," q.v.

SANGSTON, William. Private, Militia, Capt. Andrew Fountain's Company, 14th Battalion, by August 13, 1777 [Ref: M-157, which spelled the name "Sanxton"].

SATTERFIELD (SATERFIELD), Andrew. Ensign, Militia, Capt. Cornelius Johnson's Company, December 17, 1781 [Ref: I-27, M-118]. Andrew Satterfield married Deborah Stevens by license dated September 16, 1783 [Ref: X-15].

SATTERFIELD, Elizabeth. See "William Fountain," q.v.

SATTERFIELD (SATERFIELD), George. Private, Militia, Capt. Samuel Jackson's Company, 28th Battalion, by August 13, 1777 [Ref: M-153]. Subscribed to the Oath of Allegiance and Fidelity (made his mark that resembled a "D" lying on its back with a line drawn vertically through the center) before the Hon. Richard Mason on March 2, 1778 [Ref: J-1814]. See "William Satterfield," q.v.

SATTERFIELD (SATERFIELD), Hinson. Private, Militia, Capt. William Chipley's Company, 28th Battalion, by August 13, 1777 [Ref: M-153].

SATTERFIELD, Hosea. See "William Satterfield," q.v.

SATTERFIELD, Levi. See "William Satterfield," q.v.

SATTERFIELD, Matthew. See "William Satterfield," q.v.

SATTERFIELD (SATERFIELD), Nathaniel. Private, Militia, Capt. William Chipley's Company, 28th Battalion, by August 13, 1777 [Ref: M-153].

SATTERFIELD, Pleasant. See "William Satterfield," q.v.

SATTERFIELD (SATERFIELD), Solomon. Private, Militia, Capt. Samuel Jackson's Company, 28th Battalion, by August 13, 1777 [Ref: M-153]. Rendered patriotic service by providing wheat for the use of the military in August, 1782, as verified by Giles Hicks 3rd, Commissary for Caroline County [Ref: V-6636].

SATTERFIELD, William (1760-1813). Private, Maryland Line, who married Unicey Clements (or Unicy Clement) in the spring of 1781 or 1782 or 1783 (all three years were given) in Anson County, North Carolina. He died in December, 1813 in Greenville District, South Carolina and his widow applied for a pension (W1088) in Jefferson County, Tennessee on November 18, 1847, aged 89. She died there on May 16, 1849, leaving these children: Matthew Satterfield, Hosea Satterfield, Levi Satterfield (born May 28, 1787 and married Nancy Simmons on February 15, 1810), and George G. Satterfield. Also mentioned was a Pleasant G. Satterfield who was born August 28, 1812; probably a son of Levi Satterfield

[Ref: Y-2568, W-3020, which latter source inadvertently omitted the pension number. *The Index of Revolutionary Pension Applications*, which was compiled in 1980 by the National Genealogical Society (page 492), states the pension number was W1088]. He may have been related to a William Meads Satterfield who married Ann Dukes by license dated December 28, 1782 in Caroline County [Ref: X-14].

SAULSBURY, Margaret. See "James Fountain," q.v.

SAULSBURY, Mary. See "James Waddell" and "Jonathan Wilson," q.v.

SAVEN, Eliza. See "Thomas Mason," q.v.

SCOTT, Caroline. See "John Lucas," q.v.

SCOTT, Elizabeth. See "William Tallboy," q.v.

SCOTT, James. Private, Militia, Capt. Andrew Fountain's Company, 14th Battalion, by August 13, 1777 [Ref: M-157]. James Scott married Ann Shaw by license dated October 29, 1777 [Ref: X-7].

SCOTT, Priscilla. See "Stephen Cooper," q.v.

SCOTT, Sarah. See "John Mitchell," q.v.

SCOUDRICK, Thomas. Private, Maryland Troops, enrolled by Lieut. Thomas Wynn Loockerman in Caroline County in July, 1776 [Ref: D-69].

SCOWDRICK, William. Private, Militia, Capt. John Mitchell's Company, 14th Battalion, by August 13, 1777 [Ref: M-155].. Subscribed to the Oath of Allegiance and Fidelity (made his mark that resembled an upside down "V") before the Hon. Peter Richardson on February 28, 1778 [Ref: J-1814].

SEA, John. Subscribed to the Oath of Allegiance and Fidelity before the Hon. Richard Mason on March 2, 1778 [Ref: J-1814].

SELLERS, Elizabeth. See "Henry Downes," q.v.

SELLERS, Francis. See "Henry Downes," q.v.

SELLERS, Henry Downes. See "Henry Downes," q.v.

SETH, Charles. Private, Militia, Capt. Henry Downes' Company, 28th Battalion, by August 13, 1777 [Ref: M-152]. Subscribed to the Oath of Allegiance and Fidelity before the Hon. Henry Downes, Jr. on March 2, 1778 [Ref: J-1814]. See "James Seth," q.v.

SETH, Elizabeth. See "James Seth," q.v.

SETH, George Washington. See "James Seth," q.v.

SETH, Jacob. Sergeant, 5th Maryland Line, enlisted August 15, 1777, demoted to private on July 1, 1778, and discharged on August 20, 1780 [Ref: D-244]. See "Philemon Downes" and "James Seth," q.v.

SETH, James. Resided in Queen Anne's County (of age by 1762) which became part of Caroline County after 1773, was in Tuckahoe Hundred of Caroline County in 1778, and returned to Queen Anne's County by 1784. James married twice (first wife unknown) and his second wife was Sarah Winchester, daughter of Thomas Winchester of Talbot County. His children were Charles Seth, James Seth, Jacob Seth, Thomas Winchester Seth, George Washington Seth, and Elizabeth Seth [Ref: R-723]. On December 30, 1776, Isaac McHard wrote to the

Maryland Council to inform them that he had "contracted with Mr. Potter to buy me all the pork that is to be had in Caroline County [and] ... I have likewise ingaged with Mr. James Seth to get for me all the pork in Talbut and Queen Anns County, if he should want a little salt I hope you will order him a little if he should want, I dont no that he will want, for he had contracted to deliver it to Annapolis if possibly he can get it their if he cannot get it their from the badness of the weather it must be salted over here, and barreled and brought to Annapolis in the spring." [Ref: B-561]. Second Lieutenant, Militia, Capt. William Hopper's Company, 28th Battalion, by August 13, 1777 [Ref: M-151, J-1814]. Subscribed to the Oath of Allegiance and Fidelity before the Hon. Henry Downes, Jr. on March 2, 1778 [Ref: J-1814]. Rendered patriotic service by providing wheat for the use of the military in July, 1782, as verified by Giles Hicks III, Commissary for Caroline County [Ref: P-533]. James Seth represented Caroline County in the Lower House of the Maryland General Assembly, 1780-1781. He died between November 5, 1784 and January 8, 1785, probably in Queen Anne's County [Ref: R-84, R-723].

SETH, Mary. See "Philemon Downes," q.v.

SETH, Thomas Winchester. See "James Seth," q.v.

SEVORAD(?), William. Private, Militia, Capt. Vincent Price's Company, 28th Battalion, by August 13, 1777 [Ref: M-152].

SEWARD, Anna. See "Zebdiah Billetor," q.v.

SHADDEN, John. Private, Militia, Capt. Thomas Hughlett's Company, 28th Battalion, by August 13, 1777 [Ref: M-152]. See "John Shedden," q.v.

SHARP (SHARPE), Henry. Private, Militia, Capt. Vincent Price's Company, 28th Battalion, by August 13, 1777 [Ref: M-152]. Rendered patriotic service by providing wheat for the use of the military in August, 1782, as verified by Giles Hicks 3rd, Commissary for Caroline County [Ref: V-6636, which spelled the name "Sharp"].

SHARP (SHARPE), James (1760 -   ). Private, Militia, 14th Battalion, Capt. Joseph Richardson's Company, by August 13, 1777 [Ref: M-154]. Aged 26 in a 1786 deposition [Ref: T-12].

SHARP (SHARPE), John. Private, Militia, 14th Battalion, Capt. Joseph Richardson's Company, by August 13, 1777 [Ref: M-154].

SHARP (SHARPE), William (1757 -   ). Private, Maryland Troops, enrolled by Lieut. Thomas Wynn Loockerman in Caroline County in July, 1776 [Ref: D-69]. Private, Militia, 14th Battalion, Capt. Joseph Richardson's Company, by August 13, 1777 [Ref: M-154]. Aged 29 in a 1786 deposition [Ref: T-12].

SHAW, Ann. See "James Scott," q.v.

SHAW, Benjamin. Private, Militia, Capt. Andrew Fountain's Company, 14th Battalion, by August 13, 1777 [Ref: M-157].

SHAW, Mary. Rendered patriotic service by providing wheat for the use of the military in August, 1782, as verified by Giles Hicks 3rd, Commissary for Caroline County [Ref: V-6636].

SHEARMAN, John. Private, Militia, Capt. Nehemiah Andrew's Company, 14th Battalion, by August 13, 1777 [Ref: M-155]. See "John Sherman," q.v.

SHEDDEN, John, of Choptank Hundred. Subscribed to the Oath of Allegiance and Fidelity before the Hon. Benson Stainton on February 2, 1778 [Ref: J-1814]. See "John Shadden," q.v.

SHENTON, James. On May 26, 1780, he filed a certificate in Caroline County Court that he had subscribed to the Oath of Allegiance and Fidelity before the Hon. Richard Mason [Ref: N-78].

SHEPHERD (SHEPARD), William (1743 -   ). Private, Militia, Capt. William Chipley's Company, 28th Battalion, by August 13, 1777 [Ref: M-153]. Rendered patriotic service by providing wheat for the use of the military in August, 1782, as verified by Giles Hicks 3rd, Commissary for Caroline County [Ref: V-6636]. Aged 39 in a 1782 deposition [Ref: T-3].

SHERMAN, John. Rendered patriotic service by providing wheat for the use of the military in June and August, 1782, as verified by Giles Hicks 3rd, Commissary for Caroline County [Ref: V-6636]. See "John Shearman," q.v.

SHERWOOD, Francis. Private, Militia, Capt. William Haslett's Company, 28th Battalion, by August 13, 1777 [Ref: M-152].

SHERWOOD, Hugh. Private, 5th Maryland Line, enlisted June 6, 1778 and discharged in July, 1778 [Ref: D-245].

SHERWOOD, Joseph. Private, Militia, Capt. John Mitchell's Company, 14th Battalion, by August 13, 1777 [Ref: M-155].

SHERWOOD, Mabel. See "Charles Daffin," q.v.

SHERWOOD, Mary. See "James Kirkman," q.v.

SHERWOOD, Nickson. Private, Militia, Capt. Samuel Jackson's Company, 28th Battalion, by August 13, 1777 [Ref: M-153].

SHERWOOD, Philip. See "Charles Daffin," q.v.

SHIPLY, William (Captain). Rendered patriotic services by hauling corn for the State of Maryland, as certified by Richard Keene, Commissary for Caroline County, on June 24, 1780 [Ref: P-298]. This information may actually pertain to "William Chipley," q.v.

SIMMONS, Nancy. See "William Satterfield," q.v.

SIMPSON, Elijah. Private, Militia, Capt. Shadrack Liden's Company, 14th Battalion, by August 13, 1777 [Ref: M-155].

SIMPSON, John. Private, Militia, Capt. Andrew Fountain's Company, 14th Battalion, by August 13, 1777 [Ref: M-157].

SISK, David. Private, Militia, Capt. John Mitchell's Company, 14th Battalion, by August 13, 1777 [Ref: M-155].

SISK, James. Private, Militia, Capt. Nehemiah Andrew's Company, 14th Battalion, by August 13, 1777 [Ref: M-155]. James Sisk married Mary Bowdle by license dated January 3, 1791 [Ref: X-22].

SKIDMORE, Samuel. See "William Molleston," q.v.

SKINNER, Daniel. Served on the Committee of Observation for Caroline County on August 2, 1775 [Ref: A-48]. Subscribed to the Oath of Allegiance and Fidelity before the Hon. Henry Downes, Jr. on March 2, 1778 [Ref: J-1814].

SKINNER, Daniel. Private, Militia, Capt. Vincent Price's Company, 28th Battalion, by August 13, 1777 [Ref: M-152]. Daniel Skinner married Mary Casson by license dated September 29, 1774 [Ref: X-4].

SKINNER, Frederick. Private, Militia, Capt. William Haslett's Company, 28th Battalion, by August 13, 1777 [Ref: M-152].

SKINNER, John. Private, Militia, Capt. William Haslett's Company, 28th Battalion, by August 13, 1777 [Ref: M-152]. Subscribed to the Oath of Allegiance and Fidelity before (made his "\" mark) the Hon. Benson Stainton on February 2, 1778 [Ref: J-1814].

SKINNER, Thomas. Private, Militia, Capt. William Haslett's Company, 28th Battalion, by August 13, 1777 [Ref: M-152].

SLAUGHTER, Edward. Subscribed to the Oath of Allegiance and Fidelity in 1780 [Ref: L-120]. He may have been the son of Edward Slaughter who was aged 52 in a 1779 deposition [Ref: T-2].

SLAUGHTER, Elizabeth. See "Thomas Baynard," q.v.

SLAUGHTER, James. Private, Militia, Capt. John Fauntleroy's Company, 28th Battalion, by August 13, 1777 [Ref: M-154]. James Slaughter married Priscilla Harrington by license dated October 9, 1787 [Ref: X-18].

SLAUGHTER, John. Private, Militia, Capt. John Fauntleroy's Company, 28th Battalion, by August 13, 1777 [Ref: M-154]. Rendered patriotic service by providing wheat for the use of the military in August, 1782, as verified by Giles Hicks 3rd, Commissary for Caroline County [Ref: V-6636]. Subscribed to the Oath of Allegiance and Fidelity before the Hon. Henry Downes, Jr. on March 2, 1778 [Ref: J-1814]. John Slaughter married Elizabeth Hynson by license dated March 21, 1787 [Ref: X-18].

SLAUGHTER, John Jr. Private, Militia, Capt. John Fauntleroy's Company, 28th Battalion, by August 13, 1777 [Ref: M-154].

SLAUGHTER, Mary. See "Cloudsberry Matthews," q.v.

SLAUGHTER, Nathan. Private, Militia, Capt. John Fauntleroy's Company, 28th Battalion, by August 13, 1777 [Ref: M-154]. Subscribed to the Oath of Allegiance and Fidelity (made his "A" mark) before the Hon. Richard Mason on March 2, 1778 [Ref: J-1814].

SLAUGHTER, Rebekah. See "Thomas Harrington," q.v.

SLAUGHTER, Samuel. See "John Allen Sangston," q.v.

SLAUGHTER, Stephen. Subscribed to the Oath of Allegiance and Fidelity in 1780 [Ref: L-120].

SLEMARR, James. See "James Lemarr," q.v.

SMALLWOOD, General. See "Peter Adams" and "--?-- McNeere," q.v.

SMITH, --?--. See "George Turner," q.v.

SMITH, Ader. See "John Smith," q.v.

SMITH, Ann. See "John King," q.v.

SMITH, Charles Turpin. See "Joseph Douglass," q.v.
SMITH, Christopher. See "Thomas Smith," q.v.
SMITH, Ezekiel. Private, Militia, 14th Battalion, Capt. Richard Andrew's Company, by August 13, 1777 [Ref: M-156].
SMITH, George. Private, Militia, Capt. William Chipley's Company, 28th Battalion, by August 13, 1777 [Ref: M-153]. Recommended as First Lieutenant, June 12, 1781 [Ref: M-122]. Subscribed to the Oath of Allegiance and Fidelity before the Hon. Henry Downes, Jr. on March 2, 1778 [Ref: J-1814]. See "John Smith," q.v.
SMITH, Hannah. See "John Smith," q.v.
SMITH, Isaac. Private, Militia, 14th Battalion, Capt. Richard Andrew's Company, by August 13, 1777 [Ref: M-156].
SMITH, James. Rendered patriotic service by providing wheat for the use of the military in August, 1782, as verified by Giles Hicks 3rd, Commissary for Caroline County [Ref: V-6636]. See "Levin Smith" and "John Smith," q.v.
SMITH, James, of Michael. On December 27, 1776 he joined a company of men in Caroline County who marched to Talbot County to obtain a supply of salt [Ref: B-564, B-565].
SMITH, Job. Private, Militia, Capt. William Chipley's Company, 28th Battalion, by August 13, 1777 [Ref: M-153].
SMITH, John. Private, Militia, Capt. William Chipley's Company, 28th Battalion, by August 13, 1777 [Ref: M-153]. Private (draft), Maryland Troops, enrolled in Caroline County by William Whiteley, County Lieutenant, on August 14, 1781 (although reported sick at the time) to serve in the Maryland Line until December 10, 1781 [Ref: D-385]. One John Smith died in 1795 as noted in land commission records in 1795 and 1798 regarding a tract called "Wheatley's Park" in which Joseph Rogers stated John Smith died in January, 1795, leaving my wife Frances Rogers (who died between 1795 and 1798) who had daughter Elizabeth Rogers (also deceased), and James Smith (aged about 18 in 1795), George Smith (aged about 13 in 1795), Rachel Smith (aged about 7 in 1795), Rebecca Smith (aged about 5 in 1795), Ader Smith (aged about 3 in 1795), and Hannah Smith (aged about 18 months in 1795), with Levin Smith as guardians to the minor children [Ref: T-18, T-20]. One John Smith married Elonor Anthony by license dated September 11, 1780 [Ref: X-12]. Since there was more then one man named John Smith, additional research will be necessary before drawing conclusions.
SMITH, John (c1700 - after 1784). Rendered patriotic service by providing wheat for the use of the military in August, 1782, as verified by Giles Hicks 3rd, Commissary for Caroline County [Ref: V-6636]. "John Smith, Quaker, of Watts Creek" was aged 82 in 1782 and 1783 depositions, and "John Smith, Sr." was aged 74 in a 1775 deposition and aged 84 in a 1784 deposition [Ref: T-5, T-6, T-8].
SMITH, John B. See "Thomas Smith," q.v.
SMITH, Joshua. Private, Militia, Capt. Shadrack Liden's Company, 14th Battalion,

by August 13, 1777 [Ref: M-155].

SMITH, Levin. Private, Militia, 14th Battalion, Capt. Richard Andrew's Company, by August 13, 1777 [Ref: M-156].

SMITH, Levin. Private, Militia, Capt. John Stafford's Company, 14th Battalion, by August 13, 1777 [Ref: M-156]. Rendered patriotic service by providing wheat for the use of the military in August, 1782, as verified by Giles Hicks 3rd, Commissary for Caroline County [Ref: V-6636]. "Levin Smith, son of James" was aged 38 in a 1790 deposition and aged 50 in an 1800 deposition [Ref: T-14, T-21]. See "William Bell," q.v.

SMITH, Mary. See "William Bell" and "Charles Nichols," q.v.

SMITH, Michael. Private, Militia, Capt. Henry Downes' Company, 28th Battalion, by August 13, 1777 [Ref: M-152]. Michael Smith married Elizabeth Harris by license dated November 5, 1779 [Ref: X-11]. One Michael Smith was aged 56 in a 1785 deposition [Ref: T-9]. See "James Smith," q.v.

SMITH, Nathan. Private, Militia, Capt. Henry Downes' Company, 28th Battalion, by August 13, 1777 [Ref: M-152]. Private (draft), Maryland Troops, enrolled in Caroline County by William Whiteley, County Lieutenant, on August 14, 1781 (although reported "run" at the time) to serve in the Maryland Line until December 10, 1781 [Ref: D-385]. Nathan Smith married Elizabeth Keen (Keene) by license dated May 26, 1784 [Ref: X-15].

SMITH, Rachel. See "John Smith" and "Richard Swift," q.v.

SMITH, Ralph. Private, Militia, Capt. Shadrack Liden's Company, 14th Battalion, by August 13, 1777 [Ref: M-155]. Rendered patriotic service by providing wheat for the use of the military in August, 1782, as verified by Giles Hicks 3rd, Commissary for Caroline County [Ref: V-6636]. See "Richard Smith" and "Thomas Smith," q.v.

SMITH, Rebecca (Rebeccah). Rendered patriotic service by providing wheat for the use of the military in August, 1782, as verified by Giles Hicks 3rd, Commissary for Caroline County [Ref: V-6636]. See "John Smith," q.v.

SMITH, Richard. Private, Militia, 14th Battalion, Capt. Richard Andrew's Company, by August 13, 1777 [Ref: M-156].

SMITH, Richard, of Ralph. Private (draft), Maryland Troops, enrolled in Caroline County by William Whiteley, County Lieutenant, on August 14, 1781 (although reported "run" at the time) to serve in the Maryland Line until December 10, 1781 [Ref: D-385]. One Richard Smith married Sarah Banning by license dated August 6, 1778 [Ref: X-9].

SMITH, Sarah. See "John Green," q.v.

SMITH, Southey. Private, Militia, Capt. Shadrack Liden's Company, 14th Battalion, by August 13, 1777 [Ref: M-155].

SMITH, Thomas. Private, Militia, 14th Battalion, Capt. Richard Andrew's Company, by August 13, 1777 [Ref: M-156]. See the other "Thomas Smith," q.v.

SMITH, Thomas. Private, Militia, Capt. Shadrack Liden's Company, 14th Battalion, by August 13, 1777 [Ref: M-155]. Rendered patriotic service by providing wheat for the use of the military in August, 1782, as verified by Giles Hicks 3rd, Commissary for Caroline County [Ref: V-6636]. "Thomas Smith, of Ralph" died by 1809 and a son Christopher Smith was aged 23 in 1809 and a son John B. Smith was aged 25 in 1809 [Ref: T-25]. One Thomas Smith married Katharine Price by license dated October 7, 1778, a Thomas Smith married Nancy White by license dated August 31, 1780, and a Thomas Smith married Rhody Cooper by license dated January 9, 1792 [Ref: X-9, X-12, X-23].

SMITH, William. Private, Militia, Capt. Shadrack Liden's Company, 14th Battalion, by August 13, 1777 [Ref: M-155]. Second Lieutenant, Militia, Capt. Thomas Eaton's Company, December 17, 1781 [Ref: M-123, I-27]. Rendered patriotic service by providing wheat for the use of the military in August, 1782, as verified by Giles Hicks 3rd, Commissary for Caroline County [Ref: V-6636]. One William Smith married Ann Green by license dated September 28, 1778 [Ref: X-9].

SMITH, William (Turk). Private, Militia, Capt. William Haslett's Company, 28th Battalion, by August 13, 1777 [Ref: M-152].

SMITH, William Jr. Rendered patriotic service by providing wheat for the use of the military in August, 1782, as verified by Giles Hicks 3rd, Commissary for Caroline County [Ref: V-6636].

SMITH, William Sr. Rendered patriotic service by providing wheat for the use of the military in August, 1782, as verified by Giles Hicks 3rd, Commissary for Caroline County [Ref: V-6636].

SMOOT, Arrietta. See "Joseph Douglass," q.v.

SMOOT, Janet or Jennet. See "Joseph Douglass," q.v.

SMOOT, John. See "Joseph Douglass," q.v.

SNOW, William. Private, Militia, 14th Battalion, Capt. Richard Andrew's Company, by August 13, 1777 [Ref: M-156].

SOUTHERLY, Samuel. Rendered patriotic service by providing wheat for the use of the military in August, 1782, as verified by Giles Hicks 3rd, Commissary for Caroline County [Ref: V-6636]. Samuel Southray [Southley?] married Hannah Blades by license dated June 18, 1781 [Ref: X-13].

SPARKS, Richard (1750 -   ). Private, Militia, Capt. Shadrack Liden's Company, 14th Battalion, by August 13, 1777 [Ref: M-155]. Aged 45 in a 1795 deposition [Ref: T-16].

SPENCE, George. Private, Militia, Capt. William Hopper's Company, 28th Battalion, by August 13, 1777 [Ref: M-151].

SPENCE, Patrick. Private, Militia, 14th Battalion, Capt. Richard Andrew's Company, by August 13, 1777 [Ref: M-156]. Subscribed to the Oath of Allegiance and Fidelity before the Hon. Nathaniel Potter on March 2, 1778 [Ref: J-1814].

SPENCE, Pearce. Private, Militia, Capt. John Mitchell's Company, 14th Battalion, by August 13, 1777 [Ref: M-154].

SPENCER (SPEMCER?), Mary. See "Garey Leverton," q.v.

SPRY, Mary. See "Daniel Lambdin," q.v.
SPURREY, Elizabeth. See "John Spurrey," q.v.
SPURREY, George. See "John Spurrey," q.v.
SPURREY (SPURRY), John. Private, Militia, Capt. William Chipley's Company, 28th Battalion, by August 13, 1777 [Ref: M-153]. In an 1803 land commission record it stated that William Emerson had purchased the right of George Spurrey, son of John Spurrey who had died in March, 1793 seized of tracts called "Shadwell" and "Lloyd's Regulation." John left George Spurrey (eldest son, over 21), Sally Emory (under 21), William Spurrey (minor), and Elizabeth Spurrey (minor). The record also stated that John Spurrey left a wife Elizabeth and her children (by her former husband, name not given), viz., John Hobbs, Ann Hobbs (now deceased), and Elizabeth Hobbs (who married Solomon Rouse). William Kirkman married John Spurrey's widow [Ref: T-22]. John Spurrey married Elizabeth Everett by license dated October 19, 1780 [Ref: X-12].
SPURREY, Sally. See "John Spurrey," q.v.
SPURREY, William. See "John Spurrey," q.v.
STABLEFORD, Daniel. Rendered patriotic service by providing wheat for the use of the military in May, 1782, as verified by Giles Hicks 3rd, Commissary for Caroline County [Ref: V-6636].
STACK, Joseph. Rendered patriotic service by providing wheat for the use of the military in August, 1782, as verified by Giles Hicks 3rd, Commissary for Caroline County [Ref: V-6636]. One Joseph Stack married Elizabeth Banning by license dated April 5, 1780, and a Joseph Stack married Rebecca Lewis by license dated January 2, 1791 [Ref: X-12, X-22].
STACK, Thomas. Private, Militia, 14th Battalion, Capt. Richard Andrew's Company, by August 13, 1777 [Ref: M-156].
STAFFORD, Abram. Private, Militia, Capt. John Stafford's Company, 14th Battalion, by August 13, 1777 [Ref: M-156].
STAFFORD, James. Private, Militia, Capt. John Stafford's Company, 14th Battalion, by August 13, 1777 [Ref: M-156]. Ensign, Militia, Capt. Joseph Douglass' Company, August 14, 1779. Second Lieutenant, Militia, Capt. Jesse Greyless' Company, June 28, 1780 [Ref: M-124, E-493, F-207]. Rendered patriotic service by providing wheat for the use of the military in August, 1782, as verified by Giles Hicks 3rd, Commissary for Caroline County [Ref: V-6636]. James Stafford married Esther Andrews by license dated November 4, 1782 [Ref: X-14].
STAFFORD, Jervis. Private, Militia, Capt. John Stafford's Company, 14th Battalion, by August 13, 1777 [Ref: M-156].
STAFFORD, John. Captain, Militia, 14th Battalion, June 8, 1776 [Ref: M-156, M-124]. Subscribed to the Oath of Allegiance and Fidelity before the Hon. Nathaniel Potter on March 2, 1778 [Ref: J-1814]. Rendered patriotic service by providing wheat for the use of the military in August, 1782, as verified by Giles Hicks 3rd, Commissary for Caroline County [Ref: V-6636]. See "John Safford," q.v.

STAFFORD, John Jr. Private, Militia, Capt. John Stafford's Company, 14th Battalion, by August 13, 1777 [Ref: M-156].

STAINTON, Benson. Attended the Maryland Conventions in 1774 and 1775, and represented Caroline County in the Lower House of the Maryland General Assembly between 1778 and 1781. Served as a Court Justice in Dorchester County, 1770-1773, Court Justice of Caroline County, 1774 to at least March 21, 1780, and Justice of the Orphans' Court from 1774 to at least 1779. He also served on the Committee of Observation in 1776, was Collector of Gold and Silver Coin in 1776, and Subscription Officer, Continental Loan Office, in 1779 [Ref: R-76, R-78, R-80, R-84, N-70, A-5, A-132, A-481 (which misspelled the name as "Stamton"), O-4, E-140, E-249, Z-1, Z-26]. Lieutenant Colonel, Militia, 28th Battalion, January 12, 1776; Colonel, resigned March 12, 1777 [Ref: M-124]. Justice who administered the Oath of Allegiance and Fidelity in 1778 [Ref: J-1814]. Benson married by January, 1770, to Elizabeth Cambell or Campbell (widow of John Cambell or Campbell, and daughter of John Goldsborough). They had no children; his stepdaughter Margaret Cambell or Campbell married John Henry, Jr. When Benson Stainton's inventory was filed in November, 1781, a Francis Stainton signed as nearest of kin. Elizabeth Stainton, widow of Benson, stated that she knew of no other person in Maryland who was related to Benson except Francis. Elizabeth subsequently married Richard Kennard in 1783 [Ref: R-767].

STAINTON, Benson. Private, Militia, Capt. William Haslett's Company, 28th Battalion, by August 13, 1777 [Ref: M-152]. "Benson Stanton, miller" was employed for the use of the State of Maryland, as certified by Richard Keene, Commissary for Caroline County, on June 3, 1780 [Ref: P-294]. This Benson Stainton was probably the son of Francis Stainton. See the other "Benson Stainton," q.v.

STAINTON, Elizabeth. See "Benson Stainton," q.v.

STAINTON, Francis. See "Benson Stainton," q.v.

STANT, John. Private, Militia, Capt. William Hopper's Company, 28th Battalion, by August 13, 1777 [Ref: M-151]. Subscribed to the Oath of Allegiance and Fidelity before the Hon. Benson Stainton on February 2, 1778 [Ref: J-1814]. "John Stant" married Mary Ellers on June 8, 1759, and a "John Staut" married Mary Carter by license recorded on October 30, 1775 [Ref: X-7, K-27].

STANT, Peter. Private, Militia, 14th Battalion, Capt. Richard Andrew's Company, by August 13, 1777 [Ref: M-156].

STANTON, Elizabeth. See "Richard Kennard," q.v.

STANTON, John. Private, Militia, Capt. Shadrack Liden's Company, 14th Battalion, by August 13, 1777 [Ref: M-155].

STAPLEFORD, Andrew. Private, Militia, Capt. Andrew Fountain's Company, 14th Battalion, by August 13, 1777 [Ref: M-157].

STARK, Joseph. Private, Militia, Capt. Joseph Douglass' Company, 14th Battalion, by August 13, 1777 [Ref: M-156].

STAUT, John. See "John Stant," q.v.

STEEL, Peter. Subscribed to the Oath of Allegiance and Fidelity (made his "P" mark) before the Hon. Peter Richardson on February 23, 1778 [Ref: J-1814].

STEVENS, Ann. See "John Stevens," q.v.

STEVENS, Azel (Azell). Private, Militia, Capt. John Stafford's Company, 14th Battalion, by August 13, 1777 [Ref: M-156]. See "John Stevens," q.v.

STEVENS, Benjamin. Private, Militia, Capt. William Hopper's Company, 28th Battalion, by August 13, 1777 [Ref: M-151, which spelled the name "Stevins"].

STEVENS, Bentol (Benthal). Private, Militia, Capt. Shadrack Liden's Company, 14th Battalion, by August 13, 1777 [Ref: M-155, which spelled his first name as "Betel"]. Ensign, Militia, Capt. Joseph Douglass' Company, April 9, 1778. Second Lieutenant, August 14, 1779. First Lieutenant, Militia, Capt. Jesse Greyless' Company, June 28, 1780 [Ref: M-125, E-23, E-493, F-207]. Benthal Stevens married Mary Newells by license dated September 21, 1778 [Ref: X-9].

STEVENS, Deborah. See "Andrew Satterfield," q.v.

STEVENS, Elizabeth. See "John Stevens," q.v.

STEVENS, Horatio. See "John Stevens," q.v.

STEVENS, James. See "John Dillen," q.v.

STEVENS, John. Private, Militia, 14th Battalion, Capt. Joseph Richardson's Company, by August 13, 1777 [Ref: M-154]. In an 1807 land commission record regarding tracts called "Stevens' Purchase," "Stevens' Rest" and "Chance's Desire," it stated that one John Stevens had "died since October 5, 1802," leaving grandchildren as heirs at law: Nancy Stevens, John Stevens, Peggy Stevens (married William Corrie), Mary Stevens (married John Johnson), Nancy Dean (heir at law of Elizabeth Stevens who married Solomon Dean), and Horatio Stevens (under 21 and his guardian was Azel Stevens). [Ref: T-24]. Since there was more then one man named John Stevens, additional research will be necessary before drawing conclusions.

STEVENS, John (1740-1785). Second Lieutenant, Militia, Capt. Joseph Richardson's Company, resigned May 15, 1776. First Lieutenant, May 15, 1776 (same date, date company). [Ref: M-125, A-427]. Attended the Maryland Convention in 1775 [Ref: A-7, O-4, R-71]. Aged 40 in a 1780 deposition [Ref: T-3]. "John Stevens, of Walter" was Justice of the Peace in 1783 and 1784 [Ref: I-341, I-503]. He was the son of Walter Stevens and Rachel Eccleston, and married Ann Anderson by license recorded August 9, 1775. They had sons William and John and two daughters (mentioned, but names not given, in his will) before 1785. John served on the Committee of Observation in 1775 and 1776 and was a Court Justice from 1783 until his death circa March, 1785. His widow subsequently married Charles Blair in 1790 [Ref: R-775, X-6, A-48].

STEVENS, John 2nd. Subscribed to the Oath of Allegiance and Fidelity before the Hon. Charles Dickinson on March 1, 1778 [Ref: J-1418]. John Stevens, Jr. married Elizabeth Andrews by license dated March 5, 1781 [Ref: X-13].

STEVENS, John 3rd. Rendered patriotic service by providing wheat for the use of the military in August, 1782, as verified by Giles Hicks 3rd, Commissary for Caroline County [Ref: V-6636].

STEVENS, Margaret. See "John Robinson (Robertson)," q.v.

STEVENS, Mary. See "William Keene" and "John Stevens" and "Abram Evitt," q.v.

STEVENS, Nancy. See "John Stevens," q.v.

STEVENS, Peggy. See "John Stevens," q.v.

STEVENS, Rachel. See "John Stevens," q.v.

STEVENS, Walter. See "John Stevens," q.v.

STEVENS, William. Private, Militia, Capt. John Stafford's Company, 14th Battalion, by August 13, 1777 [Ref: M-156]. "William Stevens, Nicholite" was aged 52 in a 1785 deposition [Ref: T-12]. See "John Stevens," q.v.

STEWARD, Daniel. Rendered patriotic service by providing wheat for the use of the military in August, 1782, as verified by Giles Hicks 3rd, Commissary for Caroline County [Ref: V-6636].

STEWART, Athol or Athell (1741 -   ). Private, Militia, Capt. Vincent Price's Company, 28th Battalion, by August 13, 1777 [Ref: M-152]. Rendered patriotic service by providing wheat for the use of the military in September, 1782, as verified by Giles Hicks 3rd, Commissary for Caroline County [Ref: V-6636]. Aged 45 in a 1786 deposition, noting he was the son of Thomas Stewart [Ref: T-12].

STEWART, Lydia. See "Abner Clements," q.v.

STEWART, Michal. Private, Militia, Capt. Andrew Fountain's Company, 14th Battalion, by August 13, 1777 [Ref: M-157].

STEWART, Thomas. See "Athol Stewart," q.v.

STEWART, William (1744 -   ). Private, Militia, Capt. Vincent Price's Company, 28th Battalion, by August 13, 1777 [Ref: M-152]. Subscribed to the Oath of Allegiance and Fidelity before the Hon. Henry Downes, Jr. on March 2, 1778 [Ref: J-1814]. "William Steward" was aged 41 in a 1785 deposition and "William Stuart" was aged 44 in a 1788 deposition [Ref: T-9, T-12].

STOKELY, Arabella. See "Aaron Hardcastle" and "Thomas Hardcastle," q.v.

STOKES, Limuel. Private, Militia, Capt. John Stafford's Company, 14th Battalion, by August 13, 1777 [Ref: M-156].

STOKES, William. Private, Militia, Capt. John Stafford's Company, 14th Battalion, by August 13, 1777 [Ref: M-156].

STOREY, Duke. Private, Militia, 14th Battalion, Capt. Richard Andrew's Company, by August 13, 1777 [Ref: M-156].

STOREY, John. Private, Militia, Capt. William Chipley's Company, 28th Battalion, by August 13, 1777 [Ref: M-153].

STOUT, Richard. Private, Militia, Capt. William Chipley's Company, 28th Battalion, by August 13, 1777 [Ref: M-153].

STRADLEY, Griffith. Private, Militia, Capt. Samuel Jackson's Company, 28th Battalion, by August 13, 1777 [Ref: M-153]. Subscribed to the Oath of

Allegiance and Fidelity in 1780 [Ref: L-121].
STRADLEY, James. Private, Militia, 14th Battalion, Capt. Joseph Richardson's Company, by August 13, 1777 [Ref: M-154].
STRADLEY, Salathiel. Private, Militia, 14th Battalion, Capt. Joseph Richardson's Company, by August 13, 1777 [Ref: M-154].
STRAWHAN (STROWN, STRAUGHAN), Thomas. Private, Militia, Capt. Thomas Hughlett's Company, 28th Battalion, by August 13, 1777 [Ref: M-152]. Rendered patriotic service by providing wheat for the use of the military in August, 1782, as verified by Giles Hicks 3rd, Commissary for Caroline County [Ref: V-6636]. "Thomas Strangham" married Ann Harrington by license dated October 19, 1778 [Ref: X-9].
STUART, Alexander. See "John Thomas," q.v.
STUART, Elizabeth. See "John Thomas," q.v.
STUBBS, Ann. See "Nicholas Stubbs," q.v.
STUBBS, Charles. See "Nicholas Stubbs," q.v.
STUBBS, Ealy. See Nicholas Stubbs," q.v.
STUBBS, John. See "Nicholas Stubbs," q.v.
STUBBS, John Jr. Rendered patriotic service by providing wheat for the use of the military in August, 1782, as verified by Giles Hicks 3rd, Commissary for Caroline County [Ref: V-6636].
STUBBS, John Sr. Rendered patriotic service by providing wheat for the use of the military in August, 1782, as verified by Giles Hicks 3rd, Commissary for Caroline County [Ref: V-6636].
STUBBS, Mary. See "Nicholas Stubbs," q.v.
STUBBS, Nicholas. Private, Militia, Capt. Nehemiah Andrew's Company, 14th Battalion, by August 13, 1777 [Ref: M-155]. In 1808 John Dawson, of John, of Fork District, filed a petition in the land commission records that Nicholas Stubbs died on February 10, 1801, seized of tracts called "Addition to Timber Tree Neck," "Levin's Folly Enlarged" and "Addition to Miles' Swamp" and left the following children: William Stubbs, John Stubbs (minor), Mary Stubbs (minor), Ann Stubbs (minor), Ealy Stubbs (minor), and Richard Stubbs (minor). Guardians to the minors were Levin Wright, of Levin, and Charles and Nancy Stubbs [Ref: T-27]. Nicholas Stubbs married Keziah Busick by license dated January 11, 1779 [Ref: X-9].
STUBBS, Richard. See "Nicholas Stubbs," q.v.
STUBBS, William. See "Nicholas Stubbs," q.v.
STUDHAM (STEEDHAM?), Thomas. Private, Militia, Capt. John Fauntleroy's Company, 28th Battalion, by August 13, 1777 [Ref: M-154].
SULLIVAN, Daniel. Rendered patriotic service by providing wheat for the use of the military in August, 1782, as verified by Giles Hicks 3rd, Commissary for Caroline County [Ref: V-6636]. See "Daniel Sullivane," q.v.
SULLIVAN (SULLIVANE), Fletcher. Rendered patriotic service by providing wheat for the use of the military in August, 1782, as verified by Giles Hicks 3rd,

Commissary for Caroline County [Ref: V-6636]. "Fletcher Sullivane" was a private, in the militia, Capt. Nehemiah Andrew's Company, 14th Battalion, by August 13, 1777 [Ref: M-155].

SULLIVAN (SULLIVANE), James. Private, Militia, Capt. Nehemiah Andrew's Company, 14th Battalion, by August 13, 1777 [Ref: M-155]. "James Sullivane" married Margaret Wheatley by license dated August 26, 1777 [Ref: X-7].

SULLIVAN, John. Private, Militia, Capt. Joseph Douglass' Company, 14th Battalion, by August 13, 1777 [Ref: M-156]. Rendered patriotic service by providing wheat for the use of the military in August, 1782, as verified by Giles Hicks 3rd, Commissary for Caroline County [Ref: V-6636]. See "John Sullivane," q.v.

SULLIVAN, John, of John. Rendered patriotic service by providing wheat for the use of the military in June, 1782, as verified by Giles Hicks 3rd, Commissary for Caroline County [Ref: V-6636].

SULLIVAN, Owen. Private, Militia, Capt. Joseph Douglass' Company, 14th Battalion, by August 13, 1777 [Ref: M-156].

SULLIVAN, Rhoda. See "James Kirkman," q.v.

SULLIVAN, William. Rendered patriotic service by providing wheat for the use of the military in August, 1782, as verified by Giles Hicks 3rd, Commissary for Caroline County [Ref: V-6636]. See "William Sullivane," q.v.

SULLIVANE, Amelia. See "John Robinson," q.v.

SULLIVANE, Daniel. Private, Militia, Capt. Nehemiah Andrew's Company, 14th Battalion, by August 13, 1777 [Ref: M-155].

SULLIVANE, Daniel. Private, Militia, Capt. Joseph Douglass' Company, 14th Battalion, by August 13, 1777 [Ref: M-156].

SULLIVANE, Darby. Private, Militia, Capt. Nehemiah Andrew's Company, 14th Battalion, by August 13, 1777 [Ref: M-155].

SULLIVANE, Florince. Private, Militia, Capt. Nehemiah Andrew's Company, 14th Battalion, by August 13, 1777 [Ref: M-155].

SULLIVANE, Jinkins. Private, Militia, Capt. Joseph Douglass' Company, 14th Battalion, by August 13, 1777 [Ref: M-156].

SULLIVANE, John. Private, Militia, Capt. Nehemiah Andrew's Company, 14th Battalion, by August 13, 1777 [Ref: M-155].

SULLIVANE, Solomon. Private (recruit), Maryland Troops, enrolled in Caroline County by William Whiteley, County Lieutenant, on August 14, 1781 to serve in the Maryland Line for 3 years [Ref: D-385].

SULLIVANE, William. Private, Militia, Capt. Nehemiah Andrew's Company, 14th Battalion, by August 13, 1777 [Ref: M-155].

SUMMERS, Felix. Subscribed to the Oath of Allegiance and Fidelity (made his "U" mark) before the Hon. Henry Downes, Jr. on March 2, 1778 [Ref: J-1814].

SUMMERS, James. Private, Militia, Capt. Joseph Douglass' Company, 14th Battalion, by August 13, 1777 [Ref: M-156]. Private, Light Horse Troops, Capt. Henry Dickinson's Company, June 12, 1781 [Ref: M-157]. James Summers

married Abisha French by license recorded on August 9, 1775 [Ref: X-6].
SUMMERS (SOMMERS), Sarah. See "Thomas Orrell," q.v.
SUMMERS, Solomon. Private, 5th Maryland Line, enlisted on May 6, 1778 and still in the service on November 1, 1780 [Ref: D-245].
SUMMERS, William (1752 -   ). Private, Militia, Capt. Vincent Price's Company, 28th Battalion, by August 13, 1777 [Ref: M-152]. Subscribed to the Oath of Allegiance and Fidelity before the Hon. Henry Downes, Jr. on March 2, 1778 [Ref: J-1814]. Private, Light Horse Troops, Capt. Henry Dickinson's Company, June 12, 1781 [Ref: M-157]. Aged 43 in a 1795 deposition [Ref: T-16].
SUMPTION, Elizabeth. See "Benjamin Townshend," q.v.
SUMPTION, Perry. See "Benjamin Townshend," q.v.
SUTTON, Benjamin. Private, Militia, Capt. Vincent Price's Company, 28th Battalion, by August 13, 1777 [Ref: M-152]. Benjamin Sutton married Rhode Toottle by license dated January 13, 1781 [Ref: X-13].
SUTTON, James. Private, Militia, Capt. Vincent Price's Company, 28th Battalion, by August 13, 1777 [Ref: M-152].
SUTTON, John. Private, Militia, Capt. Henry Downes' Company, 28th Battalion, by August 13, 1777 [Ref: M-152].
SWAN, Arabella. See "Thomas Swan," q.v.
SWAN, James. See "Thomas Swan," q.v.
SWAN, Judith. See "Thomas Goldsborough," q.v.
SWAN, Mary. See "Able Chilton," q.v.
SWAN, Sally. See "Thomas Swan," q.v.
SWAN, Solomon. Private, Militia, Capt. William Chipley's Company, 28th Battalion, by August 13, 1777 [Ref: M-153]. Subscribed to the Oath of Allegiance and Fidelity before the Hon. Nathaniel Potter on November 17, 1778 [Ref: N-46].
SWAN, Thomas. Private, Militia, Capt. William Chipley's Company, 28th Battalion, by August 13, 1777 [Ref: M-153]. See the other "Thomas Swan," q.v.
SWAN, Thomas. Private, Militia, Capt. Thomas Hughlett's Company, 28th Battalion, by August 13, 1777 [Ref: M-153]. In a 1797 land commission record it noted that Sally Swan, James Ryall and his wife Betty, stated that Thomas Swan had died in 1796, owned tracts called "Broughten" and "Broughten's Addition" and left heirs, viz., Sally Swan, Betty Ryall, Thomas Swan (son), and James and Arabella Swan (grandchildren), minors [Ref: T-18]. One Thomas Swan was aged 66 in a 1783 deposition and a Thomas Swan was aged 80 in a 1792 deposition [Ref: T-7, T-15]. Since there was more then one man named Thomas Swan, additional research will be necessary before drawing conclusions.
SWIFF, Sarah. See "Richard Mason," q.v.
SWIFT, David. Private, Militia, Capt. Andrew Fountain's Company, 14th Battalion, by August 13, 1777 [Ref: M-157]. Private, 5th Maryland Line, enlisted on June 6, 1778 and discharged on March 1, 1779 [Ref: D-245].
SWIFT, Gideon. Private, Militia, Capt. John Fauntleroy's Company, 28th Battalion,

by August 13, 1777 [Ref: M-154].

SWIFT, James, of Choptank Hundred. Subscribed to the Oath of Allegiance and Fidelity before the Hon. Benson Stainton on February 2, 1778 [Ref: J-1814].

SWIFT, James, of John. On August 7, 1780, he filed a certificate in Caroline County Court that he had subscribed to the Oath of Allegiance and Fidelity before the Hon. Thomas Hardcastle [Ref: N-86].

SWIFT, James Jr. Private, Militia, Capt. Samuel Jackson's Company, 28th Battalion, by August 13, 1777 [Ref: M-153]. Subscribed to the Oath of Allegiance and Fidelity in 1780 [Ref: L-121].

SWIFT, James Sr. Private, Militia, Capt. Samuel Jackson's Company, 28th Battalion, by August 13, 1777 [Ref: M-153]. Subscribed to the Oath of Allegiance and Fidelity in 1780 [Ref: L-121].

SWIFT, John. Private, Militia, Capt. Samuel Jackson's Company, 28th Battalion, by August 13, 1777 [Ref: M-153]. Subscribed to the Oath of Allegiance and Fidelity in 1780 [Ref: L-121].

SWIFT, Mary. See "John Newcomb," q.v.

SWIFT, Richard. Private, Militia, Capt. Samuel Jackson's Company, 28th Battalion, by August 13, 1777 [Ref: M-153]. He may have been related to "Richard Swift, Quaker" who was aged 69 in 1776 and the son of William Swift and brother of William Swift [Ref: T-1]. One Richard Swift married Sarah Reynolds by license dated May 3, 1785, and a Richard Swift married Rachel Smith by license dated August 13, 1793 [Ref: X-16, X-25].

SWIFT, Samuel. Private, Militia, Capt. Samuel Jackson's Company, 28th Battalion, by August 13, 1777 [Ref: M-153]. Rendered patriotic service by providing wheat for the use of the military in August, 1782, as verified by Giles Hicks 3rd, Commissary for Caroline County [Ref: V-6636].

SWIFT, Sarah. See "Richard Mason" and "Solomon Clark," q.v.

SWIFT, Thomas. Private, Militia, Capt. Samuel Jackson's Company, 28th Battalion, by August 13, 1777 [Ref: M-153]. One Thomas Swift married Sarah Mason by license dated December 14, 1790 [Ref: X-22].

SWIFT, Vincent. Private, Militia, Capt. Samuel Jackson's Company, 28th Battalion, by August 13, 1777 [Ref: M-153].

SWIFT, William. See "Richard Swift," q.v.

SWIGGATE, Benjamin. Private, Militia, Capt. Andrew Fountain's Company, 14th Battalion, by August 13, 1777 [Ref: M-157]. Rendered patriotic service by providing wheat for the use of the military in August, 1782, as verified by Giles Hicks 3rd, Commissary for Caroline County [Ref: V-6636, which listed the name as "Ben Swigate"].

SWIGGATE, Harmon. Private, Militia, Capt. John Stafford's Company, 14th Battalion, by August 13, 1777 [Ref: M-156].

SWIGGATE, Henry Jr. Private, Militia, Capt. John Stafford's Company, 14th Battalion, by August 13, 1777 [Ref: M-156]. He was probably the son of "Henry Swiggett" who was aged 55 in a 1785 deposition [Ref: T-11].

SWIGGATE, James. Private, Militia, Capt. John Stafford's Company, 14th Battalion, by August 13, 1777 [Ref: M-156]. "James Swigget" married Elizabeth Priest on July 3, 1755 [Ref: K-27].
SWIGGATE, Johnson. Private, Militia, Capt. John Stafford's Company, 14th Battalion, by August 13, 1777 [Ref: M-156].
SWIGGATE, William. Private, Militia, Capt. John Stafford's Company, 14th Battalion, by August 13, 1777 [Ref: M-156].
SYLVESTER, Benjamin. First Lieutenant, Militia, Capt. Thomas Hughlett's Company, 1777, and subsequently resigned before June 19, 1777, and was a Recruiting Officer, 1779-1780 [Ref: J-1814, F-49]. Stored wheat for the use of the State of Maryland, as certified by Richard Keene, Commissary for Caroline County, on June 3, 1780 [Ref: P-294]. In an 1818 land commission record it stated that Benjamin Sylvester had died on March 17, 1795, seized of many land tracts [too numerous to mention here, but they are listed in the record] and leaving a daughter Martha Purnell and grandchildren Serena Purnell (who married Edmond Pendleton and had Isaac Purnell Pendleton and Serena Catherine Pendleton, and has since died) and Clarissa Purnell (daughters of Isaac Purnell, of Baltimore, who died August 11, 1813). Martha also had Frederick, Adeline, and Mary Purnell, and died on June 15, 1805 [Ref: T-31].
SYLVESTER, Cloudsberry. Private, Militia, Capt. William Chipley's Company, 28th Battalion, by August 13, 1777 [Ref: M-153]. Subscribed to the Oath of Allegiance and Fidelity (made his "+" mark) before the Hon. Richard Mason on March 2, 1778 [Ref: J-1814, which spelled the name "Cloudsbery Silvester"].
SYLVESTER, Daniel. See "David Sylvester," q.v.
SYLVESTER, David. Rendered patriotic service by providing wheat for the use of the military in August, 1782, as verified by Giles Hicks 3rd, Commissary for Caroline County [Ref: V-6636, which spelled the name "Silvester"]. See "Purnell Sylvester" and "Thomas Roe," q.v.
SYLVESTER, Herrington. Private, Militia, Capt. William Chipley's Company, 28th Battalion, by August 13, 1777 [Ref: M-153].
SYLVESTER, Herrington. Private, Militia, Capt. William Hopper's Company, 28th Battalion, by August 13, 1777 [Ref: M-151]. One "Kerrington Sylvester" married Sophia Mason by license dated January 1, 1783 [Ref: X-14].
SYLVESTER, James. Private, Militia, Capt. William Chipley's Company, 28th Battalion, by August 13, 1777 [Ref: M-153].
SYLVESTER, Jane. See "Valentine Green," q.v.
SYLVESTER, Julia. See "Abner Roe," q.v.
SYLVESTER, Margaret. See "Purnell Sylvester," q.v.
SYLVESTER, Martha. See "Benjamin Sylvester," q.v.
SYLVESTER, Mary. See "Thomas Roe," q.v.
SYLVESTER, Nancy. See "Purnell Sylvester," q.v.
SYLVESTER, Purnell (1754-1811). Private, Militia, Capt. William Chipley's Company, 28th Battalion, by August 13, 1777 [Ref: M-153, which spelled his

name "Purnall"]. Purnell Sylvester was aged 56 in an 1810 deposition (noting that his father, David Sylvester, was deceased). In 1811 Thomas Sylvester filed a petition in the land commission records that his father, Purnell Sylvester, had died on May 14, 1811, seized of tracts called "Grubby Neck" and "Grubby Neck Addition" and leaving the following heirs: David Sylvester (of age), Nancy Sylvester (of age; married Richard Legg), Thomas Sylvester (of age), Daniel Sylvester (aged about 18), Samuel Sylvester (aged about 14), Margaret Sylvester (aged about 14), and Sarah Sylvester (aged about 7). [Ref: T-25, T-28]. Purnell Sylvester married H. Evans by license dated November 30, 1778 [Ref: X-9].

SYLVESTER, Rachel. See "Thomas Ozmont" and "Isaac Merrick," q.v.

SYLVESTER, Samuel. See "Purnell Sylvester," q.v.

SYLVESTER, Sarah. See "Ezekiel Hunter, Jr." and "Purnell Sylvester," q.v.

SYLVESTER, Thomas. Subscribed to the Oath of Allegiance and Fidelity before the Hon. Richard Mason on March 2, 1778 [Ref: J-1814, which spelled the name "Silvester"]. One "Thomas Silvester" was a private in the 5th Maryland Line who enlisted on May 20, 1778 and died on August 21, 1778 [Ref: D-245]. See "Purnell Sylvester," q.v.

SYLVESTER, Tryphena. See "John Russum," q.v.

SYLVESTER, William (1753 -   ). Private, Militia, Capt. William Hopper's Company, 28th Battalion, by August 13, 1777 [Ref: M-151]. Aged 57 in 1810 deposition [Ref: T-26].

TALBOTT, Margaret. See "William Bell, Jr.," q.v.

TALBOTT, Samuel. See "Charles Manship, Jr.," q.v.

TALLBOY, Robert (1759 -   ). Private, Militia, Capt. Andrew Fountain's Company, 14th Battalion, by August 13, 1777 [Ref: M-157]. Aged 35 in a 1794 deposition [Ref: T-16, which spelled the name "Talboy"].

TALLBOY, William. Private, Militia, Capt. Andrew Fountain's Company, 14th Battalion, by August 13, 1777 [Ref: M-157]. Rendered patriotic service by providing wheat for the use of the military in August, 1782, as verified by Giles Hicks 3rd, Commissary for Caroline County [Ref: V-6636]. William Talboy married Elizabeth Scott by license dated February 2, 1780 [Ref: X-11].

TANNER, James. Private, Maryland Troops, enlisted by Capt. Joseph Richardson in Caroline County and passed by Col. William Richardson on August 31, 1776 [Ref: D-69].

TAYLOR, Absalom. Private, Militia, Capt. John Fauntleroy's Company, 28th Battalion, by August 13, 1777 [Ref: M-154].

TAYLOR, Clarissa. See "Richard Cooper," q.v.

TAYLOR, Robert Henry. See "William Harris," q.v.

TAYLOR, Sarah. See "Vinson Chance," q.v.

TEAT, Elizabeth. See "Richard Fisher," q.v.

TEMPLE, William. Private, 6th Company, Capt. Peter Adams, 1st Maryland Line, enlisted May 7, 1776 [Ref: D-15].

TEMPLEMAN, Henry. Private, Militia, Capt. John Stafford's Company, 14th

Battalion, by August 13, 1777 [Ref: M-156].

THARPE, John. Private, Militia, Capt. William Hopper's Company, 28th Battalion, by August 13, 1777 [Ref: M-151].

THAWLEY, Edward (1744 -   ). Private, Militia, Capt. William Hopper's Company, 28th Battalion, by August 13, 1777 [Ref: M-151]. Subscribed to the Oath of Allegiance and Fidelity (made his "L" mark) before the Hon. Henry Downes, Jr. on March 2, 1778 [Ref: J-1814]. Rendered patriotic service by providing wheat for the use of the military in August, 1782, as verified by Giles Hicks 3rd, Commissary for Caroline County [Ref: V-6636]. Aged 38 in a 1782 deposition, noting he was the son of John Thawley [Ref: T-4].

THAWLEY, John (1754 -   ). Private, Militia, Capt. William Hopper's Company, 28th Battalion, by August 13, 1777 [Ref: M-151]. Rendered patriotic service by providing wheat for the use of the military in August, 1782, as verified by Giles Hicks 3rd, Commissary for Caroline County [Ref: V-6636]. Aged 28 in a 1782 deposition [Ref: T-4]. See "Edward Thawley" and "James Barwick," q.v.

THAWLEY, Mary. See "James Barwick," q.v.

THOMAS, Ann. See "Ellis Thomas," q.v.

THOMAS, Anna Louisa. See "John Thomas," q.v.

THOMAS, Easter. See "Ellis Thomas," q.v.

THOMAS, Ellis (1755/6-1839). Private, Maryland Troops, enlisted by Capt. Joseph Richardson in Caroline County and passed by Col. William Richardson on August 31, 1776 [Ref: D-69]. Private, Militia, Capt. John Mitchell's Company, 14th Battalion, by August 13, 1777 [Ref: M-155]. Subscribed to the Oath of Allegiance and Fidelity before the Hon. Charles Dickinson on March 1, 1778 [Ref: J-1418]. "Ellis Thomas" was aged 29 in a 1785 deposition, aged 33 in a 1789 deposition, and aged 43 in a 1798 deposition, noting he was a grandson of John Richardson. "Elias Thomas" was aged 36 in a 1792 deposition, noting he was a grandson of John Richardson [Ref: T-10, T-13, T-17, T-19]. Mary Thomas, widow of Ellis, applied for a pension (W9519) in Anne Arundel County, Maryland on April 11, 1843, aged 82, stating her name was "Mary H-?-is" [Harris] before she married Ellis Thomas in Caroline County, Maryland on April 12, 1787. She was his second wife; name of first wife not stated. Ellis died on November 13, 1839 and his children were as follows, which is incomplete since family data is in poor condition in pension file: William Thomas (by his first wife; born in May, 17-?-); Ellis Thomas (first child by second wife; born August 15, 1788); John Richard Thomas (born August 15, 1790); Ann Thomas (born January 7, 1793); --?-- Thomas (a son; born October 19, 179?); James Thomas (born June 14, 1798); Easter Thomas (born in 1800); and, Mary Thomas (born in 1803). [Ref: Y-2915, and W-3462, which recommends "see National Archives Series M804, Roll #2368 for complete file," and X-18, which states the marriage license of Ellis Thomas and Mary Harris was dated March 12, 1787]. See "John Thomas," q.v.

THOMAS, Henry. See "John Thomas," q.v.

THOMAS, Isaac. On September 2, 1778, John West gave a deposition in Caroline County pertaining to "the qualification and enlistment of Isaac Thomas in Col. William Haslett's Regulars." [Ref: P-187].

THOMAS, James. See "Ellis Thomas," q.v.

THOMAS, John (1755-1799). Private, Maryland Troops, enrolled by Lieut. Thomas Wynn Loockerman in Caroline County in July, 1776 [Ref: D-69]. Private, Militia, Capt. John Mitchell's Company, 14th Battalion, by August 13, 1777 [Ref: M-155]. Subscribed to the Oath of Allegiance and Fidelity before the Hon. Thomas Hardcastle on February 27, 1778 [Ref: J-1814]. John Thomas was born in 1755 in (now) Caroline County and lived in Dorchester County (which part became Caroline County) at the time of his enlistment in 1776. He lived there until 1800 when he moved to Anne Arundel County and on June 4, 1833 he applied for a pension. Rebecca Gibson of Talbot County referred to him as John Thomas, Jr. on May 24, 1844 and Rebecca R. Gibson witnessed her affidavit. John Thomas' grandson John T. Thomas made an inquiry from Queen Anne's County on March 3, 1851 and stated his grandfather died in 1799. Nathan Allen made affidavit in 1843 in Queen Anne's County that he lived with John Thomas, Sr. (soldier's father) for several years before John Thomas, Jr. married Elizabeth Gibson of Talbot County. Henry Thomas (soldier's son) made affidavit on July 1, 1851 and referred to Capt. Woolman Gibson, a son of John Gibson (relationship to his mother not stated), and he stated that John Thomas, Jr. died October 3, 1799. Henry stated he was born on September 13, 1783 and his stepfather Dr. Alexander Stuart died in 1806 and his mother Elizabeth died on February 20, 1849 at her granddaughter Elizabeth Pratt's near Queenstown in Queen Anne's County. He also stated soldier had died leaving three children: Henry Thomas (born September 13, 1783); Anna Louisa Thomas (who was born October 18, 1786, married Charles Gibson, had children but no names were given, and in November, 1844, Anna Louisa was aged 61); and, John Gibson Thomas (who was born December 22, 1789 and was a resident of Queen Anne's County in 1844). John Thomas' widow Elizabeth (Gibson) (Thomas) Stuart applied for a pension (W27527) on May 19, 1845 in Queen Anne's County, aged 82, stating she had married John on May 9, 1779 and he died on October 3, 1799. She married second in 1804 to Dr. Alexander Stuart of Kent County, Maryland, who also served in the Revolutionary War. Alexander died on April 20, 1806. Ellis Thomas was a witness to her application, but no relationship was stated [Ref: W-3465]. See "Ellis Thomas," q.v.

THOMAS, John G. See "John Thomas," q.v.

THOMAS, John R. See "Ellis Thomas," q.v.

THOMAS, John T. See "John Thomas," q.v.

THOMAS, Joseph. Private, Maryland Troops, enrolled by Lieut. Thomas Wynn Loockerman in Caroline County in July, 1776 [Ref: D-69].

THOMAS, Mary. See "Ellis Thomas" and "William Walker, Jr." and "William Coursey," q.v.

THOMAS, Nathaniel. Rendered patriotic service by providing wheat for the use of the military in August, 1782, as verified by Giles Hicks 3rd, Commissary for Caroline County [Ref: V-6636].

THOMAS, Richard. Private, Militia, 14th Battalion, Capt. Joseph Richardson's Company, by August 13, 1777 [Ref: M-154]. Richard Thomas married Rhoda Porter by license recorded August 9, 1775 [Ref: X-6].

THOMAS, Robert. Private, Maryland Troops, enlisted by Capt. Joseph Richardson in Caroline County and passed by Col. William Richardson on August 31, 1776 [Ref: D-69]. Private, Militia, Capt. John Mitchell's Company, 14th Battalion, by August 13, 1777 [Ref: M-155]. Robert Thomas married Eleanor Alford by license dated June 3, 1779 [Ref: X-10].

THOMAS, Tamsey. See "John Diggans (Diggin)," q.v.

THOMAS, Thomas. Private, Militia, Capt. Henry Downes' Company, 28th Battalion, by August 13, 1777 [Ref: M-152].

THOMAS, William. See "Ellis Thomas," q.v.

THOMPSON, Susan. See "Joseph Douglass," q.v.

THORMAN, Elizabeth. See "John Robinson," q.v.

THORNTON, George. On August 23, 1780, he filed a certificate in Caroline County Court that he had subscribed to the Oath of Allegiance and Fidelity before the Hon. Thomas Hardcastle [Ref: N-86, L-121].

TILGHMAN, Matthew. Private, Militia, Capt. William Hopper's Company, 28th Battalion, by August 13, 1777 [Ref: M-151].

TILLOTSON, Elizabeth. See "Philemon Downes," q.v.

TILLOTSON, John. Clerk to the Committee of Observation by June 8, 1776 [Ref: A-481]. Ensign, Militia, Capt. William Hopper's Company, 28th Battalion, June 19, 1777; subsequently reported dead and was replaced by Solomon Kenton (Taylor) as ensign [Ref: V-6636]. See "Philemon Downes," q.v.

TILLOTSON, Thomas Baynard. See "Philemon Downes," q.v.

TODD, Michal. Private, Militia, 14th Battalion, Capt. Richard Andrew's Company, by August 13, 1777 [Ref: M-156].

TODD, Nathan. Private, Militia, 14th Battalion, Capt. Richard Andrew's Company, by August 13, 1777 [Ref: M-156]. Rendered patriotic service by providing wheat for the use of the military in May, 1782, as verified by Giles Hicks 3rd, Commissary for Caroline County [Ref: V-6636].

TODD, Richard. Rendered patriotic service by providing wheat for the use of the military in August, 1782, as verified by Giles Hicks 3rd, Commissary for Caroline County [Ref: V-6636].

TOLSON, John. Private, Militia, Capt. Thomas Hughlett's Company, 28th Battalion, by August 13, 1777 [Ref: M-153]. Subscribed to the Oath of Allegiance and Fidelity before the Hon. Richard Mason on March 2, 1778 [Ref: J-1814, which spelled the name "Toalson"]. Ensign, Militia, Capt. Hughlett's Company, April 18, 1780. Second Lieutenant, Militia, Capt. Robert Hardcastle's Company, December 17, 1781 [Ref: M-1130, F-144, I-27].

TOMLINSON, Bennett. See "James McQuality," q.v.
TOOLSON, Mary. See "James Boon," q.v.
TOOTTLE, Rhode. See "Benjamin Sutton," q.v.
TOWERS, Africa. See "George Morgan," q.v.
TOWERS, James. Private, Militia, Capt. Shadrack Liden's Company, 14th Battalion, by August 13, 1777 [Ref: M-155]. Rendered patriotic service by providing wheat for the use of the military in August, 1782, as verified by Giles Hicks 3rd, Commissary for Caroline County [Ref: V-6636]. James Towers married Tamsey Bland, and James Towers, Jr. married Mary Hobbs, both by licenses dated November 12, 1788 [Ref: X-19].
TOWERS, Solomon. Private, Militia, Capt. Shadrack Liden's Company, 14th Battalion, by August 13, 1777 [Ref: M-155]. Rendered patriotic service by providing wheat for the use of the military in August, 1782, as verified by Giles Hicks 3rd, Commissary for Caroline County [Ref: V-6636].
TOWERS, Thomas (1747 -   ). Private, Militia, Capt. Nehemiah Andrew's Company, 14th Battalion, by August 13, 1777 [Ref: M-155]. Rendered patriotic service by providing wheat for the use of the military in August, 1782, as verified by Giles Hicks 3rd, Commissary for Caroline County [Ref: V-6636]. Aged 50 in a 1797 deposition [Ref: T-19].
TOWNSHEND (TOWNSEND), Benjamin. Private, Militia, Capt. Thomas Hughlett's Company, 28th Battalion, by August 13, 1777 [Ref: M-152, which listed the name as "Townstind(?)"]. Private, 5th Maryland Line, enlisted February 4, 1777 or August 1, 1778 (both dates were given) and still in the service on November 1, 1780 [Ref: D-251]. Rendered patriotic service by providing wheat for the use of the military in August, 1782, as verified by Giles Hicks 3rd, Commissary for Caroline County [Ref: V-6636, which spelled the name "Townsend"]. One "Benjamin Townsend" died on January 17, 1790, possessed of tracts called "Whitbey's Hazard," "Irish Discovery" and "Dublin" and leaving children as follows: Elizabeth Sumption (wife of Perry A. Sumption), Henrietta (wife of Richard Ridgaway), William Townsend, John Townsend, Thomas Townsend, Sarah Townsend, Cecelia Townsend, and Rachel Townsend [Ref: T-20].
TOWNSHEND, James. Private, Militia, Capt. John Fauntleroy's Company, 28th Battalion, by August 13, 1777 [Ref: M-154].
TOWNSHEND, Thomas. Private, Militia, Capt. William Chipley's Company, 28th Battalion, by August 13, 1777 [Ref: M-153].
TRIPPE, James, son of John, of Dorchester County. "Marriner, belonging to Capt. Thomas Noel's sloop now lying at his wharf," subscribed to the Oath of Allegiance and Fidelity before the Hon. Peter Richardson on March 1, 1778 [Ref: J-1814].
TRIPPE, Levin, of Dorchester County. "Marriner, belonging to Capt. Thomas Noel's sloop now lying at his wharf," subscribed to the Oath of Allegiance and Fidelity before the Hon. Peter Richardson on March 1, 1778 [Ref: J-1814].

TROTH, James. Subscribed to the Oath of Allegiance and Fidelity (made his "X" mark) before the Hon. Henry Downes, Jr. on March 2, 1778 [Ref: J-1814].

TUCKER, James. Private, Militia, Capt. Nehemiah Andrew's Company, 14th Battalion, by August 13, 1777 [Ref: M-155].

TUCKER, Levi. Rendered patriotic service by providing wheat for the use of the military in June, 1782, as verified by Giles Hicks 3rd, Commissary for Caroline County [Ref: V-6636].

TULL, Levin. Private, Militia, Capt. Shadrack Liden's Company, 14th Battalion, by August 13, 1777 [Ref: M-155]. He may be the Levin Tull who was aged about 48 in an 1809 deposition [Ref: T-26].

TULL, William. Private, Militia, Capt. Shadrack Liden's Company, 14th Battalion, by August 13, 1777 [Ref: M-155]. William Tull married Mary Grace by license dated December 23, 1777 [Ref: X-7].

TURBUTT, Samuel. See "Foster Goldsborough," q.v.

TURBUTT, Sarah. See "Thomas Goldsborough" and "Foster Goldsborough," q.v.

TURNER, Edward. On March 23, 1780, he filed a certificate in Caroline County Court that he had subscribed to the Oath of Allegiance and Fidelity before the Hon. Joseph Bewley [Ref: N-75].

TURNER, Elizabeth. See "Thomas Burk," q.v.

TURNER, George. Rendered patriotic service by providing wheat for the use of the military in August, 1782, as verified by Giles Hicks 3rd, Commissary for Caroline County [Ref: V-6636]. George Turner married --?-- Smith by license dated December 31, 1777 [Ref: X-7].

TURNER, Henry. Two men with this name were privates in the militia, Capt. John Mitchell's Company, 14th Battalion, by August 13, 1777 [Ref: M-155]. Henry Turner, Jr. married Sarah Blades by license dated September 10, 1782, and Henry Turner, Jr. married Rebecca Eaton by license dated January 14, 1791 [Ref: X-14, X-22].

TURNER, John. Private, Maryland Troops, enrolled by Lieut. Thomas Wynn Loockerman in Caroline County in July, 1776 [Ref: D-69]. Private, Militia, 14th Battalion, Capt. Joseph Richardson's Company, by August 13, 1777 [Ref: M-154]. Subscribed to the Oath of Allegiance and Fidelity (made his "T" mark) before the Hon. Peter Richardson on February 28, 1778 [Ref: J-1814].

TURNER, Lucretia. See "John Blades," q.v.

TURNER, Nice. See "James Fisher," q.v.

TURNER, Thomas. Private, Militia, Capt. John Mitchell's Company, 14th Battalion, by August 13, 1777 [Ref: M-155]. Thomas Turner married Ann Andrew by license dated April 26, 1781 [Ref: X-13].

TURPIN, Ann or Nancy. See "Joseph Douglass," q.v.

TWIFORD, Brown. Private, Militia, 14th Battalion, Capt. Richard Andrew's Company, by August 13, 1777 [Ref: M-156].

TWYFORD, Charles. Private, Militia, Capt. Joseph Douglass' Company, 14th Battalion, by August 13, 1777 [Ref: M-156].

TYLER (TYLOR), Elijah. Private, Maryland Troops, enrolled by Lieut. Thomas Wynn Loockerman in Caroline County in July, 1776 [Ref: D-69]. Private, Militia, Capt. Shadrack Liden's Company, 14th Battalion, by August 13, 1777 [Ref: M-155]. Subscribed to the Oath of Allegiance and Fidelity (made his mark that resembled a large "A" with the left leg missing) before the Hon. Nathaniel Potter on March 2, 1778 [Ref: J-1814].

VAINE, Bartholomew. Private, Militia, Capt. Shadrack Liden's Company, 14th Battalion, by August 13, 1777 [Ref: M-155].

VAINE, Thomas. Private, Maryland Troops, enlisted by Capt. Joseph Richardson in Caroline County and passed by Col. William Richardson on August 31, 1776 [Ref: D-69].

VALLIANT (VALLIENT), Ansell (Anson). Private (draft), Maryland Troops, enrolled in Caroline County by William Whiteley, County Lieutenant, on August 14, 1781 to serve in the Maryland Line until December 10, 1781 [Ref: D-385, which spelled the name "Ansell Vallient"]. Honorably discharged from the service on December 5, 1781 [Ref: I-10, which spelled the name "Anson Valliant"].

VALLIANT (VALLIENT), Daniel. Private, Militia, Capt. John Mitchell's Company, 14th Battalion, by August 13, 1777 [Ref: M-155]. Daniel Valliant married Elizabeth Alford by license dated January 29, 1787 [Ref: X-17].

VALLIANT (VALLIENT), John. Private, Militia, Capt. John Mitchell's Company, 14th Battalion, by August 13, 1777 [Ref: M-155]. John Vallient, Jr. married Eliza Lowrey by license dated April 10, 1779 [Ref: X-10].

VALLIANT (VALLIENT), Thomas. Private, Militia, Capt. John Mitchell's Company, 14th Battalion, by August 13, 1777 [Ref: M-155].

VANDERFORD, Sarah Hall. See "Hawkins Downes," q.v.

VAUX (VAULX), Ebenezer (Eben). Rendered patriotic service by providing wheat for the use of the military in August, 1782, as verified by Giles Hicks 3rd, Commissary for Caroline County [Ref: V-6636].

VAUX (VAULX), John. Rendered patriotic service by providing wheat for the use of the military in August, 1782, as verified by Giles Hicks 3rd, Commissary for Caroline County [Ref: V-6636].

VAUX (VAULX), Salathiel. Private, Militia, Capt. John Stafford's Company, 14th Battalion, by August 13, 1777 [Ref: M-156, which spelled the name "Selathiel Vaulz"]. Rendered patriotic service by providing wheat for the use of the military in August, 1782, as verified by Giles Hicks 3rd, Commissary for Caroline County [Ref: V-6636].

VAUX (VAULX), William. Private, Militia, Capt. Henry Downes' Company, 28th Battalion, by August 13, 1777 [Ref: M-152, which spelled the name "Vaulx"]. Subscribed to the Oath of Allegiance and Fidelity before the Hon. Thomas Hardcastle on February 27, 1778 [Ref: J-1814, which spelled the name "Vox"]. Rendered patriotic service by providing wheat for the use of the military in August, 1782, as verified by Giles Hicks 3rd, Commissary for Caroline County

[Ref: V-6636]. "William Vaulx" married Mary Tumpillian by license dated May 29, 1789 [Ref: X-19].

VICKERS, Thomas. Private, Militia, Capt. John Mitchell's Company, 14th Battalion, by August 13, 1777 [Ref: M-155].

VINSON, David. Private, Militia, Capt. Vincent Price's Company, 28th Battalion, by August 13, 1777 [Ref: M-152].

VINSON, Jethrew. Private, Militia, Capt. John Stafford's Company, 14th Battalion, by August 13, 1777 [Ref: M-156].

WADDELL (WADDLE), Alexander (c1732-1790). Subscribed to the Oath of Allegiance and Fidelity (made his "X" mark) before the Hon. Peter Richardson on February 23, 1778 [Ref: J-1814]. Alexander Waddell was born circa 1732, married Elizabeth --?--, rendered patriotic service during the war, and died before February 8, 1790 [Ref: Y-3061].

WADDELL (WADDLE), Alexander. Ensign, Militia, Capt. Joseph Richardson's Company, May 24, 1776. Second Lieutenant, Militia, 14th Battalion, Capt. Joseph Richardson's Company, 14th Battalion [Ref: M-154, M-132, A-442, A-482]. First Lieutenant, Militia, Capt. Thomas Loockerman's Company, 14th Battalion, June 24, 1777, and Captain, December 17, 1781 [Ref: M-132, I-27, C-299].

WADDELL (WADDLE), James. Private, Militia, 14th Battalion, Capt. Joseph Richardson's Company, by August 13, 1777 [Ref: M-154]. One James Waddell married Mary Saulsbury by license dated June 1, 1792 [Ref: X-24]. One James Waddell was aged 56 in a 1786 deposition and aged 62 in a 1793 deposition [Ref: T-14, T-16].

WADDELL (WADDLE), Jesse. Private, Militia, Capt. Nehemiah Andrew's Company, 14th Battalion, by August 13, 1777 [Ref: M-155].

WADDELL (WADDLE), John. Private, Militia, 14th Battalion, Capt. Joseph Richardson's Company, by August 13, 1777 [Ref: M-154]. Subscribed to the Oath of Allegiance and Fidelity before the Hon. Peter Richardson on February 28, 1778 [Ref: J-1814]. John Waddell married Elizabeth Wright by license dated August 5, 1790 [Ref: X-21].

WADDELL (WADDLE), Robert. Private, Maryland Troops, enrolled by Lieut. Thomas Wynn Loockerman in Caroline County in July, 1776 [Ref: D-69]. Private, Militia, 14th Battalion, Capt. Joseph Richardson's Company, by August 13, 1777 [Ref: M-154]. Subscribed to the Oath of Allegiance and Fidelity before the Hon. Charles Dickinson on March 1, 1778 [Ref: J-1418]. Robert Waddell married Elizabeth Ball by license dated April 25, 1778 [Ref: X-8].

WADDELL, Rowland. Private, Militia, 14th Battalion, Capt. Richard Andrew's Company, by August 13, 1777 [Ref: M-156].

WADMAN, Susannah. See "Emanuel Cranor (Craynor)," q.v.

WADMAN (WHADMAN), Wheatley or Wheatly (1726-   ). On May 26, 1780, he filed a certificate in Caroline County Court that he had subscribed to the Oath of Allegiance and Fidelity before the Hon. Richard Mason [Ref: N-78]. Rendered patriotic service by providing wheat for the use of the military in September, 1782, as verified by Giles Hicks 3rd, Commissary for Caroline County [Ref: V-6636]. Aged 56 in a 1782 deposition [Ref: T-3].

WALES, William. Private (recruit), Maryland Troops, enrolled in Caroline County by William Whiteley, County Lieutenant, on August 14, 1781 to serve in the Maryland Line until December 10, 1781 [Ref: D-385].

WALKER, --?--. See "Hephzebah Guild," q.v.

WALKER, Ann. See "Henry Dickinson" and "John Willoughby," q.v.

WALKER, Charles. Subscribed to the Oath of Allegiance and Fidelity (made his mark that resembled a large backwards "C") before the Hon. Richard Mason on March 2, 1778 [Ref: J-1814]. Charles Walker married Susanna Price by license dated April 14, 1779 [Ref: X-10].

WALKER, Daniel. Private, Militia, Capt. Henry Downes' Company, 28th Battalion, by August 13, 1777 [Ref: M-152].

WALKER, Elizabeth. See "Henry Dickinson," q.v.

WALKER, John. Private, Militia, Capt. John Stafford's Company, 14th Battalion, by August 13, 1777 [Ref: M-156].

WALKER, John. Private, Militia, Capt. John Mitchell's Company, 14th Battalion, by August 13, 1777 [Ref: M-155].

WALKER, John. Private, Militia, 14th Battalion, Capt. Richard Andrew's Company, by August 13, 1777 [Ref: M-156].

WALKER, John. Subscribed to the Oath of Allegiance and Fidelity before the Hon. Charles Dickinson on March 1, 1778 [Ref: J-1418]. Rendered patriotic service by providing wheat for the use of the military in August, 1782, as verified by Giles Hicks 3rd, Commissary for Caroline County [Ref: V-6636].

WALKER, Michal. Private, Maryland Troops, enlisted by Capt. Joseph Richardson in Caroline County and passed by Col. William Richardson on August 31, 1776 [Ref: D-69].

WALKER, Moses. Private, Militia, 14th Battalion, Capt. Joseph Richardson's Company, by August 13, 1777 [Ref: M-154]. Second Lieutenant, Militia, Capt. Alexander Waddle's Company, December 17, 1781 [Ref: M-132, I-27].

WALKER, Nancy (Anne). See "Philip Walker," q.v.

WALKER, Philip. Son of Rev. Philip Walker (died in 1776) and Elizabeth Dickinson Richardson (widow of Anthony Richardson and daughter of James Dickinson). Philip was born after 1740 and married first to --?-- Dickinson (daughter of William Dickinson of Talbot County), and second to Margaret Dickinson (daughter of Charles Dickinson) by license dated December 5, 1780. He had a daughter Nancy (Anne) Walker who married John Dickinson [Ref: R-854, X-13]. Subscribed to the Oath of Allegiance and Fidelity before the Hon. Peter Richardson on January 26, 1778 [Ref: J-1814]. Philip was County Coroner, 1778-1791, Commissioner of Tax between 1782 and 1790, and represented Caroline County in the Lower House of the Maryland General Assembly, 1786-1790. He died between January 21, 1791 and May 5, 1791 in Caroline County

[Ref: R-854, R-91, R-92, E-172]. See "Henry Dickinson," q.v.

WALKER, William. Private, Maryland Troops, enlisted by Capt. Joseph Richardson in Caroline County and passed by Col. William Richardson on August 31, 1776 [Ref: D-69]. Private, Militia, Capt. John Mitchell's Company, 14th Battalion, by August 13, 1777 [Ref: M-155]. Subscribed to the Oath of Allegiance and Fidelity before the Hon. Charles Dickinson on March 1, 1778 [Ref: J-1418]. One William Walker married Elizabeth Green by license dated April 19, 1779, and a William Walker married Rebecca Crunan by license dated January 30, 1793 [Ref: X-10, X-25].

WALKER, William Jr. Private, Militia, Capt. John Mitchell's Company, 14th Battalion, by August 13, 1777 [Ref: M-155]. Subscribed to the Oath of Allegiance and Fidelity before the Hon. Peter Richardson on February 26, 1778 [Ref: J-1814]. William Walker, Jr. married Mary Thomas by license dated February 22, 1779 [Ref: X-10]. See "William Walker," q.v.

WALL, Levin. Rendered patriotic service by providing wheat for the use of the military in August, 1782, as verified by Giles Hicks 3rd, Commissary for Caroline County [Ref: V-6636].

WALLACE, Hugh. Private, 6th Company, Capt. Peter Adams, 1st Maryland Line, enlisted January 30, 1776 [Ref: D-14].

WALLS, John Milburn. First Lieutenant, Militia, Capt. Samuel Jackson's Company, in 1777, entered "in the continental service" on February 20, 1777 as an ensign, 5th Maryland Line, and resigned on October 13, 1778 [Ref: J-1814, D-254]. "John Milbourne Walls" subscribed to the Oath of Allegiance and Fidelity before the Hon. Richard Mason on March 2, 1778 [Ref: J-1814]. "John Melborn Walls" rendered patriotic service by providing wheat for the use of the military in August, 1782, as verified by Giles Hicks 3rd, Commissary for Caroline County [Ref: V-6636].

WALTERS (WATTERS?), Alexander. Private, Militia, Capt. William Chipley's Company, 28th Battalion, by August 13, 1777 [Ref: M-153].

WARD, Ann. See "Levin Noble" and "Henry Ward," q.v.

WARD, Daniel. See "Henry Ward," q.v.

WARD, Esther. See "Henry Ward," q.v.

WARD, Henry. Private, Militia, Capt. Vincent Price's Company, 28th Battalion, by August 13, 1777 [Ref: M-152]. Henry Ward married Mary Cooper (born July 6, 1750, daughter of Richard Cooper) in 1767 and their children were Ann (Nancy) Ward, Daniel Ward, Henry Ward, James Ward, Richard Ward, Lydia Ward, Sarah Ward, Esther Ward, and Rachel Ward [Ref: Q-32:2 (Spring, 1991), pp. 140-141].

WARD, James. See "Henry Ward," q.v.

WARD, John. Rendered patriotic service by providing wheat for the use of the military in August, 1782, as verified by Giles Hicks 3rd, Commissary for Caroline County [Ref: V-6636].

WARD, Lydia. See "Henry Ward," q.v.

WARD, Mary White. See "Levin Noble," q.v.

WARD, Rachel. See "Henry Ward," q.v.

WARD, Richard. Rendered patriotic service by providing wheat for the use of the military in August, 1782, as verified by Giles Hicks 3rd, Commissary for Caroline County [Ref: V-6636]. See "Henry Ward," q.v.

WARD, Sarah. See "Henry Ward," q.v.

WARREN, Clark. Private, Militia, Capt. William Haslett's Company, 28th Battalion, by August 13, 1777 [Ref: M-152]. Rendered patriotic service by providing wheat for the use of the military in August, 1782, as verified by Giles Hicks 3rd, Commissary for Caroline County [Ref: V-6636].

WARREN, John. Private, 5th Maryland Line, enlisted April 28, 1777 and discharged October 12, 1779 [Ref: D-254].

WARREN, Solomon (1747 -   ). Private, Militia, Capt. John Stafford's Company, 14th Battalion, by August 13, 1777 [Ref: M-156, which spelled the name "Warring"]. Rendered patriotic service by providing wheat for the use of the military in August, 1782, as verified by Giles Hicks 3rd, Commissary for Caroline County [Ref: V-6636]. Aged 38 in a 1785 deposition [Ref: T-12].

WARRINGTON, Nathaniel. Private, Militia, 14th Battalion, Capt. Joseph Richardson's Company, by August 13, 1777 [Ref: M-154]. Subscribed to the Oath of Allegiance and Fidelity before the Hon. Charles Dickinson on March 1, 1778 [Ref: J-1418].

WASHINGTON, George. See "Thomas Goldsborough" and "Robert Gilchrist," q.v.

WATKINS, Joseph. Private, Militia, Capt. Joseph Douglass' Company, 14th Battalion, by August 13, 1777 [Ref: M-156].

WATKINS (WALKINS?), Thomas. Rendered patriotic service by providing wheat for the use of the military in August, 1782, as verified by Giles Hicks 3rd, Commissary for Caroline County [Ref: V-6636].

WATSON, William. Rendered patriotic service by providing wheat for the use of the military in August, 1782, as verified by Giles Hicks 3rd, Commissary for Caroline County [Ref: V-6636].

WATTS, John. Ensign, Militia, Capt. Richard Keene's Company, December 17, 1781 [Ref: M-134, I-27].

WEATHERLY, Abnor. Private, Militia, Capt. Nehemiah Andrew's Company, 14th Battalion, by August 13, 1777 [Ref: M-155].

WEATHERLY, Isaac. Private, Militia, Capt. Nehemiah Andrew's Company, 14th Battalion, by August 13, 1777 [Ref: M-155].

WEATHERLY, Isaiah. Private, Militia, Capt. Nehemiah Andrew's Company, 14th Battalion, by August 13, 1777 [Ref: M-155].

WEATHERLY, Jesse. Private, Militia, Capt. Nehemiah Andrew's Company, 14th Battalion, by August 13, 1777 [Ref: M-155].

WEATHERLY, Job. Private, Militia, Capt. Nehemiah Andrew's Company, 14th Battalion, by August 13, 1777 [Ref: M-155].

WEATHERLY, John. Private, Militia, Capt. Nehemiah Andrew's Company, 14th Battalion, by August 13, 1777 [Ref: M-155].
WEATHERLY, William. Private, Militia, Capt. Nehemiah Andrew's Company, 14th Battalion, by August 13, 1777 [Ref: M-155].
WEBB, Ann. See "William Richardson," q.v.
WEBB, George. Rendered patriotic service by providing wheat for the use of the military in August, 1782, as verified by Giles Hicks 3rd, Commissary for Caroline County [Ref: V-6636].
WEBB, John. Private, Maryland Troops, enlisted by Capt. Joseph Richardson in Caroline County and passed by Col. William Richardson on August 31, 1776 [Ref: D-69].
WEBB, Mary. See "Edward Carter," q.v.
WEBB, William. On May 26, 1780, he filed a certificate in Caroline County Court that he had subscribed to the Oath of Allegiance and Fidelity before the Hon. Richard Mason [Ref: N-78]. William Webb married Comfort Holson by license dated December 19, 1780 [Ref: X-13].
WEBBER, Ann. See "John Webber" and "Solomon Webber," q.v.
WEBBER, John (1748 -   ). Private, Militia, Capt. William Hopper's Company, 28th Battalion, by August 13, 1777 [Ref: M-151]. John Webber, son of Joseph and Ann Webber, was born November 1, 1748 [Ref: K-26].
WEBBER, Joseph. See "John Webber" and "Solomon Webber," q.v.
WEBBER, Rachel. See "John Barwick," q.v.
WEBBER, Solomon (1756 -   ). Private, Militia, Capt. William Hopper's Company, 28th Battalion, by August 13, 1777 [Ref: M-151]. Solomon Webber, son of Joseph and Ann Webber, was born February 11, 1756 [Ref: K-26].
WEBSTER, Henry. Private, Militia, 14th Battalion, Capt. Joseph Richardson's Company, by August 13, 1777 [Ref: M-154].
WEBSTER, John. Private, Militia, Capt. Nehemiah Andrew's Company, 14th Battalion, by August 13, 1777 [Ref: M-155]. Rendered patriotic service by providing wheat for the use of the military in August, 1782, as verified by Giles Hicks 3rd, Commissary for Caroline County [Ref: V-6636].
WEBSTER, Rhoda. See "Solomon Carter," q.v.
WEBSTER, Richard. Private, Militia, Capt. Nehemiah Andrew's Company, 14th Battalion, by August 13, 1777 [Ref: M-155]. Rendered patriotic service by providing wheat for the use of the military in August, 1782, as verified by Giles Hicks 3rd, Commissary for Caroline County [Ref: V-6636].
WEBSTER, Solomon. First Lieutenant, Militia, Capt. Nehemiah Andrew's Company, 14th Battalion, by August 13, 1777 [Ref: M-155].
WEBSTER, Thomas. Private, Militia, 14th Battalion, Capt. Richard Andrew's Company, by August 13, 1777 [Ref: M-156].
WEBSTER, William. Private, Militia, 14th Battalion, Capt. Joseph Richardson's Company, by August 13, 1777 [Ref: M-154]. Subscribed to the Oath of Allegiance and Fidelity (made his "W" mark) before the Hon. Peter Richardson

on February 28, 1778 [Ref: J-1814].
WEST, John. Rendered patriotic service by hauling flour for the State of Maryland, as certified by Richard Keene, Commissary for Caroline County, on June 24, 1780 [Ref: P-298]. See "Isaac Thomas," q.v.
WHEATLEY, Henrietta. See "William Cannon," q.v.
WHEATLEY (WHEATLY), John. Private, Militia, Capt. John Stafford's Company, 14th Battalion, by August 13, 1777 [Ref: M-156]. Subscribed to the Oath of Allegiance and Fidelity before the Hon. Thomas Hardcastle on February 6, 1778 [Ref: J-1814].
WHEATLEY, Margaret. See "James Sullivan," q.v.
WHEATLEY, Mary. See "William Colscott," q.v.
WHEATLEY (WHEATLY), Nathan (1738 -   ). On December 27, 1776 he joined a company of men in Caroline County who marched to Talbot County to obtain a supply of salt [Ref: B-564, B-565]. Private, Militia, Capt. Henry Downes' Company, 28th Battalion, by August 13, 1777 [Ref: M-152]. Aged 48 in a 1786 deposition [Ref: T-12].
WHEATLEY (WHEATLY), William. Colonel, Militia, 14th Battalion, June 24, 1777 [Ref: M-135, C-299]. Appointed to be the "Collector of Cloathing" for Caroline County on November 27, 1777, by the Council of Maryland [Ref: C-426]. See "William Whitely," q.v.
WHEELAR, Charles. Private (recruit), Maryland Troops, enrolled in Caroline County by William Whiteley, County Lieutenant, on August 14, 1781 to serve in the Maryland Line until December 10, 1781 [Ref: D-385].
WHEELAR, Hezekiah. Private (draft), Maryland Troops, furnished in Caroline County by William Whiteley, County Lieutenant, on April 16, 1781 [Ref: D-368].
WHEELER, Ezekial (Ezekiah). Ensign, Militia, Capt. Nehemiah Andrew's Company, April 9, 1778 [Ref: M-135, E-23].
WHEELER, Thomas. Private, Militia, Capt. Samuel Jackson's Company, 28th Battalion, by August 13, 1777 [Ref: M-153].
WHIRRITT, Elizabeth. See "Thomas Cooper," q.v.
WHITBY (WHITBEY), Benjamin (1730 or 1731 - after 1782). Rendered patriotic service by providing wheat for the use of the military in August, 1782, as verified by Giles Hicks 3rd, Commissary for Caroline County [Ref: V-6636]. "Benjamin Whitbey" was aged 52 in a 1782 deposition, noting he was a son of William Whitbey. "Benjamin Whitby" was aged 52 in a 1784 deposition [Ref: T-4, T-9]. "Benjamin Whidbey" married Lydia Bell on June 15, 1756 [Ref: K-27].
WHITBY (WHITBEY), Joseph. Private, Militia, Capt. Thomas Hughlett's Company, 28th Battalion, by August 13, 1777 [Ref: M-153]. "Joseph Whitby, Sr." was aged 60 in a 1790 deposition [Ref: T-13].
WHITBY (WHITBEY), Nathan. Private, Militia, Capt. William Chipley's Company, 28th Battalion, by August 13, 1777 [Ref: M-153]. Rendered patriotic service by providing wheat for the use of the military in August, 1782, as verified

by Giles Hicks 3rd, Commissary for Caroline County [Ref: V-6636].
WHITBY, William. See "Benjamin Whitby," q.v.
WHITE, Edward. Private, Militia, Capt. William Haslett's Company, 28th Battalion, by August 13, 1777 [Ref: M-152]. Subscribed to the Oath of Allegiance and Fidelity before the Hon. Benson Stainton on February 2, 1778 [Ref: J-1814]. One "Edward White 3rd" married Elizabeth Fountain by license dated January 29, 1793 [Ref: X-25].
WHITE, James. Private, Militia, Capt. William Haslett's Company, 28th Battalion, by August 13, 1777 [Ref: M-152].
WHITE, James. Second Lieutenant, Militia, Capt. Shadrack Liden's Company, 14th Battalion, June 24, 1777 to at least April 9, 1778 [Ref: M-155, C-299, E-23]. Subscribed to the Oath of Allegiance and Fidelity before the Hon. Nathaniel Potter on March 2, 1778 [Ref: J-1814]. Rendered patriotic service by providing wheat for the use of the military in May, 1782, as verified by Giles Hicks 3rd, Commissary for Caroline County [Ref: V-6636].
WHITE, John. First Lieutenant, Militia, Capt. Postlethwait's Company, 28th Battalion, April 9, 1778 [Ref: M-136, E-23].
WHITE, John (1727 - after 1784). Served on the Committee of Observation for Caroline County on August 2, 1775 [Ref: A-48]. Quartermaster, Militia, 14th Battalion, January 12, 1776 [Ref: M-136]. Attended the Maryland Convention on July 3, 1776 for the "express purpose of forming a new government." [Ref: O-35]. Appointed a Judge of Elections for Caroline County at the Maryland Convention on November 8, 1776 [Ref: O-55]. Rendered patriotic service by providing wheat for the use of the military in August, 1782, as verified by Giles Hicks 3rd, Commissary for Caroline County [Ref: V-6636]. Aged 57 in a 1784 deposition, noting he was a son of John White [Ref: T-7].
WHITE, John Jr. Private, Militia, Capt. William Haslett's Company, 28th Battalion, by August 13, 1777 [Ref: M-152]. Subscribed to the Oath of Allegiance and Fidelity before the Hon. Matthew Driver on February 1, 1778 [Ref: J-1814].
WHITE, Joseph. Private, Militia, Capt. John Fauntleroy's Company, 28th Battalion, by August 13, 1777 [Ref: M-154].
WHITE, Joseph. Private, Militia, Capt. William Chipley's Company, 28th Battalion, by August 13, 1777 [Ref: M-153].
WHITE, Joseph, of Choptank Hundred. Subscribed to the Oath of Allegiance and Fidelity before the Hon. Benson Stainton on February 2, 1778 [Ref: J-1814].
WHITE, Mary. See "James Kirkman," q.v.
WHITE, Nancy. See "Thomas Smith," q.v.
WHITE, Prudence. See "Andrew Price," q.v.
WHITE, Samuel. Private, Militia, Capt. Andrew Fountain's Company, 14th Battalion, by August 13, 1777 [Ref: M-157].
WHITE, Thomas. Private, Militia, Capt. Andrew Fountain's Company, 14th Battalion, by August 13, 1777 [Ref: M-157].
WHITE, Thomas. Court Justice, 1775 [Ref: Z-1]. One Thomas White was aged 63

in a 1793 deposition [Ref: T-16].
WHITELY, Arthur. See "William Whitely," q.v.
WHITELY, Benjamin. See "William Whitely," q.v.
WHITELY, Henry. See "William Whitely," q.v.
WHITELY, Katherine. See "William Whitely," q.v.
WHITELY, Mary. See "William Whitely," q.v.
WHITELY, Sarah. See "William Whitely," q.v.
WHITELY (WHITELEY, WHEATLY), William (1752-1815). Son of Arthur Rich Whitely of Dorchester County, and wife Katherine, William was born August 27, 1752 and married first to Sarah Baynard on March 3, 1778 (license dated February 25, 1778) and second to Mary --?-- by 1799. His children were William Whitely, Henry Whitely, Benjamin Whitely, Kitty Russel (wife of Andrew R. Russel), and Elizabeth Macbeth or MacBeath (wife of John Macbeth or MacBeath). William represented Caroline County in the Lower House of the Maryland General Assembly, 1780-1792, and Senate, 1801-1810. He served as County Lieutenant, 1777-1781, Trustee for the Poor, 1792, Associate Justice, Fourth District, 1793, and Maryland Senate Elector, 1801 [Ref: R-884, R-84, R-86, R-89 (which spelled the name "Wheatly"), R-90, G-55, X-8]. First Major, Militia, East Battalion, 1776. Lieutenant Colonel 4th Maryland Battalion of the Flying Camp, August 6 to December 1, 1776. Colonel and Commander in Chief of East and West Battalions (14th and 28th Battalions) by August 13, 1777. Colonel, Militia, 19th Battalion, 1794-1801 [Ref: R-884, M-151, M-154]. Subscribed to the Oath of Allegiance and Fidelity before the Hon. Benson Stainton on January 23, 1778 [Ref: J-1814]. He died on August 19, 1815 at Newark, New Castle County, Delaware [Ref: R-884]. See "William Wheatley" and "William Whitley" and "John Allen Sangston" and "George Hutton," q.v.
WHITLEY, Benjamin. Private, Militia, Capt. Thomas Hughlett's Company, 28th Battalion, by August 13, 1777 [Ref: M-153].
WHITLEY, William. One William Whitley or Whiteley was born circa 1757 in Maryland, married Sidney Glandon, served as a lieutenant in the Maryland troops, and died before March 12, 1816 [Ref: Y-3194]. See "William Whitely," q.v. Additional research may be necessary before drawing conclusions.
WHITTINGTON, Benjamin. Private, Militia, Capt. Andrew Fountain's Company, 14th Battalion, by August 13, 1777 [Ref: M-157]. Private, 5th Maryland Line, enlisted May 14, 1778 [Ref: D-255].
WHITTINGTON, Joseph. Private, Militia, Capt. Andrew Fountain's Company, 14th Battalion, by August 13, 1777 [Ref: M-157]. Private, 5th Maryland Line, enlisted by June, 1778 [Ref: D-255].
WIETT, Thomas. Private, Militia, Capt. John Stafford's Company, 14th Battalion, by August 13, 1777 [Ref: M-156]. Subscribed to the Oath of Allegiance and Fidelity before the Hon. Matthew Driver on February 1, 1778 [Ref: J-1814].
WILLIAMS, Jacob. Private, Militia, Capt. John Fauntleroy's Company, 28th Battalion, by August 13, 1777 [Ref: M-154].

WILLIAMS, James. Private, Militia, Capt. John Fauntleroy's Company, 28th Battalion, by August 13, 1777 [Ref: M-153]. Subscribed to the Oath of Allegiance and Fidelity in 1780 [Ref: L-123]. Private (recruit), Maryland Troops, enrolled in Caroline County by William Whiteley, County Lieutenant, on August 14, 1781 to serve in the Maryland Line until December 10, 1781 [Ref: D-385].

WILLIAMS, James Jr. Subscribed to the Oath of Allegiance and Fidelity in 1780 [Ref: L-123].

WILLIAMS, Jessee. Private, Militia, Capt. Joseph Douglass' Company, 14th Battalion, by August 13, 1777 [Ref: M-156].

WILLIAMS, John (1744 -   ). Private, Militia, Capt. William Hopper's Company, 28th Battalion, by August 13, 1777 [Ref: M-151, A-48, A-49]. Aged 38 in a 1782 deposition [Ref: T-4].

WILLIAMS, Thomas. Private, 6th Company, Capt. Peter Adams, 1st Maryland Line, enlisted February 24, 1776 [Ref: D-15].

WILLIAMS, Thomas. Private, Militia, 14th Battalion, Capt. Richard Andrew's Company, by August 13, 1777 [Ref: M-156].

WILLIAMS, Thomas. Rendered patriotic service by providing wheat for the use of the military in August, 1782, as verified by Giles Hicks 3rd, Commissary for Caroline County [Ref: V-6636].

WILLIAMS, Vincent. Private, Militia, Capt. Samuel Jackson's Company, 28th Battalion, by August 13, 1777 [Ref: M-153]. Subscribed to the Oath of Allegiance and Fidelity before the Hon. Richard Mason on March 2, 1778 [Ref: J-1814].

WILLIAMS, William. Subscribed to the Oath of Allegiance and Fidelity in 1780 [Ref: L-123]. See "Levin Noble," q.v.

WILLIAMS, William. Private, Militia, Capt. John Fauntleroy's Company, 28th Battalion, by August 13, 1777 [Ref: M-154].

WILLIAMS, William. Private, Militia, Capt. Joseph Douglass' Company, 14th Battalion, by August 13, 1777 [Ref: M-156]. One William Williams married --?-- Merrick, of Queen Anne's County, by license dated May 25, 1774 [Ref: X-3].

WILLIN, William. Private, Maryland Troops, enrolled by Lieut. Levin Handy in Caroline County and passed by Col. William Hopewell on August 4, 1776 [Ref: D-69].

WILLIS, Andrew. Private, Maryland Troops, enrolled by Lieut. Thomas Wynn Loockerman in Caroline County in July, 1776 [Ref: D-69]. Private, 5th Maryland Line, enlisted February 17, 1777 and discharged February 14, 1780 [Ref: D-254]. Second Lieutenant, Militia, Capt. James Andrew's Company, 14th Battalion, June 12, 1781 [Ref: M-138].

WILLIS, Daniel. Drummer, 5th Maryland Line, enlisted February 9, 1777, reported missing on August 16, 1780 at the Battle of Camden in South Carolina, but subsequently "joined" [Ref: D-254].

WILLIS, Deborah. See "Joshua Lucas," q.v.

WILLIS, Elijah. Private, Militia, Capt. Joseph Douglass' Company, 14th Battalion, by August 13, 1777 [Ref: M-156]. Rendered patriotic service by providing wheat for the use of the military in August, 1782, as verified by Giles Hicks 3rd, Commissary for Caroline County [Ref: V-6636].

WILLIS, Eleanor. See "Henry Willis," q.v.

WILLIS, Elizabeth. See "John Willis," q.v.

WILLIS, Ezekiel. Private, Militia, 14th Battalion, Capt. Richard Andrew's Company, by August 13, 1777 [Ref: M-156]. Appointed to be Constable of Great Choptank Hundred on March 17, 1779 [Ref: N-50].

WILLIS, Henry. Private, Maryland Troops, enrolled by Lieut. Thomas Wynn Loockerman in Caroline County in July, 1776 [Ref: D-69]. Private, Militia, Capt. John Mitchell's Company, 14th Battalion, by August 13, 1777 [Ref: M-155]. In an 1806 land commission record it stated that Henry Willis had died on November 1, 1793, seized of a tract called "Painter's Range" which descended to his heirs, viz., Henry Willis (minor), Levin Willis (minor), and Eleanor Willis (who married John Gwinn of Queen Anne's County). The land was purchased by Jesse Connelly [Ref: T-23]. One Henry Willis married Ann Connerly (Connerlyd?) by license dated December 8, 1780, and a Henry Willis married Rhody Batchelor by license dated June 12, 1793 [Ref: X-13, X-25].

WILLIS, Isaac. Subscribed to the Oath of Allegiance and Fidelity before the Hon. Charles Dickinson on March 1, 1778 [Ref: J-1418].

WILLIS (MILLIS?), James. On May 30, 1780, he filed a certificate in Caroline County Court that he had subscribed to the Oath of Allegiance and Fidelity before the Hon. Nathaniel Potter [Ref: N-78].

WILLIS, Jarvis. Subscribed to the Oath of Allegiance and Fidelity before the Hon. Charles Dickinson on March 1, 1778 [Ref: J-1418]. One Jarvis Willis was aged 63 in a 1798 deposition [Ref: T-20].

WILLIS, Jarvis (Jarvus). Private, Maryland Troops, enrolled by Lieut. Thomas Wynn Loockerman in Caroline County in July, 1776 [Ref: D-69]. Corporal, 5th Maryland Line, enlisted February 17, 1777 and discharged February 14, 1780 [Ref: D-254].

WILLIS, Jervis. Private, Militia, 14th Battalion, Capt. Joseph Richardson's Company, by August 13, 1777 [Ref: M-154].

WILLIS, Jervis. Private, Militia, Capt. Joseph Douglass' Company, 14th Battalion, by August 13, 1777 [Ref: M-156].

WILLIS, John (1731 -   ). Private, Militia, Capt. John Mitchell's Company, 14th Battalion, by August 13, 1777 [Ref: M-155]. "John Willis, son of John and Elizabeth Willis, both deceased, of Dorchester County" was aged 51 in a 1782 deposition in Caroline County. "John Willis, Sr." was aged 61 in a 1793 deposition. "John Willis" was aged 53 or 54 in a 1785 deposition [Ref: T-4, T-10, T-17].

WILLIS, Joshua. Constable, 1775 [Ref: Z-2]. Private, Militia, Capt. John Mitchell's Company, 14th Battalion, by August 13, 1777 [Ref: M-155]. Gave a deposition on January 20, 1777 (age not given) before the Committee of Observation [Ref:

C-65]. "Joshua Willis (Assessor)" subscribed to the Oath of Allegiance and Fidelity before the Hon. Charles Dickinson on March 1, 1778 [Ref: J-1418]. Joshua Willis married Deborah Greehawk [Greenhawk] by license dasted May 20, 1774 [Ref: X-3].

WILLIS, Levin. See "Henry Willis," q.v.

WILLIS, Richard. Private, Militia, Capt. John Mitchell's Company, 14th Battalion, by August 13, 1777 [Ref: M-155]. One Richard Willis married Elizabeth Greenbaugh by license dated December 13, 1783, and a Richard Willis married Betany Gwoty by license dated January 22, 1788 [Ref: X-15, X-18].

WILLIS, Robert. Private, Militia, Capt. John Mitchell's Company, 14th Battalion, by August 13, 1777 [Ref: M-155].

WILLIS, Shadrack. Private, Militia, Capt. Joseph Douglass' Company, 14th Battalion, by August 13, 1777 [Ref: M-156]. Shadrick Willis married Ann Wright by license dated October 13, 1778 [Ref: X-9].

WILLIS, Thomas. Private, Militia, 14th Battalion, Capt. Richard Andrew's Company, by August 13, 1777 [Ref: M-156].

WILLIS, Thomas. Private, Militia, Capt. John Mitchell's Company, 14th Battalion, by August 13, 1777 [Ref: M-155]. Rendered patriotic service by providing wheat for the use of the military in August, 1782, as verified by Giles Hicks 3rd, Commissary for Caroline County [Ref: V-6536].

WILLIS, William. Private, Militia, Capt. Joseph Douglass' Company, 14th Battalion, by August 13, 1777 [Ref: M-156]. Rendered patriotic service by providing wheat for the use of the military in August, 1782, as verified by Giles Hicks 3rd, Commissary for Caroline County [Ref: V-6636].

WILLOUGHBY (WILLOBEY, WILLOBY), Edward (1743 -   ). Private, Militia, Capt. John Stafford's Company, 14th Battalion, by August 13, 1777 [Ref: M-156]. Rendered patriotic service by providing wheat for the use of the military in August, 1782, as verified by Giles Hicks 3rd, Commissary for Caroline County [Ref: V-6636]. Aged 42 in a 1785 deposition [Ref: T-12].

WILLOUGHBY, John. Private, Militia, 14th Battalion, Capt. Joseph Richardson's Company, by August 13, 1777 [Ref: M-154]. One John Willoughby married Ann Walker by license dated December 20, 1774, and a John Willoughby married Celia Connelly by license dated September 19, 1789 [Ref: X-4, X-20].

WILLOUGHBY, Margaret. See "James Bell," q.v.

WILLOUGHBY (WILLOBY), Richard. Private, Militia, Capt. William Haslett's Company, 28th Battalion, by August 13, 1777 [Ref: M-152]. Richard Willoughby married Elizabeth Lawrence by license dated October 20, 1781 [Ref: X-14].

WILLOUGHBY (WILLOBY), Samuel. Private, Militia, Capt. William Haslett's Company, 28th Battalion, by August 13, 1777 [Ref: M-152]. Samuel Willoughby married Amelia Howard by license dated February 23, 1791 [Ref: X-22].

WILLOUGHBY (WILLOBY, WILLABY), Solomon. Private, Militia, Capt. William Haslett's Company, 28th Battalion, by August 13, 1777 [Ref: M-152]. Rendered patriotic service by providing wheat for the use of the military in

August, 1782, as verified by Giles Hicks 3rd, Commissary for Caroline County [Ref: V-6636].

WILLOUGHBY, William. Private, Militia, 14th Battalion, Capt. Joseph Richardson's Company, by August 13, 1777 [Ref: M-154]. Private, 5th Maryland Line, enlisted on January 29, 1777 and reportedly "deserted" on March 31, 1779 [Ref: D-254].

WILSON, Ann. See "Oliver Hackett, Jr." and "James Roe," q.v.

WILSON (WILLSON), Benjamin. Rendered patriotic service by providing wheat for the use of the military in August, 1782, as verified by Giles Hicks 3rd, Commissary for Caroline County [Ref: V-6636].

WILSON, Charlotte. See "Joseph Douglass," q.v.

WILSON (WILLSON), Christopher. Private, Militia, Capt. William Haslett's Company, 28th Battalion, by August 13, 1777 [Ref: M-152]. Subscribed to the Oath of Allegiance and Fidelity before the Hon. Benson Stainton on February 2, 1778 [Ref: J-1814]. Rendered patriotic service by providing wheat for the use of the military in August, 1782, as verified by Giles Hicks 3rd, Commissary for Caroline County [Ref: V-6636]. Christopher Wilson married Sarah Dixon by license dated December 20, 1781 [Ref: X-14].

WILSON (WILLSON), Elisha. Private, Militia, Capt. Henry Downes' Company, 28th Battalion, by August 13, 1777 [Ref: M-152].

WILSON (WILLSON), George. Private, Militia, Capt. John Mitchell's Company, 14th Battalion, by August 13, 1777 [Ref: M-155]. Seaman, enlisted May 27, 1782 to serve on the barge "Fearnaught" under Capt. Edward Spedden, and was paid £3 bounty for enlisting; physical description given as 5' 8" tall with a fair complexion [Ref: D-611]. George Wilson married Sally Cooper by license dated February 8, 1785 [Ref: X-16].

WILSON (WILLSON), James. Private, Militia, Capt. Vincent Price's Company, 28th Battalion, by August 13, 1777 [Ref: M-152]. See the other "James Wilson," q.v.

WILSON (WILLSON), James. Private, Militia, Capt. John Stafford's Company, 14th Battalion, by August 13, 1777 [Ref: M-156]. One James Wilson married Sarah Cooper by license dated December 28, 1785, and a James Wilson married Elizabeth Hardcastle by license dated November 23, 1792 [Ref: X-17, X-24].

WILSON (WILLSON), John. First Lieutenant, Militia, Capt. Andrew Fountain's Company, 14th Battalion, by August 13, 1777 [Ref: M-156]. Rendered patriotic service by providing wheat for the use of the military in August, 1782, as verified by Giles Hicks 3rd, Commissary for Caroline County [Ref: V-6636].

WILSON (WILLSON), Jonathan. Private, Militia, Capt. Shadrack Liden's Company, 14th Battalion, by August 13, 1777 [Ref: M-155]. Jonathan Wilson married Mary Saulsbury by license dated June 5, 1792 [Ref: X-24].

WILSON, Peter. See "James Roe," q.v.

WILSON (WILLSON), Robert. Private, Militia, Capt. William Haslett's Company, 28th Battalion, by August 13, 1777 [Ref: M-152]. Robert Wilson married

Elizabeth Pritchett by license dated June 3, 1779 [Ref: X-10].

WILSON (WILLSON), Samuel. Rendered patriotic service by providing wheat for the use of the military in August, 1782, as verified by Giles Hicks 3rd, Commissary for Caroline County [Ref: V-6636].

WILSON (WILLSON), Solomon. Private, Militia, Capt. Henry Downes' Company, 28th Battalion, by August 13, 1777 [Ref: M-152]. Solomon Wilson married Hannah Bett or Belt by license dated August 3, 1774, and a Solomon Wilson married Elizabeth Craynor by license dated April 4, 1792 [Ref: X-3, X-24].

WILSON, Susannah. See "Charles Daffin," q.v.

WILSON (WILLSON), William. Private, Militia, Capt. Henry Downes' Company, 28th Battalion, by August 13, 1777 [Ref: M-152]. Rendered patriotic service by providing wheat for the use of the military in September, 1782, as verified by Giles Hicks 3rd, Commissary for Caroline County [Ref: V-6636]. One William Wilson died in December, 1789, leaving heirs with the surnames of Wilson, Causey, and Blake, as noted in a 1795 land commission record [Ref: T-18].

WINCHESTER, Jacob. Rendered patriotic service by providing wheat for the use of the military in August, 1782, as verified by Giles Hicks 3rd, Commissary for Caroline County [Ref: V-6636].

WINCHESTER, Sarah. See "James Seth," q.v.

WINCHESTER, Thomas. See "James Seth," q.v.

WING, Roxanna. See "William Kelly," q.v.

WISE, Anthony. Private, Militia, Capt. William Haslett's Company, 28th Battalion, by August 13, 1777 [Ref: M-152].

WITH, Ann. See "Joseph Dixon," q.v.

WLS(?), Robert. Private, Militia, Capt. William Hopper's Company, 28th Battalion, by August 13, 1777 [Ref: M-151].

WOLSON, William. Rendered patriotic service by providing wheat for the use of the military in August, 1782, as verified by Giles Hicks 3rd, Commissary for Caroline County [Ref: V-6636].

WOOD, Ann. See "Richard Loockerman," q.v.

WOOD, Jacob. Rendered patriotic service by providing wheat for the use of the military in August, 1782, as verified by Giles Hicks III, Commissary for Caroline County [Ref: P-539].

WOOD, Joseph. Private, Militia, Capt. Thomas Hughlett's Company, 28th Battalion, by August 13, 1777 [Ref: M-153]. Ensign, Militia, Capt. Robert Hardcastle's Company, December 17, 1781 [Ref: M-139, I-27]. Subscribed to the Oath of Allegiance and Fidelity before the Hon. Thomas Hardcastle on February 27, 1778 [Ref: J-1814].

WOOD, Tabatha. See "James Kirkman," q.v.

WOOLFORD, David (1746 -   ). Private, Militia, Capt. Nehemiah Andrew's Company, 14th Battalion, by August 13, 1777 [Ref: M-155]. Aged 38 in a 1784 deposition, aged 40 in a 1786 deposition, and aged 48 in a 1793 deposition [Ref: T-7, T-12, T-16].

WOOTTERS (WOOTERS), Aaron. Private, Militia, Capt. Andrew Fountain's Company, 14th Battalion, by August 13, 1777 [Ref: M-157].
WOOTTERS (WOOTERS), Benjamin. Private, Militia, Capt. William Hopper's Company, 28th Battalion, by August 13, 1777 [Ref: M-151].
WOOTTERS (WOOTERS), Elijah. Private, Militia, Capt. Andrew Fountain's Company, 14th Battalion, by August 13, 1777 [Ref: M-157].
WOOTTERS (WOOTERS), Hannah. See "Christopher Jump" and "Matthew Chilton," q.v.
WOOTTERS (WOOTERS), James. Private, Militia, Capt. William Hopper's Company, 28th Battalion, by August 13, 1777 [Ref: M-151].
WOOTTERS (WOOTERS), John. Private, Militia, Capt. Andrew Fountain's Company, 14th Battalion, by August 13, 1777 [Ref: M-157].
WOOTTERS (WOOTERS), John. Private, Militia, Capt. William Hopper's Company, 28th Battalion, by August 13, 1777 [Ref: M-151]. One John Wootters married Elizabeth All by license dated August 18, 1779 [Ref: X-10].
WOOTTERS (WOOTERS), Lemuel. Private, Militia, Capt. William Hopper's Company, 28th Battalion, by August 13, 1777 [Ref: M-151].
WOOTTERS (WOOTERS), Reuben. Private, Militia, Capt. Andrew Fountain's Company, 14th Battalion, by August 13, 1777 [Ref: M-157].
WOOTTERS (WOOTERS), Richard. Private, Militia, Capt. William Hopper's Company, 28th Battalion, by August 13, 1777 [Ref: M-151]. Richard Wootters married Mary Price by license dated August 21, 1782 [Ref: X-14].
WOOTTERS (WOOTERS), Sarah. See "Matthew Deroachbrune," q.v.
WOOTTERS (WOOTERS), Solomon. Private, Militia, Capt. Andrew Fountain's Company, 14th Battalion, by August 13, 1777 [Ref: M-157].
WOOTTERS (WOOTERS), Thomas. Private, Militia, Capt. William Hopper's Company, 28th Battalion, by August 13, 1777 [Ref: M-151]. A "Thomson Wootters" married Elizabeth Jarman by license dated April 26, 1785 [Ref: X-16].
WRIGHT, Alexander. Private, 6th Company, Capt. Peter Adams, 1st Maryland Line, enlisted January 23, 1776 [Ref: D-14].
WRIGHT, Ann. See "William Hopper" and "Shadrack Willis," q.v.
WRIGHT, Captain. See "--?-- McNeere," q.v.
WRIGHT, Celia. See "Isaac Nichols" and "Joseph Douglass," q.v.
WRIGHT, Coursey. Private, 5th Maryland Line, enlisted April 20, 1778 and reportedly "deserted" on June 19, 1778 [Ref: D-255].
WRIGHT, Edward. Private, Militia, Capt. Joseph Douglass' Company, 14th Battalion, by August 13, 1777 [Ref: M-156].
WRIGHT, Elizabeth. See "John Waddell," q.v.
WRIGHT, Isaac. Ensign, Militia, Capt. Thomas Eaton's Company, 14th Battalion, December 17, 1781 [Ref: M-140, I-27].
WRIGHT, Jacob. Private, Militia, Capt. Joseph Douglass' Company, 14th Battalion, by August 13, 1777 [Ref: M-156].
WRIGHT, James. Private, Militia, Capt. Joseph Douglass' Company, 14th

Battalion, by August 13, 1777 [Ref: M-156].
WRIGHT, James. Private, Militia, Capt. Joseph Douglass' Company, 14th Battalion, by August 13, 1777 [Ref: M-156].
WRIGHT, Joshua. Private, Militia, 14th Battalion, Capt. Richard Andrew's Company, by August 13, 1777 [Ref: M-156].
WRIGHT, Lamuel. Private, Militia, 14th Battalion, Capt. Richard Andrew's Company, by August 13, 1777 [Ref: M-156].
WRIGHT, Levin. Private, Militia, 14th Battalion, Capt. Richard Andrew's Company, by August 13, 1777 [Ref: M-156]. Rendered patriotic service by providing wheat for the use of the military in August, 1782, as verified by Giles Hicks 3rd, Commissary for Caroline County [Ref: V-6636].
WRIGHT, Levin. Private, Militia, Capt. Joseph Douglass' Company, 14th Battalion, by August 13, 1777 [Ref: M-156]. See "Nicholas Stubbs," q.v.
WRIGHT, Mary Anne. See "William Hopper," q.v.
WRIGHT, Solomon. See "Robert Gilchrist" and "John Allen Sangston," q.v.
WRIGHT, Susan. See "John Allen Sangston," q.v.
WRIGHT, William. Private, 5th Maryland Line, enlisted May 4, 1778 and discharged June 1, 1779 [Ref: D-255].
WYAT, John. Rendered patriotic service by providing wheat for the use of the military in August, 1782, as verified by Giles Hicks 3rd, Commissary for Caroline County [Ref: V-6636].
YEWELL, Solomon. Private, Militia, Capt. Vincent Price's Company, 28th Battalion, by August 13, 1777 [Ref: M-152]. Subscribed to the Oath of Allegiance and Fidelity before the Hon. Henry Downes, Jr. on March 2, 1778 [Ref: J-1814]. "Solomon C. Yewell" was a private in the 5th Maryland Line who enlisted on June 4, 1778 [Ref: D-259].
YOUNG, Jacob W. (1762 - after 1832). Applied for pension (S3954) on December 12, 1832 in Maury County, Tennessee, stating he was born in Queen Anne's County, Maryland on November 21, 1762 and lived in Caroline County, Maryland at the time of his enlistment in the Maryland Line; he also served on a privateer [Ref: W-3996].
YOUNG, John. Private, Militia, Capt. Joseph Douglass' Company, 14th Battalion, by August 13, 1777 [Ref: M-156]. Rendered patriotic service by providing wheat for the use of the military in August, 1782, as verified by Giles Hicks 3rd, Commissary for Caroline County [Ref: V-6636].
YOUNG, William. First Lieutenant, Militia, Capt, John Fauntleroy's Company, 28th Battalion, June 19, 1777 [Ref: J-1814].

Other Heritage Books by Henry C. Peden, Jr. :

A Closer Look at St. John's Parish Registers [Baltimore County, Maryland], 1701–1801

A Collection of Maryland Church Records

A Guide to Genealogical Research in Maryland: 5th Edition, Revised and Enlarged

Abstracts of the Ledgers and Accounts of the Bush Store and Rock Run Store, 1759–1771

Abstracts of the Orphans Court Proceedings of Harford County, 1778–1800

Abstracts of Wills, Harford County, Maryland, 1800–1805

Baltimore City [Maryland] Deaths and Burials, 1834–1840

Baltimore County, Maryland, Overseers of Roads, 1693–1793

Bastardy Cases in Baltimore County, Maryland, 1673–1783

Bastardy Cases in Harford County, Maryland, 1774–1844

Bible and Family Records of Harford County, Maryland Families: Volume V

Children of Harford County: Indentures and Guardianships, 1801–1830

Colonial Delaware Soldiers and Sailors, 1638–1776

Colonial Families of the Eastern Shore of Md.: Vols. 5, 6, 7, 8, 9, 11, 12, 13, 14, and 16

Colonial Maryland Soldiers and Sailors, 1634–1734

Dr. John Archer's First Medical Ledger, 1767–1769, Annotated Abstracts

Early Anglican Records of Cecil County

Early Harford Countians, Individuals Living in Harford Co., Md. in Its Formative Years Volume 1: A to K, Volume 2: L to Z, and Volume 3: Supplement

Harford County Taxpayers in 1870, 1872 and 1883

Harford County, Maryland Divorce Cases, 1827–1912: An Annotated Index

Heirs and Legatees of Harford County, Maryland, 1774–1802

Heirs and Legatees of Harford County, Maryland, 1802–1846

Inhabitants of Baltimore County, Maryland, 1763–1774

Inhabitants of Cecil County, Maryland, 1649–1774

Inhabitants of Harford County, Maryland, 1791–1800

Inhabitants of Kent County, Maryland, 1637–1787

Joseph A. Pennington & Co., Havre De Grace, Maryland Funeral Home Records: Volume II, 1877–1882, 1893–1900

Maryland Bible Records, Volume 1: Baltimore and Harford Counties

Maryland Bible Records, Volume 2: Baltimore and Harford Counties

Maryland Bible Records, Volume 3: Carroll County

Maryland Bible Records, Volume 4: Eastern Shore

Maryland Deponents, 1634–1799

Maryland Deponents: Volume 3, 1634–1776

Maryland Public Service Records, 1775–1783: A Compendium of Men and Women of Maryland Who Rendered Aid in Support of the American Cause against Great Britain during the Revolutionary War

Marylanders to Carolina: Migration of Marylanders to North Carolina and South Carolina prior to 1800

Marylanders to Kentucky, 1775–1825
Methodist Records of Baltimore City, Maryland: Volume 1, 1799–1829
Methodist Records of Baltimore City, Maryland: Volume 2, 1830–1839
Methodist Records of Baltimore City, Maryland: Volume 3, 1840–1850 (East City Station)
More Maryland Deponents, 1716–1799
More Marylanders to Carolina: Migration of Marylanders to North Carolina and South Carolina prior to 1800
More Marylanders to Kentucky, 1778–1828
Outpensioners of Harford County, Maryland, 1856–1896
Presbyterian Records of Baltimore City, Maryland, 1765–1840
Quaker Records of Baltimore and Harford Counties, Maryland, 1801–1825
Quaker Records of Northern Maryland, 1716–1800
Quaker Records of Southern Maryland, 1658–1800
Revolutionary Patriots of Anne Arundel County, Maryland
Revolutionary Patriots of Baltimore Town and Baltimore County, 1775–1783
Revolutionary Patriots of Calvert and St. Mary's Counties, Maryland, 1775–1783
Revolutionary Patriots of Caroline County, Maryland, 1775–1783
Revolutionary Patriots of Cecil County, Maryland
Revolutionary Patriots of Charles County, Maryland, 1775–1783
Revolutionary Patriots of Delaware, 1775–1783
Revolutionary Patriots of Dorchester County, Maryland, 1775–1783
Revolutionary Patriots of Frederick County, Maryland, 1775–1783
Revolutionary Patriots of Harford County, Maryland, 1775–1783
Revolutionary Patriots of Kent and Queen Anne's Counties
Revolutionary Patriots of Lancaster County, Pennsylvania
Revolutionary Patriots of Maryland, 1775–1783: A Supplement
Revolutionary Patriots of Maryland, 1775–1783: Second Supplement
Revolutionary Patriots of Montgomery County, Maryland, 1776–1783
Revolutionary Patriots of Prince George's County, Maryland, 1775–1783
Revolutionary Patriots of Talbot County, Maryland, 1775–1783
Revolutionary Patriots of Worcester and Somerset Counties, Maryland, 1775–1783
Revolutionary Patriots of Washington County, Maryland, 1776–1783
St. George's (Old Spesutia) Parish, Harford County, Maryland: Church and Cemetery Records, 1820–1920
St. John's and St. George's Parish Registers, 1696–1851
Survey Field Book of David and William Clark in Harford County, Maryland, 1770–1812
The Crenshaws of Kentucky, 1800–1995
The Delaware Militia in the War of 1812
Union Chapel United Methodist Church Cemetery Tombstone Inscriptions, Wilna, Harford County, Maryland

www.ingramcontent.com/pod-product-compliance
Lightning Source LLC
Chambersburg PA
CBHW060518090426
42735CB00011B/2283